D1187271

On the Banks of the Wabash

The Life and Music of Paul Dresser

On the Banks of the Wabash

The Life and Music of Paul Dresser

CLAYTON W. HENDERSON

Indiana Historical Society Press
Indianapolis 2003

Printed in the United States of America

This book is a publication of the
Indiana Historical Society Press
450 West Ohio Street
Indianapolis, Indiana 46202-3269 USA
www.indianahistory.org
Telephone orders 1-800-447-1830
Fax orders 317-234-0562
Orders by E-mail shop.indianahistory.org

The paper in this publication meets the minimum requirements of American National Standard for Information Sciences—Permanence of Paper for Printed Library Materials, ANSI Z39.48–1984. ∞

Library of Congress Cataloging-in-Publication Data

Henderson, Clayton W., 1936-
On the banks of the Wabash : the life and music of Paul Dresser / Clayton W. Henderson
p. cm.
Includes worklists (p.), bibliographical references (p.), and index.
ISBN 0-87195-166-5 (alk. paper)
1. Dresser, Paul, 1858-1906. 2. Composers—United States—Biography. I. Title.

ML410.D8133H46 2003
782.42164'092—dc21
[B]

2003041656

To Elizabeth and our grandchildren
and to the memory of Clyde P. Henderson

Contents

Part Five: The Songs

Preface

My debt to friends, colleagues, and institutions is considerable. This book would have been much longer in the making and far less enjoyable to write without their aid, prodding, and encouragement.

My first thanks go to the Indiana Historical Society. It offered me the opportunity to present some of my preliminary work on Paul Dresser at one of its meetings in 1996 and accepted for publication in its magazine *Traces of Indiana and Midwestern History* my article on the centennial of "On the Banks of the Wabash, Far Away," Indiana's state song.[1] Most important, it gave me generous support and encouragement with a Clio Grant. My debt to this splendid organization is substantial. The late Dr. Robert M. Taylor, Jr., then the director of the Society's Education Division, was most gracious and generous in his support of my work.

As a teenager I read Theodore Dreiser's *An American Tragedy*. His awkward, dark, and convoluted writing style—much like the author himself—annoyed me at times. But as he followed all sorts of side and back roads, he strangely drew me into that poignant story, holding me captive. Nonetheless, I went on to other things and didn't return to Dreiser for years. That I did return to him is owing to summer study I did in 1991 at the University of North Carolina at Chapel Hill. Townsend Ludington and John and Joy Kasson directed a summer institute there on "The Emergence of the Modern: American Art and Culture from the Columbian Exposition to the Armory Show, 1893–1913." Sponsored by the National Endowment for the Humanities (NEH), my colleagues and I spent five weeks reading, listening to lectures, and viewing art from this heady period in American culture. One of the books we read was Dreiser's *Sister Carrie*. Some attributes of Paul Dresser, the author's oldest brother, surface in George Hurstwood, one of the book's main characters. Knowing only that Dresser had been a songwriter around the turn of the century, I decided to study him and his songs. Ludington and the Kassons encouraged my interest, and it is because of them and our discussions about Dreiser's *Sister Carrie* that I began to think about an article on Dresser.

I thank the NEH for a second opportunity to spend a concentrated period of time working on Dresser and his music. In 1994 I participated in an NEH summer seminar at Johns Hopkins University and the Peabody Conservatory of Music. There I was able to piece together some of the materials on Dresser I had collected since my time in Chapel Hill and to begin to make some sense of where I was heading. Working in Johns Hopkins's extensive Lester Levy Collection of sheet music, at the Smithsonian Institution, and at the Library of Congress gave me the chance to collect more songs and music composed by Dresser and his contemporaries. John Spitzer and Ronald Walters, the directors of the seminar, helped me considerably with their suggestions at that stage of my work.

Saint Mary's College has been generous in its support of my work. Faculty development grants have allowed me to continue my work during the summers. I thank Sister Bernice Hollenhorst, C.S.C., retired director of the Cushwa-Leighton Library at Saint Mary's, for providing me with space and resources of the library to carry out my work. Robert Hohl and Jill Hobgood, Saint Mary's reference librarians, and John Kovach, archivist and Saint Joseph County historian, were unfailingly helpful to me; I will always be amazed at their resourcefulness in finding information when I just knew I had reached a dead end. Rebecca J. Klest, a music major at Saint Mary's, worked her magic with the computer-generated music examples.

I spent four weeks during summer 1996 as a visiting research fellow at the American Music Resource Center at the University of Colorado at Boulder, where I pored through the popular songs in the Morris E. Dry and Charles Krolek sheet-music collections, looking for music about mother and home, precisely the kinds of song in which Dresser excelled. Thomas Riis, the director of the center, was helpful in suggesting areas for research. William Kearns, senior fellow at the center and its former director, was especially generous with his time and help. I will long remember our Thursday hikes on various trails in the foothills of the Rocky Mountains and, in particular, the long days climbing Twin Sisters and Bear Peak, during which time we talked at length about Dresser and his place in American music. Some of what I have written about American popular song in these pages owes much to the remarks Kearns made during those two long hikes. I thank him and his wife, Sophia, for the hospitality they so graciously extended to me. They, and the lovely setting of Boulder, made it hard for me to return to Indiana with its less-dramatic scenery.

Anyone studying the Dreiser family soon realizes the importance of the Dreiser archive in the Van Pelt–Dietrich Library Center at the University of Pennsylvania. Nancy M. Shawcross, curator of manuscripts in the Rare Book and Manuscript Library there, was most generous in allowing brittle typescripts of Dresser's plays to be scanned and reproduced. She always met my Dreiser-Dresser questions with great patience and with enviable knowledge of the library's holdings. John Pollack and Daniel G. Traister were especially helpful to me during my periodic visits to the center to search the Dreiser collection for material about Paul Dresser. I should remark at this point that I have left intact Dresser's writing idiosyncrasies in my quotations unless something was not clear; then I made only appropriate changes, marking each with editorial brackets. I was thrilled and dismayed to see one of Dresser's pianos in the collection: thrilled because I was seeing the instrument on which Dresser had composed some of his music; dismayed because Theodore Dreiser had turned it into a desk, removing the keyboard and the inner workings of the piano.

I am particularly beholden to a number of public libraries and historical societies. Without their collections of Dresser-Dreiser materials this book would have been far more difficult to write and less complete. Susan Dehler, special collections archivist at the Vigo County Public Library in Terre Haute; Donna Adams, Sullivan County historian and genealogy and local history specialist at the Sullivan County Public Library in Sullivan; Jack Buckley of the Sullivan County Historical Society in Sullivan; Lyn Martin at the Willard Library in Evansville; and John L. Selch, newspaper librarian at the Indiana State Library in Indianapolis all helped make my work easier. Marylee Hagan, executive director of the Vigo County Historical Society in Terre Haute twice took me to the recesses of the attic in the Society's building and allowed me to photograph the plaster model for the Arch housed there, the Arch that had once been proposed as a memorial to

Dresser; she graciously took me for a personal tour of Dresser's birth home. Jack and Ilena Buckley and Mary Jane Moon generously took me on a tour of Sullivan and Merom, Indiana, and introduced me to the area where the future composer spent part of his boyhood. I thank Ralph Woodward for sharing with me a ledger from his great-grandfather William Griffith's general store in "Depot Town" in Sullivan and Mrs. Merle Thompson, who showed me the deed to the property on North Broad Street that Johann Paul Dreiser once owned. The Sullivan County Public Library possesses a remarkable series of scrapbooks that Dr. James Brian Maple (1879–1970), a local physician, assembled. Consisting of newspaper clippings rich in Sullivan history from the nineteenth and early twentieth centuries, the Maple scrapbooks are a treasure trove of material that chronicles life in this small town. Without his assiduous work, these views of Sullivan history might have been lost.

Richard Dowell, professor emeritus at Indiana State University and Dreiser scholar, graciously shared information about the Paul Dresser Memorial Association and its work during the 1920s and 1930s. B. Michael McCormick, Vigo County historian, was especially helpful with matters related to Terre Haute locations and times. He found and shared with me the reference to Dresser's enrollment at St. Bonaventure's Lyceum in Terre Haute in 1872. This seemingly small piece of information filled in what had been a gap in my knowledge about Dresser's life during the time he still lived in Terre Haute. Annette Fern, research and reference librarian at the Harvard Theatre Collection, gave me a photocopy of a playbill of Dresser's appearance at a benefit concert for Daniel Decatur Emmett in 1882—the first substantial evidence I had of a Dresser performance; Riva Pollard, archival specialist of the Special Collections and Preservation Division of the Chicago Public Library, provided me with camera-ready copy of that same playbill; Francis Edwin Lapka, public services assistant at the Lilly Library, Indiana University, Bloomington, found materials I needed from some of Theodore Dreiser's days as editor of *Ev'ry Month*. Larry and Mary Kay Burton, Kiki Fisher, and John Palmer, friends all, helped me by reading an earlier version of my work on "On the Banks of the Wabash, Far Away." Their comments and the extra sets of eyes they provided prevented me from making embarrassing mistakes then. I thank Richard Lingemen, Vera Dreiser, and Tedi Dreiser Godard for their helpful replies to my questions about both Theodore and Paul. Excellent editing is a major ingredient in producing a book. I have been most fortunate in having had Paula Corpuz, George Hanlin, Kathy Breen, and Judith McMullen of the Indiana Historical Society Press apply their skills to this endeavor, and I heartily thank them for their superb work.

In welcoming me into their home and never complaining about my distractedness, my daughter and son-in-law, Jennifer and Mark Brandyberry, provided me with much welcome relief when I was working in Baltimore, Washington, D.C., and Philadelphia. My visits there were even more pleasant because I could enjoy three of my grandsons. Ethan Henderson read the entire manuscript and offered suggestions that improved the flow of certain sections of the book. He and I took a lengthy jaunt through Dresserland in New York City one cold February morning, with father pointing out various Dresser sites to a most patient son. Gregory, Christopher, and Joshua Henderson offered gentle prodding, together with the encouragement I needed at those points when I had doubts that I would ever say farewell to Paul Dresser.

I owe my greatest debt to my wife, Elizabeth. Her patience with my Dresser obsession and with my long absences from home doing research have been unfailing. Musical partners for more than forty years, we have collaborated on many performances over those years, including programs of mother-and-home songs by Dresser and his contemporaries. She is my favorite singer and my best critic.

Clayton W. Henderson
South Bend, Indiana
Summer 2003

Introduction

By the time Paul Dresser died in 1906, his sentimental song style, embodied in such hits as "On the Banks of the Wabash, Far Away" and "Just Tell Them That You Saw Me" had fallen out of fashion, replaced in the public's affections by breezy, slangy, topical songs, some with the rhythms of ragtime, the newest craze. Dresser's effusions, as they were sometimes called, brought to a peak and simultaneously concluded a golden age of American popular song only a decade or so after Tin Pan Alley began to become a powerful, centralized publishing force in American popular music.

Another group of song composers, four to five decades younger than Dresser and dominated by Jerome Kern, Irving Berlin, Cole Porter, George Gershwin, and Richard Rodgers, created another golden age of popular song that reigned largely unchallenged from the second decade of the twentieth century into the 1950s. Before Dresser and his contemporaries came along, an earlier generation of popular-song composers—some American born, others only recently removed from their native roots—constituted yet another golden age. Many of this group, of whom Stephen Collins Foster was the most prominent, succeeded in establishing American popular-song styles that owed much to the music of the preceding era. This generation emulated many of the songs and arrangements of the Irish and Scottish music of Thomas Moore, Henry Bishop, and John Howard Payne.

Italian opera arias also served as models. American audiences, especially in the major cities of the East, were acquainted with some of the music of Gioacchino Antonio Rossini, Vincenzo Bellini, and Gaetano Donizetti, for example. Performed in Italian or in English with other music sometimes interpolated, *Cinderella, The Barber of Seville, La sonnambula,* and *Lucia di Lammermoor* became known to their ears. When native-born American composers turned to opera for inspiration, the results sounded quite familiar to those who had already heard their Italian models.[1]

Beginning with the Foster generation, composers found an outlet for their songs in the developing blackface minstrel shows. Songs with dance origins, those passed down through oral tradition, and newly composed efforts all provided music for minstrelsy. Thomas Dartmouth Rice's "Jim Crow," George Washington Dixon's "Coal Black Rose," and the many songs of Daniel Decatur Emmett, the composer of "Dixie," come to mind. Foster and his colleagues took up and extended that tradition.[2]

Nostalgia was a favorite topic for musical settings. For many Americans, only recently removed from foreign shores or to the city, the longing for home or for the old village was painfully strong. Composers who expressed such yearning in music could count on a large audience. The titles of many express much of the sentiment contained in the song: "The American Exile," "Carry Me Home to Die," "The City's Too Crowded Too Sultry for Me," "My Dear My Native Home," "Delaware, My Delaware," and "Erin Is My Home." The list could be extended manyfold.

Idealized mother was a rich lode that numerous composers mined. Late-nineteenth-century culture placed the figure of an all-forgiving, wise, angelic, and saintly mother—a kind of Protestant Madonna—on a pedestal. Mother songs were so prevalent by the 1860s that an H. DeMarsan published a parody of the genre, "Mother on the Brain." Sung to the tune "The Bonnie Blue Flag," the words are a compilation DeMarsan took from various mother songs, well-known in their time.

In the 1860s the Civil War became a powerful subject for song composers, northern and southern. Parting, death, and sorrow all became part of the song narrator's vocabulary, especially for the four years of the conflict but continuing for decades afterward.

Composers writing in the 1870s tended to emulate Foster and his colleagues, but the musical and poetic talents of these newcomers generally fell short of those of the earlier generation. The newer poetry often descended to the bathetic: a bereaved mother sings, "Gone to the heavenly garden, / Far from this world and its sin, / Two little faces we cherished, / Angels have ushered within." The two little faces become "Four pretty eyes that were bright," "Four little hands that were busy," "Two lisping tongues," "Four tiny feet," "Two goodly souls," and "Two little sunny-haired darlings."[3]

The songs of Dresser and his generation have received neither the scholarly attention nor the contemporary popular acceptance that Foster and the twentieth-century Tin Pan Alley composers have. Some minstrel and Civil War songs by Foster and others are still part of an aural treasury of our nation's past more than a century after Americans first sang them; think of "The Battle Hymn of the Republic," "My Old Kentucky Home, Good Night!," "Tenting on the Old Camp Ground," "The Battle-Cry of Freedom," "Old Folks at Home" ("Swanee River"), and "De Camptown Races" for examples. Even though the heyday of Tin Pan Alley ended nearly a half century ago, many can still hum a Gershwin, Porter, Berlin, Rodgers, or Harold Arlen tune. In the 1940s and 1950s—fifty years or so after Dresser and colleagues such as Charles K. Harris and Harry Von Tilzer wrote *their* songs—some Americans could sing *some* of that music, but no longer. Now, most would be hard-pressed to sing much from the late nineteenth and early twentieth centuries.

With some rare exceptions, audiences, and most scholars, pass over the rich heritage of late-nineteenth-century popular song. Individual articles, chapters in some books, and an occasional book or two have helped the interested reader begin to understand some things about American popular song from around 1875 to just past the turn of the twentieth century, but this music needs more study, especially in the context of late-nineteenth-century American popular culture, if only to help better understand that exhilarating period in American history.[4]

The study of individual composers, of the publishing industry, and especially of the vast amount of the music itself would create an extensive and inclusive panorama of that golden age of American popular song. Additionally, singing the songs would add the important aural dimension to the broader picture and invigorate the music as only live sound can.

Paul Dresser's life was a rags-to-riches-to-rags tale. The oldest of ten children in a family that was often poor, Dresser became a wealthy celebrity by using his modest musical abilities to compose songs an adoring public readily embraced. Not blessed with either the business sense to be a competent steward of his riches or with the ability, or perhaps desire, to change his musical style to meet a fickle public's changing tastes, he precipitously fell to a poverty-stricken has-been far more rapidly than he ascended from his childhood environment. While Dresser's story is neither unique to

America nor to the nineteenth century, it is an interesting one, coming early in America's fascination with celebrity and demonstrating what often happens to an individual once the public's interest has waned and moved on to embrace someone new.

My first purpose in writing this book is to bring the reader's attention to an important figure in late-nineteenth-century American songwriting and to place Dresser and his creations within a broad context of the American popular culture of that era. Called at various times the "greatest of American popular song writers," the "ballad-maker of a nation," and the composer who "managed to reach the popular heart," Dresser wrote sentimental music and coupled it with wistful language recalling the halcyon days of youth, home, village, mother, love, and innocence. It succeeded, as very little music since the time of Foster had, in touching the emotional and cherished places of many Americans.

I have written this book for the general reader and have kept the technical language of music to a minimum. In order to discover what "makes" a Dresser song, however, a certain amount of musical analysis is unavoidable. The interested reader should find no great difficulty following my thoughts there. For the most part I have dealt with Dresser's songs in a separate section of the book. This has the advantage of allowing the reader who cares little about the workings of music to spend most of her or his time in the life-and-times portion of the book and to dip into the song section only when interested. The disadvantage in this method, however, is in removing the songs from their immediate chronological and cultural context and treating them as isolated entities. I have tried my best to avoid too much segregation between the two bodies.

Unlike those who have written biographies of reasonably famous people and bemoan the fate of having too much primary material from which to flesh out their subject, I have found myself with precious little of that kind of information for Dresser. Biographers of Theodore Dreiser, his famous brother, have quite understandably treated Dresser as a peripheral part of the author's life. Dresser's generosity to Dreiser when the latter was suffering from severe depression has been well documented, and writers on Dreiser have mentioned other brief episodes of Dresser's life when those events have informed Dreiser's life.

Newspaper articles about Dresser, written during his life and shortly after his death, tend to be encrusted with the effusive language so typical of the period, making it difficult to get an objective picture of the composer. Some of Dresser's childhood friends wrote letters about him long after he died. More often than not, the correspondents were quite elderly when they wrote, and although a number of the letters are interesting and touching, they often contain statements that fail to stand up to fact—inaccuracies in remembering events from a distant past. Dresser was not very helpful to a biographer. In some newspaper interviews he mixed up dates, locations, and situations or exaggerated stories about himself. He was quite reticent about divulging some details of his childhood, perhaps thinking his adoring public might find his youthful indiscretions unacceptable.[5]

Dreiser was the best, if often exasperatingly inaccurate, chronicler of Dresser's life and career.[6] A couple of examples of his carelessness with facts will suffice. In 1919, thirteen years after his brother's death, Dreiser wrote that Dresser died in November at the age of "not quite fifty five."[7] In fact, Dresser died the next-to-last day of January 1906, two and a half months before his forty-eighth birthday. In *Newspaper Days*, Dreiser has his brother appearing in Charles Hoyt's play *A Midnight Bell* and as the composer of "The Bowery." Dresser *did* tour in a Hoyt play, but it was *A Tin Soldier*. Both Hoyt and Percy Gaunt, the poet and composer, respectively, of "The Bowery," would have been greatly dismayed to have their hit song of 1892 attributed to someone else, but they were both dead by the time Dreiser was writing these reminiscences.[8] Written by a loving yet critical and oftentimes jealous brother, Dreiser's essay "My Brother Paul" gives the reader a look at the composer and his environment; at the same time the sketch illustrates Dreiser's ambivalent feelings about Dresser's lifestyle and the kind of music he wrote. Much of Dreiser's commentary in *The Songs of Paul Dresser* replayed material he had written for "My Brother Paul."[9] Other Dreiser essays or books in which Dresser and his career feature more or less prominently are "Whence the Song" in *The Color of a Great City*; *A Hoosier Holiday*; and a sketch that Dresser probably dictated to Dreiser in late 1905.[10]

Dreiser's errors are certainly not willful ones; rather, as a novelist, he placed greater stock in the grand sweep of his narrative than in some of the more mundane details. Although the author often ignored or played loose with facts when recounting some of his brother's life, Dreiser's chronicles give a substance and flavor to Dresser's times and to the world of popular song that no other writer at the time equaled; since his day, few have been as eloquent.

H. L. Mencken, usually an acerbic curmudgeon, found Dresser's sentimental songs unusually attractive and told Dreiser that he should write a book about his brother: "We have biographies of all sorts of eighth-rate politicians, preachers, cheesemongers, etc. Why not a full-length book on a genuine American original, what we Huns call a Kopf?"[11] Alas, Dreiser never got around to doing that.

A researcher frequently spends countless hours in dimly lit rooms reading page after page on microfilm. The images may be beautifully clean and clear, or just as often they may be so dim or dark as to challenge even the most assiduous reader with perfect eyesight. This long and often tedious job is rewarded when a gem or two of relevant information pops to the surface. I found it fascinating, if not always fun, paying some of my scholar's dues by reading pages of the *New York Clipper* and the *New York Dramatic Mirror*. Both are wonderful repositories of information about entertainment in America during the second half of the nineteenth century. *Mirror* founder Harrison Gray Fiske and his reporters dealt primarily with the world of theater—popular and serious—with tidbits about music thrown in from time to time. Harrison Fulton Trent founded the *Clipper* as a sporting paper in 1853. Frank Queen bought the paper in 1855 and turned it into a resource rich in reviews of chess matches, marathon pedestrian races, prizefights, baseball games, drama, circuses, freak shows, music, and more. I imbibed deeply from many volumes of both papers, gaining some of the flavor of popular culture in late-nineteenth-century America. There I found much information about Dresser's whereabouts as a solo performer when he shared bills with animal acts, jugglers, acrobats, novelty acts, dancers, and melodramas.

I took vicarious pleasure in joining Dresser as he toured the nation with a variety of theatrical companies for eleven long years.

I joined thousands of people in palatial theaters as well as in those makeshift affairs, laughing at Dresser's jokes and listening to his songs. In those pages I learned about his work as a playwright and, through advertisements for his songs, about his growing involvement in the business of popular music.

While these bits of information helped give flesh to Dresser's already substantial size, the papers seldom told me what sorts of receptions audiences gave to Dresser and his colleagues. Negative criticism is but rarely found in those pages; the unwary reader could easily be led to believe that only the best and brightest of talents appeared in front of American audiences and that spectators always responded to entertainers' efforts with universal praise and acceptance.

In my attempt to reconstruct Dresser's life, I visited some of the places that featured prominently in it. My travels took me to New York City, where I attempted to get a feel for his haunts, long since vanished or altered. On a brisk February morning, with a windchill below zero, I walked along Broadway trying to imagine what it might have been like a century ago—the Broadway where he was hailed as one of the most celebrated figures of his day. I walked to the location where he, Pat Howley, and Fred Haviland established the firm of Howley, Haviland and Company (later Howley, Haviland and Dresser), half expecting in my imaginary world to hear the popular music of Dresser's time, a century removed from the present. Tin Pan Alley may be gone, but the heady vitality of the city's popular entertainment still permeates the air and daily life much as it undoubtedly did when Dresser walked those streets and inhabited those spaces. I visited the magnificent Church of St. Francis Xavier on West Sixteenth Street, Dresser's place of worship when he lived in the city and the church from which he was buried. Visually, little has changed in St. Francis Xavier since Dresser's day, and one might without too much difficulty imagine oneself transported back in time to that February day of Dresser's funeral.

Although Dresser was the friend and confidante of many, was the talk of New York City, and was generously rewarded for his songs, he had mixed emotions most of his adult life about his worldly success and acclamation. In song after song, but perhaps more tellingly in letters he wrote to friends back home, he repeatedly expressed his longing to return to his roots in Indiana. I spent considerable time in Terre Haute, Dresser's hometown, which sits on the banks of his beloved Wabash River. In my attempts to find the sometimes elusive Paul Dresser and to recapture some of the atmosphere of his haunts, albeit more than a century after he was there, I returned often to Terre Haute to walk along the banks of the Wabash in autumn, spring, and summer, spending time at what little is left of the Paul Dresser Memorial, once a grand dream, regrettably never realized. Modern lights shine through the sycamores, replacing the flickering candlelight of Dresser's time, but imagination can help one relive, if only for a moment, some of the memories expressed in "On the Banks of the Wabash, Far Away." Leaving Terre Haute, I traveled south on U.S. 41, once named the Paul Dresser Memorial Highway. I left the highway at Sullivan, where Dresser lived from ages five through twelve and from whose center he probably made the twelve-mile trip to the Wabash River, below the bluffs at Merom. Returning to the highway, I continued south to Evansville, a young, boisterous, and already cultured Ohio River town during Dresser's life, many of whose citizens embraced and encouraged the young singer and comic and where he lived with the great love of his life.

My second reason for writing this book is to attempt to come to grips with the two Paul Dressers. Like all human beings, Dresser combined a mixture of moods, impulses, and psychological and emotional makeups. He was, on one hand, an extremely generous, compassionate man—almost maternal in his care for others—who freely gave to those less fortunate than he. After the turn of the century he grew increasingly concerned and agitated about the plight of the dispossessed, especially the immigrants who lived on New York's Lower East Side. He talked about the inequitable division of wealth and goods and criticized, through interviews and in song, those who ignored or took advantage of the destitute. This Dresser was a mama's boy, greatly influenced and psychologically dominated by his mother. The other Dresser was a promiscuous womanizer, given to flaunting his own sexuality and even introducing his brother Theodore to sexual practices that late-nineteenth-century standards of behavior considered aberrant. Dreiser commented more than once on this dark side of his brother, calling him an "unregenerate sex enthusiast."[12]

In his careers as medicine-wagon showman, minstrel, comic actor and singer, composer, publisher, and playwright, Dresser embodied the exuberance and immense variety of America's popular culture in the latter part of the nineteenth century. His move from a rural, somewhat provincial, existence to important player in the broad life of American popular culture mirrored, in small, the nation's gradual transition from a position of insularity to one of political, military, and economic power. The loose parallel ends there, however. The Horatio Alger quality of Dresser's move from the meanness of his childhood to the rank of one of the wealthiest, most successful composers in America, one who often enjoyed the riches that any number of people yearned for, had a sad conclusion, its own American tragedy. In his descent from the zenith of celebrity, that transitory mistress, to its nadir—to the pitiful poverty and neglect he could never again overcome—Dresser suffered a fate not dissimilar to that which many others experienced before and after him.

That story is reflected in his fate after he died. At his death and for three decades after, many thought of ways to honor this poet of the people. Most of the plans were well meant, and many were ambitious in scope. As those thirty and more years wore on, however, with few of the projects brought to fruition, Dresser and most of his music slipped into an undeserved obscurity. It is wishful thinking to hope for a revival of those Dresser songs that became high-water marks in American popular music during the late nineteenth and early twentieth centuries. Nevertheless, if only a few readers of this book decide to look at—or better yet, sing—"On the Banks of the Wabash, Far Away," "My Gal Sal," or "Just Tell Them That You Saw Me" and are brought back, if only for a moment, to that heady period in America's cultural history, I will have accomplished my goal of championing the man, his music, and those intoxicating times.

Prelude

New Yorkers had been enjoying a respite from winter's hold, but by Friday, 2 February 1906, the recent temperatures in the thirties and forties had been replaced by gradually colder weather, pushed to bone-chilling discomfort by brisk winds blowing from the northwest. Shortly before ten o'clock that morning, with the thermometer at fifteen degrees, family, friends, musicians (including "more than a hundred well-known vaudeville performers and singers"), representatives of Tin Pan Alley's publishing houses, and the merely curious gathered inside the welcome warmth of the Church of St. Francis Xavier at Sixteenth Street and Sixth Avenue. They were there to say farewell to "the greatest of American popular song writers," the "ballad-maker of a nation," the composer who "managed to reach to popular heart," "perhaps the most voluminous writer of successful popular songs of the day," the man whose "name is familiar in nearly every home where popular songs are sung." One obituary stated: "Not in years has a death among the music trades occasioned greater regret."[1]

Paul Dresser, whose songs represented the last descendants of the grand tradition of nostalgic and sentimental ballads, had died. Dresser's song successes had made him a wealthy man, but before he died many of his former admirers had deserted him and his music to embrace a new kind of popular song whose style left little room for sentiment and nostalgia. Dresser, whose creative abilities were not matched by business acumen, had died virtually penniless; the *New York Telegram* remarked that he "was liberal to a fault and gave away his money almost as fast as he made it."[2]

Arthur Gillespie of the Witmark music-publishing company—one of Dresser's major competitors—wrote a lengthy "Tribute to Paul Dresser." It read, in part:

> Amid the flow of song and rhyme,
> 'Midst verse and melody sublime,
> The hand of death hath cast a pall
> Upon the father of them all—
> For Dresser's songs were of the kind

That left sweet memories behind. . . .
To Dresser, who of song was king,
We bow to you, departed Paul,
You were the LEADER of us all.[3]

Many of the mourners who arrived early had time to take in the magnificent interior of St. Francis Xavier, to marvel at the many frescoes on the walls—scenes from the Annunciation, Nativity, Crucifixion, Resurrection, and Ascension, together with depictions of various Jesuit saints. When their eyes traveled farther upward, nearly seventy-five feet to the ceiling, they viewed a large painting of angels bearing St. Francis Xavier into heaven. Four smaller paintings surrounded the larger one, each bearing symbols of the virtues of this patron saint. Statues of St. Joseph and the Virgin Mary stood above the side altars; the Stations of the Cross were "startling in their realism"; even an unbeliever would have been impressed with the frescoes—how magnificent they were! Painted by William Lamprecht, a medal of honor recipient from the Royal Academy of Art in Munich, they "fill[ed] the space between the pilasters around the sides of the entire church." The columns of "blue, mottled and snowflake granite" shone softly even on such a dreary day as this. And the high altar. Most had probably never seen anything as magnificent as this. Made of "blue-veined Italian marble and dotted with Mexican onyx," the massive high table exuded immense strength, but in its proportion to its surrounding, it did not intimidate the viewer.[4] The opulence of the grandest of theaters these performers had played in paled in comparison to the grandeur of St. Francis Xavier. The soft music from the magnificent Hook and Hastings organ, with its towering pipes standing in the loft, provided a lovely aural background to this visual splendor and to the thoughts of the mourners.

A few minutes before ten a hearse from the Anthony Huhna funeral home arrived at the church. Two by two, six pallbearers removed the coffin bearing Dresser's body. These colleagues from Dresser's White Rats entertainers' fraternity trudged up the twenty steps from West Sixteenth Street into the narthex of the church and after a few minutes bore his body down the long center aisle. Dresser's large body, still weighing close to three hundred pounds at death, and the massive coffin in which it was encased, tugged mightily on the arms of those men. His friends placed the coffin upon the bier standing immediately outside the communion rail. Six of Dresser's brothers and sisters followed the coffin; Al and Rome Dreiser, the wanderers, were missing, their whereabouts unknown. Their sister Theresa had died in 1897. Then followed the clergy party of acolytes, thurifer, torchbearer, and Paul's good friend, Father Henry Van Rensselaer, S.J. The private thoughts of each of the Dreisers that day remain just that. All remembered their brother in different ways. Theodore surely thought about a much happier time, nearly twelve years earlier, when a proud brother took the diffident twenty-three year old on long walking tours of the marvelous city. One of their stops on a warm summer's day had been in this very church, its cool interior providing welcome relief from the cloying humidity outside. Today, as Theodore saw St. Francis Xavier for but the second time, much was familiar, but there were also things he noticed for the first time.

As he walked behind his brother's coffin, Theodore, the observant journalist, took in the profiles of some of the mourners closest to the aisle. There was Louise Dresser, née Kerlin, Paul's professional "sister." At the news of Paul's death, Louise had canceled her stage appearances at Proctor's Fifty-eighth Street Theatre for the rest of the week. Theodore knew some in the congregation as employees of his brother's own publishing company. Mose Gumble was there, representing the Jerome Remick publishing house, and the Music Publishers' Association was represented. And, of course, there was Charles K. Harris, one of Paul's dearest friends and competitors—it was Harris whose judgment of "On the Banks of the Wabash, Far Away" Paul first trusted. Theodore couldn't see them from where he was, but surely Pat Howley and Fred Haviland were there. They had been Paul's friends and partners for more than a decade, but the three had had a series of fallings-out in the past two years, each going his own way in the music-publishing business. From his place in the procession, Theodore could make out Eddie Foy, one of the pallbearers and another of Paul's good friends. Theodore was fully aware of the smells on this winter morning—odors of damp clothing made more intense by the warmth of the church and the acrid, yet sweet, scent of incense, its smoke pouring from the thurible and spiraling upward to form a gray transparency high overhead. He was also aware of the sounds—the muffled coughs, the muted weeping of more than a few mourners, and the rich music of the magnificent organ. This was the first time Theodore had heard this impressive instrument. The soft music the organist had chosen to play before the service and during the procession were lovely, comforting to the congregation with their gentle sweetness.

The Dreiser brothers and sisters, their bodies enlarged in heavy winter clothing, the women's faces shrouded in black veils, shuffled into the first pew. With the Introit, *"Requiem aeternam dona eis Domine"*—"Grant them eternal rest, O Lord," the Requiem Mass began. In his homily, Van Rensselaer, the celebrant and pastor of St. Francis Xavier, remembered Dresser fondly: Dresser always met his obligation of First Friday Holy Communion whenever he was in the city, and coincidentally today was such a day; on some occasions, when Dresser was in the city and had stayed away from church too long, Van Rensselaer sought him out at the Howley, Haviland and Dresser offices, leaving only when Dresser promised to go to church the next day. Dresser had been a great benefactor of St. Francis Xavier, sometimes giving minstrel shows for the benefit of a day nursery there.

Closing his homily, Van Rensselaer read the words of Dresser's last song, "The Judgment Is at Hand":

> Yonder the Father now sits on the throne, Justice devine [*sic*] is He,
> And when asked what good have ye done! what will the answer be,
> And have ye clothed and fed the hungry or turned them from your sight,
> Or have ye robbed the orphan and the widow of her mite,
> Ye who have struggled so hard in my name then shall find peace and rest,
> The Masters [*sic*] arms are opened wide come to the throne with the blest!
> And then came an Angel Majestic, pure and grand,
> Calling "Arise ye!" Judgment is now at hand,
> As ye have sown, so shall ye reap, Just as the Maker planned,
> Arise ye all seek not to hide, the Judgment is at Hand.[5]

Newspaper accounts of the funeral service interpreted those words as Dresser's omen of his own death. The Paul Dresser Publishing Company later issued the song with a cover that bore the figure of an angel with tilted scales of justice and upraised hand. The inscription on the title page read:

> This song was completed by Mr. Dresser January 27, 1906, and seemed to be a premonition of his death, which came three days later. It was thought by many, that he knew the end was near and this last inspiration of his might rightly be termed as his own requiem.[6]

The Mass concluded, and the pallbearers carried Dresser's coffin out into the raw New York morning. The body was taken to Calvary Cemetery in Long Island, placed in a holding vault, and buried on 6 February—one week after Dresser's death. Theodore Dreiser remembered that "it was so cold and dreary there, horrible."[7]

For at least two decades this small-town boy who had enjoyed enormous celebrity as a composer and entertainer had wanted to return to the scenes of his youth, to the innocence of his rural roots. Now, even in death, fate would bar him from Indiana soil.

PART 1

Youth: 1858–1876

CHAPTER 1

Terre Haute Days

The composer whose songs idealized mother, home, and the joys of small-town youth was born Johann Paul Dreiser, Jr., in Terre Haute, Indiana, the fourth son and first surviving child of Sarah Mary Schänäb and Johann Paul Dreiser.

Johann Paul Dreiser was born in 1821 in Mayen, Germany, a predominantly Roman Catholic city about a hundred miles from Frankfurt and not far from Koblenz. He was one of twenty-two children born to Johann Dreiser and a succession of three wives. The Dreiser family was among the oldest families in Mayen, where six Dreisers had served as mayor at various times since 1571. After his youth, there was little to hold Johann Paul in Mayen. In such a large family he certainly had to fend for himself often, but in doing so he developed a valuable self-sufficiency that would hold him in good stead in the future. When he took up the trade of wool weaving and dyeing, he was able to get out of the house and away from his strict stepmother and, more important to the family, was able to help it financially.

The young Dreiser's future in Mayen looked bleak, however. Because the Prussian government controlled the city and pressed the eligible males into military service, it was just a matter of time before Johann Paul would be drafted. At the same time, some mills in the district were closing, making a continuing profession as weaver and dyer somewhat tenuous, especially for the younger workers. Those two facts, combined with the stress and tension of living under the same roof with so many siblings and a loving but strict stepmother, forced Johann Paul's hand. As for so many others, America seemed to hold the promise of work and prosperity for this twenty-three year old. So it was in 1844 that Johann Paul, filled with optimism for his own future and more than a little anxiety and a certain amount of sadness, said farewell to his family and Mayen and embarked on his exciting adventure. Immigrating to the United States, he left his ship at Castle Garden, New York, where officials processed his application in the old theater building that would soon become the formal immigrant reception center.[1]

Van Pelt-Dietrich Library Center, Univ. of Pa.

Johann Paul Dreiser, Paul Dresser's father.

Van Pelt-Dietrich Library Center, Univ. of Pa.

Sarah Mary Schänäb Dreiser, Paul Dresser's mother.

Sometime after his processing Dreiser traveled to Somerville, Massachusetts, to work in a local woolen mill for a few years. Before too long, feeling that there might be more opportunities for advancement for young workers beyond the settled communities of the East, he joined other adventurers in their westward exodus and around 1849 arrived in Middletown, Ohio. There he found work in a woolen mill at Miamisburg, just south of Dayton. George Ellis, the owner of the mill, immigrated to America eight years before Johann Paul and had operated his mill for about a decade before Dreiser moved to Ohio.[2] Ellis found in the young Dreiser a good, trustworthy worker unafraid of hard work, one who demonstrated an ability to get things done. Dreiser's future would be tied to Ellis and his mills for at least the next three decades—now in the Dayton area and before long even farther west in Indiana. After his experience in Miamisburg, the young Johann Paul would assume increasing responsibilities in the business, working up to the positions of foreman and then manager.

Around 1850 Johann Paul met sixteen-year-old Sarah Mary Schänäb, "a ravishing country belle, lovely as a garden of roses or a field of wheat, and he fell madly in love with her."[3] Sarah's parents were living west of Dayton when she was born on 8 May 1833. By the time she was nine, she and her family had moved westward to a farm near the village of Silver Lake, Indiana, west of Fort Wayne and directly south of Warsaw. Sarah's parents immediately opposed Dreiser once they learned of the relationship. Not only was Dreiser twelve years older than Sarah, he was also a staunch Roman Catholic who followed the dogmas of his religion with a rigidity that later would appall some of his children. The Mennonite Schänäbs considered Dreiser to be an unacceptable suitor for their daughter's hand. Sarah, however, was strong willed—a trait that would surface repeatedly when it came to her own family—and eloped with her beloved to Piqua, Ohio, thirty miles north of Dayton, where they were married on 1 January 1851. Although Sarah's father disowned her, some of her siblings kept in touch with her and even provided a home for one or more of her children when the Dreisers suffered financial problems. On that January day, however, the future held only the promise of unlimited possibilities for this happy couple—the serious German and his "ravishing country belle." Soon they moved to Fort Wayne, where Dreiser worked in another mill.

In 1853 Ellis left the Dayton area, moving to Terre Haute to establish the Riverside Woolen Mills at the corner of First and Walnut Streets, close to the Wabash River. In that same year, or by 1854 at the latest, Johann Paul and Sarah Dreiser, probably at Ellis's invitation, removed to Terre Haute, and Dreiser once again went to work for Ellis. Sarah, Johann Paul, and their babies moved into a home on First Street, near Walnut Street and very near to the mill.

IHS C9071

Terre Haute in the 1850s.

Great misfortune visited the young couple in their first four years of marriage. By 1855 the twenty-two-year-old Sarah had given birth to three children, all sons, but two of them died in 1854 and the third a year later. The grieving mother firmly believed God had punished her because of a wish she had uttered in a moment of absolute exhaustion and depression. At the end of her tether, the young mother had wished she could be rid of such responsibilities. As she later recalled, Sarah had no sooner pronounced this terrible oath when she saw three lights bobbing nearby. The superstitious mother knew, without a doubt, that these represented her three babies and that they would soon die. Theodore Dreiser wrote that as the last of the three children was being taken for burial, young Sarah "threw herself on her knees beside it and made a solemn promise to God—or Life, or Fate—that if He—or It—would have mercy on her and grant her forgiveness for her rebellious complaint, she would henceforth bear herself as an humble servitor to His or Its will: even though she were given as many as ten children, and the rearing of them proved difficult, she would not complain!"[4] In the next seventeen years, Sarah got her ten children—five daughters and five more sons—but for the time being she could not conceive. During that time she must have worried she might not bear any more children. When she discovered in late summer 1857 that she was pregnant, she was both overjoyed and apprehensive at the news.

On Tuesday, 22 April 1858, Sarah became a mother for the fourth time, giving birth to another son, whom the joyful Dreisers named Johann Paul, Jr. On 24 May, in St. Joseph Catholic Church, Father J. A. Koenig baptized the baby, whom he incorrectly identified in the parish records as James Paul Dreiser. James Bell, a local physician, and Margaret Breen were the baby's godparents.[5] St. Joseph, an imposing brick building on South Fifth Street in Terre Haute, was only about twenty years old at the time. Described as having "stained glass windows, a good organ, and beautiful altars and furniture," this was the Dreisers' church, where the greatly loved Father Simon P. Lalumiere had been a resident pastor from 1842 until a year before Paul's birth. At his death in 1857 the good priest was laid to rest in the church.[6]

Vigo County Historical Society

Paul Dresser birthplace, Terre Haute.

CHAPTER 2

Sullivan

In July 1863 Johann Paul Dreiser sold his house and shortly afterward moved twenty-five miles south to Sullivan, Indiana, to work at another woolen mill. George Ellis had bought a factory there and refitted it with new machinery. Known initially as a branch of the Terre Haute Woolen Factory and shortly afterward as the Sullivan Woolen Mills, Ellis's enterprise sat near the train depot, an ideal spot from which Ellis could ship his woolen goods to markets throughout Indiana and beyond its borders. Impressed with Dreiser's hard work and diligence in the past, Ellis had undoubtedly asked him to go to Sullivan, and Dreiser must have seen this move as advancing his career even though it meant selling his home and uprooting Sarah and their four children. By spring 1864 the six Dreisers—with yet another child on the way—were living on North Broad Street in an area known as Depot Town, a place the *Sullivan Union* remembered as "one of the best residential sections in town" at that time. Ellis's personal connection with the Sullivan operation was short lived, however, for he sold the mill in March 1864. The new owners, D. M. and E. D. Jewett, brothers from Terre Haute, boasted that their "machinery [had] been put in the best order," and the foreman—most likely Dreiser—had had "many years experience both in Europe and this country."[1]

Only 350 people lived in Sullivan when it was incorporated in 1853, about a decade before the Dreiser family arrived, and Sullivan County had a population of slightly more than 15,000 in

Sullivan Woolen Mills.

PAUL DREISER,

Woolen Dealer and Manufacturer of Woolen Goods,

Sullivan, Indiana.

Keeps constantly on hand, and for sale at the lowest cash prices,

JEANS AND SATINETS,

Cassimeres, Blankets, Coverlets,

Stocking Yarn, &c.,

Or, I will take wool in exchange for any of the above articles, or for custom work, at its cash value. Particular attention given to

CUSTOM

CARDING AND SPINNING,

Which we will do on as short notice, and as well as any Factory in the State, and at customary prices.

The Highest Cash Price Paid for Wool.

PAUL DREISER.

June 2, 1870.–3mo

DIVORCE NOTICE.

The State of Indiana, Sullivan County, In the

Newspaper ad for Johann Paul Dreiser's woolen mills.

1860. The region offered potential, however, and experienced steady growth. Named the county seat in 1842, Sullivan, at the time of the Dreisers' arrival, was experiencing the pains that frequently accompany growth when a clear plan for the future has not been made. Thomas J. Wolfe, a chronicler of Sullivan's early history, wrote, "The streets were not different from the highroads through the country, except that increased travel upon them made them more nearly impassable."[2] Sidewalks to protect pedestrians from the inevitable mud that followed a rainstorm were practically nonexistent. Temporary plank walks were placed along a few streets and gravel or cinders thrown on others, but the planks had been poorly made and were soon worthless; and the stones were hardly enough "to keep the feet from burying in the mud."[3] By November 1864 the *Sullivan Democrat* cried out: "The side-walk mania is prevailing in Sullivan to an alarming extent these days. Almost every individual you meet has a subscription for the construction of a plank walk out his street. The most important one projected is to reach to the depot, and will cost about $500."[4] Less than two years later four thousand feet of plank walks and twenty-five hundred square yards of brick pavement had been laid. Sidewalks to the railroad station had been completed.[5]

Of course electric lighting did not yet exist so those who ventured out after dark had to carry a lantern or torch to illuminate their way over these planks or through the dirt and mud. Water was available only at the town pump in the public square or in the wells and cisterns of private homes. "The slops and garbage were disposed of after the fashion of each individual home," Wolfe wrote, "and while each citizen had ample space about his doors it was not a matter of grave concern whether his home and premises were strictly sanitary."[6] In the same month the *Sullivan Democrat* exclaimed about sidewalk mania, it also criticized the condition of the town's burying ground:

> Our graveyard (though the public commons in which our dead are interred does not merit that name) has never been enclosed; hogs wallow above neglected graves; cattle roam through it, and eat off what little shrubbery the hands of affection have planted there; no care whatever is taken to

> protect the stones and monuments there from defacement, and the graves are huddled together without order and in utter confusion.[7]

The summer of 1864—the Dreisers' first full summer in Sullivan—was so hot and dry that merchants around the square attempted to sprinkle the streets of the town, but there was precious little water in the cisterns to do this.

In this same year Sullivan business comprised the "well filled stores of eleven merchants, three jewelry shops, two merchant tailors, mechanics of all kinds, three hotels, one flouring mill, sawmill and woolen factory and a steam stave and heading factory."[8] William Griffith, who had started a general store in Sullivan by 1856, was the owner of one of those "well filled stores." Johann Paul and Sarah shopped frequently at Griffith's store, and the Jewett brothers bought many of their goods there as well. One of Griffith's ledgers lists numerous purchases by Paul Dresser (i.e., Johann Paul Dreiser) and, on occasion, Mrs. Dresser. Never is the family identified as Dreiser. Most of the Dreisers' purchases were for staple items such as sugar, salt, butter, coffee, milk, oil, and candles.

By 1865 Sullivan had not only several schoolhouses and churches, but also six saloons, something that said much about the opportunities for culture and recreation in town. In April of that

Van Pelt-Dietrich Library Center, Univ. of Pa.

One of the Dreiser family homes in Sullivan.

year the residents of Sullivan, and of the nation, scarcely had time to absorb the news of the end of the Civil War before the dreadful accounts of President Abraham Lincoln's assassination reached them. Reminiscing forty years later, Paul Dresser remembered the funeral train with its "engines in black."[9] The closest the train came to Sullivan was Indianapolis, some 125 miles away, and it is unlikely that Paul or any of his family actually traveled to the capital to view the train at its stop there. Paul undoubtedly was recalling newspaper pictures and accounts of that mournful procession, which bore Lincoln's body through the Indiana communities of Richmond, Indianapolis, Lafayette, Westville, and Michigan City to Chicago and ultimately to Springfield, Illinois, for burial.

Paul lived in Sullivan from approximately age five to twelve. The young, rambunctious Paul probably thrived on life in the small village, reveling in the relatively short springtime when new growth and flowerings suffused the senses with magnificent color and delicious scents as no other season could. In the long, hot, and nearly always humid summers, Paul could enjoy the laziness of dawdling, scuffing his feet in the dust of the dirt streets or, after a heavy rain, sinking his feet in that deep mud that felt so cool and delicious to youngsters. When a bit older and school was out and when work did not interfere, he could have gone off to the "old swimming place at Morrison Creek,"[10] crawled under the tent of a traveling circus, or gawked at the snake-oil pitchman who set up his wagon near the town square. From a quartet of male singers traveling with the medicine wagon, he would have heard some Stephen Foster tunes, the patriotic songs left over from the recent war, and the latest minstrel songs. He would have laughed with others at the jokes he heard—at least at the humor he was capable of comprehending.

On those rare days when he was lucky enough to have all the time to himself, perhaps he and some boyhood chums hitched a ride on a wagon plying its way toward Merom, the old county seat. The twelve-mile trip would have seemed to take forever, but once they were in the village, the boys could have looked down from their vantage point, high on the Merom bluffs, to see the Wabash River, magical and mighty in the eyes of the more imaginative of them. Across that water lay Illinois, another world.

Scampering down the steep slopes, they could have stood on the banks of the Wabash, trying to skip stones over its surface and letting the scene and scents saturate their imaginations. If they could build a raft and launch it on this mighty river, where would it take them? What adventures they would have! These youngsters could have been the early Huckleberry Finns of Sullivan County. Later, when he returned to Terre Haute as a teenager, Paul would have his first chance to spend long stretches of time playing on, and daydreaming along, the banks of the Wabash. For now, however, such a rare trip to Merom would have to suffice.

If his father had had similar boyhood experiences in Mayen, they would have seemed as if from another lifetime, for now his life was mostly work. In spite of the problems that existed in the raw, new community, Dreiser and his growing family must have been reasonably happy about the move. If nothing else, the confidence the Jewett brothers placed in Dreiser, making him foreman of the woolen mill and the financial advantages that this promotion carried with it, must have overcome any regrets he may have had about leaving Terre Haute. The sanguine present, however, was to be brief; the Dreisers' stay in Sullivan would be marked by more reversals than advances.

On Sunday, 22 June 1865, at around four in the morning, fire destroyed the Sullivan Woolen Mills and all its contents, including the account books. The Jewett brothers carried no insurance on the wool stock, and their coverage of four thousand dollars on the structure and machinery was far less than the estimated loss of five times that amount.[11] But the Jewetts persevered. Within three months Dreiser was assisting in rebuilding the factory—"brick, three stories high and considerably larger than [the] one that burned,"[12] an effort that guaranteed Dreiser some continuing income to provide for his family's needs; now there were five children to feed. But more misfortune befell Dreiser less than a year later. On 28 April 1866, only six days after his oldest son turned eight, Dreiser was seriously injured. He was struck on the head and knocked "senseless" by a falling timber as workers were erecting a scaffold to finish the cornice of the new woolen mill.[13] The injuries were not fatal, but his son Theodore was convinced the accident brought on a "long and painful brain illness,"[14] one that resulted in a fanaticism toward his Catholic faith—"a man concerned much more with the hereafter than with the now . . . a man . . . obsessed by a religious belief."[15] The facts, however, do not support Theodore's contention of an incapacitating "brain illness."

Less than a year after the accident, Dreiser was on top again, his fortunes having taken an about-face when he became a partner with the Jewetts in the new Sullivan Woolen Mills.[16] His status as partner and his improved financial standing were reflected in his purchase, from Hardy and Ally Hill, of two pieces of property in the Snow and Cochran addition to Sullivan for $140.[17] There he built a house "larger than the small cottage near the depot and the old mill the family had previously occupied."[18] Even with the larger house, quarters were probably somewhat cramped, for Sarah and Johann Paul now had seven children. In this good year, Johann Paul also helped raise money to build a church for the small Catholic community of Sullivan. The Dreisers, one of only five or six Catholic families in Sullivan, were impressive, if only by their numbers, as they made their way to the small wooden church on Sunday mornings. Johann Paul, Sarah, and young Paul, leading his six brothers and sisters—a seventh was soon on the way—presented an awesome "spectacle" as they took their places in their seats, like "so many peas in a pod."[19] The church building, only twenty-five by fifty feet, must have seemed filled with the clan.

Father Herman Joseph Alerding was one of the priests who supplied the small Sullivan church in its early days. Alerding eventually became one of the leading prelates of the Catholic Church.[20] Ordained in 1868, the twenty-three-year-old Alerding was something of a circuit rider, ministering to the faithful not only in Sullivan but also in other small Catholic mission churches in the area. The young priest probably stayed with the Dreisers when he was in Sullivan. At the time, no one had any notion of the significant influence Alerding would play in young Paul Dresser's life in the very near future or later when Paul was in straitened circumstances.

Paul attended school in Sullivan in the old seminary. The poor condition of the schoolhouse probably forced Paul and his schoolmates to have more vacation times than most schoolchildren would normally have had. A two-story structure built in 1845, with two rooms on each floor, the old seminary was already in deplorable shape by the end of the Civil War, referred to as " 'a complete old rookery,' which had never been suitably arranged and ha[s] now become almost worthless."[21] During the winter of 1865–66 school was canceled because of the dilapidated state of the building. In December 1866 Sullivan residents were told that, because of a lack of furniture, school would not be in session until the beginning of 1867. The old seminary had lent its desks and seats to local private schools, and most of those items had somehow been destroyed. Now the old seminary had to be equipped with new furnishings. Not only was the condition of the building awful, but the school property and its surroundings were also terrible: "The school house lot and its approaches . . . are in a most shocking bad condition," wrote the editors of the *Sullivan Democrat*. "Some of the little fellows, barely six years of age, will sink in that 'mash,' or slough, some of these days." In a tone of sharp sarcasm, the editorial continued, "As the primary department is overcrowded this may be an end devoutly wished by the trustees. Or it may be they have no funds to build the walk."[22]

Because public funds to support free education were severely limited, dictating a short school year of three or four months, some teachers opened private schools at the conclusion of the regular school year to continue educating the children as well as to supplement their own meager incomes. Paul was probably unable to take advantage of such an opportunity because of the shifting financial fortunes of his father and the demands that a growing family placed on whatever money his father made. Once the children reached the age when they could help, they were all expected to pitch in to bring in additional money for the family. Paul, for example, worked in the woolen mill twisting strands of wool together. Such chores and the relative poverty of the family would most assuredly have prevented the Dreiser children from taking advantage of the supplementary education the private schools offered.

Paul's schoolmates remembered him as a popular youngster and a favored friend. A fellow student recalled Paul, who had been "one of [her] boy admirers," swimming with the neighbor boys in Black Creek, a popular bathing spot in the county, and remembered his singing and dancing—talents that made him "the Irving

Berlin and the Al Jolson of his day"—and "the star performer at the school entertainments . . . of the district schools of the county."[23] Another reminisced that even as a boy "Paul . . . was a great jokester and kidder—keeping everyone in a good humor."[24] Around the turn of the century, Ophelia Moore, then around sixty years old, wrote to Paul about

> the fair-haired little boy that was so hard to keep in the school room. You did well enough when I could get you in, but I had to watch or else you would slip away. You always had too much business to attend to in those school days to mind the voice of your teacher.

Paul must have chuckled as he got to his teacher's account of his arriving at school after the late bell rang. The locked hall door barred late students from entering, but Moore let him in through the back door, and "one very cold morning I took you in through the window." Any student wanting to leave the classroom had to get the teacher's permission and "one day you held up your little hand and said, 'Cuse me.' I did and walked to the door with you." She could still remember her affection for this little boy: "You reached up and put your arms around my waist as I said good-by to you." Paul was still one of Moore's favorites even nearly forty years after he had been in her classroom.[25]

Close friends in Sullivan were James and Mary Bulger and their children, a family with whom the Dreisers shared the bonds of Catholicism and poverty and shopping at Griffith's general store. James Bulger worked as a section hand for the Evansville and Terre Haute Railroad. He and Mary had four children by 1870, including the second oldest, red-haired Jimmy, born around 1867. The Bulgers' oldest son was killed in Sullivan in a mining accident shortly before the Dreisers arrived in town. Years later in a book, Theodore Dreiser wrote that James Bulger (renamed Thomas Dooney in the account), was, like Theodore's father, a "priest-ridden Catholic who had been befriended by my father in earlier days."[26] Dreiser recalled the elder Bulger as an abusive man who occasionally punished Jimmy by beating him with a heavy horsehide whip.[27] When tragic circumstances in Jimmy's life brought him to Paul's attention many years later, Paul referred to him as a close "boyhood chum." Because Jimmy was nine years younger than Paul, it is unlikely the two were that close, but Paul *did* know Jimmy and in later years knew about some of his troubles with the law.

The Sullivan of Paul's youth attracted entertainments of various kinds, many of which would have appealed immensely to this youngster. Traveling medicine-wagon shows regularly stopped in Sullivan. The Hamlin Wizard Oil Company, with its gaily decorated wagon filled with cure-alls, songbooks, and costumes, was the most impressive of the lot. And what a show the "doctor" and his singers put on! The male quartet entertained with a few boisterous songs, perhaps Foster's "If You've Only Got a Mustache," or something similar to amuse the crowd. Changing to a more sentimental mood, the quartet might then have sung "Backward, turn backward, O Time, in your flight, / Make me a child again just for to-night! / Mother, come back from the echoless shore, / Take me again to your heart as of yore"—words that would have brought tears to even the most hardened members of the audience.[28]

Now, with the crowd in their hands, the singers might have offered yet another poignant song, perhaps William Willing's "Twenty Years Ago," with its sentiments about a man's return to the old village where he and his best friend played such a short time ago. Memory after memory is evoked about that idyllic village and the friends they knew, especially those who lie buried in the old churchyard. "When our time shall come . . . and we are called to go, / I hope they'll lay us where we played just twenty years ago" likely would have brought lumps to the throats of those gently transported to their own childhoods.[29] Then it would have been time to brighten the mood; the quartet would have launched into another jolly song, perhaps Foster's "Oh! Susanna." The nonsensical "It raind all night the day I left, / The weather it was dry, / The sun so hot I frose to death" may have left Paul puzzled, trying to figure out what on earth they meant. More than likely the crowd would have been encouraged to join in: "Oh! Susanna Oh! dont you cry for me / I've come from Alabama wid mi banjo on my knee."[30]

With the crowd warmed up, it would have been time for some more group singing. The troupe would have passed out copies of a gaudily illustrated booklet of a dozen or so pages boasting of the magical cures of the company's nostrums. Interspersed every so often among the advertisements were words to songs—no music was needed, for these were songs everyone knew. The raucous out-of-tuneness of many of the voices would have somehow blended with the lovely, pure sound of many of the women and the almost golden quality of a few of the men's voices. This is what Paul could have heard when he walked the short distance from home to the town square with or without his parents, brothers, and sisters. Then there would have been the magic tricks that left the crowd gasping with wonder—pulling a coin unexpectedly out of a child's ear and then making it disappear, only to reappear in another's ear; pulling small animals out of the top hat of one of the quartet singers; and so many more that would have dazzled the audience. The troupe might have performed short dramas that delighted and amused. In a final bid to win favor, the troupe would have passed among the townspeople, distributing free gifts. There would have been something for everyone: the inexpensive trinkets, toys, and dolls would have been winners among the youngsters and the candy a delight to all. Perhaps a lucky few could even win a blanket or kitchen utensil in a drawing that night.

The events of the night would have certainly mesmerized young and old. Then it was time to go home. Children would have found it hard to sleep because of the exciting time they had had. In the meantime, the doctor would have placed some of his "medicines" in a local store where townspeople might buy them after the company left. That night the troupe would have prepared its wagon for the move to another town the next day, or it might have stayed in Sullivan for a couple more days. If it was in town over the weekend, the quartet would have made itself available for church services on Sunday, thus further ingratiating the company in the eyes of the residents. Smaller snake-oil operations, some consisting of only the "doctor" or the pitchman and a partner, would later come and go, but they certainly would not be as impressive as the Hamlin or Lightning Liniment companies were.

Medicine-wagon operations were not the only show in town. Wild West troupes, called Smith and Wesson opera companies, visited. And there were the rare extravaganzas. Little more than a year after *The Black Crook* opened at Niblo's Garden in New York

City, a Genuine Black Crook company played in Sullivan, attracting more than two thousand people.[31] What the audience thought about such big-city entertainment is unknown, but some were certainly shocked at the female cast members, some wearing flesh-colored tights, who flaunted their beauty and alluring charms; others were no doubt mesmerized by the wonder of the music, drama, and dance. Sullivan had never before seen the likes of such a show.

The circus, with its panoply of animals, jugglers, acrobats, and instrumental music, played an important role in entertaining Sullivan audiences. In summer 1868, when Paul was ten years old, three different circuses visited the town in only three months: the Stowe Brothers company began the processional in June, DeHaven's Circus followed in August, and the wonders of the Great Oriental Circus and Egyptian Caravan unfolded in September.[32] What an experience for Paul and the other youngsters—to watch as the circus pulled into town, and if one were old and big enough, to help put up the tent. What sights, odors, and sounds one remembered for the rest of one's life. The circus band may have played some of the rousing music popular from the recent war. The patriotic musical fervor of "The Battle-Cry of Freedom," "The Battle Hymn of the Republic," or "When Johnny Comes Marching Home" would have swelled the hearts of those on the sidelines. A county fair was held in Sullivan beginning in 1865 and continued during the years the Dreisers lived in town. Though probably not as fascinating as the circus or the medicine-wagon shows, the fair would have been another way for a youngster to pass time on a sultry summer's day.

Minstrel troupes, more modest in size than those playing Terre Haute, Indianapolis, or Evansville, included Sullivan in their itinerary as they crisscrossed the Middle West. If Paul had the opportunity to see even the smallest of the companies, he would have marveled at these players parading around the stage, singing to the cacophony of tambourine, fiddle, banjo, and bones. And strangest to his eyes might have been the black faces he saw on that stage. Even as a youngster, he would have known that these were not real blacks, that these imposters had merely darkened their faces with burnt cork. Some of them, however, looked like the real thing, and was not the language they spoke the authentic speech of blacks? It certainly would have sounded like it to him. Minstrels sang sentimental ballads as well as humorous songs—just like what he would have heard at the medicine-wagon shows—and offered fractured renditions of Shakespeare or a bit of some other drama. But the spectacle of the closing act was something no one could forget. Here was the entire troupe—small or large in numbers—strutting around the stage like so many black-faced peacocks, dressed in gaudily colored clothing of some outlandish style, each member trying to outdo the other. The young, impressionable Paul could have held on to these images and later selected from them to create his own brand of humor and music.

Band music was also a vital feature of small-town life, especially after the Civil War, when regimental bands continued their music making, now for the pleasure of the audience rather than to rally the troops to battle.

While some of these entertainments required the purchase of a ticket, something undoubtedly beyond the Dreisers' reach, there were any number of opportunities to see and hear much of this entertainment free.

Hearing and singing the exuberant and sentimental songs of his day likely colored Paul's auditory sense and helped forge his musical style as a neophyte entertainer and, later, as a composer. To him the visual and aural wonder and appeal of these Sullivan entertainments offered the promise of excitement and recognition. How different the life of an entertainer was, he must have thought; how unlike his own existence that was too often drab, depressing, and just plain hard. Later in life, in his letters and songs, Paul chose to remember the carefree days of his youth. There are few stories, and certainly no songs, about those times when he had to scour fields for vegetables for the dinner table or had to make coffee out of rye grass. The boyhood experiences that filled his senses with wonder and joy created indelible imprints on him—so much so that he repeatedly sought, through his songs, to relive the innocence of his youth where his beloved and all-forgiving mother and the small village of Sullivan would always protect him from the vicissitudes of life.

All this is not to say that Paul's youth was nothing but poverty and hard work. To the contrary, his father's financial situation at times was quite good. In those months when it was, the happiness and relative prosperity of the Dreiser clan must have been palpable to them and to their neighbors. In January 1869 Dreiser's partnership in the woolen mill allowed him to buy an adjacent lot from Ralph and Mary Thompson.[33] Perhaps Dreiser had planned to enlarge his house on some of this land. His growing family could always use more space. If this was his intention, nothing came of it; once more, money became scarce. Shortly after he bought his new lot, Dreiser and the Jewett brothers dissolved their partnership. It is not known why they decided to do this, but in April the Jewetts advertised their Sullivan Woolen Mills, this time without mentioning Dreiser. What Dreiser did after the dissolution is unknown, but without his full-time job, he and his family had to tighten their belts yet again, experiencing the deprivations of life lived on the edge of poverty. Mary Frances "Mame" Dreiser Brennan, the eldest Dreiser daughter, claimed years later that the Jewett brothers ruined the business during her father's illness—undoubtedly the "brain illness" to which Theodore referred.[34] Certainly this became part of the family legend surrounding the breakup of the partnership, but there is nothing to substantiate those claims.

Within thirteen months Dreiser's financial situation was reversed once more. In May 1870 Chauncey Rose, successful businessman and a beneficent figure in the history of Terre Haute, bought the Sullivan Woolen Mills from the Jewett brothers for more than ten thousand dollars and hired Dreiser as its manager. Johann Paul bought a lot and house from David Jewett and his wife—property that some have called the mill owner's lot and house in the Gray, Watson, and Bloom Addition to the town of Sullivan. Rose, perhaps Terre Haute's leading figure—certainly its wealthiest—had been responsible for bringing substantial railway lines and traffic to the city, linking Terre Haute with the important market capitals of the Midwest. Earlier he had built the Terre Haute House, considered to be the finest hotel in the city and, many thought, in the entire Midwest. Later, Sarah Dreiser would toil there, scrubbing, cleaning, and working herself to exhaustion in the place locals referred to as the Terrible Hot House.

Alas, Dreiser's good fortune was short lived, for in the late autumn of 1870 or early winter of 1871 he lost his position after a storm blew away the mill's top story. Not wanting to continue his investment in the factory or to sink money into its repairs, Rose, a shrewd businessman who knew how to cut his losses, sold the mill to Peter Hill and Eli and Anthony Milner on 8 February 1871 for seven thousand dollars, walking away with a loss of three thousand dollars.[35] Within the next two months Dreiser sold his Sullivan properties but had not completely given up, for in May the *Sullivan Democrat* carried an ad asking that "Persons having Wool to sell for Cash, or exchange for Goods, will find it to their interest to call on Paul Dreiser, at the Warehouse of W. H. Power & Son[,] Sullivan, Ind., Near the Depot. . . . Paul Dreiser, Formerly of Sullivan Woolen Mills."[36] Dreiser was now competing with Hill and the Milners; mindful of his business reversals in the recent past, he was not certain about his chances with this new venture, for he ran the ad for just a single issue.

This attempt at a comeback lasted only a short time. By August 1871 the Dreisers had moved back to Terre Haute, soon with nine children to feed. Theodore Dreiser was born that very month. Johann Paul had had success as a worker in woolen mills in Dayton, Fort Wayne, Terre Haute, and Sullivan, but he only rarely enjoyed similar accomplishment as a businessman and manager.

The *Sullivan Union* recalled Johann Paul as "a good citizen, but a poor business man and his family suffered at times. The mother was courageous and with the aid of friends and relatives managed to care for her large family."[37] Part of that statement would become no less true of Johann Paul's namesake, who also became a good citizen and compassionate human being but a poor businessman. Another Sullivan resident remembered Sarah "as a splendid woman [whose] life was one long battle against poverty."[38] While Theodore blamed his father's religious zealotry for the family's precarious situations, Mame blessed her father as "a man of stability whose word was his bond . . . [who] lived his Christianity 7 days a week." She especially recalled "the morning and evening prayers when all would gather around hearing again [his] earnest voice raised and noting the spiritual glow in his face."[39]

Theodore and Mame were merely responding in opposite ways to their father's practice of his Roman Catholic faith. Paul Dresser, on the other hand, tended to mask whatever feelings he had about his father even when the two were at loggerheads with each other. While the growing Paul generally kept his own counsel, he would soon rebel against his father in ways that were affronts to Johann Paul's religious beliefs as well as to his old-world ways. In those rebellions, Sarah could be counted on to take her son's side, exacerbating the tensions in the Dreiser household. Young Paul's first serious act of defiance was but a short time in coming.

CHAPTER 3

St. Meinrad Abbey and Rebellion

It was probably in early autumn 1870 that young Paul Dresser entered St. Meinrad Seminary. In the flush of success as manager of the Sullivan Woolen Mills, Johann Paul Dreiser's decision to send his oldest son to become a priest was perhaps his act of thanksgiving for God's rewards, an act bearing witness to his abiding, unquestioning belief in his Catholic faith. German-born Father Herman Joseph Alerding, the priest in Sullivan, had become friends with the Dreiser family and may have played some part in this decision. A recent graduate of St. Meinrad, the slender, handsome twenty-five year old was an impressive young man who soon came to the attention of members of the Roman Catholic hierarchy. Alerding was appointed pastor of St. Joseph, a prestigious parish in Indianapolis, when he was but twenty-nine, and in 1900 he became the fourth bishop of the Diocese of Fort Wayne.

During his days at the seminary, Alerding had played E-flat cornet in the student brass band, at that time a fledgling group. Initially, the sound of the group caused the "people [to stop] their ears and [keep] their distance." That did not bother Florentin Sondermann, a classmate and organizer of the band: "We did not let that worry us and kept on blowing lustily, and . . . after two months, [the band was] presentable. Hurrah for the St. Meinrad brass band!"[1] We do not know what Paul's musical ability was at this time, but if he showed any inclination toward music during Alerding's time in Sullivan, the young priest, remembering his own modest music making, may have encouraged the youngster and won his confidence. This compassionate and good priest, only thirteen years Paul's senior, might have seemed to him to be a wise, older brother. Certainly, the Dreisers loved Alerding. In the end it was father Dreiser's decision to send Paul to the seminary, but Alerding might have helped nudge the family in this direction, realizing that this could be young Paul's way out of the straitened circumstances that often threatened to overwhelm the family.

The Benedictines (Order of St. Benedict) had founded St. Meinrad in 1854, less than two decades before Paul arrived there. Settling in deep southern Indiana, about fifteen miles north of the Ohio River, the Benedictines had ambitious plans to make the region a center of Catholicism, especially for the Germans who populated the area and for those they hoped to attract. Named in honor of the ninth-century founder of Maria Einsiedeln, a Benedictine monastery in Switzerland, St. Meinrad would serve as a place of worship, and its seminary would educate young men for the priesthood. At its beginning, St. Meinrad was very modest, with only two priests to operate the undertaking that was housed in the two rooms of an old log house already standing on the property. There was great promise here, however, for the Anderson

IHS C9070

St. Meinrad in the 1860s.

River flowed nearby, offering the possibilities "for milling purposes and for flat-boat service."[2]

Shortly before young Paul arrived, Pope Pius IX had elevated the status of St. Meinrad from a priory to that of an independent abbey and had appointed Father Martin Marty its first abbot, actions reflecting the growth, stability, and promise of St. Meinrad. Unaware of the pope's appointment of Marty, the fourteen professed members of the priory gathered together and elected an abbot who would guide the fortunes of the abbey. Fortunately, these men also chose Marty. The solemn blessing of the abbot took place on Sunday, 21 May 1871, an event witnessed by "a mighty throng" of students, visiting clergy, members of the St. Meinrad community, and "the faithful from near and far."[3] The bishop of the Diocese of Vincennes officiated, assisted by the abbots of St. Vincent Abbey and the Trappist Abbey of Gethsemani in Kentucky.

If Paul had enrolled at St. Meinrad the previous fall—and much evidence points to that probability—he would have been witness to the grandeur, solemnity, and celebration of that great day. It is impossible, however, to know unequivocally if Paul was already a student then, for a disastrous fire on Friday, 2 September 1887, destroyed the abbey, many of its records, and much physical evidence of its students to that year. Thus we have no evidence of when Paul matriculated, what courses he studied, or how long he was there. At various times in later life, he said he had been a student at St. Meinrad for two years. Paul's brother Theodore Dreiser recalled his being there for six months, but that information would have come from family members since Theodore was not born until 1871.

At some point Paul realized the priesthood was not his calling. Whether he found study too difficult, the religious life oppressive and too reminiscent of the atmosphere of his own home and father, or his temperament in conflict with the goals of the religious community is not known. His sister Mame told the story that Paul, whom she affectionately called Pudley because of his chubbiness, was caught teaching some of the smaller boys "monkey shines, negro minstrelsey [*sic*] and tricks of various kinds. Finally one fine day he was missed at refectory, having joined a troupe of minstrels in real earnest when they were passing thru Kentucky."[4] While this is a nice story, it probably is only that. If there is even a grain of truth to it, one can almost see dismay, tinged with amusement, playing on Alerding's face.

***

Although the Dreisers returned to Terre Haute in late summer 1871, Paul kept his Sullivan-area connections, working during the summers of 1871 and 1872 on the farm that Jesse and Julia Rector owned east of Dugger, Indiana, in Greene County. Julia Rector and Sarah Dreiser were close friends, and the families had traveled the short distance between Sullivan and Greene Counties to visit one another often. After he left St. Meinrad, Paul may have initially returned to Sullivan or neighboring Greene County. He could, thereby, avoid what would be the considerable wrath of his father. After he finally worked up the courage to return to his family in Terre Haute, probably during the summertime, 1872, the fourteen year old took a variety of odd jobs to help bring in money for the family that then numbered nine children. A tenth, Edward, would arrive the next year. Paul shoveled corn in a distillery one winter and worked for the Evansville and Terre Haute Railroad as a train butcher and selling newspapers, candy, cigarettes, and cigars. The 1874 Terre Haute city directory lists his occupation as blacksmith. Paul also worked at the Ellis Woolen Mills, coming in early to light the gas. When she was ninety years old, Sarah Pierce reminisced about working with young Paul and also remembered "Paul making his first singing adventure on the back end of a wagon from which Modoc oil, 'good for man or beast,' was sold." After he became successful, she remembered him returning "in all of his sartorial splendor and call[ing] on his old friends in the neighborhood of First and Walnut streets."[5] The necessity for Paul to work so much undoubtedly prevented him from finishing the 1872 academic year at the St. Bonaventure Lyceum in Terre Haute. He and Charley Parrott, a boyhood friend and fellow musician, are both listed in the school's catalog as students for that year. None of the four Terre Haute newspapers of the time, however, mentions his name again in connection with St. Bonaventure's.[6]

It was probably during this time that Paul received his only formal music instruction, taking piano lessons from Fannie Hartung.

Fannie was about twenty-nine then, the daughter of German-born parents, George and Anna Hartung. Born in Ohio around 1845, Fannie had moved with her family to Terre Haute by 1860. There George Hartung taught music at home and later at the Indiana Conservatory of Music in Terre Haute.[7] Later in life Paul recalled his formal music study: "I studied music for six months; I think they call this period 'two terms.' At the expiration of the second term I had mastered the 'Sack Waltz.' That is about the limit of my musical education." He mentioned that Fannie later became a nun and added humorously that perhaps his "bad playing or the anticipation of some of the music I have written drove her into the retirement of a convent."[8]

The year 1873 was more than likely marked by continuing conflict between father and son, with the lively and irrepressible young Paul running afoul of his father's strict standards of behavior. Probably as a result of some sort of trouble in Terre Haute—perhaps between father and son, or even between Paul and the law—the elder Dreiser sent Paul back to the Rector farm to work. Judging from the caring letters he wrote to them in years to come, it is likely that Jesse and Julia Rector had by then become surrogate parents for Paul, perhaps giving him a kind of understanding and warmth missing from his own home. The Rectors' daughter Emma, with whom Paul often corresponded later in life, became a special friend. Jesse Rector paid Paul eighteen dollars a month for his work, and when he was ready to return to Terre Haute in 1874 after harvest time, Rector gave Paul a "few clothes, [a] couple of sides of beef, [a] couple [of] logs & 50.00 dollars."[9] When he returned home, his ever-critical father destroyed whatever sense of accomplishment young Paul must have felt; when his son gave him the fifty dollars, the parent scolded in his thick accent: "Iss dat all vot you got?"[10]

After having been isolated on the farm for such a time, Paul felt somewhat intimidated by the size and bustle of Terre Haute. He felt very much like a "country yokel," as he later told his brother Theodore. Additionally, he had no money to spend, while his younger, freewheeling, troublemaking brother Rome had money to burn, money—from who knows where—that he did not often share with the family. On the occasion of Paul's return, however,

Rome generously bought him a suit of clothes. Perhaps to prove he was not the bumpkin he envisioned himself to be, Paul began to hang around with some young delinquents, drinking, carousing, and "raising hell." He later wrote a song that touched on this period in his life. A boy ignores his mother's good advice, goes astray, and wanders down "the path that leads the other way."[11] His wayward life leads him to a prison cell.

Before Paul could continue down his own dangerous path, help came in the person of Father Meinrad McCarty, who was pastor at the Catholic church in Brazil, Indiana, northeast of Terre Haute. Supply priests had celebrated Mass for the faithful few in private homes in Brazil and its rural districts for less than a decade, but now Brazil had its own Catholic church. McCarty, a graduate of St. Meinrad, came to Brazil from St. Mary-of-the-Woods in Vigo County and was the person largely instrumental in establishing that church—the Church of the Annunciation. McCarty now needed a schoolteacher and, perhaps with the recommendation of Alerding, offered Paul the job. The twenty dollars a month and board and wash would certainly have been attractive to the sixteen year old.

If Paul had any qualms about his lack of qualifications, he put them aside, accepted the job, and took the train, whose fare the priest had paid, to Brazil. Dressed in a new suit that may have given him the confidence he needed at this moment—he had to have some feeling of trepidation—Paul went to work immediately. Later, he recalled his strenuous life in Brazil. Rising at four in the morning, he went to work in the garden and cleaned the horses' stall before breakfast. Then at seven, his day already three hours old, Paul assisted McCarty at Mass, after which he returned to work in the garden for about an hour. His teaching responsibilities began at nine, and he was with his young charges until noon. Afternoons were given over to lunch, more work in the garden, more teaching, a return to the garden at six and, at long last, supper. Josephine Walzer, the cook, rewarded his long, exhausting day with a wonderful meal. He remembered that she always gave him "good things to eat."[12] After supper he was free to go to his room, happily filled with his ample meal, but with the knowledge that he would have to begin this long and demanding schedule again in only a few hours.

After following what he called a "beaut" of a routine for three months with little, if any, relief, Paul decided to go see the circus that had just arrived in Brazil. He asked McCarty's permission for this absence, but the priest refused to allow him to go, telling him to stay home. Paul probably felt that his superior was merely being arbitrary, not unlike his father back in Terre Haute. That being the case, he did what he would have done to his father: he ignored McCarty's orders and went to the circus. Seeing Paul there, some neighbors betrayed him to McCarty, who immediately sent for Paul's father. The senior Dreiser arrived in Brazil in a rage. First, Paul had disappointed him by leaving St. Meinrad; then he had taken up a dissolute lifestyle. Now, McCarty had rescued Paul, had been generous to him, had helped him begin a worthwhile life, and how had he repaid the good priest? This was absolutely unacceptable! Dreiser gave his son the choice of coming home and going to a house of correction or of going wherever he pleased. What a choice! As Paul later recalled, "you would have thought I had committed murder."[13]

Paul made his decision: he would leave home. After packing the few things he had brought to Brazil, the reality of his decision hit him. What could he do? Where would he go? He had no money, no prospects. He certainly did not want to return to work on the farm. He began to cry as the enormity of the decision he had made sank in. As he stood on the street corner, tears coursing down his face, a woman approached him and asked if she could help. Maria Shattuck, who had heard him play the organ, consoled him and, learning he had no place to go, invited him to stay with her and her large family until he could get something to do. Counting himself exceedingly lucky for his rescue, Paul stayed with the generous Shattucks for four weeks, for which they charged him fourteen dollars for his room, board, and washing. Without a job, Paul could not pay even this little amount, but he did repay Maria and Frank Shattuck in later years.[14]

Panic-stricken about his future, Paul did not know where to turn. But his music abilities were about to rescue him. One night he heard Charley Kelley, a wandering banjo-playing minstrel and patent-medicine salesman, playing on the street corner. If he could only hook up with Kelley, this might be the way out of his predicament.

Thanks to his piano lessons with Fannie Hartung, Paul could read a little music; furthermore, he had a natural aptitude for music, being able to pick up "all sorts of songs. If he heard one once [he] would get it."[15] Paul approached Kelley and asked if the banjo player could use a partner. On hearing Paul play the piano in the Shattucks' parlor, Kelley hired him, and the two traveled throughout central and southern Indiana, playing anywhere they could. Working with Kelley, who "once in a while went on sprees," must have been an invigorating and exciting experience for young Paul.[16] The two itinerant musicians made up handbills announcing their appearances, and on good nights they made as much as seven dollars. All was not roses, however, for they sometimes lost as much as two dollars. This was a bare-bones medicine-show operation, for Kelley had no wagon, and he and Paul nearly always walked to their next stop unless they could hitch a ride with someone going their way.

One Friday night Paul was singing for a crowd when he became aware that Kelley was nowhere to be seen. Kelley should have been standing nearby, ready to sell the few medicines he carried, but instead he had abandoned Paul, taking the till of seventy-eight dollars they had accumulated. Paul was stuck with the bills for room and board and hall rent. The local sheriff, unmoved when Paul explained what had happened and learning that he could not pay his debts, put the young minstrel in jail. Paul must have felt a kind of fear he had never experienced before, hundreds of miles from family and friends, knowing no one, and uncertain when he might be free again. Two days later, the sheriff, in a moment of kindness, released Paul.

The grateful youngster immediately left town. He headed north, thinking that Indianapolis might have something to offer. Even though he had never been to that large city, there *must* be something he could do there, he thought. Certainly he did not want to return to Terre Haute to face yet another ugly confrontation with his father. The teenager began his trek in a drizzly cold rain, walking the remainder of that Sunday afternoon and early evening without food. One can only imagine the loneliness of walking long, remote stretches of Indiana countryside in the early winter. The enveloping darkness was unrelenting except when the moonlight, if there was any, provided some illumination. The cold was nearly unbearable, and the hunger rumbling in his belly was something he could not ignore! Long after dark Paul saw a light in a house, went to the door, knocked, and asked the elderly householder if he could stay the night. The "old guy's" less-than-cordial response: "Get out of here or I'll sic the dog on you—God damn you."[17]

Paul turned around and resumed his trek. Sighting some haystacks on this "old guy's" property, he sought shelter and warmth under the straw. The old farmer, however, had seen what Paul had done and came after him with a pitchfork. Escaping unharmed but still dreadfully cold and hungry, Paul wandered the dark path for another half hour before he saw another house. Rapping on its front door, he roused the owners—a farmer and his wife. When Paul asked to stay overnight, the farmer warily responded that he was not sure he had room. With tears in his eyes, Paul turned to go, but the farmer's wife came to his rescue, saying to her husband, "Silas, that's only a boy." The husband relented and the couple took Paul in, made him exchange his wet clothing for a suit of clothes from the husband, prepared supper for him, and gave him a bed. After two nights of sleeping in a jail cell, this was more than a little welcome, and Paul woke the next morning with spirits raised. The farmer returned Paul's clean and dry clothes to him and wished him well. When Paul offered to repay the farmer's kindness by helping with the chores, the old man would hear none of it and went out to begin his work for the day. While her husband was outside, the farmer's wife reached into an old tin can, pulled out a quarter, and slipped it to Paul. Paul had truly been blessed finding these Good Samaritans. He would remember these acts of unexpected kindness, repeating them to others time after time in years to come.[18]

Paul's step was lighter when he left the farm and walked the fourteen miles to the nearest railroad track. Unseen by the authorities, he hopped aboard a train heading north and rode "from 10 a.m. to evening." Then he slipped off the train and began once again his nightly search for a place to stay. This night his efforts were quickly rewarded by a black man who gave him a quilt and let him sleep on the floor of his cabin—another act of generosity from a total stranger. Paul remembered that he slept well that night. Early the next day he continued his travels north. He again hopped on a train, but this time his luck abandoned him; he was kicked off early in the day and spent the next five days walking, riding, and begging his way to Indianapolis.[19]

On Sunday evening at seven, one week to the day after he had been released from jail, Paul arrived in Indiana's capital. Knowing no one there, having neither a place to stay nor a job, the impact of his aloneness hit him hard, but he could not stop now. A short walk brought him to the new courthouse under construction and a brief distance beyond that to a church on East Vermont Street. In great weariness and sinking spirits, he sat down on the steps of the large building that housed St. Joseph Catholic Church, its school, seminary, and parsonage. Before very long two priests walked by, lost in conversation. As they passed Paul, one of them looked at him, walked on, looked back again at the disconsolate young man, and retraced his steps. "Isn't this Paul Dresser?" At the priest's question, Paul began to weep. Father Alerding, this good man of God, had come to his rescue. Paul must have been elated for he did know someone in Indianapolis after all.

As luck, or divine intervention, would have it, Alerding had been transferred to Indianapolis from Cambridge City, Indiana, just months before and was now the procurator for St. Joseph Seminary and pastor of the congregation. Alerding's teacher at the school had left because of illness, and the priest offered the job to his former parishioner—this sixteen year old whose past record would not have impressed a less compassionate and perceptive individual. Alerding was certainly well aware he was taking a gamble in offering the job to Paul. This youngster, likable though he was, had finished little he had started in life, had dropped out of Alerding's alma mater, had already had scrapes with the law, and had largely been abandoned by his father. Nonetheless, Alerding came to Paul's rescue, continuing his forceful and guiding presence in the young man's life. The priest took Paul to a store the next day to buy him a new suit and other clothing appropriate for his new position as teacher.

During the year Paul taught at St. Joseph, Alerding saw to it that he saved the money he earned and provided the kind of guidance and caring that this young man needed at this point in his life.

At the end of 1875, or the very early part of January 1876, Alerding made Paul a gift of the suit, fixed him up in other ways, gave him the four hundred dollars he had saved from his earnings, and sent him on his way back to Terre Haute, undoubtedly paying his train fare from Indianapolis. Paul had been gone from home for at least a year. No one had known where he was, and for all that anyone knew, he might have been dead. But here he was, much to the joy of his mother; even his father saw him in a different light when his prodigal son gave him a generous portion of the money he had saved. The rejoicing at Paul's return was to be short lived, however. Even though Alerding had done much to set Paul on the right path during their year together, the young man almost immediately resumed his former ways, drinking and squandering the rest of his savings.[20]

On Saturday night, 19 February, Paul was drinking heavily in one of Terre Haute's saloons. After the town's bars closed, he broke into two of them, stole bottles of whiskey, and helped himself to some checks. Much later in life Paul told Theodore the preposterous story that he had had a key that "accidentally fitted [the] door" to one of the saloons.[21] Even in his last months Paul was unwilling to admit the deliberateness of his act. The police immediately suspected Paul, arrested him, and charged him with burglary. Paul confessed to entering "the saloon of a man named Miller, on Third Street [and] also the Woodruff Saloon on Ninth and Main" but falsely claimed that Marshall Smith, "a well known character," had been the one who got Paul drunk, had instigated the crime, and had used Paul as his accomplice.[22] Smith had an alibi and was exonerated.

Unable to raise three hundred dollars for bail, Paul was sent to the county jail, where he spent ten weeks before his trial. Near the beginning of May, Paul was found guilty of the charges, and the judge sentenced him to an additional thirty days in jail and a fine. Released at the very end of May or early in June, Paul, smelly and dirty, walked to his home at Twelfth and Walnut but could not bring himself to enter the house, knowing what his father would say and do. Hiding in the outhouse, he beckoned his five-year-old brother, Theodore, and told him to go inside and tell their mother that he was out of jail. Sarah, ever the all-forgiving mother, embraced her oldest boy, burned the clothes that he had probably worn for the past four months, "scrubbed him, [and] gave him some old clothes." This done, they "both cried."[23]

Johann Paul's embarrassment and shame must have been considerable. First, Rome had become the town rowdy, a ne'er-do-well who never fit into the Dreiser family and could never be counted on to do anything except cause trouble. Now his firstborn had brought dishonor to the family. Even the *Sullivan Democrat* reported Paul's arrest. The thought that friends in Terre Haute and Sullivan must certainly be condemning him and his family preyed mightily on Johann Paul's mind. Young Paul, however, still had not learned his lesson, for he returned to his rounds of drinking in the saloons of Terre Haute, perhaps admired by his hooligan companions because of his newly acquired reputation as a jailbird. Before long, however, music rescued Paul from the path that threatened to lead him to self-destruction.

PART 2

Apprenticeship: 1876–1886

CHAPTER 4

Of Medicine Wagons and Minstrelsy

During the summer of that trying year of 1876, Paul Dresser and his father were at their wits' ends, the son wanting to get out from under the oppressive hand of the old man and the father convinced that his stern punishment was what this rebel needed. Johann Paul Dreiser's method of punishing his oldest child had not worked in the past, and it was not now going to change the behavior of this spirited eighteen year old. Something had to break the impasse that existed between the two, a stalemate that undoubtedly affected the entire household. Tenderhearted Sarah was not much help; her unequivocal love for her children, no matter what they did, served to work at cross-purposes to father Dreiser's strict discipline, even though she never overtly challenged her husband in such matters. Still, the children knew, as children nearly always do, where to turn for unstinting love. In the end, music broke the impasse, or at least separated father and son from each other, allowing Dresser to break free from the household.

That summer the Lemon brothers from Marshall, Illinois, just across the Wabash River, came to Terre Haute with their minstrel-medicine show.[1] Needing an organist and principal singer, the leader of the Lemon troupe, upon hearing Dresser play and sing, offered him the job for five dollars a week with food and washing. Dresser would even play the bass drum with the troupe, accompanied by his Terre Haute friend Charley Parrott on the tenor drum. Dresser hurriedly accepted the offer and immediately recommenced the hurly-burly life of a traveling musician. He was in the glamorous situation of working with a group. Here he was part of the male quartet of singers; here he could interact with his colleagues in short humorous or dramatic skits as the troupe entertained the crowds, softening them up for the inevitable medicine pitch that would follow. The Lemon brothers played the street corners of Terre Haute for the next four weeks—locations where Dresser was "applauded by [the very] people who had roasted him [before]." In later years Dresser remembered "Hungry Man from Marshall" and "Gilfillow, the Big Buck Goat" as two of the crowd's favorite songs.[2] Although he never claimed to have had anything to do with writing the music or words for these songs, Dresser was a keen observer of what pleased the public, and he would put his observations to practical use before long in both his performances and the songs he would write. The troupe played in other cities, towns, and villages in Indiana, traveling as far south as Evansville, a city that would soon play an important role in Dresser's development as a musician, actor, and comic.

Sometime during the spring of 1877 the Lemon brothers disbanded, their money having run out.[3] At that time Dresser most likely went to Chicago, where yet another exciting chapter in his life was about to unfold. Perhaps he was already there, having traveled to the city with the Lemon brothers; perhaps he had joined a minstrel troupe that went to Chicago. In any event, he arrived in a city that was then in the throes of rebirth after the devastating 1871 fire. This was the place to be for the young, for the entrepreneur, for those willing to gamble on this new phoenix; this was the most exciting place Dresser had ever been.

One of the shrewdest of the many businessmen who populated this new, vital Chicago was John Austin Hamlin, the inventor of Wizard Oil. The son of a Cincinnati physician, Hamlin invented his elixir while a teenager, moved to Chicago in 1861 when he was twenty-four, and with his brother Lysander founded the Wizard Oil company, an organization that "represented the acme of piety and rectitude."[4] Producing his formula in mass quantities, Hamlin claimed Wizard Oil could cure "All Pain in Man or Beast." Various Hamlin pamphlets touted the benefits of Wizard Oil. A combination of camphor, ammonia, chloroform, sassafras, cloves, turpentine, and goodly quantities of alcohol, the nostrum could be used, its inventor boasted, to relieve rheumatism, lame back, headache, neuralgia, toothache, earache, sore throat, diphtheria, catarrh, inflammation of the kidneys, ulcers, fever sores, cholera morbus, and all "Inflammation or Pain from whatever Cause."[5]

Hamlin soon used his considerable talents for promotion to bring his product to a wide public, and he began traveling to villages and towns in the Midwest. The entrepreneur was so successful that before long he had seventy troupes plying the roads. According to one researcher, "Each troupe included a driver, a lecturer, and a male quartet, traveling in a covered wagon drawn by four or six horses. Packed in the wagon were a wardrobe trunk, an organ, and a supply of torches for night performances."[6] Most important, the wagon was filled with Wizard Oil, other cure-alls Hamlin had invented, and songbooks published by the company. At each location, the quartet entertained the audience with music, comedy sketches, and skits—not unlike the kinds of entertainment one found in the blackface minstrel shows of the time. The performers were flexible, playing inside a hall sometimes, but more often they performed on street corners, where "from the wagon, which could be quickly converted into a stage, [they] would sing a medley of songs, decked out in silk top hats, frock coats, pinstripe trousers. And patent leather shoes with spats."[7]

The audience frequently participated in the entertainment for the evening. The members of the troupe passed out the company's songsters to the crowd and asked it to join in singing old favorites, the words of which were printed in the free booklet. In one Wizard Oil collection, "Swing Low, Sweet Chariot," "The Old Doorstep," "Only a Dream of the Old Home," "Carve Dat 'Possum," and "Steal Away" alternate with descriptions of symptoms of various ailments, testimonials from those "cured by Wizard Oil," instructions for using the medicines—"For Croup.— . . . mix together equal quantities of Wizard Oil and goose oil or sweet oil, and apply externally to the throat and chest with a feather or camel-hair brush. Bathe the feet in warm water, and keep the body warm"—and advertisements for other Hamlin products.[8]

After the entertainment, the "professor" or "doctor"—initially Hamlin himself—gave a brief lecture on the benefits of Wizard Oil, supported perhaps by testimonials from some people—often planted in the crowd—who claimed to have been cured by this wonderful elixir. After the doctor's pitch, many in the audience, anxious to try this marvelous medicine that promised so much, lined up to buy it, either in fifty-cent or one-dollar bottles. Finished with their work for the evening, the entertainers then settled in for a stay in the community or began their travel to the next location. "It was to the showman's benefit to stay in one place as long as possible, especially in bad weather, and operators tried to remain in small towns at least a week and preferably two," notes one historian. "Large important companies that could draw huge crowds would work cities for as long as two months at a time."[9]

Because unscrupulous medicine-wagon showmen had given the profession a bad reputation by leaving town without paying their bills or by selling worthless snake oils, troupes frequently planned escape routes out of town in case emergencies arose. Certainly Charley Kelley had done this; Dresser had been the unwitting dupe of Kelley's emergency escape. Perhaps the Lemon brothers had also done this. The Hamlin company, however, was a different sort of operation, known for its fairness and quality products. Even though it was common knowledge that there existed no bottled or packaged panacea—not even with the Hamlin company—Hamlin troupes were nearly always welcomed for repeat visits. If nothing else, the quality of their entertainments assured them a warm reception.

Dresser took a job with the Hamlin organization as a singer and organist for fourteen dollars a week.[10] Already familiar with music in the songbooks and knowing many other tunes as well—he was a quick study when it came to music—Dresser soon composed his own songs. The company issued these songs, certainly imitations of other composers' works, in a Paul Dresser songbook that was "full of parodies" and for which Dresser got half the royalties.[11] The six to ten dollars a week he made from his share of the sales of his songster, together with his weekly pay, brought him a generous financial reward on top of the nightly approval he received from appreciative audiences. If he had not known it before, he must have recognized now that this was the life for him.[12]

Traveling with a rival medicine show at about the same time was fellow Hoosier James Whitcomb Riley. Riley wrote to a friend about his adventures with the C. M. Townsend Magic Oil Company: "I am having first rate times considering the boys I am with. They, you know, are hardly my kind, but they are pleasant and agreeable and with Doctor Townsend for sensible talk occasionally, I have really a happy time. We sing along the road when we tire of talking, and when we tire of that and the scenery, we lay ourselves along the seats and dream the happy hours away." While traveling with Townsend, Riley came up with a novel idea for advertising the "doctor's" products through illustrations and words on a blackboard.[13] Riley's and Dresser's paths would cross from time to time during the next decade, first as they both traveled the medicine-wagon circuit, and later when Dresser was a solo singer-actor and Riley pursued a career as half of a duo with humorist Bill Nye.

Apparently Dresser stayed with the Wizard Oil company for just one season, for by August 1878 he was back in Terre Haute, where a local newspaper informed its readers that he had written a song and dance called "Where the Orange Blossoms Grow."[14] Because the tune has been lost, we do not know what an early Paul Dresser song sounds like, but it was almost certainly based on music Dresser would have sung with the Lemon brothers and with the Wizard Oil troupe. Writing much later, an unidentified reporter claimed that the tune was "almost literally taken from 'Way Down Upon the Suwanee River.' "[15] Certainly the allusion to Stephen Foster's tune is wrong, for a scan of Dresser's words reveals that they do not fit that particular melody:

I just arrived in town today,
I'm a stranger to you all,
And hearing such sweet music
I thought I'd make a call.
I came from that sweet, sunny clime,
Where you never see deep snow;
I just arrived from Dixie,
Where the orange blossoms grow.
Now very soon I'm going home,
And then no more will you see me roam;
For I want to see that dear old spot
Where the summer winds do blow,
And I'm going back to Dixie,
Where those orange blossoms grow.[16]

The reporter recalled that George H. Primrose and William H. West, two blackface minstrels, were in the audience when Dresser sang his song.[17] Primrose and West were in town performing with Milt Barlow, George Wilson, and other musicians. Twenty-year-old Dresser was singing for two of the leading entertainers in America at that time—half of what would become the Barlow, Wilson, Primrose, and West minstrel company. Primrose was pleased with "Where the Orange Blossoms Grow," said that he wanted to add it to his repertoire, and gave Dresser "a fine diamond ring" as payment for it.[18] Even though the value of the ring was probably negligible, Dresser was undoubtedly ecstatic that this great star liked the song. One can imagine the pride young Dresser must have felt at the moment. Primrose, that stellar burnt-cork artist, would now be singing a Paul Dresser song to countless numbers of people all over the nation. The only catch was that Dresser had given away all the future rights to this song—royalties as well as acknowledgment as its composer—all for that ring. Without documenting their sources, most of Theodore Dreiser's biographers claim that Dresser went on the road with a minstrel troupe at about this time. If this is accurate, Primrose may well have given Dresser more than "a fine diamond ring" in return for the song.[19] He may have offered Dresser a job with his company.

The Barlow, Wilson, Primrose, and West minstrel troupe became one of the most popular and successful of the blackface organizations, easily bringing in a hundred thousand dollars a year. Its manager claimed that the company brought in more than five hundred dollars a night and often made more than a thousand. Successful minstrel managers brought matters of economy to bear to make as much money as possible for their troupes. By staying in one city for more than a night, the company got better rates at hotels and saved on railroad fares. The troupes guaranteed freshness to theater managers and audiences by changing their programs somewhat each night they stayed. The salaries the company paid its performers ranged from twenty-five to two hundred dollars per week, and a newcomer's salary was probably at the lowest end of the scale. Nonetheless, twenty-five dollars a week was more money than young Dresser previously had made except when his *Paul Dresser Songster* sold extremely well for the Hamlin company.[20]

Dresser himself provided scant information about this time in his life and never mentioned traveling with a specific blackface minstrel company. In an interview from around April 1898, Dresser said that he "had traveled with all sorts of bum troupes out of Terre Haute until [he] became ambitious and went to New York." Possessing no little amount of self-assurance, Dresser decided to start at the top in New York City. That meant Augustin Daly's theater, where he was thwarted time and again as he sought an audition. Annoyed at the stage-door manager there who repeatedly turned down his request for entrance with a haughty "No, mah deah boy, we have all the talent we desiah," Dresser spent some of his meager savings to print cards that read:

> MR. PAUL DRESSER,
> DALY'S THEATER.
> Stage Entrance—No Farther.

"One of these cards finally reached Mr. Daly himself. He sent for me and I was engaged. That's how I came to get my first, good job."[21]

Daly's theater was located in the heart of the Broadway and Union Square Rialto theater district. In 1879, as the theater district migrated northward, Daly moved his stock company to Broadway and Thirtieth. Broadway, the main north-south thoroughfare of the city, where one could see or purchase almost anything imaginable, must have overwhelmed the young comic singer from Indiana. The magnificent stores of Brooks Brothers, B. Altman, A. T. Stewart, and Lord and Taylor, so many Broadway sirens beckoned passersby, luring them with their tantalizing offerings. Dresser may have trod Chicago's State Street in the past, but even that experience would have fallen short of the visual grandeur, the spectacle, and the sheer volume of sound he encountered when he first set foot on Broadway. Dresser left no impressions of New York City from this point in his life, save what he said above, but in the words of a writer of the time:

> its tread is elastic, buoyant, and almost rhythmic, as it follows the rattle and roar of the vehicles; and that rattle and roar, made by the pressure of hundreds of wheels and hoofs

> on a resonant pavement, are like the *crescendo* movement of a heroic symphony. . . .
>
> If in some way the rest of the city should be demolished, Broadway could supply the survivors with every necessary and luxury of life.[22]

At the same time, in all of the hubbub, with people scurrying to and fro, the overwhelming number of buildings, and the noise, one could find occasional oases of calm. Parts of Union Square offered

Van Pelt-Dietrich Library Center, Univ. of Pa.

The Casino Theatre, on the corner of Broadway and Thirty-ninth, one of the many attractions lining the Great White Way in the late nineteenth century.

places, where one could, in warm weather, settle amidst the carpet of grass and the graceful foliage and be renewed by the gentle sounds of the fountain. Here the sounds of nature hushed those of the nearby world only a few steps away. Here nannies pushed their tiny charges in carriages during the mornings and afternoons, idlers wasted away hour upon hour, and weary souls sat for a few moments of reflection. After dark, pairs of lovers replaced the nannies, the whole scene illuminated by lamps.

Dresser may have taken the opportunity to enjoy the peace and relative quiet that part of Union Square had to offer, but it was Broadway with its entertainment district that drew him in. Wallack's Theater sat just south and west of Union Square, while Tony Pastor's and the Germania Theater lay close by. If Dresser had, indeed, laid siege to Daly's, he was bidding high, for Daly was a major player in the dramatic world of nineteenth-century New York City. Success at Daly's theater carried with it an entrée into other theaters in the city and beyond. No evidence exists to verify Dresser's claim of having performed there, and his circa April 1898 interview is the only one in which he mentioned appearing there. Theodore Dreiser recalled that Dresser had been a "monologue artist" at Tony Pastor's and Niblo's Garden, but he never repeated Dresser's story about Daly's theater.[23] Even here, however, Dreiser's memory cannot be trusted, for there is, similarly, no evidence that Dresser ever appeared at either Pastor's or Niblo's Garden. Dreiser recalled that when he first visited his brother in New York City in the summer of 1894, Dresser talked about Daly's as they passed the theater. The initial part of Dresser's comments, as recalled by Dreiser, might seem to suggest that he had actually worked for Daly:

> [Daly] is a manager. He makes actors—he don't hire them. He takes 'em and trains 'em. . . . When you work for him you're just an ordinary employe [*sic*] like any one else and you do what he tells you, not the way you think you ought to do.

The last portion of Dresser's words, however, appear to indicate that he had been only an observer at Daly's, not that he had actually worked for Daly:

> I've watched him rehearse, and I know, and all these fellows tell the same story about him. But he's a gentleman, my boy, and a manager, a manager, see? Everybody knows that when he finishes with a man or woman they can act.[24]

Whatever the accuracy of Dreiser's omissions or inclusions, precious little can be documented about Dresser's life and whereabouts between 1878 and December 1880. By the latter date Dresser had gained enough experience as an entertainer to be hired as a solo artist at the Apollo Theatre in Evansville.[25] To gain that exposure as a singer, to build on his abilities as a blackface artist—both areas he had cultivated as a medicine-wagon-show entertainer—and to possess even a reputation sufficient enough to gain entrance to the Apollo, Dresser must have been with some sort of performing troupe or working alone at his craft between August 1878 and his opening at the Apollo. The fact that he is listed in the Terre Haute city directory for 1879–80 as a musician is a clear sign that this is what Dresser considered his profession to be.

Thus Dresser left behind that difficult period of his youth with its rebellious side and became a professional entertainer. Of course he had been on his own in the world before, but in the past, Indiana and mother had been his anchors. That they would continue to be his foundations was certainly true, but he would never again return to his beloved state for extended stays, and he would lose contact with his family for long periods of time. Yet as his celebrity grew, memories of those places and of his mother would become dearer to him. They, not New York City, would ever be the stable influences in his existence, ones to which and to whom he returned time and again in his songs.

CHAPTER 5

Evansville

At some point during his travels before 1880, Paul Dresser landed in Evansville, Indiana, a thriving city on the banks of the Ohio River. Evansville had been an important transportation center for nearly three decades by the time Dresser arrived there. With steamboats plying the Ohio River and the Evansville and Terre Haute Railroad joining the Chicago and Eastern Illinois Railroad to form a connecting line from the south and southwest to Chicago and beyond, Evansville was able to transport goods and passengers both north and south. It also sat in the center of a vast coalfield, was known for its building stone and iron deposits, and at the time was the largest hardwood lumber market in the United States. A vital economy along with a temperate winter climate, the existence of numerous churches and parks, boat excursions during the more clement time of the year, and numerous kinds of entertainment, including an active baseball season, made Evansville an attractive place to live. By the late 1880s the city was home to nearly sixty thousand people.

The city's active theater and entertainment life provided Dresser with opportunities to advance his career as a performer. Diversity prevailed in the city's cultural offerings. On a given evening, the great Norwegian violinist Ole Bull or the eminent Hungarian violinist Eduard Hoffmann, known professionally as Remenyi, might perform a potpourri recital of classical music together with arrangements of popular and folk tunes. Theatergoers could attend a performance by a touring company of

Uncle Tom's Cabin; a band concert over in Salt Wells; a minstrel show featuring the Barlow and Wilson troupe, the Thatcher, Primrose, and West company, or Haverly's Original Colored Minstrels; a variety show at the Apollo Theatre; a lecture perhaps by someone of Robert Ingersoll's stature; Thomas W. Keene in Shakespeare's *Richard III*; the circus; or a variety show replete with singers, acrobats, jugglers, animal acts, and a concluding dramatic presentation. Sunday was the only day when one usually could not find this sort of entertainment, although there were numerous attempts to change this with calls to repeal the Sabbath laws.

Univ. of Southern Indiana Special Collections and University Archives, Tom Mueller Collection

Fischer's Hotel and Fourth Street Market, Evansville, ca. 1890.

The Apollo Theatre, the Opera House, and Simon Cahn's usually attracted large audiences. The Apollo, with a company of thirty-five actors, singers, and instrumentalists, was where Dresser most frequently appeared. An open beer garden during warm-weather months, it could be enclosed for the winter season. At various times local newspapers praised Apollo manager John Albecker for operating a clean theater: "[Albecker gives] the people the best variety amusement untainted with anything immoral," the *Evansville Daily Journal* reported in 1879. "The standard of propriety is so much above that usually found in such theaters that all the performers marvel that the theater is so popular." The paper concluded by suggesting that Albecker set aside one evening when he would close the bar and invite the ladies to see his excellent entertainment.[1] It later encourged the public to support Albecker and his entertainments "from which vulgarity and double-entendre are eliminated."[2]

With the installation of electric lights in part of the city in the early 1880s, a measure of safety was added for those who wished to venture out after dark. Before this, one made one's way through the darkened and often dusty or muddy streets of the city aided by whatever light was thrown by lanterns or by the rush candles—a kind of reed torch, dipped in grease and set alight—one carried. Even after the city added masts with electric lights, however, a certain inconsistency in lighting prevailed, leaving many dark areas where the light could not reach. A writer complained, "The two masts on the river front are worthless, if it is intended they shall light the entire front of the city not provided for by the up town lights, for they only light one block in each direction."[3] The lights were not turned on when the moonlight provided sufficient illumination. Still, the addition of electric light in the streets brought an increase in theater attendance, and after theater owners installed electric lighting in their entertainment palaces, the number of theater fires decreased.

Just how Dresser got to Evansville is now unknown, but at least four accounts written after he died had him arriving there with a medicine-wagon show. A local obituary read, "He came to Evansville with a patent medicine doctor and it was his work to sing and entertain the crowds that gathered around the flimsey [*sic*] stage in front of the tent of the medicine vender, which was placed near the old court house at Main and Third streets."[4] A 1922 article, written at the time when there was great interest in erecting a memorial to Dresser, noted, "The memory of Hamlin's Wizard Oil is kept alive by the memory of Paul Dresser's songs and humor for his performance was the real drawing card that attracted the crowds." People would walk downtown, one resident remembered, "every night there was a medicine show announced just to hear Paul Dresser sing. A great favorite with the people was his song 'Mary Ann's a Teacher in the Great Big Public School.' "[5] If this song was, indeed, by Dresser, it has been lost. In two other reminiscences, the writers had Dresser coming to Evansville with the Lightning Linament Company.[6] He was remembered as the organ player for the troupe, and more than one person commented on his habit of scribbling verse at any opportunity.

Given the fact that even the earliest account of Dresser's coming to the city was written more than two and a half decades after his arrival and the last more than seventy years after he got there, it is not surprising that the writers' memories were hazy when it came to remembering specific dates. It is interesting that each account recalled Dresser arriving with a medicine-wagon show; nowhere is there mention of his coming to town first with a blackface minstrel troupe. If Dresser *did* travel with the Barlow, Wilson, Primrose, and West Minstrel Troupe as his niece Vera Dreiser suggested, or with any other troupe after August 1878, it is most likely that he had left organized minstrelsy for some reason and had returned to performing with a medicine-wagon show by the time he arrived in Evansville.[7]

In February 1880, some ten months before Dresser made his first known solo performance in Evansville, management began work to improve two of the most popular theaters in the city. At the Apollo, carpenters added an elevated floor and gallery and more seats to increase the audience capacity to more than a thousand. Not to be outdone, the Opera House underwent renovations at the same time. Workers repaired the old scenery that had been in continuous use for more than a decade and painted over the gaudy and blatant advertising that had decorated the drop curtain. The *Evansville Daily Journal* reported: "Many theatre-goers will rejoice at this intelligence, and the JOURNAL is assured that no more advertising curtains will be displayed in the Opera House under its present management."[8]

When it reopened, the Apollo, located on upper Third Street, became increasingly known as a place for family entertainment. Albecker added matinee performances that were planned with a specific audience in mind. Now women and children would not have to venture out after dark to attend the theater. Furthermore, they were guaranteed a show that would in no way offend their sensibilities. A reviewer of a matinee performance later in the year remarked, "There was a goodly sprinkling of ladies present, whose manifestations of approval, though less demonstrative than those of the men, were equally as perceptible, and testified to the high character of the performance."[9]

The autumn of 1880 was marked with the frenzy surrounding forthcoming local and state elections. Even more important to many was the presidential contest between two Civil War veterans, Winfield Scott Hancock of Gettysburg fame and James A. Garfield, who had fought in the battle at Shiloh. Dresser was one of those caught up in campaign fever. Volunteering for the Democratic campaign, he helped lead torchlight processions that wound through the city, the marchers cheering lustily for General Hancock, "Hancock the superb." As interest and involvement in the campaigns increased, theater audiences dwindled in size to such an extent that Albecker decided to close the Apollo until after the elections. He would simply lose too much money keeping his theater open to ever smaller audiences. The approaching election brought more celebrations—"Jollifications" as they were called—including a separate one for the black community. More torchlight parades, bonfires, illuminations, triumphal arches, and grand pyrotechnic displays filled the city.[10]

Election time concluded (Dresser's man lost to Garfield), the Apollo, newly painted and made ready for the winter season, reopened during the third week in November. Two weeks later Dresser appeared there as a solo performer. His first-night audience was somewhat small, but he gave patrons their money's worth. With "his humorous songs, [he] literally took the house by storm, and made a great hit." On closing night "the largest house of the week witnessed the performance . . . and manifested its appreciation of the bill by liberal applause, of which Mr. Paul Dresser, or *Driesser*, received the lion's share."[11] Why the reviewer spelled Dresser's name two different ways is uncertain, but others, including the publishers of city directories and the proprietor of one of the Sullivan general stores, had done the same thing in the past. Perhaps Paul himself was uncertain as to what name he should use. Whatever the case, he had decided on Dresser, for that is the way his name always appears in ads and reviews after 1881.[12]

Dresser or Driesser notwithstanding, not even this promising young entertainer could keep the Apollo open by himself. Attendance was still low, in part because of competing attractions at the Opera House. Albecker, an astute businessman, knew when to cut his losses. In spite of the investment he had made in refurbishing the building, he reluctantly closed the Apollo for the season after Dresser's last night, less than one month after the theater had reopened. A local newspaper regretted this necessary action because it felt local citizens should lend Albecker the kind of support his "first class specialty show[s], . . . his energy and enterprise justly entitled him to."[13]

During his Evansville years, Dresser's infectious humor, his talent, and especially his generosity to others won him many good friends and admirers. Regarding his abilities as a composer, John Mackey, a clarinetist, remembered playing "many of the compositions composed by Paul which at that time were not published."[14] For Dresser, "composition" took the form of singing his tunes to the leader of the Apollo orchestra who would then copy and arrange them for the orchestra. At the time Dresser knew little about the fundamentals of music and could not write down the music that he had in his head and could sing and play. Another musician recalled, "To get the real beauty of [the] songs, one had to sit with [Dresser], he playing the piano and singing the song himself. He was not a good pianist nor singer but he knew how to do the stuff and get all out of it."[15] One Evansville resident remembered some of Dresser's doggerel from the time: "The festive Dudelet With his poodlet, Took a walklet down the Streetlet, Dude got so rudelet, Cop nabbed the Dudelet: And stuck him in the cooler with his poodlet."[16] Such "poetry" and other Dresser humor also appeared in a column he wrote for a time for a local newspaper.

Dresser's generosity had few limits. He often got passes for youngsters to see a show for free at the Polly Garden, as the Apollo was called by some. On a walk through Evansville one day, Dresser and Mackey came upon a crippled beggar to whom Dresser gave his last dollar, money he had intended to use to buy himself a couple of pairs of socks. Dresser noted that the unfortunate man probably had no feet for socks, but that the man certainly needed the money more than he did.[17] On another occasion Dresser paid for lessons for a young girl who was appearing at Simon Cahn's. Emma Kane had, he thought, a marvelous voice, but her poor stage presence made it impossible for her to sell a song. Dresser arranged for a local music "professor" to give Kane lessons in stage deportment to improve her "rough and awkward appearance." Six months after the lessons, Kane repaid Dresser, writing to thank him for what he had done and to let him know that "thanks to your kindness . . . I open at [the] Whalen Theatre in Louisville Ky next week under contract for $75 per week and just six months ago I opened at Cahan's [*sic*] Winter Garden for 15 per week and as I now understand things, if it had not been for you and your kind heart I would now at this time have a much different story to tell."[18] Dresser practiced similar acts of generosity and kindness throughout his life, a trait that some took advantage of. As Theodore Dreiser said later, Dresser "was generous to the point of self-destruction."[19]

Sometime during his early days in Evansville, Dresser wrote a weekly humor-and-advice column, called "Plummy's Pointers," for the short-lived *Evansville Argus*.[20] The contents of the paper are unknown, for it has vanished like so much of the ephemera of the period. It was probably something of a gossip sheet. Founded in November 1879, the weekly *Argus* was published on Saturdays, and Dresser's entertainment column, for which he was paid eight dollars a week, was the one many people turned to first when they opened the paper. Dresser's column treated readers to chitchat about local happenings, to gossip about who was seen with whom, and to the latest, often preposterous, jokes. Although many looked forward to their weekly dose of the *Argus*, others viewed the upstart paper with disdain. "The *Argus* should be content with its proud pre-eminence of perennial dullness," sniffed a columnist for the *Daily Journal*. Suggesting that the addition of intelligence to the editor's brass would enable him to sell lightning rods, the same columnist concluded "we see no future before him. As a journalist he is a dead failure."[21]

Dresser's combination of singing, humor, wit, and personal warmth quickly made him a local favorite, one Evansville audiences looked forward to seeing, hearing, and reading. In turn, he had gained much experience in this river city. He had learned how to read audiences—what was successful with them and which parts of his act and what songs and jokes did not work. He could then alter his routines to make them more appealing to the crowd. He had had the opportunity to try out songs that were forever circling in his brain—melodies and words that seemed to possess him. People liked many of them, and perhaps that was where his future lay. He had gained a certain degree of celebrity that would have astounded the good people of Terre Haute, not to mention his own family. Moreover, he had attained a maturity that enabled him to make the choices that moved him ever farther from that dangerous path he had so recently traveled. This was a new Dresser people back home would hardly recognize. By the spring of 1881, just before his twenty-third birthday, he decided he was ready to try his wings beyond the Middle West. Even though he was often on the road during the next few years, Evansville remained his new home until the summer of 1886. He retained his local addresses in this southern Indiana city where the love of his life lived and where he would soon move some of his family.

CHAPTER 6

Beyond Evansville

In March 1881 an Evansville newspaper noted that Paul Dresser, the "very promising young comic vocalist" had left for Chicago, where he was to open at the Academy of Music on the fourteenth of the month.[1] We do not know what his reception was at the Academy because there are no reviews of that, his first solo performance in Chicago. We *do* know that anyone playing that city could count on stiff competition for an audience, and the rivalry during Dresser's stay there was no different from that found in other weeks. One could attend a performance of Sprague's Georgia Minstrels ("18 Famous Colored Artists! 6 End Men 6") at Sprague's Olympic Theatre or see the "Original Sensation Play entitled The Cuban Spy" at the grand reopening of the Lyceum. Central Music Hall had "The Musical and Literary Event of the Season" with a testimonial to "the Popular Young Reader, Miss Jennie Hunter." Hooley's Theatre had booked a series of plays, including *I Wish I Had a Clove* and *Dreams; or, Fun in a Photograph Gallery*, and Professor Liesegang's orchestra was performing at Brand's Hall. Those with more classical tastes could go to Haverly's Theatre to see an Augustin Daly student, Fanny Davenport, in *Camille*. Chicagoans who preferred the opera looked forward to a visit from a New Orleans opera company the following week. Beauplan's Grand Opera repertoire included *Aida, Robert le Diablo, Carmen*, and *Faust*, and the company assured its Chicago audience it would perform all of them "in their entirety, with complete Ballets as written. [N]othing cut."[2]

The variety of entertainment was nothing short of astounding for this city that fire had all but leveled only a decade ago. Chicago had been given a second chance, and city fathers had grand plans for its future. Two nights before Dresser was to open, these movers and shakers gathered at the Palmer House to discuss ways the city could commemorate the tenth anniversary of its great fire. Among the proposals considered were a monument in Lincoln Park, "inscribed [with] the names of all the States and countries which had given succor to Chicago in her extremity," and the building of a new public library that would hold the seventy-five thousand volumes the city then owned and that would provide additional space for what was projected to be a quarter of a million books within twenty years.[3] This was the heady atmosphere in which Dresser found himself. To be sure, it was not New York City, but Chicago boasted a different sort of atmosphere than that of that great, more settled, eastern city. In the process of its rebirth, Chicago was bursting with the vitality that surrounds new opportunities; it had an almost palpable collective belief in its future; it exuded the confidence of a new frontier settlement even though its frontier days were long past. In its rush to rebuild, the city had not forgotten the role it should play as a cultural resource. Business entrepreneurs not only built buildings for commerce, they also turned their attention to constructing the theaters and halls that would attract entertainments of all sorts for Chicagoans and its visitors.

Playing Chicago in March 1881 marked the true beginning of Dresser's rise as a singing and comic star. It was perfectly fine to secure a reputation in Evansville, but that was a place of apprenticeship, where one paid one's dues as a young performer. To establish himself as a major figure in the world of entertainment, however, Dresser would have to win over the more critical audiences in the large cities on, or near, the eastern seaboard. In the next twenty-two months Dresser took his act to Boston, New Haven, New York, and Philadelphia, as well as to Pittsburgh and the smaller cities of Cincinnati, Indianapolis, and Louisville. When he next played Chicago, he appeared as one of the featured stars in a benefit concert for Daniel Decatur Emmett, the beloved blackface minstrel and composer of "Dixie." But paying homage to "Ol' Dan" was still in the future as Dresser sang and did his comic routines for his Chicago audience this late winter. As a beginner in the profession, his work schedule could be somewhat irregular, with weeks when he was not booked anywhere. During those dry spells he could return to Evansville to fill in at the Apollo or wherever his talents could be used.

After his Academy of Music engagement, the next we hear about Dresser is three months later when he played for a week at Gilmore's Zoo in Indianapolis, opening on Monday, 20 June. Charles Gilmore ran the Zoological Garden, Theater, and Saloon on North Mississippi Street, a place with the reputation for furnishing "fine attractions for the amusement-loving people" and for its refreshing coolness during the hot, humid summer months.[4] While reviews of the variety show did not single Dresser out for mention, his colleagues were highly regarded: the audiences loved Fannie Beane and Charles Gilday, Indianapolis favorites who were paying a return visit to the capital. "Miss Allie Ballinger and Mr. Clark Hillyer, in their solos, duets and mimicry, [were] immense," the *Indianapolis Sentinel* reported, and "Miss Drucie Gilmore [undoubtedly the proprietor's daughter], the bright little star, appears in a pathetic musical specialty entitled 'The Soldier's Orphan Child,' and is winning more and more praise."[5]

The emphasis of this zoo production appears to have been on providing a show that all members of the family could attend without fear of embarrassment. Many theater owners and managers were booking similar shows, attempting to remove theater experiences from their former connections with the coarse, the vulgar, and the saloon atmosphere. A leader in this movement was New York's Tony Pastor, whose touring company was playing in Indianapolis at the same time Dresser was there. While decrying the noticeable decline in quality apparent in many variety shows of late, the reviewer of the Pastor show at Dickson's Park Theatre remarked that Pastor had succeeded in making "his attractions of a higher grade than the average . . . [with] an abundance of fun, frolic and at times a wild hilarity . . . but they never approach the coarse or vulgar, and in this we are glad to mark a commendable advance."[6] Closing in Indianapolis after their Saturday-night performance, Dresser and most of his colleagues made their way to Louisville to play for the next week at Woodland Garden.

Two and a half months later H. C. Miner's Theatre, then celebrating its fifth season at 165–169 Bowery in New York City, welcomed the "First appearance at this Theatre of the Eccentric Comique, Paul Dresser."[7] Writing later, but in words that were equally appropriate to the 1880s, Benjamin Franklin Keith, a founder of vaudeville, described the sort of entertainment that had the greatest appeal to audiences: "light, frothy acts, with no particular plot, but abounding in songs, dances, bright dialogue and clean repartee."[8] Another wrote: "The most serious thing about the programme is that seriousness is barred. . . . From the artist who balances a set of parlor furniture on his nose to the academic baboon, there is one concentrated, strenuous struggle for a laugh. No artist can afford to do without it."[9]

Dresser and his colleagues were attempting to do no less. After leader Thomas Maguire and Miner's orchestra concluded the overture, fourteen acts and a concluding drama followed, the name or names of each written on a placard placed on an easel for the audience to see. In some of the larger theaters, players' names were displayed above the proscenium arch. It was the orchestra leader's responsibility to know the entrances, cues, tempos, accelerations, ritards, cuts, and exits for each of the acts, all this accomplished in a comparatively brief rehearsal before opening night. By the end of the week, after matinee and evening performances, orchestra and performers felt quite comfortable with one another. But then a new week brought changes to the bill and new musical challenges to the leader and his ensemble. It also meant that some of the week's performers moved on to a new theater with its own orchestra and leader and a new set of challenges for both.

Dresser's "melange of original Songs and Parodies, entitled Mirthful Morsels" was the next-to-last act—a strong spot for this youngster—and marked his solo debut in this capital of popular entertainment.[10] Waiting backstage for his entrance must have seemed interminable; trying to quell his nervousness, he likely paced and mentally rehearsed his routines—what was that next line?—was that *really* funny? Then he was on and had but a brief time to win audience members over—to make them laugh with his funny business and then to bring them to tears by singing nostalgic songs of mother and home. We do not know what Dresser's "Eccentric Comique" act was like, but perhaps he included in it his "festive dudelet" routine that an Evansville friend recalled him having done earlier. Perhaps he did his trick of "hooking his derby hatbrim under his back collar so that when he nodded his head the derby would lift miraculously . . . as he sang:

> Let me tell you of a fellah, lah-de-dah!
> A fellah who's a swell, ah, lah-de-dah!

At each 'lah-de-dah' his hat would flip, making observers roll in merriment."[11] His parodies may well have included "Dutch" comedy, with its heavy, outlandish pseudo-German dialect. His songs were undoubtedly modeled on those he had sung in his days with medicine and minstrel shows. Perhaps every now and then one of his tunes took on an original shape that the audience found greatly appealing. All in all, this must have been a very exciting time for this twenty-three year old. His colleagues for the nine performances—six nights with matinees on Tuesday, Friday, and Saturday—reflected the variety of entertainments typically found in this sort of theater. The "lightening [*sic*] vocal and terpsichorean artiste" Maggie Bursel combined singing, jig dancing, and skipping rope in her "unrivalled" act; Press Eldridge brought out his "mammoth Dry Goods Box filled to the brim with new songs, humorous anecdotes, local hits and dramas"; the Cawthorn brothers did Irish, Dutch, Negro, and other types of songs and dances; an Irish comedy team had the audience howling at their "Drill of the Murphy Guards of N.Y."; and the popular comic and singer Dyllyn performed his brand of genteel Irish comedy. At the end of the fourteenth act a comic sketch, "Married in the Dark," concluded the show.[12]

Edwin Milton Royle's assessment of vaudeville is refreshingly candid:

> Vaudeville is very American. It touches us and our lives at many places. It appeals to the business man, tired and worn, who drops in for half an hour on his way home; to the

> person who has an hour or two before a train goes, or before a business appointment; to the woman who is wearied of shopping; to the children who love animals and acrobats; to the man with his sweetheart or sister; to the individual who wants to be diverted but doesn't want to think or feel; to the American of all grades and kinds who wants a great deal for his money. The vaudeville theatre belongs to the era of the department store and the short story. It may be a kind of lunch-counter art, but then art is so vague and lunch is so real.[13]

After New York City, Dresser's move to the Grand Central Theatre in Troy, New York, was an anticlimax. As a performer, though, Dresser had to learn to live with the fact that the euphoria of playing in a superb location could often be followed by a dark mood—sometimes depression—brought on by the next week's booking in an inferior one. To succeed in the business, one had to rise above the lows and to take advantage of emotional peaks when they occurred. In Troy, Dresser shared the bill with new colleagues, including Monroe and his talented cats. After the show closed on Saturday, 17 September, Dresser had three weeks before he was scheduled to play next in Philadelphia.

Only two days after Dresser's final Troy performance, news of the inevitable began to spread: James Garfield, twentieth president of the United States, had died. The victim of Charles J. Guiteau's crazed attack on 2 July, the president had lingered near death for such a long time that few were taken by surprise at the announcement. Dresser was caught up in his memories of marching through the streets of Evansville such a short time ago, parading in support of Winfield Hancock for the presidency. Now Hancock's opponent was dead, shot only a few months after his inauguration. For the second time in scarcely more than a decade and a half, the nation mourned an assassinated leader. Theater attendance dropped during this week, but soon it recovered.

After the hiatus following Troy, it was on to Philadelphia for a week playing nine shows—six evenings and three matinees—at the National Theatre, where Dresser, "in his eccentric comicalities [received] considerable praise from Manager T. F. Kelly for the success he made of his act."[14] The *New York Clipper*, reporting on the appearance, also noted that Dresser intended to protect his song "Can You Skate?" Had someone tried to steal the song, or did the word merely mean that Dresser would "protect" his song through publishing it? Nothing is known of the song beyond this brief mention. It may well have existed in sketch form only, enough for the pianist or a few instrumentalists to follow as Dresser sang it in his act. Immediately following Philadelphia, Dresser returned to New York City where he and his Mirthful Morsels played for two weeks at the National Theatre in the Bowery, billed as "The Cosiest Family Resort in the City."[15] Dresser appeared as the fifth act this week, following the Sparks Brothers, "Celtic representatives [with their] famous recitations, hits at the times, and executing their Songs, Dances, funny sayings, etc., as only these gentlemen can." He preceded vocalists Theresa and Ada Lanier and "The world's greatest Canine instructor, H. M. Parker and his Wonderful Mastodon Dog Circus (8 Canine Wonders). The best trained dogs on earth. Gymnasts, Acrobats, Athletes, Comedians."[16] The show's playbill described the closing act:

> This monster entertainment will conclude . . . with a Magnificent Spectacular Production. Return of the Universal favorite, N. S. Wood supported by the Eminent Tragedian, Joseph P. Winter and the Cultured Tragedienne, Miss Kate Estelle. Introducing his two thoroughbred steeds, Hassan and Abdallah. In the Romantic and truly Sensational Border Drama, in 3 Acts and Twelve Tableaux, written expressly for him by Miss Maggie Weston, entitled "The Boy Scout of the Sierras." This Drama will be produced in Magnificent Style. 40 Supernumeraries in Splendid U.S. Uniforms. A Full Brass Band on the Stage. Lightning Lew and Fritz mounted on their Indian horses. 2 Horses. A complete Uniformed Military Co.[17]

With only Sunday intervening, Dresser then moved on to Boston's Boylston Museum, appearing for a week with a new group of performers, including one with the unlikely name of Yakoob El Bazoozie. Here the "museum was filled to its utmost capacity at each evening and afternoon performance."[18]

By the close of 1881 Dresser, at twenty-three, and not so far removed from his medicine-wagon days, had played in theaters in the major cities and had won high praise as an up-and-coming comic and singing sensation. He was to enjoy these heady successes and the inevitable accompanying public adulation for at least the next full year, for his performance calendar included numerous appearances in eastern and midwestern cities throughout 1882. That next year also held in store a reunion for Dresser and part of his family.

CHAPTER 7

Sarah and Evansville

Paul Dresser had been on his own for three years and had not kept in touch with his family. Unknown to him, his mother had moved from Terre Haute in the spring of 1879, taking Edward, Theodore, and Claire—her youngest children—with her. Sarah and Johann Paul Dreiser had decided on the rather strange scheme of separating the family, feeling that each parent would be able to better support a smaller group. The Dreisers sent Al to live with a relative, Rome was off somewhere—where he was, no one seemed to know—and Paul was out in his own world, far removed from Terre Haute. Johann Paul remained in Terre Haute with Mame, Emma, Theresa, and Sylvia. Sarah and the three younger children moved south.

Traveling to Vincennes, scarcely more than fifty miles from Terre Haute, Sarah and her children moved in with Sue Bellette and her husband Frank, a captain with the local fire company. Earlier, Sarah had befriended Mrs. Bellette when the two lived in Sullivan; now Mrs. Bellette repayed that kindness by letting the Dreisers occupy rooms in the local firehouse where she and her husband lived. Unknown to Sarah at the time, however, the upper floor of the building doubled as a haven for prostitutes brought in by the firemen. When she learned this, the horrified Sarah took her family to the only place she thought held any chance for their immediate future. Though it had been almost a decade since the Dreisers had lived there, Sarah took her family to Sullivan—the spot that once had held so much promise for them. The four

Dreisers lived for a short time with James and Mary Bulger, their old Sullivan friends, but soon they settled into their own house.

To make ends meet and with hopes of saving enough money to be able to reunite her family, Sarah did laundry for neighbors, took in boarders, and set about trying to create a good life for her reduced family. This was not easy, however, for new family problems beleaguered the hapless Sarah. Most of the older Dreiser daughters, probably chafing under their father's strictness, came to Sullivan for brief visits. First Sylvia appeared at the door, then Emma came for a short time until she ran off to Chicago. Mame arrived, quite obviously pregnant. Sarah helped her oldest daughter through the remainder of her pregnancy, and when Mame gave birth to a stillborn child, Sarah helped her bury the infant in their backyard. In spite of all that Sarah did to try to improve life for this unfortunate tribe, emotional and economic demons constantly threatened its very existence. Extra money was unheard of, and meals were sometimes unbearably meager—Theodore remembered having to eat cornmeal mush without milk. Clothing consisted of hand-me-downs and makeovers of apparel that kind neighbors gave them—sometimes that clothing had been repeatedly patched. Theodore was painfully aware that his mother was behind on paying the rent and that the family was refused credit at all the grocery stores.[1] The more thoughtless and less compassionate members of the Sullivan community thought this poor band scarcely better than white trash, something of which the observant and impressionable Theodore was aware. To Sarah, the relative happiness of their first adventure in Sullivan less than two decades earlier—those days when her husband had frequently been successful, that time when the children were yet small and still innocent—must have seemed as a dream, a hallucination that reality now cruelly mocked.

Then came a last-hour rescue so incredible that a melodrama would have had difficulty duplicating it. Sometime in February 1882, after playing for a week in New Haven, Connecticut, Dresser returned to the Midwest, and he decided to visit his family in Terre Haute. Although he knew nothing about their dreadful straits, he had a premonition that something was not well with the family. Upon learning that Sarah had moved to Sullivan, Dresser quickly boarded a train for his old hometown. Appearing at the door of the Dreiser cottage on a cold and snowy day, the errant son amazed and delighted his family, appearing to the impressionable ten-year-old Theodore "like the sun, or a warm, cheering fire."[2] In Theodore's eyes, his eldest brother, dressed in the finest of clothing, including fur coat and silk hat—things the family could only dream about—filled the doorway with his new Falstaffian stoutness and seemed the very essence of worldly success. The laughter, embraces, and tears of happiness that filled that shabby little dwelling were unlike anything Theodore had ever before seen.

Seeing his mother so happy, happiness brought to her by a son who had all but been banished from their Terre Haute home, created an impression on Theodore that he never forgot. Ah, the stories Paul told! Accounts of his adventures, his journeys, the places he had seen and people he had met and worked with—stories Paul recounted with theatrical flair—filled his family with awe and pride. If only all of Sullivan could have witnessed this day! Perhaps Theodore and his siblings, still possessing that innocence of childhood in spite of their recent hard times, had a sense that all was not lost, even though they could not articulate this at the time. With business to take care of, the prodigal son could stay but a few hours. Dresser pressed his mother with money she so desperately needed, gave the boys copies of *The Paul Dresser Songster*, promised to return to the family soon, and left. After his visit Dresser sent packages of clothing and groceries to Sarah and the three youngsters, extending his beneficence far beyond his mere presence on that cold February day. He would continue to support his mother with gifts and money until the day she died. Sarah was his angel, the one woman he could count on to accept him as he was.

Dresser probably went to Evansville after the visit, with no more touring for the present. The train trip south gave him some time to refine a plan he had devised to help his family and to move them closer to him. An Evansville lover he had met undoubtedly had something to do with the plan, for she soon journeyed north to Sullivan to meet Sarah and some of Dresser's siblings. Paying a call at the Dreiser home between trains to and from the area, the Evansville woman impressed Sarah and the children. To the child

Theodore, she was a wonder, a "handsome woman of perhaps twenty-seven or eight—which seemed very old to me at the time . . . [with] clear, incisive, black eyes, and . . . exaggerated whiteness of her face and hands."[3] Following the woman's visit the Dreisers received packages of fruit, groceries, and clothing, including, as Theodore remembered, "a number of cast-off and rather remarkable garments, the source and exact use of which were not discovered by my mother for some time, if ever."[4] If Sarah had any inkling of this woman's profession as a madam in an elegant house of prostitution, she never let on. Even if she did somehow know, the woman was, after all, Paul's friend, his love, his confidante; furthermore, she had been kind to the family. That was enough for Sarah.

Sometime in late spring that year, Dresser moved his mother, Theodore, Ed, and Claire to Evansville. When their train arrived in the city late at night, Dresser ushered them to a streetcar that took them to their new home. Dresser had worked his magic yet again. He and his lover had completely furnished the one-and-a-half-story brick cottage at 1413 East Franklin Street. Sarah could set up housekeeping at once, for all her immediate needs had been met, including kitchen furnishings such as pots, pans, dishes, and uten-

Univ. of Southern Indiana Special Collections and University Archives, Tom Mueller Collection

Former Dreiser family residence at East Franklin Street near Main Street, Evansville, 1919.

sils. The house had been decorated and carpeted and was completely furnished with even a piano in the parlor! Dresser had become Sarah's guardian angel; he had become to his mother what she had been to him when he was young—someone who would always watch out for her, take care of her, and protect her from the vicissitudes of life. Could life have any greater reward or satisfaction than a child who returned a mother's unquestioning love? Sarah certainly loved all her children, saw the good things in all of them, even if her daughters *did* do things that brought more than a hint of scandal to the family and utter shame to old Johann Paul. But Paul was her oldest; to bask in the light of his obvious love for her, his success, and his happiness must have brought great joy to Sarah. And the children! To have a brother whose pictures graced the gaudily colored posters announcing his appearance at the Apollo Theatre and the Opera House and to read their brother's humorous columns in the pages of the *Evansville Argus*. To share in Paul's celebrity, no matter how vicariously, and to be able to tell their new friends about their famous brother was such a turn of events—something they could never do until now. After years of being pointed out as the poor white trash of their neighborhoods, after the tauntings they endured about this and about their shameless sisters, and of being the brother of Rome Dreiser, a town drunk and ne'er-do-well, Dresser's siblings must have exulted in their newly found status.

Perhaps Sarah's portion of the Dreiser clan had moved to Evansville by the time Dresser appeared at the Apollo Theatre for the second week of May 1882. Performing a new specialty, titled "Fish Cakes," Dresser shared the bill with Parker and Donovan, who acted out blackface plantation routines. The Gillmore sisters performed their athletic skipping-rope songs and dances, and the comedy team of Emerson and West did their Dutch act—stereotypical German comic characters, complete with thick, ridiculous accents.

During the warm, almost tropical summer days in Evansville, the Dreiser boys shared in Dresser's newest passion for baseball. Dresser bought his two brothers bats, balls, baseball caps, and material that Sarah fashioned into baseball uniforms, with "Evansville Reds" emblazoned on their fronts. Dresser, now bearing a waistline that betrayed his prosperity, hit fungoes to Ed and

Theodore; he would have had some difficulty in running very fast to catch a fly or to field a grounder. At other times the children could wile away sultry hours just being children, walking along the levee, picking up stones that were wonderfully cool to the touch, stones worn smooth by the ebb and flow of the water—winding up and sidearming those same stones across the river's surface. They watched visitors streaming into the city from the many steamers that visited, observed the stevedores unloading cargo, and then in late afternoon viewed the same scenes as if played backward.

Not all was pleasant, however. Residents were terrified by accounts of smallpox in this river city and looked with fear at the dreaded plague boats that lay anchored in the river—vessels crowded with those suffering from this dreadful disease. Each day the newspapers carried a tally of the dead from the previous day, together with the numbers of the newly ill who now took their places on the boats.

And then there was another sort of plague for the Dreisers—Rome. Markus Romanus Dreiser, two years younger than Paul, was the family's black sheep, the one who seemed to be in trouble all of the time. Rome was known for his drunken sprees, his disappearances, and his sudden reappearances at the Dreiser doorstep. Now he was back again, "advertis[ing] himself as [Dresser's] brother, borrowing money, drinking, gambling, passing worthless checks, and presently landing in jail." Soon police jailed him yet again, this time on a charge of grand larceny. Greatly embarrassed by all this, Dresser used his influence with a judge to secure his brother's freedom, with the provision that Rome would leave Evansville. This he did, departing for another lengthy period, to the great relief of the family but to the great worry of Sarah. Rome would repeat this pattern time and again until his alcoholism reduced him to a shambling recluse. Theodore then took care of his brother from a distance, until Rome's personal demons finally destroyed him in the 1940s.[5]

For the most part, Dresser enjoyed the life his family and his lover brought him, but he had to remain active professionally. As comfortable as life in Evansville was, he could ill afford to become provincial if he wanted to gain a reputation as a major figure in the entertainment world. He had to build on his early successes, to become more versatile, but it had to be beyond this southern and western city. This, of course, meant more travel, but that was not altogether onerous to him; he rather enjoyed the peripatetic existence of week-by-week entertaining in new cities. Besides, he was not the sort to settle down into some sort of routine existence. Certainly not yet. He was scarcely twenty-four. Yes, his family and his lover were terribly important to him, but he would never be ready to sacrifice everything for them, no matter how loving, compassionate, and generous he might be. He could be those things from places beyond Evansville, Indiana.

CHAPTER 8

The Lady in Black

Theodore Dreiser identified Paul Dresser's Evansville lover as Annie Brace, the proprietor of one of the most elegant and "very successful, even imposing," brothels in that city.[1] As the madam of the establishment, her professional name, according to Dreiser, was Sallie Walker. Many, including Dreiser, have written that Dresser's last hit song, "My Gal Sal," was a recollection of the romance he and Annie/Sallie had had more than two decades earlier. The Sal of his song was "A wild sort of devil, / But dead on the level."[2] Was Dresser really referring to his Evansville lover? If so, was Sal her real name, or had Dresser merely used that as a logical rhyme for "gal"? It is important to know that Dreiser was the person who identified this woman as Annie Brace or Sallie Walker and that there is no account of Dresser ever having mentioned his lover by name in the newspaper interviews or in his letters that have survived. Subsequent writers have taken Dreiser at his word.

There is little doubt that Dresser had a great love in Evansville, but were Annie or Sallie her real names? The answer may well be no since Dreiser often invented names to disguise the identities of those he wrote about. In *Dawn*, for example, he referred to his sisters as Janet, Eleanor, Ruth, Amy, and Trina rather than by their real names of Emma, Mame, Theresa, Sylvia, and Claire, respectively. In *Dawn* he also wrote about a Sullivan resident, Thomas Dooney. In reality, Dooney was James Bulger, a good friend of the Dreiser family. While a desire to protect his own family and, possibly, the real identity of a family friend is understandable, is it plausible for him to offer the same anonymity to a madam of a house of prostitution? Again, it is important to remember that Dreiser was the person who established Annie/Sallie's identity for his readers, for there is no trace of any woman by that name living in the Evansville area during the time Dresser was there. No one by that name is identified in the Evansville newspapers or in birth and death records of the area for that period. Of course, this woman could have been buried in an unmarked grave or have left the Evansville area and died elsewhere. While the lack of a paper trail for a prostitute is not unusual, it was reasonably common for prostitutes' names and addresses—at least those arrested and named in articles in the local papers—to appear in the Evansville city directories, without, of course, betraying their occupations. Between 1876 and 1886, Lizzie Fine's name appears for six different years and Annie Griffith's on four occasions; Maria Caldwell and Martha Lockwood are included in the directories three times and two times, respectively. A few other known prostitutes' names appear for one year. Minnie Holland, whose name is in the directory four different years, was a madam whose reputation was well known. In September 1882, for example, the *Evansville Journal* reported that "a young girl in her seventeenth year—very pretty and having much the appearance of a child—was found at the bagnio of the woman Minnie Holland by the officers last night, and taken to the lockup and assigned quarters for the night."[3] Neither newspaper accounts of prostitution arrests nor city directories, however, mention the names Annie Brace or Sallie Walker or any combination. One might argue, of course, that Annie/Sallie and her business were financially successful enough to be able to buy protection from such kinds of exposure.

Long after the fact, Theodore Dreiser described Dresser's Evansville lover who visited them in Sullivan in February 1882 as a "handsome woman of perhaps twenty-seven or eight."[4] If his memory was correct, Annie/Sallie would have been born around 1854 or 1855, making her three or four years older than Dresser. To have already established herself as the madam of an elegant and "imposing" brothel at such a young age strains credulity, but anything is possible considering the young age at which many women became prostitutes. Assuming that Annie/Sallie lived somewhere in Indiana sometime from 1860 through the mid-1880s—and, of course, such an assumption is only that—census records for that period of time show the name Brace to be quite uncommon. The 1860 census for Aurora, Indiana—in the southeastern part of the state bordering the Ohio River—yields an Ann E. Brace and her husband, Martin C. Aged around twenty-six and forty-eight, respectively, the Braces were the parents of two daughters, Alvah, born around 1858, and her sister, Johanna, born a year earlier. Ann E. Brace, the mother, would have been approximately forty-eight years old in 1882, one year younger than Sarah Dreiser. This makes it unlikely for her to have been Dresser's Annie/Sallie. A desperate researcher might see daughter Johanna as the mystery lady. Traveling south and westward along the stretches of the Ohio River, settling in Evansville, assuming a diminutive of Johanna as Anna or Annie (or having been called this affectionately as a little girl) and becoming involved in one of Evansville's more lucrative businesses as Madam Sallie Walker, this Brace *could* have been Dresser's Annie/Sallie. This, however, still begs the question of someone so young operating a major brothel. She would have been only a year older than Dresser when Theodore Dreiser first met her.

Could Holland have been the lady in black? As we have seen, a local newspaper identified her as a madam of a house of prostitution, and her name was listed in the Evansville city directories for some of the years Dresser lived in the city. The Indiana census for 1900 lists a Minnie Holland, then living in Columbus, Indiana, 150 miles northeast of Evansville. Born in Ohio in June 1848, she would have been in her early- to mid-thirties if she was the woman Theodore Dreiser met. Her age would have been in keeping with one experienced enough to run a brothel, certainly more so than that of the Annie described above. This, of course, is merely speculation, but speculation in the absence of hard facts is a tempting recourse for a researcher. The true identity of the great love in Dresser's life may never be known, and she may forever be referred to as Annie Brace or Dresser's "Gal Sal."

Evansville had a thriving prostitution trade, helped, to a considerable extent, by its location on a major river; the city had a larger than average population of transients. Packets, excursion steamers, and freighters stopped at Evansville on a regular basis. The population often swelled by five to ten thousand, especially on summer holidays when "strangers"—as one newspaper called them—flocked to the city to take in its many entertaining attractions or simply to stroll along the levee.[5] Baseball was one pastime of note, and some of the games featured unusual competitions, as when the "Blondes and Brunettes" from Philadelphia played each other. Some visitors who stayed overnight lodged at the Sherwood House or, money permitting, at the elegant St. George Hotel, often Dresser's home during his years in Evansville.

A different sort of entertainment for those so inclined could be had in the numerous brothels located near and along the riverfront. Local newspapers regularly identified the city's areas of prostitution. In addition to the places on the levee, one could find bagnios in Cat Alley, at the "Sooner" House, at the "Little Jessie," at the "Bull Yard," at the "chute" to Madison Street, on Jackson Street, on Fifteenth Street, on "Madden's Alley," on "O'Neal's Alley," on "Congress Alley," on Fifth Street between Cherry and Oak Streets, on Church Street between Cherry and Oak Streets, in areas of the eastern expansion of the city, and in Rowleytown. From time to time police arrested "soiled doves," the "dizzy girls," the "frail females," the "bad'nes" of Cat Alley, the "notorious characters," the "females of the stripe," the "women of the town," the "fallen angels," the "undesirable daughters of Baal," the "nymphes du pavé"—those who plied their trade in the houses or more blatantly in the streets. The fine for the offense of prostitution was around fifteen to twenty dollars—not an inconsiderable amount at that time—but probably paid more often than not by the madam of the house or by one of the johns.

The houses ranged from hovels, barely fit for human occupation, let alone any other activity, to the most elegant of establishments, such as Sallie's. When he was about eleven, Theodore Dreiser delivered to this mysterious lady in black a gift from his mother; it is from this experience, written down long after the fact, that we have a brief description of the place and young Dreiser's reaction to the women he saw there. The boy found Sallie's brothel on a street that ran parallel to the Ohio River; once there, a black woman ushered him into the entryway. The two climbed the staircase and proceeded down the hall to the madam's suite, whose windows provided a grand view of the Ohio.

> Everything in [the rooms was] rich and wonderful, a marvelous place. Striped awnings were at the window to shut out the hot morning sun, and the living-room was furnished with comfortable-looking wicker furniture, covered with tan linen. There were potted plants and a piano, strewn with music. Silver-backed toilet articles graced a dresser in the nearby bedroom and beyond this was a bathroom such as I had never seen before, large and bright and equipped with toilet accessories in great profusion. It seemed a kind of fairyland.[6]

Dresser and his lover were both there, Dresser dressed in "trousers of a light, summery suit and a silk shirt" and Sallie "in a pink and white, heavily beflounced dressing gown."[7] More exciting to the impressionable Dreiser had been what he had seen while walking through the passageway to Sallie's suite. Glancing into several rooms through their partially opened doors, he could see beds in disarray, a "yellow-haired siren half naked before her mirror . . . in chemisette, her arms and breast exposed, 'making up' her cheeks and eyes." Dreiser wanted to see more of "these pink-meated sirens, however vulgar they might have been in their physical as well as mental texture," but had to content himself, for the time being, with his imaginings of what went on in such a place.[8]

Dresser often lived with Sallie, but when the two lovers quarreled, or it was more convenient for him, he moved to the elegant St. George at the corner of First and Locust Streets. Sometime during the summer of 1884, Dresser and Sallie had one of those quarrels—a falling out, precipitated, according to Dreiser, by Dresser's sexual affairs with other women—even one of Sallie's own girls. Dreiser wrote:

> I have never known a man more interested in women from the sex point of view (unless perchance it might be myself), nor one to whom women were more attracted. . . . He was a genial and lovable Lothario or Don Juan, devoting his time, thought, energy and money to his unquenchable desire.[9]

When Dresser began an affair with a wealthy Evansville woman, Sallie's patience with her lover was at an end. She ordered him out of her brothel and out of her life. In a passage that he omitted from the published version of *Dawn*, Dreiser recalled that his brother contracted syphilis about this time.[10] If this is accurate, it could account for Dresser's being "sick in the south" as he later claimed. Or "sick in the south" might have been a euphemism Dresser concocted for some other difficulties he encountered in Evansville. In any event, the single intense love affair in Dresser's life came to an end, and the exotic woman in black vanished from Dresser's life, but certainly not from his memory.

CHAPTER 9

Chicago

The end of Paul Dresser's protracted love affair was still nearly two years in the future when he traveled to Chicago the first week of October 1882 to appear at the Lyceum Theatre on Desplaines Street near Madison. Dresser and his colleagues faced stiff competition from the "Jesse James" combination that was at the Olympic Theatre, playing "in the lurid drama" that blatantly capitalized on the death of the famous outlaw only six months earlier. Advertisements boasted that "two horses owned and ridden by the desperado are to appear in the play."[1] Not to be outdone, the Ford brothers, advertised as the "Removers of Jesse James," soon plied the theater circuits with their own act, taking advantage of their infamy but having to brave the hissing from many in the audiences who cursed the cowardly manner in which the Fords had "removed" the outlaw.[2] The next week saw Dresser, still in Chicago, performing at the Criterion—the "Palace Theatre of the North Side"—at the corner of Sedgwick and Division Streets. He played in the olio—that potpourri of musical numbers—that preceded the melodrama *Escaped from Sing Sing*. Once again the show included an animal act, this time a Professor Moore and his "educated dogs."[3]

Dresser spent the third week of October yet in Chicago, returning to play the Lyceum, with still another combination of performers. Some of the competition Dresser and his colleagues faced that week included eight midgets; "A fine, healthy male child 19 months old, with a Perfectly Transparent Head!"; a monster whale weighing forty tons; and the Zulu warriors, all stellar attractions at the Chicago Museum. Mary Anderson appeared at McVicker's Theatre, starring in six shows—*Love; or, The Countess and the Serf; The Hunchback; The Daughter of Roland; Romeo and Juliet; Pygmalion and Galatea*; and *The Lady of Lyons*—in six days; and Emma Thursby, "America's greatest Concert Prima Donna," accompanied by pianist Teresa Carreno, appeared in concert at the Central Music Hall.[4]

What made this month singular in Dresser's young career, what made one night more important than much of his previous work, was his appearance on Thursday, 5 October, at Hamlin's Grand Opera House at 119 North Clark Street. John Austin Hamlin, the famous Wizard Oil entrepreneur, had built his opera palace, situated opposite Chicago's new courthouse, only a decade earlier. In one sense Dresser's performance marked an opportunity for the young comic singer to show his stuff to his former boss, to demonstrate to Hamlin how much he had grown since his Wizard Oil days. Perhaps Hamlin himself had something to do with contracting Dresser for this one night. What made the evening even more important was that Dresser performed a number of his comic songs in a benefit concert for Daniel Decatur Emmett, one of the founders of blackface minstrelsy and famous throughout the world as the composer of "Dixie." While the *Chicago Tribune*'s review of Dresser's performance was brief, consisting of merely the line, "Paul Dresser sang several songs well," accompanied by a full orchestra led by Otto Vogler, the opportunity to appear that evening must have been exhilarating for this twenty-four year old.[5] To appear in front of Hamlin, who gave him one of his first breaks, and to be on the stage of this particular opera house with an assembled company of stars was certainly a significant honor, but to sing for Emmett, one of the preeminent names in minstrelsy, had to have been one of the most exciting experiences in Dresser's early career.

Emmett's music was featured in the opening overture, "Dixie Quadrille," that Vogler conducted; then Emmett, just three weeks shy of his sixty-seventh birthday, came onstage carrying his fiddle. The applause that greeted him was deafening, continuing "until he struck up an old-fashioned reel. The time was tapped by feet all

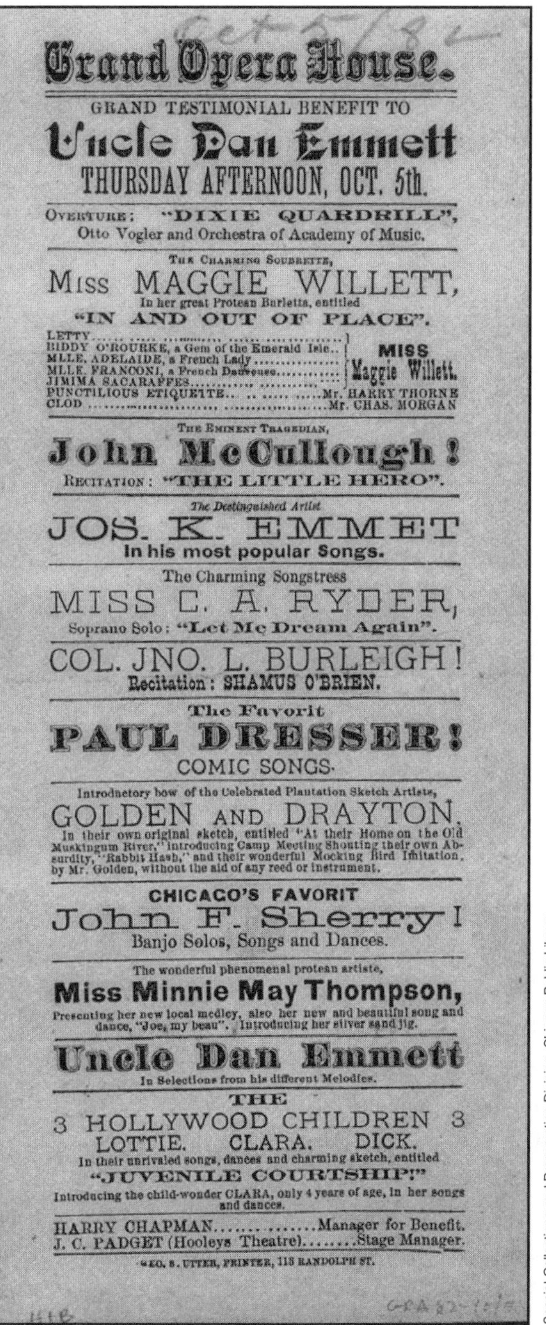

Grand Opera House.

GRAND TESTIMONIAL BENEFIT TO

Uncle Dan Emmett

THURSDAY AFTERNOON, OCT. 5th.

OVERTURE: "DIXIE QUARDRILL",
Otto Vogler and Orchestra of Academy of Music.

THE CHARMING SOUBRETTE,

MISS MAGGIE WILLETT,
In her great Protean Burletta, entitled
"IN AND OUT OF PLACE".

LETTY }
BIDDY O'ROURKE, a Gem of the Emerald Isle }
MLLE. ADELAIDE, a French Lady } MISS
MLLE. FRANCONI, a French Danseuse } Maggie Willett.
JIMIMA SACARAFFES }
PUNCTILIOUS ETIQUETTE .... Mr. HARRY THORNE
CLOD .... Mr. CHAS. MORGAN

THE EMINENT TRAGEDIAN,

John McCullough!
RECITATION: "THE LITTLE HERO".

The Destinguished Artist

JOS. K. EMMET
In his most popular Songs.

The Charming Songstress

MISS C. A. RYDER,
Soprano Solo: "Let Me Dream Again".

COL. JNO. L. BURLEIGH!
Recitation: SHAMUS O'BRIEN.

The Favorit

PAUL DRESSER!
COMIC SONGS.

Introductory bow of the Celebrated Plantation Sketch Artists,

GOLDEN AND DRAYTON,
In their own original sketch, entitled "At their Home on the Old Muskingum River," introducing Camp Meeting Shouting their own Absurdity, "Rabbit Hash," and their wonderful Mocking Bird Imitation, by Mr. Golden, without the aid of any reed or instrument.

CHICACO'S FAVORIT

John F. Sherry!
Banjo Solos, Songs and Dances.

The wonderful phenomenal protean artiste,

Miss Minnie May Thompson,
Presenting her new local medley, also her new and beautiful song and dance, "Joe, my beau". Introducing her silver sand jig.

Uncle Dan Emmett
In Selections from his different Melodies.

THE

3 HOLLYWOOD CHILDREN 3
LOTTIE. CLARA. DICK.
In their unrivaled songs, dances and charming sketch, entitled
"JUVENILE COURTSHIP!"
Introducing the child-wonder CLARA, only 4 years of age, in her songs and dances.

HARRY CHAPMAN .... Manager for Benefit.
J. C. PADGET (Hooleys Theatre) .... Stage Manager.

GEO. S. UTTER, PRINTER, 118 RANDOLPH ST.

Playbill from testimonial benefit to Dan Emmett, Grand Opera House, Chicago, 5 October 1882.

over the house, and when the old man struck up 'Dixie' the audience yelled and he smiled with pleasure and conscious pride."[6] That night Dresser did not have to share the bill with any animal acts or acrobats. His colleagues were singers, instrumentalists, and dancers, some of them, such as Joe Emmet, very well known at the time. Emmet, who was not related to Dan Emmett, was a German-dialect comedian then appearing at Hooley's Theatre in Chicago, playing a lead role in an audience favorite, *Fritz among the Gypsies*. Tonight this Emmet was paying homage to *the* Emmett, and the audience greeted his rendition of his "Cuckoo Song" and "Wilhelmina Strauss" with riotous applause that was "difficult to quell."[7] The concert realized at least a thousand dollars for Emmett, and the beneficiary was even serenaded outside the opera house by the Nevans' Band, a well-known Chicago group.

One can only conjecture that when Dresser finally returned to his room and reflected on the evening, he must have been pleased with himself, honored that he had had the chance to demonstrate his abilities and charged emotionally to continue his rising career. But it is likely he was also feeling somewhat let down by the prospects of returning to the hodgepodge of nightly routines shared with acrobats, freak shows, and animal acts. What lay immediately ahead for Dresser was a Thanksgiving-week appearance in Cincinnati at the Vine Street Opera House. There he was to share the stage with yet another group of entertainers—Billy Maloney, Mabel Gray, and Frank Chavret—not the sort of performers he had hobnobbed with only recently in Chicago, but then the young Dresser was now back in the "real" world.[8]

In late spring 1883 Dresser was back in Evansville for a while, but he returned to Chicago in early June to appear at Kohl and Middleton's West-Side Museum on West Madison Street, near Halsted Street. The museum was divided into two sections, the museum proper, located upstairs in the building, and the theater. The museum featured freaks and odd assortments of attractions that were certain to lure large audiences. A Fiji family of children was there that week; so were Josephine, the fat lady, and the amazing Edward Payson Weston, the noted pedestrian who had fashioned a career out of walking incredibly long distances in rapid times over periods of weeks and months at a time. Weston had begun his feats of endurance in 1861 by walking from Boston to Washington, D.C., in only ten days to witness the inauguration of Abraham Lincoln; forty-nine years later the lithe septuagenarian walked from Los Angeles to New York City in an amazing seventy-eight days. When he appeared in Chicago as a Kohl and Middleton's museum attraction, Weston was the most prominent name in that age of pedestrianism when large purses were offered to those who covered extraordinary distances in extraordinarily fast times. By then he had become an American hero and a household name. Management typically kept the entrance fee to museum offerings low to attract a large crowd, but they could have charged higher prices and still been guaranteed a crowd with Weston's name on their bill.

When the prices to see performances in the theater were no higher than those charged for the museum, some performers rebelled. Fanny Janauschek—Madame Janauschek—the renowned and quite intimidating actress, later refused to perform in a New Haven, Connecticut, theater until the admission fee was raised to fifty cents. She stated imperiously that "people can see a museum for a quarter, but they cannot see me for that small sum."[9] In Chicago, however, Dresser and his colleagues, Thatcher and Adair, Emma Lamouse, James Goodwin, John Leach, and the De Van brothers—certainly not in Madame's league—appeared in the theater where admission was cheap and "business was good."[10]

Chicagoans, then and now, have always had a variety of entertainments to choose from, and this week was no different from others. Barlow, Wilson and Company's Mammoth Minstrels were appearing for the week at Shelby's Academy of Music. There the audience was not only treated to the talents of Milt Barlow, George Wilson, and Luke Schoolcraft, but they could also marvel at the amazing Francis Leon, the female impersonator, famous for his "feminine grace and fragility, . . . especially when he danced in the classical ballet style."[11] Tony Pastor's company, making its nineteenth annual tour, was playing at Hamlin's Grand Opera House. A young May Irwin, "all curves and plumpness"[12] and soon to be a star of the musical stage, was part of Pastor's company; ads boasting "A Light and Sparkling Entertainment, Replete with Mirth, Melody, and Motion" also assured the public that Pastor himself would be present at every performance.[13] A reviewer, however, was not impressed with Pastor's work, suggesting that he would do better to devote his entire attention to the company and stay off the stage: "[Pastor] persists . . . [in] springing his vapid and silly topical songs upon an unsuspecting audience just as the performance begins to be enjoyable. The applause he receives is for the excellent judgment he shows in selecting his people and not for his excellence as a singer."[14]

The master showman Phineas Taylor Barnum and members of his "Greatest Show on Earth" were appearing at the lakefront for ten days of "1,000 Wonder Marvels," including "30 Cages of Rare Wild Animals and Every Cage a Carved Chariot"; "33 Golden Tableau Cars 33"; "6 Zulu Warriors with Princess and Babies"; Goshen, the eight-foot giant; and "A Tribe of Sioux Indian Savages, Mexican Vaqueros and Cow Boys from the Plains." Most of these attractions, however, paled in comparison to Barnum's centerpiece, Jumbo, a magnificent elephant weighing six and a half tons and standing eleven and a half feet tall. Purchased from the London Zoological Society for the extravagant sum of ten thousand dollars, Jumbo would be available for Chicago children to ride. "While the favored few only of our foreign cousins could have the privilege," wrote the *Chicago Tribune,* "our more democratic ideas give every child in the land the opportunity to mount his back." How many youngsters actually climbed aboard the mighty elephant is unknown, but all Chicagoans were treated to a "$1,350,000 Matchless Parade," leaving from the lakefront at 8:30 A.M. on Monday, 4 June. Emphasizing the high moral tone set by the company, ad copy remarked, "Its people are better behaved and dressed; even the supernumeraries wear button-hole bouquets in their lapels." Thus the competition for large audiences was great, and Dresser and his cohorts were probably pleased that business was reported to be good at both venues at Kohl and Middleton's that week.[15]

By August 1883 Dresser had composed three songs that the *Evansville Daily Journal* wrote were to be published by Arthur P. Schmidt.[16] "See That No One Plucks the Flowers from My Grave" and "Essie, over the Sea" have been lost and probably were not published after all, but "My Mother Taught Me How to Pray" most certainly resurfaced as "When Mother First Taught Me to Pray," a Willis Woodward and Company publication of 1892, although there is no evidence, other than similarity in titles, to support this. Theodore Dreiser mentioned the song "'Wide Wings' (published by a small retail music house in Evansville, Indiana)" as also being among his brother's early efforts, a song, if in fact by Dresser, that has vanished.[17] Others have referred to this song as "White Wings" and claim that it was published by the G. W. Warren Music Company. Some mention Schmidt as the publisher. A song titled "Wide Wings" *was* composed by Banks Winter and published by Willis Woodward and Company in 1884, just around the time when Dresser was writing some of his very early songs. When Dreiser wrote briefly about "Wide Wings," more than two decades had passed since his brother's death, and Dreiser may have mistakenly claimed the song for Dresser as he had claimed Percy Gaunt's "The Bowery" for his brother. This may be yet another example of Dreiser's carelessness with the facts. In any event, it might well be that these early songs existed only in sketch form and were never published. The year 1886 is the first year in which a published Dresser song can be documented.

On 25 August the *New York Clipper* announced that Baylies and Kennedy's Bright Lights company was to open its season in Chicago at the Lyceum Theatre on Saturday, 1 September, for a ten-day run. Dresser was listed as the variety organization's stage manager and as one of fourteen performers in the troupe.

Again, competition for audiences was fierce. European actress Helena Modjeska "invested [Friedrich Schiller's *Maria Stuart*] with dignity" at the Grand Opera House; Thomas W. Keene, appearing in a variety of Shakespearean characters at Haverly's, was panned by a critic as a "wearisome elocutionist" whose place in the "dramatic firmament" was that of a "falling rocket. The noise of his ascent marred the artistic calm."[18] Playwright-producer-actor Nat C. Goodwin's comedy *A Terrible Time* was on the boards at Hooley's, the Female Mastodon Minstrels were at the Olympic Theatre, and actress Adah Richmond was at the Academy of Music. Additionally, Chicagoans were abuzz over a visit to the city by the president during this first week of the month. Following a schedule of speeches and meetings, President Chester A. Arthur attended a performance of *The Hunchback of Notre Dame* at McVicker's Theatre. The star of the evening was Margaret Mather, known for her performances in leading roles in *Romeo and Juliet* and *Jeanne D'Arc* and as a dramatic partner of Otis Skinner, with whom she toured in a variety of plays. This evening she was in prime form and greatly charmed the president, who congratulated her on her fine performance.[19] Tragically the future would not be so kind to her, for Mather was to die penniless.

Baylies and Kennedy's company *did* open on the first and then toured through the Midwest and the East during the remainder of the year, but Dresser's name appeared neither in reviews of the company nor in its various advertisements. The only time his name was mentioned in association with the company was in the *Clipper*'s initial remark of 25 August. Did Dresser leave Baylies and Kennedy's company shortly after the season began? Did he ever go on the road with it? No one knows.

What is known with certainty is that Dresser, "an old time favorite here," was scheduled to appear in a benefit concert for John Morrissey at Evansville's Apollo Theatre on Friday, 21 September. Morrissey, a song-and-dance man in his youth, was to be feted and to perform on the stage of the Apollo in his own sketch titled *The Monster Concert*. Morrissey played five separate parts, including send-ups on Oscar Wilde and Ole Bull, the famous Norwegian violinist who had toured America in the 1840s. His Wilde Oscar and Ole Bully Wild brought howls of laughter from the Apollo audience that night. While Dresser's name appeared in the program as "a favorite's return," one of fourteen performers scheduled to pay tribute to Morrissey, he "was the only disappointment. He was too ill to appear in character, as he had been advertised to do, and simply made a neat apology."[20] With this letdown began a period in Dresser's life that no one knows much about—the period from late 1883 to summer 1886. In later years Dresser's only explanation was that he was "sick for two years in the south."[21]

CHAPTER 10

The Mystery Years

No one, let alone Paul Dresser or his inquisitive brother, Theodore Dreiser, ever explained what Dresser meant when he said he was sick in the south. Whatever the illness was, it was serious enough to prevent Dresser from continuing his career for the time being—this after he had made such an impressive start. Dreiser claimed that his brother contracted syphilis at one point in his life but gave no details about when or where this occurred. Did that disease cause Dresser to withdraw from the stage for two years? While there is no documentation to account for Dresser's hiatus, his "illness" may well have involved a woman and possibly a child. In his autobiographical *Dawn*, Dreiser mentioned a blowup between Annie Brace/Sallie Walker and Dresser in the summer of 1884, an argument that grew out of Dresser's affair with one of Sallie's girls.[1] This, however, was nearly a year after Dresser last appeared on stage and too late to coincide with the beginning of his being ill—unless Dreiser had his dates wrong, always a possibility. Dreiser continued:

> As I learned afterwards, his stage or, as one might otherwise see it, his industrial life, had been affected by his disastrous love life. Certainly he was all but felled temporarily by the desertion of his Annie and for a number of months, as he told me later, could barely endure this fleeting thing we call life. Actually, a few years later—as many as five or six—he embodied his bitterness in a most melodramatic and yet somewhat arresting song which he titled "The Curse."[2]

Sometime after Dresser died, an article appeared in the *Terre Haute Gazette* in which the author claimed that Dresser had once been married to burlesque queen May Howard and that their infant daughter died shortly after Howard deserted Dresser for the manager of her burlesque troupe.[3] The author neither provided documentation nor mentioned the time this was supposed to have happened. At least three other authors repeated this story. Edward B. Marks claimed that Howard and Dresser separated after their child—whose gender Marks did not give—died.[4] With a sense of the melodramatic, a Sullivan, Indiana, newspaper story ornamented the tale, comparing Howard's desertion to that of a Hollywood star recently in the news:

> May Howard, like Ingrid Berman [*sic*], had fallen "head-over-heels" in love with her producer, leaving, . . . Paul with their little daughter, whom he worshipped, at death's door. At his child's deathbed the feelings of an outraged husband and broken-hearted husband were soon written into a song.[5]

As recently as the early 1980s, another author, Ronald Davis, wrote:

> In the early nineties Dresser had wed burlesque queen May Howard. The musician was soon made aware that his wife was incapable of fidelity, although he chose to ignore her extramarital entanglements. When she deserted him and their child for another man, Dresser incorporated his bitterness into a ballad, "The Curse."[6]

Howard, born in Toronto in 1862, made her professional debut in 1883 as Katy in *Muldoon's Picnic*. The following season she toured with the Rentz-Santley company but left them suddenly "on account of a severe illness."[7] What Howard's illness was is not known, but it occurred during the time Dresser claimed to have been sick in the south. Was it more than a coincidence that Howard and Dresser were both ill at around the same time? In 1890 a newspaper mentioned that Howard had married for a fourth time to a Harry Morris.[8] Only a year earlier she and her third husband, George G. Emmerle, had taken a honeymoon cruise up the Delaware River on Emmerle's yacht. Her second marriage to an Albert Lewis, the son of a wealthy physician, lasted only three weeks. Nowhere is the name of a first husband given.[9] Had it been Dresser? Probably not as we shall see.

Three of the writers mentioned a song as one of the outcomes of Dresser's supposed abandonment. Dreiser said it was "The Curse" and connected the song with Annie Brace/Sallie Walker. Davis, probably taking his information from Dreiser, repeated the title but tied it to Howard. The Sullivan paper merely mentioned "a song." It is important to note that Dresser wrote "The Curse" in 1887, earlier than the dates Dreiser and Davis gave. The chronology and the words to the song seem to indicate that something apparently did happen between Dresser and Howard, especially considering Dresser dedicated the song to Howard. The male narrator of the song, one who has loved deeply but has been abandoned, cries out:

> You have broken ev'ry vow,
> The babe that sleeps in yonder grave,
> Fails to bind us together now.
> May the curse of misery follow thee,
> May your head with shame yet bow,
> For as madly as I loved you once,
> So do I hate you now.[10]

Subsequent verses damn the former love, hoping that "not a helping hand comes nigh" to comfort her in her misery and despair; that when she appears "on that last great day, / These words won't be forgot," and the most damning of all denunciations, "May that babe look straight at you and say, / Oh! woman I know thee not." The unchanging words of the chorus curse her yet three times more with:

> So when judgement day rolls 'round
> And you stand trembling there,
> I trust no baby face will greet you,
> In your wild despair.
> But I'll be there to meet you,
> To tell you of a blow.
> That you so cruelly struck and broke,
> A heart, long, long ago;
> My curse will follow thee.
> My curse will follow thee.[11]

The dedication to Howard, together with the sentiments of the song—very strong words unlike any other Dresser song—suggests a relationship, a birth, and a painful separation. If these conjectures are accurate, those in the know would certainly have recognized the autobiographical character of the song when Howard sang it publicly, as she is said to have done. *If* "The Curse" was autobiographical, it might point to the reason for Dresser's claim of illness in the south—he could have been in Evansville attempting to reconcile differences between Howard and himself, in addition to caring for his child. If this theory is correct, a relationship between Howard and Dresser, with a child born from the affair, would most certainly have destroyed Dresser's relationship with Annie/Sallie.

If a child was born from a liaison between Howard and Dresser, did the infant really die as the song clearly states? Whatever the relationship between the two, Howard featured two of Dresser's recent compositions during her 1889–90 season.[12] *If* Howard had deserted Dresser, the rebuke carried in the words of one of these songs would have seemed biographical: a young man, in "the springtime of his life," returns home to his "modest little cottage, where love alone did dwell" to find that his beloved "Nellie" has left him "like a bird [who has] taken wing." Never abandoning hope that his wife will return, the man, now "growing old and gray," sings "I can't believe her faithless; those eyes of tender blue, / Could not be so deceiving; I don't think she's untrue; / I'm watching for her coming from dusk till break of day; / The hours are very lonely since Nellie went away."[13] By the time she sang the song, Howard was ending her third marriage and soon to be married yet again. *If* Dresser and Howard had had a relationship, it was now far in her past, and she could probably sing Dresser's sentiments of "I Can't Believe Her Faithless" with a certain detachment, yet very much aware of the irony of her performing such a song. Perhaps she chose it merely for its possibility of musical success for her.

One writer has suggested that "a theory, unproven," had Dresser as the father of Louise Kerlin, who claimed to have been born in Evansville on 5 October 1882.[14] If one accepts this premise, it suggests that Dresser might have remained in Evansville for the period in question to care for his young daughter. During the summer of 1899 Kerlin, by that time a singer with hopes of becoming a professional stage entertainer, went to the Chicago office of Howley, Haviland and Company, Dresser's publisher, looking for new songs. There she met Dresser, who was in the city on company business. Taken with her, especially after she told him that her father was William Kerlin, a railroad engineer who had befriended him years ago, Dresser decided to help Kerlin's career. He forcefully suggested she change her last name to Dresser as an entrée into the entertainment world, and thereafter he always referred to her as his kid sister. Kerlin could not have been Dresser's daughter, however, for by the time Dresser was sick in the south, Kerlin was actually between five and six years old. The Indiana census for 1880 lists her under her real name of Lulu Josephine Kerlin, the two-year-old daughter of William and Ida Kerlin.

Conjecture, assumption, and speculation all share shaky ground in the absence of evidence. Based on those ingredients and on "The Curse," the best explanation for Dresser's illness is that during these years he may have had a severe case of syphilis and/or had a relationship with Howard that may or may not have produced a child. Sometime later, but before 1887, Howard deserted Dresser. Other than that speculation, these two years in Dresser's life remain a mystery.

PART 3

On the Road: 1886–1896

CHAPTER 11

The Two Johns

"He Cleaned Out the Safe. One of Chapin & Gore's Clerks Disappears with $3,500 and Some Jewelry." "A Woman in the Case. Chapin & Gore's Embezzling Employe [*sic*] Said to Have Left with a Fair Companion." So screamed headlines in the *Chicago Mail* on 15 and 16 February 1886. The clerk, L. A. Hopkins, was married and the father of a daughter. His "fair companion" and lover was Emma Dreiser. Fourteen years later the two lovers appeared again, long after Chicago had forgotten them, as the characters Carrie Meeber, the opportunistic young woman from Columbia City, Wisconsin, and George Hurstwood, a thief and Carrie's second lover, in Theodore Dreiser's novel *Sister Carrie*. By featuring them in his book, Dreiser bestowed literary immortality on his sister and her lover, shocking the literary moralists of the genteel tradition and creating the literary scandal of the turn of the century. For this "biographical" novel, Dreiser also included characteristics of another member of the Dreiser clan. Hurstwood is, in fact, a composite of Hopkins *and* Paul Dresser. The ebullient, gregarious side of Hurstwood is clearly Dresser. With the theft and the flight of the lovers on Valentine's Day 1886 and the attendant publicity it brought to the Dreisers, twenty-three-year-old Emma Dreiser added to the dysfunctional qualities of that unfortunate flock. Although young Theodore, then fourteen, could fathom Emma's infamous celebrity, he would not, for some time to come, fully comprehend the different sort of celebrity of his oldest brother.

At the time Emma ran off with Hopkins, Dresser was still ill in the south. Four months later John Stewart Crossy, a veteran actor and writer known professionally as "Fattie" Stewart, offered Dresser a role in his three-act comedy *The Two Johns*. Dresser, as Peter Johns, would play opposite Stewart's Philip Johns. The visual spectacle of the two "brothers" guaranteed unrestrained laughter from the audience, for Stewart and Dresser both had extravagant girths on which they capitalized at every opportunity—in action, dialogue, and song. How Stewart came to know of Dresser's abilities is unknown; perhaps he had seen Dresser on the Evansville stage, or perhaps Dresser auditioned for the role. After Dresser's long hiatus from the stage, this was a wonderful opportunity to perform as an actor and singer in a company that had, for the past four years, won steady audiences with this play.

Traveling to various theaters for one-night stands and occasionally staying put for an entire week would be nothing new to Dresser, for he had played similar schedules in the past, but then he often had long stretches of time between engagements. Now he was about to embark on the frenetic and bone-wearying schedule of constant travel; of playing night after night, with at least two matinees thrown in; of living out of his trunk; and of sleeping and eating in hotels and in boardinghouses along the route. But this was big-time theater! Before 1886 ended, Dresser would travel to Nebraska, Colorado, Arkansas, Texas, Louisiana, Tennessee, and Georgia—all places he had never been before. He would play one-nighters in theaters in small villages and towns such as Titusville, Pennsylvania; Maquoketa and Ottumwa, Iowa; and Pana, Illinois. But Stewart and his company also were booked for weeklong stays in Des Moines during the Iowa State Fair, where they packed Foster's Opera House every night; into the Standard Theatre in St. Louis; and in an unidentified theater in New Orleans. Dresser would later equate an actor's existence with a "dog's life," but that was in the distant future; now he was ready for the glamour of the stage, where he could, for the moment, disguise himself as someone else. He could escape from whatever had pained him during the last few years. This was the tonic he had needed for so long.

Early that summer Dresser left Evansville, never to return for long. Evansville would never hold fond memories for Dresser the way Sullivan and Terre Haute did. His first and most prolonged love affair had occurred in that southern city, but that was now a thing of the past. At twenty-eight, Dresser was ready to hold on to that usable part of his past that would serve him well in the future as actor, singer, and composer, but he was more than ready to rid himself of the more painful parts.

Leaving Evansville early that summer, Dresser traveled to Stewart's farm in Potters Landing, Maryland, where rehearsals were about to begin for the 1886–87 season. The time in Maryland proved productive for Dresser, a sure sign to him that he had not lost his touch. Not only did he learn his role, but here he began to compose in earnest. From then until he left Stewart's company three years later, Dresser composed at least sixteen songs, some of which became quite popular, bringing him modest public acclaim if little financial reward. Dresser and Stewart certainly incorporated some of this music into the performances of *The Two Johns;* interpolating new material into the flexible structure of a comedy or melodrama was a common practice of the time, providing for a freshness that would have offered some relief from the tedium of literal repetition night after night after night. Too, such a practice got Dresser's songs in front of a larger public than would have been the case if he had relied solely on his publishers to get his songs out.

Opening night for Dresser, and the fifth season for *The Two Johns,* was a single performance in Niagara Falls, New York, on Monday, 23 August 1886. This performance was followed by nine more one-nighters before the troupe arrived in Des Moines for the week's stay. One can imagine the exciting, yet frenetic, pace of life, traveling with colleagues in a railcar specially reserved for the Two Johns Company. When they were ready to move on, troupe members struck the scenery and gathered up personal belongings and wardrobe. Upon arriving in town, sometimes at the last minute, they had eleventh-hour rehearsals for those segments of music that needed the help of local musicians, directed by the pianist cum conductor who traveled with the troupe. The duties of the local leader of this pickup group were reduced to conducting the overture and any extra musical padding that might be used between acts. One writer complained about the conductor's game of musical chairs, saying that this practice led to "much restlessness and chair-sliding—to say nothing of music-stand upsetting in leaders' in-and-out procession."[1] And then there might be only modest crowds to greet the performers—small houses because of the vagaries of the weather or because of the more predictable events such as elections and religious holidays. Houses were nearly always quite small during Lent, for example. A reporter, writing about theaters in Bridgeport, Connecticut, in 1887, complained that "the Lenten season struck amusements here with a 'dull thud,' and everybody feels it more or less."[2]

The number of companies active on the road added to the intense competition for audiences. In the season before Dresser went with *The Two Johns*, at least 393 companies were traveling and one paper estimated that the American public was spending between thirty-eight and forty *million* dollars on entertainment during a forty-week season! With this kind of activity and rewards of this scale, live entertainment had become a major industry.[3]

Townspeople were alerted to the coming attractions through newspaper ads in addition to posters pasted on almost any surface that would hold them. Theater managers tried to outdo one another in devising ever more clever schemes to announce their attractions. The manager of the Academy of Music in Baltimore, for example, placed a one-thousand-candlepower red electric light in front of his billboards, illuminating the board itself as well as the surrounding area. Advertising in more conventional ways, the academy deluged the city with "400 three sheet posters, 2,500 lithographs, 1,000 half sheet hangers and any quantity of small work."[4] Trade papers in New York City complained about the speed with which bill posters covered all available vertical spaces in new construction areas. Recalling his days in Evansville in the early 1880s and the popularity of his brother there, Theodore Dreiser wrote about some typical announcements of forthcoming attractions: "Paul has a big name. His pictures are all over town on the theatre billboards. . . . The fences and billboards everywhere attested to his popularity. Large red and yellow and black single-sheets bore his picture."[5]

The theaters for these entertainments varied considerably. At one end of the spectrum were those barely adequate makeshift spaces—often located on an upper floor of a building that served many purposes—with crudely decorated and cheaply painted house curtains, uncomfortable seating—often no more than benches—no real orchestra pit, and the ever present threat of fire from the gas lighting. Then there were the theaters that had been constructed as such, spaces that enjoyed the talents of a resident scenic artist, a spacious stage, and dressing facilities. Electric lighting had become an important element in the theater interior, having been introduced in the Bijou Theatre in Boston in December 1882. In the period between then and when Dresser went on the road with *The Two Johns*, the number of theaters with electric lighting increased dramatically and was something of which managers boasted with understandable pride. Not only did electric lighting greatly reduce the chance of fire, but illumination by electricity was far superior to the older system. In H. C. Miner's People's Theatre in New York, "an extra chandelier of twenty four lights has been placed in the lobby, making three in all, and measurably heightening the effect of the illumination there." Additionally, "all over the house are additional electric-light fixtures. Indeed, it is the People's boast now that not a gas-burner is used in the theatre. Nor is there chance of fire otherwise, for both the steam and the electricity are generated outside of the building."[6]

While devastating theater fires still occurred, rebuilding nearly always carried with it the prospect of dramatic improvements to all aspects of the interior. Fire or no fire, theater managers often remodeled their spaces, building in the process elaborate pleasure palaces to attract patrons. Thick velvet carpets were laid, chairs with plush seats or with patent-leather seats were installed, and gilded, ornamented frames were placed in the choice areas of the theater; frescoed ceilings were added; new drop curtains and scenery, painted by well-known scenic artists, graced the stage; the latest devices in mechanical effects were installed; and dressing rooms were improved to include washstands and running water. The older, darker colors were replaced by vibrant hues, whose opulence readily caught the viewer's eye. Thus, in Miner's People's Theatre, "formerly the prominent colors in the house were of the gloomy shades. Dark green may have been aesthetic, but it certainly was not cheerful to the eye. It is different now, and delightfully so."[7] Now there were lighter shades, bronzes, and dashes of crimson, gold, and blue satins.

Theodore Dreiser remembered the magical world of the theater as he experienced it in Warsaw, Indiana, in the mid-1880s. He and his brother Ed went to the Opera House as often as the two could wrangle the fifteen-cent ticket price out of their mother. Taking his seat and looking at the stage, Theodore was unimpressed with the clutter of painted canvas and the make-do scenery of paper, wood, tin, and cloth. Once the lights dimmed, however, the magic of lighting, of sound effects, and of music transformed those same crude items into "a mountain view of unparalleled grandeur," "a woodland cottage of great beauty" threatened by "a thunderstorm . . . almost more real than about our own door."[8]

Music was an important part of any production, whether it was a variety show or a dramatic presentation. In Warsaw a local carpenter conducted the small orchestra-band combination of "two violins, a trombone, a cornet, a bass viol, a 'cello, a flute and several drums of different sizes" that, as Dreiser remembered, played overtures to *Carmen, Poet and Peasant*, and *William Tell*. Dreiser was impressed not only with the sound the orchestra made, interpreting the "hieroglyphics of their music pages before them," but also with the musicians, who were "barbers, clerks, [and] grocers" by day but who dressed in their suits for the performances and played in a way that they "seemed more related to paradise than to life."[9] It was, of course, important for the music to support as far as possible the sentiments of the stage action. Critics recognized that appropriate incidental music could do much to enhance the playwright's words, but certain musical figures rapidly became clichés. The more dramatic the sentiments, the more obvious and predictable the music. The loss of a loved one, the touching scene of parent and child, and the premonition of disaster all evoked predictable musical responses from those in the orchestra. The melodramatic order of "Surrender!," followed by the hero's or heroine's "Never!," most often gave way to a "stormy dose of instrumental 'hurry' as a flavoring to the industrious slaughter prevailing on the stage."[10]

As the romantic and impressionable Dreiser fell under the spell of the music, however, *he* imagined "imperial stallions thundering over immensities of space; cloud castles lying bathed in the sapphire of unknown moons; . . . hosts of angels in ordered and rushing flight winnowing the immensities of time and eternity."[11] It is impossible to know what such an ensemble sounded like or how well or poorly the musicians played, but a jaded reviewer referred to such small-town music groups as "morphine orchestras."[12]

For the next decade Dresser would become acquainted first-hand with such "morphine orchestras" and those wretched, small opera houses with amenities and spaces so meager as to discourage even the heartiest of souls, but he would also experience the joy of playing in the opulent pleasure palaces that one hated to leave. It was all in the life of a touring performer.

Many managers, seeking to offer shows for the entire family, had strict policies that discouraged rowdiness among the audience and rules that forbade anything of a questionable nature onstage. A playbill of 1882 for the Lyceum Theatre in Chicago warned the audience, "Whistling and Stamping Positively Prohibited," and claimed, "No feature is ever introduced or tolerated that can be construed, by the most fastidious, as objectionable," and, "The Best of Order is Kept."[13] At the same time, however, many managers were aware of the impact that feminine beauty could have on attendance. A review of the offerings at the Zoological Garden, Theater, and Saloon in Indianapolis in 1886 gave a long list of names of specific performers, together with the notice that "female statuary is also announced."[14] A reporter commented about the bill at Hooley's Theatre in Chicago: "Outside of its pretty girls, 'Clio' found but little favor here. Never were more shapely forms lavishly displayed, consequently for two weeks 'Clio' played to large returns."[15] Stewart, however, was known for his clean, if slapstick, farces, and *The Two Johns* could be counted on to provide all in the audience, regardless of gender or age, an evening of enjoyable, "safe" entertainment. There would be no female statuary in his shows. No one would be embarrassed to be seen in the theater when Stewart and his company were playing.

Reviews of *The Two Johns* nearly always mention the size of the audience, rather than anything substantial about the performance or the comedy itself. Playing at Crawford's Theatre in Leavenworth, Kansas, the troupe "had a fair house. This was the first presentation here of the piece, and it was well received."[16]

In St. Louis the comedy "drew fairly well," and Little Rock, Arkansas, provided a "good house, considering the fact that rain poured down from 5 p.m. to 9."[17] The show "convulsed" two "fair" Galveston, Texas, audiences at the Tremont Opera House "with laughter . . . Mr. Stewart . . . reports that his company has been doing a big business this season."[18]

"The Letter That Never Came," published in 1886 amid controversy.

Dresser soon began to feel at ease in his new role and with his constant travel. Little more than a month after he started with Stewart's company, however, that newly found comfort was disturbed when Dresser became embroiled in his first serious problem as a composer. The 30 October 1886 issue of the *New York Clipper* advertised the publication of "The famous success, The Letter That Never Came[;] Written and Sung by Miss May Howard; [published by] T. B. Harms; 819 Broadway."[19] This is a song Dresser claimed he composed at Stewart's farm.[20] Based on Dresser's encounter with an old Civil War veteran who lived at the Dayton, Ohio, soldiers' home, the song tells the poignant tale of a man who awaits "from early morning's light, . . . till dark at night / For that letter" he hopes the postman will deliver. Waiting in vain many years for the missive, the disconsolate man finally dies, his hand clenching a note "with the last words that he wrote, / 'Should a letter come, please place it by my side.' " But a letter from whom?: "a gray-haired mother, / A sister or a brother"? Although Dresser knew the old soldier was looking for a letter from the wife or child he left behind when he enlisted in the Union army, the listener is kept in the dark; our abandoned man tells us "surely she / Must sometimes think of me." All this makes for a song much more appealing than one in which nothing is left to the listener's imagination. The refrain repeats the sad conclusion that "the letter that he longed for never came."[21]

This song won an immediate following, but its real creator was the subject of considerable controversy from the start. Four weeks after the ad for the song first appeared, the *Clipper* carried a notice from Dresser claiming the song as his own. Dresser asserted that Max Sturm, violinist, musical director of the Rentz-Stanley Company, and Howard's husband, "came to me while I was in New York last August (Sunday the 15th) and begged me to give him a song for his WIFE, that she might for once in a life-time do something new." Dresser continued that he wrote the song and "reserved the right of publication" and now, "instead of being grateful [Sturm and Howard] show the mean side of their character by claiming it as original." Dresser concluded, stating the song "is my original words and music, and will be published by Messrs. Balmer & Weber of St. Louis, Mo., and these gentlemen, I would also state, have ample funds to protect my interests."[22] A week later Sturm countered in the same newspaper. Dresser, he said, had asked him to

> arrange two songs for him, which, with a small amount of cash, was the price to be paid for the WORDS of ["The Letter That Never Came"]. I arranged the music and paid the CASH, and the words were mine. I immediately wrote a melody and gave it to Miss Howard to sing. . . . Mr. Dresser perhaps feels sorry that he disposed of the words, but they are clearly MINE by right of purchase, and the music is of my own composition. I have both the WORDS and MUSIC duly copyrighted. . . . Miss Howard had the song published with T. B. Harms & Co.[23]

The song was indeed published by Harms, never by Balmer and Weber; additionally, it carries the designation, "Written for and sung by May Howard." Dresser's name is given as the author of the words, with music composed by Sturm. The 1927 publication *The Songs of Paul Dresser,* with an introduction by Theodore Dreiser, contains this song, reprinted from the Harms publication.[24] Sturm's name is not included here, however. Instead, someone has removed the printed attributions to Sturm and Dresser and has handwritten, in cursive, "Words & Music by Paul Dresser." The handwriting is clearly Dreiser's. In an unnamed, undated newspaper, an interviewer quoted Dresser:

> The first song I ever wrote was "The Letter That Never Came." I did it in June, 1886. . . . I gave the song to a man whom I no longer love. He was to arrange the song and return it to me in the form of orchestration and piano score for purposes of publication. I went on the road with a theatrical company, and after writing many times for the return of my manuscript song and receiving no reply, I one day picked up a copy of the New York Clipper, and there, in staring type, was the announcement of my song, . . . but with the other fellow's name tacked on it. I never received a penny for that song.
>
> I remember standing at the corner of Eighth street and Broadway, New York, one evening, conscious of the fact that

> my sole worldly possessions amounted to sixty-five cents and the clothes I wore. I was an absolute stranger in New York but everywhere I went I heard some one singing "The Letter That Never Came." Another man was getting the money and I was getting the laugh.[25]

A 1902 newspaper article about Dresser remarked that "he did not receive the financial benefit [of this hit song], . . . but his first experience was one never forgotten, and since that time he has published most of the songs he has written." "Since that time" is a bit of an exaggeration, for Dresser did not begin publishing his own material until seven years later.[26]

Exactly who wrote what in "The Letter That Never Came" is difficult to sort out. *If*, as Sturm claimed, Dresser gave him the words to that song in return for Sturm's arrangements of two other songs, why does Dresser's name appear as the author in the Harms publication? Since it was "Miss Howard [who] had the song published with T. B. Harms," did she tell the publisher to credit the words to Dresser? Dresser referred to Sturm as Howard's husband and pointedly referred to Howard as Sturm's "WIFE"; in his response to Dresser, Sturm never called her Mrs. Sturm (if indeed she was), but always called her Miss Howard. *If* Sturm was merely using Howard's stage name as a professional courtesy and *if* Dresser's reference to **WIFE** was accurate, one is led to believe that Max Sturm was Howard's first husband; as we saw earlier, newspaper accounts tell us she married a third and fourth time in 1889 and 1890, respectively; undoubtedly she had wedded her second husband, Albert Lewis, sometime between the Dresser-Sturm conflict of 1886 and the date of her third marriage.

If Dresser wrote the music and words of "The Letter That Never Came," Howard and Sturm clearly had stolen his song. *If* Dresser and Howard had been lovers and she had abandoned Dresser for Sturm, Dresser had double reason for his anger. *If* a child had been born of an affair between Howard and Dresser and then had died in infancy, Howard would have become a pariah to Dresser. So many "ifs," however, are only circumstantial evidence, but in this context, "The Curse," Dresser's next song—with its words and its dedication to Howard—makes sense as Dresser's musical revenge.

Following the controversy over "The Letter That Never Came," *The Two Johns* played for a week in New Orleans before closing out 1886 with a one-nighter in Plymouth, Massachusetts, on the last day of the year. There was no respite for a weary troupe. At the conclusion of the Plymouth engagement the performers left Massachusetts immediately for Wilkes-Barre, Pennsylvania, where the show opened on Saturday, New Year's Day 1887. The Stewart company remained on the East Coast for three months of one-night stands, relieved only by four one-week stays, including very welcome back-to-back weeks at Philadelphia's National Theatre and the Howard Athenaeum in Boston. The Athenaeum certainly was impressive, remodeled extensively less than four years earlier at a cost of between twelve and fifteen thousand dollars. The old wooden balcony and gallery fronts had been replaced by delicate iron latticework painted in "pearly gray, with panels of pink and handsome scroll and stucco work in light blue and gold," a new brass chandelier with cascading glass pendants adorned the foyer, new dressing rooms had been built, and new scenery and draperies had been hung. The new flooring of the entire house (including a new stage floor) was made of hard pine, and the seats were improved. Additionally, a new curtain, designed and painted by the well-known scenic artist Henry Reid, had been hung.[27] After playing for a week in these luxurious surroundings, *The Two Johns* returned to the road for a succession of one-nighters before it finished its season with a week in Pittsburgh. After closing night the troupe dispersed, and Dresser had the summer to work at composing before he returned for his second tour in the fall.

The 1887–88 season proved to be largely an uneventful one. Uneventful, that is, except for the incredible blizzard that all but buried the East Coast between 11 and 14 March 1888. By the time residents were able to dig themselves out of snow and drifts, some more than fifteen feet deep, at least four hundred people had died, and property damage was set at more than twenty-five million dollars. That part of the nation was marooned in an immense, beautiful, and treacherous sea of white cold. Performers who closed in the East on Saturday night, the tenth, found themselves stranded the next day. Those who were scheduled to open in Philadelphia, New York, New Haven, or Boston on Monday, the twelfth, could not get there and were forced to cancel their performances. Even if they could have arrived at their destinations, empty and closed theaters would have greeted them. Story upon story, some elaborated beyond the extravagant, gradually entered the mythology surrounding the natural disaster of that late winter.

The blizzard notwithstanding, Dresser was enjoying his work in the Two Johns Company. Other than playing the same show night after night, the one constant for the group was the camaraderie the players had established among themselves. As they spent hour after hour traveling from location to location, sharing stories, jokes, and their joys and hopes, the cast members became not unlike a family for Dresser. Once the season ended in May, Dresser returned to the other pleasure of his life—his composing. By 1888 Dresser was probably convinced he had a talent for writing songs the public wanted to hear. With the exception of three songs he had placed with New York publisher Willis Woodward and Company, Dresser's publishers had been from the Midwest: Balmer and Weber in St. Louis and Lyon and Healy in Chicago. During 1888 Dresser cast his lot with Woodward, then housed in the Star Theatre Building. This was an astute business move on Dresser's part, for New York's Music Row, or Tin Pan Alley as it would be called later, was becoming the capital of song publishing. Dresser remained with Woodward through nearly three dozen songs.

In July, just before the 1888–89 season was about to begin, there was an outbreak of yellow fever in the South, this time beginning in Jacksonville, Florida. Nearly five thousand cases were reported, bringing death to well over four hundred victims. By the last part of October the epidemic had subsided, and southern theaters were advertising that they were safe. Eugene Robinson's Museum and Theatre stated boldly: "Scare Is Over And No Fever. All danger has past and left New Orleans without having a case of yellow fever, which in itself proves that city to be entirely healthy."[28] Most performers could be counted on to donate their time and their abilities to the many concerts that were given to aid victims of one disaster or another. Such benefits nearly always drew large audiences and generous receipts, and the ones given to help those in the cities plagued by yellow fever enjoyed no less success. The manager of New York's Lyceum Theatre, for example, reported over nine hundred dollars in gross receipts from one performance of *Lord Chumley* on 26 September. The receipts represented a capacity audience at the Lyceum.[29] The trade newspapers ran impressively long lists of performers who had participated and managers who had given over their theaters for these deeds.

The 1888–89 season, Stewart's seventh with his Two Johns Company, was to be Dresser's third and last for the time being. Reviewers were beginning to mention Dresser's name, often the only cast member other than Stewart to be singled out. One wrote of the company's weeklong stay at the Brooklyn Theatre: Stewart and his company, "including Paul Dresser, filled the week . . . with [their] well-known humours."[30] Such remarks were certainly encouraging to Dresser, perhaps making him think that it might be time to move on to something more ambitious than playing Peter Johns. After nearly three years in the same role, night after night after night, Dresser was ready for a chance to do something else, something different. Even though the Two Johns Company had by now attained a status that enabled it consistently to play longer stands, Dresser was getting weary of the routine. Interpolations of new dialogue and new songs might bring a freshness to a performance, but there was always the danger of growing stale in a part.

Between August 1888 and the end of that year, for the first time in Dresser's tenure with the company, *The Two Johns* played no one-night stands, and it toured part of the H. R. Jacobs theatrical circuit in a series of two- and three-night engagements. Theater impresario Jacobs was just about to dissolve his partnership with F. F. Proctor. The two had been a team for more than four years, and now they had decided to go their separate ways. By year's end Proctor was advertising eleven theaters, most of them in the Northeast. Not to be outdone, Jacobs announced his "Own Imperial Circuit" of twenty-two "Amusement Temples" in New York, New Jersey, Pennsylvania, Ohio, Illinois, and Rhode Island. Additionally, his empire spread to Canada with proprietorship of the Toronto Opera House and the Theatre Royal in Montreal. Soon Jacobs was off on a tour of the West, traveling in his own railroad car, "The Amusement King," looking for houses to add to his already impressive list of theaters.[31]

Immediately before *The Two Johns* entered the Jacobs circuit, it enjoyed acclaim in a one-week stay in Boston, where the Grand

Opera House's audience was "finely treated."[32] Then it was on to Jacobs's houses. At the Third Avenue Theatre in New York City, "large audiences greeted [them]" at their opening matinee and evening performances on 24 September and continued to treat this "most capable" troupe with sustained laughter throughout the week.[33] Stewart's company continued to draw large, sometimes packed, houses on the circuit in Albany, Syracuse, Rochester, and Troy, New York.

In early November the players made a northern swing to the Toronto Opera House, where they drew big houses for the entire week. The remainder of the month saw the company in one-week performances in Buffalo at the Court Street Theatre, where it was met with "incessant rain, accompanied by [the] political excitement"[34] of the presidential race between Benjamin Harrison and Grover Cleveland, in Philadelphia, and in Hoboken, New Jersey, where a reviewer wrote that the company "is a very good one and the presentation was received with great laughter."[35] The troupe then went outside the Jacobs circuit to two Proctor theaters, working Christmas Day in Wilmington, Delaware; then it was on to Brooklyn's Criterion Theatre—that "really charming little snuggery" where the cast brought 1888 to a close and rang in the new year. The company "drew well and pleased thoroughly."[36]

The year 1889 began with Dresser and his colleagues firmly ensconced for full-week stays in Brooklyn, a return visit to the National Theatre in Philadelphia, a run at Harris's Bijou Theatre in Washington, D.C., where they "packed the house, . . . the 'S.R.O.' [standing-room only] sign being displayed at every performance," and performances to close out the month in Pittsburgh.[37] With the exception of a one-nighter at De Give's in Atlanta, where the company "had a small and dissatisfied house," according to one review, *The Two Johns* continued to do well for the remainder of the season.[38] The show drew capacity crowds at the Avenue Theatre in New Orleans and at performances in Fort Worth, Galveston, Houston, Little Rock, St. Louis, and Louisville, where the play closed its 1888–89 season at Harris's Theatre on 20 April, the day before Easter. The poem "The Manager's Lament," published in the *Clipper*, spoke for the many theater managers who complained about the small audiences and reduced revenues that nearly always accompanied "Holy Week, with its usual frost":

"In one week more Lent will be o'er,
And a fasting it's been to me,"
This manager said, as he bent his head,
With eyes quite tearfully.
Then he peeped through a hole in the curtain—
Empty seats, not even the rent;
So again he cried, and mumbled and sighed:
"I wish it was after Lent!"[39]

But this year *The Two Johns* went against the Lenten tide, attracting exceptionally large audiences during all of Holy Week.

Now, at the completion of his third season touring with Stewart, Dresser felt the time was right for something new, something fresh that would challenge his abilities and recharge his energies. It was nice to end on the high note of a succession of one-week performances, all of which audiences applauded, but Dresser's decision to move on was probably made easier when Stewart decided to divide his energies between two different plays and companies. Stewart would no longer be playing his Philip Johns against Dresser's Peter Johns night after night. As early as late December 1888 the *Clipper* announced that Stewart's new four-act play, *The Fat Men's Club*, would tour the following season, "displacing, it is said, 'The Two Johns.' "[40] A later issue of the same paper informed readers that Stewart's new comedy would open sooner than previously had been expected and that both his companies would tour during the remainder of the 1888–89 season.[41]

Stewart would henceforth divide his time performing in the two comedies, with *The Fat Men's Club* to open on 13 February with a large cast of twenty-four players.[42] The article stated that Dresser would be cast in this new piece, but it is more likely that he continued with *The Two Johns* and finished the season with it, rather than going with *The Fat Men's Club*. His name never appears in reviews of Stewart's new show, and a *Clipper* ad of 13 April announced that Dresser, "the popular author and singing comedian," planned to leave *The Two Johns* after his third season with the company and would be available for bookings for the 1889–90 season.[43] Willis Woodward and Company advertised Dresser's new song in that same issue of the *Clipper*. "A Stitch in Time Saves Nine" was touted as "a rousing encore every time you sing it."[44] Now thirty-one years old, Dresser had reached a level in his abilities as comedian, actor, and composer that made him a very attractive and versatile figure, one in a position to call the shots for his next move, a situation that was not long in coming.

Once *The Two Johns* finished its season, Dresser returned to New York City, which was in the throes of celebrating the centennial of the federal Republic and the beginning of the second century of its existence. Dresser joined in the rousing, patriotic spectacles, which included parades, fireworks, and parties. Scarcely before the commemorations ended, however, Americans experienced the pall of a disaster of immense proportions. On the last day of May a flood roared through Johnstown, Pennsylvania, sweeping more than two thousand people to their deaths. Throughout the next month, performers from the world of popular entertainment and that of classical theater and music gave benefit concerts, the proceeds of which went to benefit the victims of the catastrophe. Joseph Jefferson's company in *Rip Van Winkle*; Augustin Daly's company; J. H. Rice's Royal Circus; Powers's Grand Opera House in Decatur, Illinois; the Brooklyn United Singers; Edwin Booth; pianist Rafael Joseffy; a large orchestra led by Anton Seidl, Theodore Thomas, and Walter J. Damrosch; and the Metropolitan Opera House were only a few of the thousands upon thousands of performers and organizations to join in the effort. Albert and Alexandra, the Prince and Princess of Wales, and their daughters, and Mrs. Levi P. Morton, wife of the vice president of the United States, were among those who attended the benefit performance in Paris of Buffalo Bill's Wild West show. The gross proceeds from that single performance were two thousand dollars.[45] At least six New York theater managers promised flood victims their gross proceeds from benefit performances in the first week of June. During the second week of June, the Casino, the Broadway Theatre, Daly's Theatre, Proctor's Twenty-third Street Theatre, the Metropolitan Opera House, the People's Theatre, the Theatre Comique–Harlem, Madison Square Garden, and the London Theatre all held special benefit performances for the victims, promising their audiences "an interesting bill at each house."[46] On 15 June the *New York Dramatic Mirror* reported that the theatrical profession throughout the nation had given nearly one hundred thousand dollars to help the flood sufferers.[47]

Thus the entertainment season drew to a close that year, later than usual, and on an emotional note that brought the community of performers together, closer than their individual egos usually allowed. Now it was on to other things for the next couple of months. Will H. Shade wrote a poem to mark the end of that season, a year in which the profession again brought enjoyment to millions, and one that concluded with a tremendous outpouring of help for the victims of the latest disaster:

> Now do we part, seeking home and rest,
> Some going Eastward, some to the West,
> Bidding adieu to the footlights' glare,
> Over the ocean some will go;
> Many will tread the classic "Square,"
> Some will meet on "the Rialto";
> Some of "the gang," ere a week, will be
> Promenading the Bowery;
> And some, perchance, of our little band
> Now say goodby till the last, last stand.
> Yet, who can tell?
> So in cheerful grasp,
> Our hands we clasp,
> As we say: "Farewell!"[48]

CHAPTER 12

A Tin Soldier

Paul Dresser spent the better part of the summer of 1889 in New York City, for upon his arrival there he was immediately offered a job. Recalling the circumstances, Dresser remarked later, "I wasn't in [New York] twenty-four hours when Frank McKee, manager of [Charles] Hoyt's productions, sent for me and told me he wanted me to play 'The Plumber' in [*A Tin Soldier*]. I signed for the season. We opened on the 26th of . . . August at Detroit and I have made a success of the part ever since."[1] As a player in a Hoyt production, Dresser was ready to ascend to stardom. While Fattie Stewart had won a certain reputation as playwright and actor, his plays were considered to be second-tier work. He simply was not in Hoyt's league. Only twenty-nine years old, Hoyt was in the front ranks of writers of farce-comedies and, more often than not, had more than one play on the boards during any given theatrical season. In the 1889–90 season three Hoyt plays were touring the country; little more than a decade later he had a phenomenal fourteen separate plays produced in the 1900–1901 season.[2]

Hoyt's play *A Tin Soldier* was starting its fourth season when Dresser joined the cast. The play contains elements of mistaken identity between a husband and his servant and the complications that ensue at a masked ball. Typically, musical, comedic, and performance interpolations were earmarks of the production—not unlike Hoyt's other productions and those of countless others. "As the [*New York*] *Dramatic Mirror* noted, the evening metamorphosed into 'a sugar coated variety olio punctuating the act with charming inconsistency.' One character was named after the spanking new masterpiece that was the talk of New York. To this figure, Brooklyn Bridge, . . . fell the 'inevitable topical song with verses ad libitum.' "[3]

The farcical, slapstick element that was a hallmark of a Hoyt production is revealed by some of the names of the characters in *A Tin Soldier*: Rats, "a perfect little gentleman"; Vilas Canby, the "Professor," a practical plumber—the part Dresser played; Brooklyn Bridge, "a gentleman of high position," and his daughter Victoria; Col. I. B. Boosey; Wright Handy; Steele Coffin; Rob Graves; Violet Hughes, "a domestic earthquake"; Carrie Story; and Mrs. Fulton Ferry, the "mother-in-law to Brooklyn Bridge." Only Patsy, described as "a young thing," has a conventional name. Subtlety, after all, was not the point in Hoyt productions or of others in this genre. Here was a play that could be counted on to evoke laughter, groans, hisses, and even good-humored booing from the audience at such outlandish names and the even more outrageous puns. Dramatic integrity, after all, did not carry the play. A writer offered the following description of some of the goings-on:

> Apparently a tar-and-feathering committee was conspicuous in that plot because [W.] Jordan's role was that of Steele Coffin, "secretary of the tar-and-feathering committee." . . .
>
> Musical "interruptions" included "Irish Reel," "I'm Waiting and Whistling for Kate," "All Ocean Gleaming," "Dancing Mad," "March of the Plumbers," "Generosity," "There You Are," "Borrowing," "Sailor Boy," "I'm So Shy" and "Golden Sword."
>
> The presentation, managed by Frank McKee, was described in a footnote as "a collection of incidents, with musical interruptions, and is called 'A Tin Soldier' because somebody has already used the title, 'Jibbanainoisy,' and is announced as a musical, etc., giving everybody a chance to exercise individual taste and fancy in describing it."[4]

Rehearsals for the twelve cast members took much of August before the farce-comedy opened at the Whitney Grand Opera House in Detroit for a week, beginning on the twenty-sixth. There it played to good business for three of its night performances, but it drew sparce audiences during the matinees. The quality of the performances was substandard according to a reviewer: "While allowance must be made for the newness of the co., at the same time it must be stated frankly that the same degree of satisfaction was not experienced at the performance as one was accustomed to when the co. was here before."[5] Such criticism was nothing compared to what often happened to a company that gave substandard performances. Two months after *A Tin Soldier* opened, the twenty men of the Howard Comedy company, playing in Johnstown, New York,

> were hissed from the stage. As the actors were leaving the Opera House they were pelted with rotten eggs, covered with flour and run out of town. All their musical instruments, including drums, were taken from them, broken and thrown into the mud. One of the players was taken to the hydrant and "ducked."[6]

And, in an incident at the Punxsutawney, Pennsylvania, Opera House, a Mr. Fish, the manager, "pummelled Palmer [whose panoramic exhibit of the Johnstown flood Mr. Fish deemed to be poor] in a very pugilistic manner until the latter took to the scene loft to escape."[7] Unruly audience members and theater managers were not the only ones that performers sometimes had to contend with. Shortly after the incident just described occurred, a scheduled performance of *Uncle Tom's Cabin* enraged the citizens of Bonham, Texas. The play itself, while still unpopular in the South, was not the sole cause of the unrest. Rather, the troupe had booked a performance on the night before the burial of Jefferson Davis, the president of the Confederacy.

> Just as the Opera House doors were opened the town band came marching down the street, and, halting in front of the Opera House, began playing "Dixie." Someone sounded the fire alarm, and [in] less than ten minutes the streets were thronged with about 2,000 men and boys, all of whom were ringing bells, popping cannon crackers and shouting, the band still continuing to play "Dixie."

The mayor was unable to do anything to quiet the thunderstorm, and

> The members of the company extinguished all the lights and huddled in one corner of the building to await until the storm was over. The crowd finally dispersed, after demonstrating, as they stated, that no company could play "Uncle Tom's Cabin" in this city the night before the burial of Jeff Davis. At no time since the war has such a spirit been aroused.[8]

Perhaps the criticism of *A Tin Soldier* was owing to an unsettled cast, upset by something that had occurred a bit earlier. The company most likely proceeded in Detroit without the presence of its stage manager, Charles F. Lorraine, and with an understudy playing Violet Hughes. Just before the play opened in Detroit, police in Long Island, New York, arrested Lorraine and his wife, St. George Hussey, who was to play Hughes. Both were held in lieu of a two-hundred-dollar bail, accused of assaulting their neighbor, Richard Canton, described as a farmer in Newtown, Long Island. Part of the account sounds like a comic routine one could have seen on stage: when Mr. Canton refused to keep his cattle from pasturing on the Lorraines' lawn, Mr. Lorraine attempted to drive the cows off his property by throwing green apples at them.

> The cows ate up his ammunition. Then Mr. Lorraine hunted up Mr. Canton, who was armed with a hoe. In the course of the argument Mr. Canton struck Mr. Lorraine across the face with the back of the blade, cutting the flesh to the bone. He had Mr. Canton arrested, and Mr. Canton brought a counter suit against both Mr. and Mrs. Lorraine, alleging that they both assaulted him, one with a hoe, and the other with a stick, and that they then pushed him through a fence.[9]

The outcome of the grand jury's deliberations are unknown, but the Lorraines returned to the company, continuing with it beyond Detroit. This was not the last time Hussey's name appeared in the newspapers in connection with a court case, for she and Dresser were adversaries in legal proceedings less than a year later.

In addition to problems with these two members of the troupe, *A Tin Soldier* gained few admirers during its stay at the Haymarket in Chicago the first week in September. There, the manager was infuriated with Hoyt for the poor performances of the cast; the *New York Clipper*'s reporter echoed the criticism in a damning review: " 'A Tin Soldier' was presented with a dime museum company, or near it, to bad business all week."[10] Because Hoyt's farce-comedies and companies had established solid reputations as excellent drawing cards known for their high quality, the Chicago black marks appear not to have been harmful. Manager McKee undoubtedly minced no words in his own comments to the cast, perhaps even going so far as to threaten to fire the poorest of the lot. Without doubt the actors got the message and improved their performances, for such scathing criticism was not heard again.

Booked for weeklong stays during the rest of September, October, and November, *A Tin Soldier* drew standing-room-only houses in Kansas City, where the company was called "fully up to the standard" and where Dresser and Louis Wesley were singled out for their work.[11] Theater audiences in St. Louis, Chicago, Louisville, Cleveland, and Cincinnati were likewise big, and reviewers praised Dresser's work: "Paul Dresser was funny as the plumber" [at Pope's Theatre, St. Louis][12]; "Dresser as the Plumber made [a] big hit" [at H. R. Jacobs's Theatre, Cleveland][13]; and "Paul Dresser made a very heavy Professor" [at Havlin's Theatre, Cincinnati].[14] At Cincinnati, however, the cast members of the production, together with John H. Havlin, the manager of the theater, were arrested for breaking the city's Sunday Amusement Law. Havlin's two recent arrests for breaking the law had not "dampened his ardor in the fight to encompass the defeat of the law"; he was "still out with his battering ram."[15] Dresser, his cohorts, and manager Havlin were hustled to the station house and registered as prisoners. The next day they were arraigned, "sandwiched between petty criminals."[16]

Freed on bail, the artists had to pay court costs, and Havlin was fined ten dollars. Already arrested twice for breaking the local prohibition against Sunday performances, Havlin was a fearsome advocate for keeping theaters open seven days a week. He and the managers of two other Cincinnati houses broke the law yet again the following Sunday and were fined fifteen dollars each. Now boldly advertising Sunday performances, Cincinnati's theater managers would gradually win their battle.[17] Sunday laws in other cities were soon struck down, and by late October 1890 Sunday had "come to be the greatest showgoing night of the week."[18] More than a decade later, however, the *Dramatic Mirror* continued to express its opposition to Sunday performances: "It is not so much a question of Sunday observance with this journal as it is a question of justice to members of the theatrical profession. Every actor or performer should be permitted to rest one day in the week."[19] The paper's stand had little effect on the profession, and Sunday performances continued to be part of an actor's schedule.

Good houses greeted the production in its short stays in other midwestern cities. On 22 November the company visited central Illinois, playing the new Grand Opera House in Decatur. Built by Orlando Powers, one of the city's wealthiest residents, the three-story building was given over entirely to the enterprise of entertainment. An elegance, both intimidating and inviting, characterized the Grand. The imported tiles that made up the lobby floor were arranged in a design that gave the appearance of a "fine Turkish rug." Throughout, carved cherry and old oak woodwork surrounded the theatergoer; frescoes decorated the walls, the proscenium arch, and most other vertical spaces. The theater had seating for sixteen hundred in upholstered chairs; the stage was provided with twenty sets of scenery and two drop curtains, and the entire theater was lighted by five hundred lights in a combination of electric and gas fixtures. Especially important to the players were the eleven dressing rooms, "conveniently located, four on the stage, sumptuously furnished. They [were] provided with fixed water basins, nicely ventilated and heated."[20] Powers's Grand Opera House was a luxury for the city. For the performers, who were not accustomed to finding such a pleasure palace out in the hinterlands, the Grand was a delightful oasis. Two weeks before *A Tin Soldier* came to town, fire had nearly destroyed Powers's magnificent house. The theater's drop curtains and the scenery for a performance of the Ullie Akerstrom company burned, but theater workers' quick actions saved the building from destruction.[21] New curtains and scenery had been hung in time for Dresser's appearance. Six years later fire revisited the Grand, this time destroying it and the entire surrounding block of businesses, at a loss calculated at a half million dollars.[22]

After packing their personal belongings, costumes, sets, props, and music, the company members boarded their train and traveled eastward from Decatur, bound for Terre Haute. Dresser had only rarely returned to the city of his birth since his rebellious youth, and now he was going to have the opportunity to play before some of the same people who had thought that he would not amount to much in life. Not only had he succeeded far beyond their meager expectations, but he was traveling throughout the nation as a featured performer in an important farce-comedy, written by one of the major figures in the theater. Dresser had traveled to places many Terre Hauteans did not even know existed, had met celebrated figures from many walks of life, and was himself something of a celebrity as an actor and composer. *A Tin Soldier* played at Naylor's Opera House 27 November, the day before Thanksgiving. Four days earlier a local newspaper remarked that the play "has lost none of its attractive features since presented here last and a great deal of new music and new business have been introduced, making it . . . better and funnier than ever." With understandable pride over one of the town's own, the newspaper trumpeted: "Paul Dresser, who appears as the plumber, is an old Terre Haute boy and has made quite a reputation for himself"—certainly a far different "reputation for himself" than the one the newspapers had reported back in 1876.[23]

On the day of the performance, a reporter for the *Terre Haute Evening Gazette* wrote about an aspect of Dresser's physical appearance that bedeviled the songwriter for most of his adult life. Remembering Dresser as weighing about two hundred pounds when he was in Terre Haute eleven years previously, the writer commented: "Paul was on the streets today looking as big as the side of a house. He weighs 300 pounds."[24] If Dresser's girth bothered him, he hid it well, for he was "as jolly a Paul as he always was, and he got many a warm grasp of the hand today from those who are glad to know that he has made a big hit in the theatrical world."[25] In addition to being treated to seeing a local boy in this major farce-comedy, the audience at Naylor's that evening had the

Van Pelt-Dietrich Library Center, Univ. of Pa.

Paul Dresser showing off his notable waistline.

pleasure of hearing the first performance of a new song its hometown star had composed. Robert C. Vernon, as Brooklyn Bridge, sang Dresser's latest creation, "The Cradle Belongs to Baby; or, Days Gone By," probably composed specifically for interpolation into *A Tin Soldier*. Willis Woodward and Company published the song a year later as "Days Gone By."

There was to be no day off to observe the Thanksgiving holiday, for after the performance in Terre Haute the troupe made the seventy-mile trip to Indianapolis, where it "had a profitable engagement" during its three days at English's Opera House.[26] Then, with

Sunday off for traveling, *A Tin Soldier* moved to Philadelphia's National Theatre, where it "drew large audiences" in its stay for a week.[27] After three nights in Albany in the middle of the month, the cast had a break from 21 to 26 December. The *Clipper* reported that "most of 'A Tin Soldier' Co. went to New York, where they rest this week. Paul Dresser is visiting a friend [in Bridgeport, Connecticut]."[28] The year ended and a new one began in Monday-through-Saturday performances at the Grand Opera House in Boston.

While Dresser had enjoyed the benefits of staying in theaters for weeklong performances during his time with the Two Johns Company, that troupe, more often than not, followed an exhausting schedule and a frenetic pace of long successions of one-nighters. The more substantial reputation of Hoyt and his productions, on the other hand, ensured a greater number of longer stays in one spot and brought with them a guaranteed audience appeal that translated into financial success at the box office. Theaters *wanted* the various Hoyt troupes and signed them to longer tenures more frequently than Dresser had enjoyed in his three years with Stewart. Between opening night in August and the end of December 1889, for example, *A Tin Soldier* played ten one-week stands in the midwestern states, Pennsylvania, and Boston.

Very late in 1889 an event occurred with which Dresser would have had considerable empathy, in light of his having been cheated out of his due rewards for "The Letter That Never Came." The 4 January 1890 issue of the *Clipper*, the trade paper Dresser regularly read, carried an article about a lawsuit that Stephen Foster's widow and daughter had brought in Indianapolis federal court in late December. The suit sought "to enjoin Kinsley & Pauley, of *The Lafayette Echo* Co. from further infringing the copyright on that old time melody, 'Way down on Suwanee River.' "[29] Having been stung himself, Dresser would undoubtedly have felt much sympathy for the Foster family.

Rather painfully, Dresser had become aware of the need for more control over his finished product. To him, this meant becoming closely involved with the publication and promotion of his own songs and working for stringent copyright laws that would afford protection of his work. Before much longer, he would become involved in both arenas—as the publisher of his songs and as a leader in efforts to extend copyright protection beyond American borders. For the present, however, he had to hold his involvement in such matters in abeyance because his life was filled with the immediate business of *A Tin Soldier* and with composing when he had the time. In early 1890, following its appearance in Boston, *A Tin Soldier* moved immediately to New York City for eight shows at the Bijou Theatre, where "a large house did full honor to . . . Hoyt's [play]. The piece is popularly interpreted, and the outlook for remunerative business . . . seems most auspicious."[30] Two more weeklong stays followed, at Harris's Bijou Theatre in Washington, D.C., and a return to New York City at the Windsor.

On the day *A Tin Soldier* closed its second run in New York City, the *Clipper* announced that Dresser was leaving the show on that date and "has already received several advantageous offers for the balance of the season."[31] An ad, carried in the same issue, read:

> Paul Dresser Singing Comedian, at liberty for balance of season and '90 and '91. . . . Farce Comedy, Burlesque, Minstrel or Variety. Author and composer of Famous Ballads. . . . Some press comments: "Jolly Paul Dresser is now playing the Plumber, and playing it well."—Cin. Enquirer. . . . "His is an unctious humor that finds its way across the footlights and sets the audience a laughing."—Cin. Com. Gazette. . . . "He plays the part with much originality, which is more than can be said of some of his predecessors."—Cleveland Plain Dealer. . . . "He is a corker."—Cin. Times Star. . . . "Paul Dresser made a hit."—Republic, St. Louis. . . . "The Plumber was capitally done by Paul Dresser."—Courier-Journal, Louisville, Ky. . . . "He is original and makes them laugh."—St. Louis Globe Democrat. . . . Space (and money) forbid the introduction of the many flattering comments received. Address to the Morton House, or care of Clipper.[32]

Why did Dresser plan to leave *A Tin Soldier*? Perhaps he felt he should get more credit as the composer of some of the songs that were interpolated in the production; considering his value to the company as composer and actor, he may have thought his salary should be higher than it was. More likely, his decision may well have been connected with the bad blood that was developing between him and Hussey. The *Clipper* would later comment that "Paul Dresser and St. George Hussey . . . seem to be anything but friends."[33]

Whatever the reasons for the January notice, Dresser changed his mind within the following week and had "reconsidered his resignation and is to continue with 'A Tin Soldier' Co. until the end of the season."[34] During the first week in February, the company "amused a large audience" at the Bijou Theatre in Milwaukee, where "Louis Wesley, Paul Dresser and St. George Hussey [received] the bulk of the applause."[35] Following that date, Dresser and his colleagues began a long tour that took them to the far West, the only time in his life that Dresser made such a journey. In addition to appearing in Nebraska and in Salt Lake City, *A Tin Soldier* stopped in Leadville, Colorado. There it played to slim audiences at Tabor's Opera House. Horace Tabor, silver magnate, former lieutenant governor of Colorado, and former senator pro tempore, had built his magnificent opera palace on the second and third floors of the Tabor and Bush building. Advertised as "the most inspiring edifice in the city, . . . and conceded by all to be the finest theater west of the Mississippi,"[36] Tabor's Opera House was little more than ten years old when Dresser played there, and the immense wealth of its owner could be seen everywhere one looked. Tabor had spent sixty thousand dollars building his opera house, and even with that sum he had barely touched his vast fortune in silver. Eight hundred eighty patrons could settle themselves in thick, plush seats, could gaze, awe-stricken, at the visual splendor of the frescoed ceiling, and could marvel at the newest of lighting that seventy-two gas jets provided. There was even a connecting walkway to the adjoining Clarendon Hotel.

The accommodations for the performers could be compared to only the most lavish of quarters the cast had seen in the largest cities they had played. Most of the residents and transients in this raw frontier town had never in their lives witnessed such a display of the power of money, the exhibition of such self-indulgence. When the Forrester Dramatic Company's production of *The Rough Diamond* inaugurated the theater on 20 November 1879,

Tabor and his wife, Augusta, were present, ushered into their lavishly appointed box with great ceremony. Leadville's great benefactor acknowledged the audience's applause with a gracious bow and the wave of his hand, perhaps with the prim Augusta registering thin-lipped disapproval of her husband's profligacy.

When Dresser opened in Leadville, any pleasant memories Augusta might have had of the theater's inaugural night had turned sour. Less than a year after the Tabors seated themselves in box number one for the first time, Horace began his scandalous love affair with the infamous "Baby" Elizabeth Doe. By the time Dresser appeared in Leadville, Horace's financial empire and personal life were in disrepair; the public's sympathies lay for the most part with Augusta, the wronged woman, and the country's gradual move to the gold standard was to strike an ominous and disastrous note for Horace's future.[37] Now, in mid-February 1890, with the Horace Tabor–Baby Doe scandal a permanent part of Colorado's lusty history, a new generation of residents and transients braved the frigid Colorado night to come to the Tabor Opera House. As they warmed themselves inside the theater that evening, perhaps a few in that small group nudged one another knowingly. The Tabor-Doe affair had had more than a few tragic moments, but in retrospect one could see something of the ludicrous, the theatrical, in those carryings-on. Tonight a small audience at the opera house would see *A Tin Soldier*, the ludicrous quality of which must have seemed quite pale if anyone present had thought about the recent past.

Reaching California, *A Tin Soldier* drew large audiences in San Francisco during the first two weeks of March when it played at the Alcazar Theatre, a venue advertised as "Unquestionably, Positively and Emphatically the Handsomest Theatre West of the Rockies."[38] The company then moved to Portland, back to Stockton, California, and on to Seattle, enjoying crowded houses in all those cities. During April, Hoyt's farce-comedy began its trip back to the East, enjoying good audiences in short stops in Montana, Minnesota, and Iowa before concluding the month with a week at the Bijou Theatre in Minneapolis.

It was during the company's tour of Montana that the animosity that had been building between Dresser and Hussey reached its peak and exploded. Admitted to the Union as its forty-first state only five short months before, Montana still carried with it an aura of the Old West. After playing a night in Philipsburg, hardly more than a village with fewer than nine hundred inhabitants—about the capacity of Leadville's Tabor Opera House—and following with two performances in Anaconda, *A Tin Soldier* moved on to the capital, Helena, for three nights, 10 through 12 April, at Ming's Opera House, before concluding the Montana segment in Butte.

Helena, a major stop on the Northern Pacific and Great Northern Railroad line, had a population of nearly fourteen thousand and could boast of having more amenities for the cast to enjoy than they had been accustomed to thus far in their tour of the state. At the same time, it still had the character of a frontier town, and the conflict between two "citified" actors may well have seemed somewhat comical to those old-timers who were accustomed to the rough-and-tumble existence of territory days. Whatever the troubles between Dresser and Hussey were, they boiled over into downright hostilities in Helena. Hussey charged Dresser with disturbing the peace and carrying concealed weapons. Arrested and taken to jail, Dresser pleaded guilty to the former charge and was fined twenty-five dollars by a Justice Woodman. After Dresser declared his innocence as to the weapons charge, a jury heard testimony and deliberated the case for about five minutes before acquitting him. The *Clipper* concluded its story with the pithy remark, "There is, or was, a great deal of antipathy between the parties."[39]

Dresser and Hussey remained in the cast for the last month of the 1889–90 season, but one can only speculate on the atmosphere that must have existed during the performances. Finally the players, physically exhausted from the extensive cross-country tour they had just concluded, and, more likely than not, emotionally drained from the Dresser-Hussey quarrels and the inevitable attempt by both to gain supporters, closed the season in a one-night stand in Wilmington, Delaware, at Proctor and Soulier's Grand Opera House. While Dresser continued with *A Tin Soldier* for one more season, Hussey left the company. An ad in the *Clipper* for 5 July 1890 announced that Hussey, "A Striking hit in 'A Tin Soldier' season of 1889–90 [was now] At Liberty."[40] By September

Hussey was back on her feet, playing at Tony Pastor's Theatre in New York.[41]

During Dresser 's break for the summer months, he turned his attention back to his songs—he would compose fifteen during this year. He then rejoined *A Tin Soldier* for the 1890–91 season, his last with the company. It began in the South with a one-night performance at the De Gives Theatre in Atlanta.

While audiences throughout the country enjoyed Hoyt's numerous farce-comedies, the playwright was no friend of the *Dramatic Mirror* and had taken to withholding the company's advance performance dates from that paper's correspondents. Acknowledging the enmity that existed between the playwright and the paper, the *Dramatic Mirror*'s response to Hoyt's actions was to point out that the paper had "not found intellectual pleasure—or even rational amusement—in [Hoyt's] knockabout conglomerates." Noting that it secured the performance dates in spite of Hoyt's lack of cooperation, the paper remarked rather snidely that "it would be a gross oversight if the readers of this journal were not forewarned of the hazardous proximity of these double-jointed phantasms" and concluded, "[Hoyt] can no more help being fantastic off the stage than can the stuff that he shovels on to it."[42]

Less than a week after these comments appeared, *Dramatic Mirror* and *Clipper* critics wrote many columns to praise Dion Boucicault, the English dramatist and actor who died at his home in New York City on 18 September 1890. That the stage could have room for both a Hoyt and a Boucicault said much for the democratic qualities of American theater and the publics that applauded these playwrights whose works were antithetical of one another in the extreme. Twice Hoyt's age and a greatly revered figure, Boucicault had written or adapted more than a hundred plays during his long career, and while he freely admitted to being a "wholesale borrower and sometimes a plagiarist from the French," he "was a most skillful workman with others' tools," as an obituary pointed out.[43]

Such criticism of Hoyt as appeared in the *Dramatic Mirror* probably did not reach readers in the hinterlands. If it did, it certainly did not deter large audiences from flocking to *A Tin Soldier* in its appearances at New Orleans's St. Charles Theatre and its stays in Alabama, Mississippi, Arkansas, and Kansas. Upon moving on to

Memphis for performances the week of 6 through 11 October, the company played in the New Lyceum Theatre. Here was an opportunity for the actors to play in an elegant theater, opened just one week before they arrived. Occupying the ground floor of a six-story brick building at the corner of Union and Main Streets, the New Lyceum seated nearly twelve hundred people. Six boxes flanked either side of the large twenty-five-by-twenty-five-foot proscenium opening, which featured drapes of a rose-colored plush fabric. The boxes had fronts of "burnished brass rail, supported by bronzed standards and scrolls, and at the top of each [was placed] an arch of ornamental fret work."[44] Each of the first-floor folding chairs had plush backs and hat, overcoat, and umbrella racks. Woodwork, finished in antique ivory, met moquette-covered aisles, and the walls and ceiling were frescoed in a Byzantine-like style. In the balcony were bronzed folding chairs placed atop a Brussels carpet. "Seven bracket cluster lights, illuminated by either electricity or gas, and twenty intermediate electric lights [were] arranged around the gallery facing."[45] The stage was large, measuring seventy feet wide by thirty-three feet deep, with a height of forty feet. Eight traps were set in the stage together with four sets of grooves for the movement of sets. Under the auditorium were fifteen dressing rooms. The drop curtain for the theater depicted, in lavish artistic rendering, Mark Antony and Cleopatra. Having just arrived from a series of single performances in Mobile, Alabama; Little Rock, Arkansas; and Vicksburg, Mississippi, the cast welcomed a week in this spanking new theater and the cosmopolitan atmosphere of Memphis.

Between the beginning of October and the end of the year, the company played a series of one-week performances in Memphis; in Kansas City, where it had "smooth sailing"; at Pope's Theatre in St. Louis, where the show "proved as popular as ever . . . and the audiences tested the capacity of the house";[46] at H. R. Jacobs's Academy at Madison and Halsted in Chicago; and on Chicago's north side at Jacobs's Clark Street Theatre, beginning with a Sunday matinee on 9 November. *A Tin Soldier* played for a total of twelve nights and four matinees at Jacobs's two "Amusement Temples," with their combined seating capacity of four thousand, and turned a tidy profit for Jacobs as well as for Hoyt. All of this must still have been exhilarating for Dresser—to be playing for extended stays in a variety of large metropolitan areas and to be a member of the cast of this company that met with audience acclaim night after night.

On the other hand, the last month and a half of 1890 was certainly among the most difficult times of Dresser's life. His mother died on Friday, 14 November. Sarah Dreiser, the woman who forgave Paul's indiscretions and his downright sins, the one who had always protected him, the person whom he elevated to saintly status in many of his songs, had died at fifty-seven. At the time of her death, Sarah lived in Chicago, close to where her eldest son was performing with *A Tin Soldier*. Dresser was at his mother's bedside for parts of her last few days, although in her fevered state she did not realize he was there.

While Dresser's sisters and brother Theodore Dreiser were happy that he could be there, they were greatly dismayed that he had brought home his current lover, someone from the company of *A Tin Soldier*. After all, this was a time for family, and the woman's presence was intrusive. She did not belong there; she was not family. Her "tailored perfection," her self-absorption with her own beauty, and her embarrassing "sexual interest in Paul" greatly upset the family, but she gradually won them over with gifts, even though her feigned affection for them was obvious. Theodore's feelings could best be described as ambivalent. On one hand, her presence at so private a moment for the family was disturbing, but he also wished "sex-wise, that I might enjoy so beautiful a woman."[47]

Sarah died during the morning of the fourteenth. The trauma was evident. "I never saw a house more shaken or disrupted than was ours by this event," Theodore wrote. "It was as if an explosion had occurred and many had been killed or injured. We were beside ourselves with grief, worry, perhaps fear of new and worse disasters to follow."[48] Dresser, her beloved son, the first of her children to survive infancy, was not with her at the moment of death. He had thanked God that "he was good enough to allow me to be [in Chicago] . . . during her last two weeks illness," but he was already at the Clark Street Theatre preparing for his afternoon show when she died.[49] Immediately following his performance and perhaps fearing the worst, Dresser rushed to 61 Flournoy

Street and arrived there around six o'clock. Upon hearing his mother was dead, he was devastated, "so stricken that he could scarcely say a word, or even make a sign. He merely stared at her body in silence, pressing his lips together and finally, unable to restrain himself, wiping away the few tears that ran down his cheeks. Then he left the room."[50]

The family's plans for a burial sanctioned by the Catholic Church were immediately met with resistance from a priest, whom Theodore acidly described as a "low-browed, dogmatic little Bavarian, panoplied with the trashy authority of his church." The local church denied permission for Sarah to be buried in consecrated ground. After all, the priest argued, had not Sarah long been absent from confession and communion? Why had the family not called a priest to give her the last rites?[51] Old Johann Paul Dreiser suffered doubly. Already grief stricken over the death of his wife, he now had to face the thought of Sarah having died in sin. After much figurative "belly-crawlings" and Dresser's probable intervention with local Catholic authorities, the church relented, and at 12:30 on Sunday, the sixteenth, carriages carrying Sarah's body and her mourners traveled to the church for funeral services. After the Mass, the funeral party headed north on Clark Street and stopped at the new German Roman Catholic cemetery—St. Boniface—"laid out on a dreary waste on the North Side—lots so much per square foot," where Sarah's body was placed in a vault.[52]

Dresser did not attend the funeral, for he and his theatrical company left that Sunday for Louisville. Given his professed love for his mother, one wonders why he did not turn his role over to an understudy for a day or two and leave for Kentucky after the funeral. Perhaps he felt there was nothing more he could do for his good mother. If he had, in fact, won permission for a church funeral for his mother, that single act would have won Johann Paul's gratefulness and, for the time being, secured some peace within the family. Sarah Mary Schänäb Dreiser was now at rest, and Dresser remembered her goodness and character for the rest of his life, calling upon her time and again as the model for his idealized mother in song.

Now, the professional in Dresser had to submerge his intense sorrow in the daily and nocturnal routine to which he had become so accustomed. After Louisville, *A Tin Soldier* played a week in Cleveland and then a series of one-nighters in New York state, concluding the year two days after Christmas in Norristown, Pennsylvania. The travel to city upon city, some of them faceless and hardly recalled afterward, the periodic rehearsals to freshen the show and to work up new songs, putting on makeup and costume, performing the show, then packing up and heading to the train depot for travel to the next spot—such order in his life must have helped Dresser to deal with his grief. Nevertheless, the guilt he felt over spending so little time with his mother in the past eight years must have been difficult to overcome. He could, however, temper that grief when he recalled the unalloyed happiness his visits and his help had brought her.

A Tin Soldier began 1891 with two very successful one-week stays in New York City. Playing for eight engagements from 5 through 10 January at the Windsor Theatre between Canal and Bayard Streets in the Bowery, the farce-comedy "reopened wide . . . the gates of mirth, with Arthur Dunn and Paul Dresser leading the fun."[53] An enthusiastic *Clipper* reviewer wrote that the play "is always sure of a hearty welcome from its East Side admirers of its rather boisterous fun. The company contains some cleverly adapted people, and the farce is given with an entertaining touch and go from beginning to end."[54] The more reserved *Dramatic Mirror* complimented the company in a backhanded way: "That hackneyed and improvable absurdity . . . is the attraction at the Windsor. . . . The cast . . . was fully capable to inject the necessary horse-play and specialties with which the skit abounds."[55] The Windsor Theatre program listed a series of "musical interruptions" throughout the performance. In the first act, a quartet consisting of Rats, Patsy, Violet Hughes, and Dresser's character performed an Irish reel. The sight of the three-hundred-pound Dresser skipping through the dance must have been, in itself, enough to open those "gates of mirth" for the audience. Dresser was called upon again in the second act's song interruption—"March of the Plumbers"—and twice in the concluding act, where he sang "Generosity" and "Sailor Boy," the latter as part of yet another quartet.[56]

There is no mention of a Dresser composition having been sung at the Windsor performances, but given the custom of musical interpolation, it would not have been unusual for one of them to have been included, if only spontaneously. After a week off following its appearance at the Windsor, the troupe moved to Jacobs's Theatre at the corner of Thirty-first Street and Third Avenue, where the show was called "one of the most laughable of C. H. Hoyt's productions," and many in the cast were singled out for praise. The critic lauded Dresser's performance as "very funny in makeup and manner."[57]

February was an exceedingly slow month with only three single performances, save for a three-night stand in Rochester, New York. The company spent the remainder of the 1890–91 season in stays of one week in Pittsburgh, where it "delighted large houses" at Harris's Theatre, and in Cincinnati, where it "did very well" at Havlin's Theatre, in spite of bad weather, and where Dresser was called "exceptionally clever."[58] Three days after the cast left Cincinnati came the news that overshadowed everything else—news that Phineas Taylor Barnum had died at his home in Bridgeport, Connecticut, at the age of eighty-two. With his uncanny ability to read an audience, to offer through his American Museum and his circus the kind of spectacle and sensation people had never before seen, Barnum presented formidable competition to other companies that might have the bad luck to perform in the same city as his shows. Often, Barnum simply dominated the scene. Perhaps Dresser thought of that week less than a decade earlier when he played Chicago and witnessed tens of thousands flock to the lakefront to see Barnum's circus and its main attraction, Jumbo.

CHAPTER 13

The Danger Signal

After he concluded his commitment to *A Tin Soldier* in late April 1891, Paul Dresser turned his attention to his summer vocation—songwriting. For the past five years he had spent most of his free summer months composing, and by 1891 he had written and published at least forty songs. His growing reputation received a boost late that spring when an advertisement in the *New York Clipper* associated one of his songs with Julia Mackey, a young singer known especially for her rich contralto voice. Mackey had been attracted to Dresser's "I Can't Believe Her Faithless," had begun to include it regularly in her stage performances, and by May had won a large following for both herself and the song. "I Can't Believe Her Faithless," in fact, did much to establish her reputation as a performer and became one of her early signature tunes.[1]

Although the advertisement was neither objective nor a review of the song, its real value was that it brought Dresser's work as a composer to the attention of the thousands who read this paper. Exciting as the growing acclaim for his songs was, Dresser knew he was not yet successful enough to leave his life in the theater and commit most of his energies to writing music. The fraternity of song composers had seen more than its fair share of one-shot successes, and, though he knew his worth and his abilities, that prospect made him nervous. The fact that others published his songs also meant that they, not he, had the real control over the profits the songs made. To give up his livelihood as an actor at this point in his life was a gamble he simply could not take.

Sometime during the summer Dresser agreed to tour the next season with *The Danger Signal*, a four-act comedy-melodrama. This time he took on double responsibilities. He was to play Cpl. Heinrich "Pretzels" Yost, one of the leading roles, and he would be the stage manager of the company. Playwright Henry DeMille loosely based *The Danger Signal* on his own play *The Main Line*, introducing "new characters, with brightened dialogues and a general transposition of the salient features of the play [to] make it . . . almost an entirely new piece" in which special effects played the dominant role.[2] Dresser and his cohorts took a decided back-seat to the locomotive and snowplow in the play.

The situation, however, was scarcely different from that found in other plays of the time, many of which emphasized spectacle over dramatic substance. Between 1891 and 1892, for example, at least three other railroad dramas were playing throughout the country. Florence Bindley's *The Pay Train* toured in 1891, and the very next year saw *The Limited Mail*, written by Elmer E. Vance. Another train show of 1891 was Lincoln J. Carter's *The Fast Mail*. Advertised as "the Acme of Realism," *The Fast Mail* featured a full-size locomotive, an illuminated caboose, and fourteen freight cars. When DeMille's play appeared at H. C. Miner's People's Theatre in New York City during the second week in September, a critic wrote, "The Danger Signal cast its warning . . . with Rosabel Morrison, Tillie Barnum, Marjorie Leigh, Helen Hall, Adolph Lestina, John F. DeGez and Paul Dresser as mere actors competing with a 'full-size locomotive' and a 'Cyclone Snow Plough at work.' "[3] Later, in 1893, Good's Opera House in South Bend, Indiana, breathlessly advertised that

> the Greatest of all Realistic Plays . . . [would be] Presented with all its Magnificent Scenic And Mechanical Effects Requiring Two Cars in Transportation. With Its Life-like Railroad Scenes, Monster Iron Locomotive, Great Snow Plow And The Cannon Ball Train, 180 feet long, 12½ feet high, Crossing The Stage in 5 Seconds.[4]

A year after this ad appeared, the same paper announced a return performance at Good's, adding to the information about the scenic effects:

> See The Life-Like Railroad Scenes, The Genuine Full-Sized Monster Locomotive, Constructed of steel, Propelled by steam. The Great Rotary Snow Plow and Cannon Ball Vestibuled Train consisting of a full-sized Locomotive, Tender and three Coaches, Flying across the stage at the rate of FIFTY MILES AN HOUR.[5]

One reviewer wrote: "The locomotive which is seen in the first act, is an excellent piece of stage mechanism, and the passage of the express at the end of the second act was sufficiently realistic to arouse great enthusiasm and a call of the curtain."[6] Another added:

> The realism is more real than the average of similar plays and the action introduces a life-size locomotive, a side-tracked freight train, a lightning express at full speed and a cyclone snow plow, all of which were successfully engineered across the stage, and the climaxes were abundantly thrilling and well executed. The stage settings were excellent and the snow storm of the third act was well contrived and carried out.[7]

The drummer in the orchestra-band was charged with the task of providing special effects to heighten the realism of the stage action. To imitate the sound of a puffing engine, the drummer held in each hand blocks shaped like bricks with steel wires protruding from them. As the locomotive began to move, the drummer struck a piece of sheet iron with the blocks, alternating his hands. Beginning quite slowly to duplicate the locomotive's initial struggle, the drummer increased the tempo of his striking motions as the train increased its speed. When the locomotive attained its top speed, the drummer matched that tempo, his hands becoming a blur to the eye. But, of course, few were watching the drummer at such moments.[8] Humans played second fiddle to the marvels of technology and theatrical magic. One wonders if Dresser, being placed in such a secondary role, recalled the times, a decade earlier, when it was Professor Parker and his dogs who stole the show from the human acts.

Opening night for the 1891–92 season was in New Haven, Connecticut. There the company spent two nights before moving on for a similar stay in Bridgeport, Connecticut, followed by a one-week stand at the Bijou Theatre in Pittsburgh. After this tryout, it was time to test the play in New York City, where audiences at Miner's would be the first New Yorkers to see this new spectacle. Opening there on Labor Day afternoon, the company was greeted by a sizable audience that was even larger for the evening show only a few hours later. Before the curtain opened for the first act,

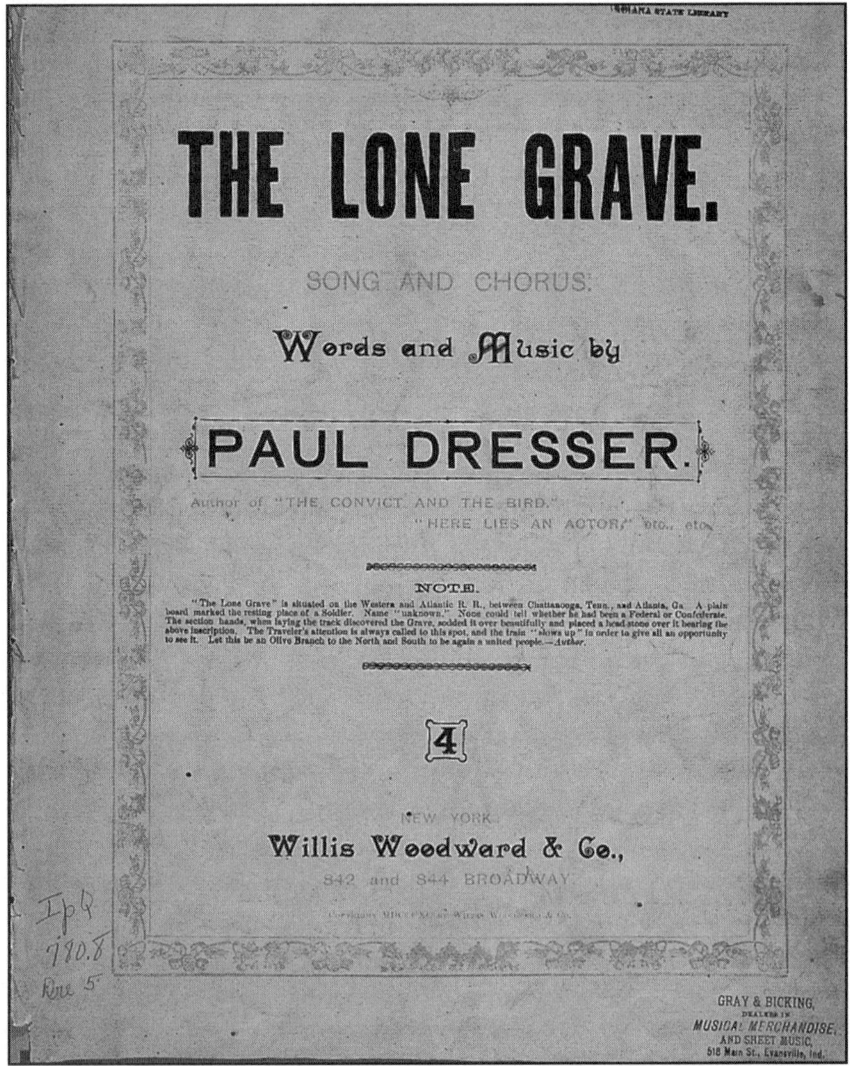

"The Lone Grave," published in 1890.

the People's Orchestra treated the audience to a program of instrumental music. The people, many of them still inattentive, talking and laughing loudly, only gradually settled in their seats as Thomas W. Hindley, the house conductor, led the ensemble in performances of the overture from Franz von Suppé's *Pique Dame*, Émile Waldteufel's "Barcarole," Robert Planquette's "Paul Jones," and Otto Langey's intermezzo "On Tip Toe." Adjusting their eyes to read their programs in the dimmed light, the members of the audience saw those titles, a précis of the play, and an advertisement for seven of Dresser's songs: "The Letter That Never Came," "I Believe It for My Mother Told Me So," "The Lone Grave," "Here Lies an Actor," "The Pardon Came Too Late," "I Can't Believe Her Faithless," and "Just to See Mother's Face Once Again."[9]

When the orchestra concluded the last measures of the Langey intermezzo, the audience members applauded somewhat halfheartedly. They were there, after all, to see the locomotive and cyclone, not to hear a concert. Curtains parted on a scene from Laramie Bend, a mountain station on the line of the Montana and Cheyenne Railroad, and the audience was immediately caught up in the stage magic. At the end of this evening, and so many others, the audience agreed that the special effects had lived up to their advance billing and that Rosabel Morrison and Dresser, "mere actors," had carried the human part of the show well. Morrison, as Rose Martin, nearly always garnered praise for her acting skills, while critics often praised Dresser for his songs, which tended to counter the "rather tiresome" dialogue of the play.[10] But writers also recognized Dresser's acting abilities: "The action of the piece is gloomy to the end, but is relieved occasionally by gleams of comedy in the appearance of Paul Dresser as Corporal Heinrich Yost with a Dutch [i.e., German] accent."[11]

During *The Danger Signal*'s run at Miner's, a *Clipper* reviewer praised Morrison, "the Wild Flower of Laramie Bend," writing, "Her lines were rendered with unusually clear and natural enunciation. It was a pleasure to witness her avoidance of straining for theatric effect, and her method shows the effects of careful training." The remainder of the review was far less encouraging to Morrison's colleagues, calling them "fair."[12] The reviewer for the competing *New York Dramatic Mirror* excoriated Morrison as having "neither the voice, nor the stage presence, nor the ability which only could justify her in occupying such a position." Furthermore, the play was "one of the worst conglomerations of cheap melodramatic rubbish that has ever been inflicted on a suffering public." Continuing, the reviewer wrote:

> Story there is none worthy of the name; of comedy there is still less, and as for scenic effect—for which so much was promised—alas! it was worse than ghastly. The card-board locomotives shook as if afflicted with palsy, while in the great snow-plough scene—the lurid posters outside the house led one to believe that the snow-plough would be seen at work shoveling up tons of snow—a wretched cardboard arrangement wobbled on, got stuck without a vestige of snow being visible, and wobbled back to the fall of the curtain, and the derision of the gallery boys.
>
> Mr. DeMille viewed the sorry spectacle from a box.[13]

Notwithstanding such adverse criticism, audiences and reviewers in many cities loved the special effects and clearly saw Morrison as the star of the company. If any name appeared in advertising for forthcoming performances, it was hers. Morrison was the daughter of actor Lewis Morrison, then well known for his national tour of *Faust*, in which he played Mephisto. Rosabel Morrison had previously played Marguerite in her father's company, and after she left the cast of *The Danger Signal*, she rejoined her father for another tour. For the present time, however, she and Dresser were together day after day, week after week, and Dresser soon became infatuated with her. Sometime during the next year, or in early 1893 at the latest, he wrote two waltzes in honor of her. "Rosie, Sweet Rosabel" is a love song with an unconventional tale: the male narrator marries a girl who had been abandoned, as a baby, on his doorstep many years before. What would Rosabel Morrison have thought about this? Was there any autobiographical content to this one? Was the thirty-four-year-old Dresser telling Morrison, then in her early twenties, that difference in ages should not be a deterrent to one's love for another? Around the same time Dresser composed "I Told Her the Same Old Story" and dedicated it "respectfully" to Rosabel. Here, a father recounts the story of his love of "a lovely maiden" and their quarrel, reconciliation, and happiness as husband and wife. Their "three golden-haired babes" cling to every word of this "sweet little dear, interesting old story, / That folks call love!"[14]

That Dresser was infatuated, if not in love, with Morrison is quite certain, but then he chased innumerable young "lovely maidens" throughout his life, never, it seems, enjoying a deep, committed relationship after his experience in Evansville. Morrison seems to have been merely another of his conquests. When Theodore Dreiser saw his brother in *The Danger Signal* in St. Louis in January 1894, he recalled that "a very petite actress—one Rosabel Morrison" was with Dresser, "one of his passing flames."[15] One wonders who Dresser's "passing flame" *really* was then, for Morrison had already left the company by that time.

The Danger Signal enjoyed mostly one-week stands for the remainder of 1891, moving in October to Brooklyn to Holmes's Star Theatre where the play and "Rosabel Morrison won the plaudits of an appreciative audience."[16] Then it was on to Philadelphia for the first of two visits the company made to the city that fall. A week and a half of temperatures that were unseasonably hot for a Philadelphia October had affected box office receipts; people who might be counted on to go to the theater could, instead, enjoy the last throes of good weather out-of-doors. Residents and visitors could walk along the banks of the Schuylkill River, enjoy the fall colors, visit some of the many historic sites the city had to offer, and perhaps take pictures of these scenes with Kodak cameras the Eastman Company had begun offering the public only a couple of years earlier. Available in seven styles and sizes, these cameras were simple to use: press the button, George Eastman said, and his company would do the rest.

By mid-October, however, a cold wave had chased many people into the theaters, so that by the time Dresser and his colleagues arrived at the Grand Opera House on the twelfth, a large audience was there to greet them. While the gathering was appreciative, a reviewer was not pleased with Morrison's performance: "The work of Miss Morrison in her new play is hardly as good as we expected from this lady, after seeing her with her father's co. as Marguerite." But with a note of resignation the writer continued,

"Still it seems to please the masses, which, I suppose, is all that is necessary." Dresser "capably filled" a leading role.[17] The company returned to Philadelphia during the first week of November and then moved to Baltimore, where it "opened to a packed house [at the Holliday Street Theatre] for a matinee, . . . which was duplicated at night" and where it had an entirely prosperous stay.[18]

Little over a week after Dresser and *The Danger Signal* played in Baltimore, the entertainment world lost another major figure with the death of Tony Hart. Born Anthony J. Cannon in Worcester, Massachusetts, in 1855, Hart, still in his teens, joined Edward Harrigan in 1871 to form a team that enjoyed immense success, especially with the *Mulligan* series of plays they began in 1879. These entertainments, with music composed by David Braham, were based on an Irish family, the Mulligans, and their adventures as they interacted with other ethnic groups. Hart's short stature and fair face allowed him to play female roles with considerable success—in the Mulligan series as well as in other Harrigan plays. Harrigan and Hart dissolved their partnership in 1885, shortly after which Hart's career began to fail, "chiefly on account of the worthlessness of the plays in which he appeared" and his gradually declining mental state.[19] Late manifestation of his syphilis, exacerbated by his acting failures, led to his increasingly bizarre behavior; finally, his family and friends committed him to the insane asylum in Worcester, where he died. In their peak years Harrigan and Hart could always be counted on to draw large audiences wherever they played, and they often appeared in the same cities and at the same time Dresser was performing as a solo act.

After Baltimore, the company moved the short distance over to Washington, D.C., to play Harris's Bijou Theatre, thence to Newark, New Jersey, at Jacobs's Theatre, where a *Dramatic Mirror* writer—obviously not the one who reviewed the play for the same paper three months earlier—found the production and the sets very convincing: "The Danger Signal is a very true portrayal of Western life. . . . A locomotive, a steam snow-plough, and a freight train invest the play with unusual realism."[20] Then, in early December, it was on to the Williamsburg section of Brooklyn to perform in the new and elegant Bedford Avenue Theatre, which had opened just three months earlier. The Bedford provided a "remarkably large [house that] showed its appreciation of [Morrison's] efforts with liberal applause. The improved stage fixings . . . made it possible to set the piece with all its elaborate mechanical effects."[21]

The Danger Signal spent the week before Christmas in New York City at Jacobs's Theatre at the corner of Thirty-first Street and Third Avenue. Glowing reviews of the "realistic scenery," the "thrilling climaxes," the company, and Morrison certainly pleased everyone involved.[22] On 20 December, the day after closing, Dresser performed for a Ladies Session of a Brooklyn Order of Elks in the Bedford Avenue Theatre.[23] Then, undoubtedly exhausted after this marathon schedule of ten one-week stands in four months, interrupted by occasional one- and two-night performances, the company welcomed the break for the Christmas holidays, after which it moved to the Griswold Opera House in Troy, New York, for performances on 28 and 29 December.

The company followed this busy performance schedule for the remainder of the 1891–92 season, playing one-week stands in Toledo, Toronto, Detroit, Chicago, Kansas City ("Paul Dresser, the heavy-weight comedian, provoked considerable mirth"),[24] St. Louis ("'S.R.O.' was the sign at Havlin's and 'The Danger Signal' caught the crowd"),[25] St. Paul and Minneapolis, Milwaukee, Jersey City, and Philadelphia. During the last two weeks of April the company spent an extended stay in its second visit to Chicago. The first of the two weeks was spent at the Clark Street Theatre, where it did well for a week beginning on 17 April. The troupe then moved to the Academy of Music, where a reviewer marveled at its "snow storm, snow-plow, rushing railway trains, switches and lanterns . . . realistic enough to please the most exciting disciple of modern realism on the stage. . . . The comedy work [was] in the hands of Paul Dresser, whose songs did much to keep the audience in good humor."[26] The troupe then moved to the Clark Street Theatre, where it did well for a week beginning on 24 April. In Philadelphia "a big audience applauded . . . 'The Danger Signal' during its closing week of the season at the Empire Theatre."[27] After Philadelphia, the various cast members went their separate ways.

The 21 May 1892 issue of the *Clipper* announced that Dresser would continue with *The Danger Signal* for the coming season but would now spend the summer months in Hoboken, New Jersey, composing new songs.[28] In late July and early August, Dresser took a working vacation at Narragansett Pier in Rhode Island. There he could enjoy the area's resort atmosphere while he made contacts with new entertainers, enticing them to feature his songs in their acts.[29] One of the songs he composed during 1892—and likely during these summer months—was "He Was a Soldier," advertised with considerable hyperbole by Willis Woodward and Company as "Paul Dresser's latest and greatest song . . . destined to achieve a popularity never before equalled in the history of songs."[30] Before long, Dresser's thoughts turned to another season with *The Danger Signal*. Summers always seemed too short, but then he always looked forward to returning to touring, to seeing new cities and theaters and people, and to his growing list of new "young maidens."

In its opening season *The Danger Signal* had played at least twenty-one one-week stands with a few one- and two-night performances interspersed. Part of the reason for the extended run of full-week performances may well have been the sheer size of the production—and the theater space needed for successful operation of the many mechanical properties. It took two railway cars just to move the scenery and sets for the play. Striking such a set and moving it to new locations for one-nighters would have been difficult at best. It could, of course, be done, but life was much simpler when the cast and crew could stay in one spot for a week. So, for the first time in his life, Dresser could enjoy the relative luxury of playing these extended stays mostly in theaters appropriate to the grandiose proportions of *The Danger Signal*'s technical demands.

The special effects, however, could be scaled back somewhat when a long series of dreaded one-nighters was forthcoming, especially in smaller theaters. For example, the 1892–93 season began with two nights in Troy, New York, followed by a week in Boston at the Globe Theatre. After that week, however, *The Danger Signal* traveled throughout Massachusetts, and then to Rhode Island, New Hampshire, New York, Pennsylvania, Ohio, and Indiana to play for audiences in thirty different theaters in only thirty-three days! This was a horrendous schedule for the actors and an expensive one for the company as well. In addition to the two railway cars needed to transport the scenery, a third was set aside for the actors. The special rate of two cents a mile most railroads charged companies of ten or more certainly helped keep costs down, but even with that, touring a show such as *The Danger Signal* was not cheap. And the traveling was not without its share of cold cars and a certain amount of dirt and grime. For the company's trips along the eastern corridor, rail travel was appreciably faster and cleaner. The Jersey Central, the Reading, and the Baltimore and Ohio lines that plied the tracks between New York and Washington, D.C., boasted that they were free of dust and cinders, and they touted a speedy five-hour trip between those two cities. But that was of little consolation to actors who had to follow the cruel schedule of a month or more of one-nighters. Even in his earliest days as actor and singer, Dresser had never had to follow such a nightmarish schedule; now, with his acting and singing chores added to his duties as stage manager of *The Danger Signal*, the pace of his life must have seemed overwhelming at times.

As Dresser's company traversed the state of Massachusetts during the last week in September, the nation's papers were reporting the sudden death of Patrick S. Gilmore, who had died on the twenty-fourth when he was in St. Louis for the Great Exposition. Gilmore and his Twenty-fourth Massachusetts Regiment band were mainstays during major campaigns of the Union army during the Civil War. At the conclusion of the hostilities, Gilmore went to Boston, where he was in charge of the music for the first Peace Jubilee in 1869; there he demonstrated a remarkable ability for organization, gathering together eleven thousand musicians who served as a massed ensemble for concerts. He surpassed that feat three years later to celebrate the end of the Franco-Prussian War, conducting a musical force of twenty-two thousand instrumentalists and choristers for a concert in a coliseum built to seat a hundred thousand spectators. In 1873 he went to New York where he became the bandmaster of the Twenty-second Regiment band, which continued under his name and proceeded to give more than six hundred concerts in the succeeding three years. He and his band were major attractions at the Centennial Exhibition in Philadelphia in 1876, and two years later the Gilmore band toured Europe, performing in all the major cities.

Through his massed concerts and his touring, Gilmore had done more than any other individual to bring the ring of patriotic instrumental music to a wide American public. Under the pseudonym of Louis Lambert, Gilmore had already won a place in Americans' hearts with his song "When Johnny Comes Marching Home," which he published in 1863 in the midst of the Civil War. Dresser and his Sullivan friends had probably sung this song as youngsters, and even though they had not marched to Gilmore's band, the kind of spell that such music cast had formed an important part of Dresser's own musical background. Like other famous performers who had recently died, Gilmore had also been a competitor of Dresser when both appeared in the same city at the same time. Now people wondered who would, or could, succeed Gilmore. Before the next month was out, Col. David W. Reeves, leader of the American Band and composer of the well-known "Second Connecticut Regiment March" of 1880, was named as the new conductor of Gilmore's Famous Band. Advertisements announced that Reeves was ready to begin a Grand Columbian Tour of the United States on 31 October. There was no danger that Americans would be without their band music, for in the very same year John Philip Sousa, the director of the U.S. Marine Band, formed his own band, which rapidly became better known than the older Gilmore organization.

A week at Chicago's Windsor Theatre from 16 through 22 October, where the company was greeted by good houses and where a critic praised it for "presenting the well known melodrama in excellent style," provided the first relief from the rigorous routine of one-nighters the cast and crew had followed for so long. They would not have another such respite until they played in Buffalo's Lyceum Theatre the second week in November.[31] From that date to the end of 1892 the production enjoyed four more full-week engagements: in Baltimore (at the Holliday Street Theatre), Williamsburg [Brooklyn] (at the Lee Avenue Academy), New York City (at the People's Theatre), and Philadelphia (at the People's Theatre). A series of one-night performances were interspersed.

Beginning with the new year, 1893, Willis Woodward and Company started to advertise Dresser's songs regularly. The January issue of the *Clipper* announced that W. H. Windom, a tenor with Haverly's Minstrels at Haverly's Casino in Chicago, had sung Dresser's "Little Fannie McIntyre" twice daily for 240 consecutive days since May 1892—"an unparalleled record for both singer and song."[32] In April Woodward plugged "Just to See Mother's Face Once Again" in two separate issues of the paper. At the same time Charles K. Harris advertised his waltz "Hearts." Only four months earlier the *Clipper* had carried an ad for the same composer's "After the Ball," his "Greatest of Descriptive Waltzes," which would soon astound the industry with a success never seen before in the history of popular song.[33]

Now that song publishing was on the threshold of becoming a big business, publishers began to increase their advertising, their hyperbolic statements of this or that "greatest hit" becoming the norm. Harris's ads are a good case in point. Working out of Milwaukee and not yet part of the New York Music Row group, Harris was a master of self promotion whose motto was "Men of Brains Originate. Monkeys Only Imitate."[34] He touted his "Is Life Worth Living" as a "worthy successor to 'After the Ball' "; "After Nine" as "The Latest and Best Topical Song Ever Written"; "Kiss and Let's Make Up" as "An Enormous Success"; "Creep, Baby, Creep" as "A Great Hit Everywhere"; and "Hello, Central, Hello" as "A Positive Hit." These are only five of the thirteen songs he advertised in the 26 August 1893 issue of the *Clipper*![35]

Anything that was attracting a large audience or was thought to have the potential of doing so became the subject of the newest song. Some composers and publishers believed that immediacy was the key to success and piggybacked on the latest sensation in their mad scramble to produce a hit song. The World's Columbian Exposition of 1893, for instance, inspired numerous songs, nearly all of them short-lived in popularity and now forgotten. "Christofo Columbo," "Naughty Doings on the Midway Plaisance," "The World's Fair Fatal Fire," "After the Fair," "The World's Fair," and "I'm the Man That Wrote 'After the Ball,' " the latter a shameless attempt to capitalize on the popularity of Harris's big hit song of the exposition, are but six examples. Willis Woodward and Company, a big name in the song industry, still published Dresser's music, but that would soon change. Even though he was not a very good businessman, Dresser already realized that the composer provided the creative spark for a hit song, but it was the publisher who made the real money.

The remainder of the 1892–93 season was scarcely any different from Dresser's first year and a half with *The Danger Signal*. The company enjoyed a week's performance in each of nine locations, but single-night engagements prevailed. By the time the season closed after the third week in May, the cast members were glad to go their separate ways. As he did the previous summer, Dresser went to Hoboken to resume his activities as a summer composer. One of the results of these efforts, as reported in the *Clipper*, was a composition "of the comic order, . . . to be called 'C.O.D.' "[36] Dresser was undoubtedly the source of this information, but the song was never published.

After those welcome three months, it was time for Dresser to return to the road again. During the summer, Morrison had left *The Danger Signal*. She and her father each led their own *Faust* companies, one to tour the East and the second to travel throughout the western states.[37] When Morrison's replacement, Ethel Gray, had to withdraw because of illness, Georgia Gardner assumed the role of Rose Martin. The company opened its 1893–94 season on 19 August for one night at the Grand Opera House in Bridgeport, Connecticut, in weather that was "still too warm to assure a large attendance."[38] The schedule for this season was scarcely different from that of 1892–93, with the company playing only eleven one-week performances between August and the first week in June. With the exceptions of rare two-night stays, the remainder of the entire season consisted of single-date performances—truly a horrendous schedule given travel conditions at the time.

Chicago, one of Dresser's favorite places, was conspicuously missing from the itinerary. In past years Dresser could look forward to playing Chicago for at least one full week, if not more. This year, however, was to be different. Theatrical agents may have been concerned that audiences would be drawn away from typical theater productions, attracted more to the World's Columbian Exposition, which opened on 1 May 1893. *The Danger Signal* did not play Chicago again until the first week of April 1894, long after the exposition had closed.

If Dresser was not in Chicago, the same could not be said for his young brother Theodore Dreiser, then twenty-one and working for the *St. Louis Republic*. Dreiser attended the World's Columbian Exposition as a reporter and wrote about it for his newspaper. From two of his hotel windows, Dreiser's eyes took in some of the visual feast of the great White City. The buildings made of staff, brilliantly white, almost to the point of painfulness, shimmered in the sun; those buildings that were reflected in the lagoon, the ponds, and the basin gave back their luminosity manyfold; at eventide, when tens of thousands of incandescent and arc lamps were turned on, the White City became absolutely enchanting. The number of exhibitions, concerts, programs, lectures, and attractions was overwhelming. Visitors marveled at reproductions of the *Niña, Pinta,* and *Santa Maria*. Audiences viewed moving pictures through Thomas Edison's Kinetoscope and roared at Buffalo Bill's Wild West show. The midway—the raucous Midway Plaisance—held incredible temptations. Here, on the Fifty-ninth Street side, at the Street in Cairo attraction, one could see Little Egypt perform her famous *danse du ventre*—the "hootchy kootchy" dance.

In addition to the Street in Cairo, one could also see on that side of the Plaisance exhibitions from Java, Germany, Algeria, and Tunis. At midpoint between the Fifty-ninth and Sixtieth Street sides stood George Washington Gale Ferris's marvelous invention. Two hundred sixty-four feet in height, the Ferris wheel dwarfed every other exhibition and carried thirty-six cars round and round, affording riders unparalleled views of the exposition grounds and parts of Chicago. Each car could hold 60 people; when fully loaded, the wheel carried 2,160 riders from ground to sky over and over in a thrilling twenty-minute ride. With an admission price of fifty cents, the wheel was the most financially successful attraction in Chicago, grossing more than three-quarters of a million dollars by the time the exposition closed on 31 October of that year.

Walking from the wheel to the Sixtieth Street side of the Midway Plaisance, east toward Lake Michigan, one could visit a Bedouin Encampment, travel through Old Vienna, see the Moorish Palace and the Turkish Village, and watch the Hagenbeck Animal Show. On the midway, Scott Joplin and a number of his piano-playing colleagues gathered to play ragtime, that jaunty new music that would soon become all the rage. At the other end of the musical spectrum, in the magnificent Court of Honor's Music Hall, the young Polish pianist Ignacy Paderewski astounded audiences with his playing of Chopin. Chicagoans and exposition visitors may have heard the musical send-ups that Will H. Fox presented as "Padewhiskie" beginning in the 1890s, but here was the real thing. For the first time, thousands of people heard "After the Ball," the song Harris had published only five months earlier. Now, thanks to the exposition, it seemed as if everyone were singing it.

In the early 1890s the nation was undergoing some of the most rapid changes and turmoil in its history, even if the architecture at the World's Columbian Exposition gave little hint of the future. Commercial telephone lines shortened communication times between New York City and Chicago. To the entertainment world, this meant that rapid contact between the two cities and those along the way could be made to secure dates and venues for theater seasons and performers. Labor unrest, manifested in the 1892 Homestead Strike in Pennsylvania and the 1894 Pullman Strike in Illinois, caused some Americans to think about the appropriate balance between labor and management, hardening the prolabor positions of those of a liberal bent and convincing the more conservative to adopt an equally intransigent attitude in favor of management. Before much longer, stage performers would stand strong against the abusive policies of theatrical circuit magnates and bring disruption to part of an entertainment season.

Some change was more subtle than that brought about by technology or in the arena of labor. Throughout its history America had offered an expansive frontier, seemingly unlimited, for those restless and adventurous souls who wanted new places to explore and to settle. Now, on a hot Wednesday in July at the World's Columbian Exposition, a young historian said that the limitless frontier was, in effect, no more. Frederick Jackson Turner had traveled down from the University of Wisconsin to deliver that message to a group of his fellow historians.[39] That pronouncement, as disturbing as it would become to a succeeding generation, was minor when compared with the news coming from the world of business.

Two months before the exposition opened, the panic of 1893 began, an economic depression that would endure for four years.

Economic woes belied these Gay Nineties. Although the White City and the less genteel midway gave little outward hint of these financial woes, their severity was increasing with alarming speed. During this decade of excess and of miserable deprivation, technology expanded in American society: the telephone lines that linked American cities, Edison's development of motion pictures, and Henry Ford's first automobile were the most obvious manifestations of that technology.

The music-publishing industry narrowed its operations geographically and expanded phenomenally at the same time. In the 1880s an increasing number of song publishers located their operations in lower Manhattan, then gradually moved northward until by the last decade of the century the area around the West Twenties became Music Row, as the *Dramatic Mirror* termed it. The firms of T. B. Harms, M. Witmark, Joseph W. Stern, F. A. Mills, and Howley, Haviland and Company could all be found in that area or very close by. Once in Music Row, many firms became specialty houses, concentrating their energies on popular songs rather than publishing the varieties of music they had in the past.

With the gathering of a number of music-publishing firms in a small geographic area, in developing new ways to market their product (whether in packaging the song or getting it sung by important entertainers in a variety of venues), in becoming ever more aggressive in their search for new songs that would prove to be hits, the music-publishing industry entered the world of big business and became not dissimilar to other large industries. And yet only a short time before, a writer had stated with confidence, "With the introduction of 200-page books of well-selected compositions for fifty cents, there would seem to be but little inducement to enter the music-publishing business just now."[40] How wrong that assessment proved to be! With its control over, indeed its monopolization of, American popular song, music publishing was following the leads of John D. Rockefeller and Andrew Carnegie. As oil and steel were commodities to be bought, sold, and controlled, so, too, was music. The rapid growth that numerous companies enjoyed was unparalleled in the history of music publishing. The secret to successful music publishing was to listen carefully to what audiences wanted and to accommodate them with song after song in that style, ever mindful that their preferences could change rapidly. For much of the decade, the lilting strains of hundreds upon hundreds of waltzes captivated listeners, but the exotic sound of ragtime, jaunty, saucy, insinuating, and exuberant in its rhythm, would soon share the spotlight; before long it would dominate popular music and become the favored style. In their efforts to succeed, publishers constantly sought new ways to promote their wares.

In the end, success depended upon a combination of shrewd business sense and the ineffable touch that went into writing songs the public could not resist. Dresser was about to add his energies and talents to one of the new publishing houses. Certainly he possessed the requisite musical ability, but he was far from a hard-headed businessman.

CHAPTER 14

Howley, Haviland and Company

The year 1893 was not the most propitious time to start a business. The financial woes of the country were considerable. Theatrical companies—especially those on the road—abruptly concluded their seasons, at least six hundred banks closed, more than seventy railroads were forced into receivership, and businesses by the thousands failed in that first year of the depression. Nevertheless, Frederick Benjamin Haviland and Patrick J. Howley opened a music-publishing house at 4 East Twentieth Street between Broadway and Fifth Avenue. At the time the two worked for other music publishers, Oliver Ditson and Company and Willis Woodward and Company, respectively. Haviland and Howley kept their jobs and named their new firm the George T. Worth Company to hide their enterprise from Ditson and Woodward.

Invited to become a silent partner in the firm, Paul Dresser severed his connections with Willis Woodward and Company and immediately went to work "selling" the George T. Worth Company as its outside man. Now that Dresser was helping to publish his own songs, his life as a composer was about to change, bringing him into a period of unprecedented wealth and celebrity. The Worth Company gave "Rosie, Sweet Rosabel," the first of Dresser's songs it published, the kind of advertising coverage most of his music had not seen in the past. The exception to this was Woodward's repeated ads for "Just to See Mother's Face Once Again," Dresser's last song for that company. Perhaps Woodward wanted to capitalize on Dresser's growing celebrity on the stage or intended to wring the last bit of money it could from his name and work before he jumped ship to his new music-publishing firm.[1]

In September the Worth Company, now openly identifying Howley ("For the past seven years with Willis Woodward & Co.") as its manager, announced that "Rosie, Sweet Rosabel" was a hit for J. Aldrich Libbey, "America's Great Baritone." Libbey was playing in Hallen and Hart's *The Idea*, a farce-comedy that had opened at New York's Park Theater the previous April.[2] In an ad that ran in the *New York Clipper* for three weeks in late winter of 1894, the new company also touted Allen May's performance of "Rosie, Sweet Rosabel" during his seventh, eighth, and ninth weeks at Herrmann's Theatre, where he was "making a tremendous hit." Plugging a forthcoming Dresser composition, the Worth ad claimed that May would sing Dresser's "He Didn't Seem Glad to See Me" during the next week.[3]

In the past Dresser had often received a flat payment, and sometimes modest royalties, from his publishers. Now as part of the publishing team, albeit as a silent partner, Dresser would share in the financial successes of his songs as well as those of other composers in the Worth stable. He was about to become one of those early music-industry magnates who combined the roles of songwriter, author, and publisher.

Severing their ties with Oliver Ditson and Company and Willis Woodward and Company in the second half of 1893, Haviland and Howley began calling their firm Howley, Haviland and Company. The name George T. Worth had served its purpose and was retired. The young entrepreneurs soon added other composers to their fold, including Charles B. Lawlor. Lawlor proved his value to the new company almost immediately with "The Sidewalks of New York," which became a tremendous hit in 1894, bringing considerable financial reward to the company. A recent phenomenon, the "hit" song often became an end in itself for the New York houses; for some firms, a single hit meant the difference between survival and bankruptcy. Howley, Haviland and Company, with Dresser as its front man, was obviously on its way.

Becoming his own publisher was yet a couple of months away when in the summer of 1893 Dresser returned to his regular routine of composing songs. This summer was busier than the others, however, for Dresser decided to try writing a play. After all, he thought, he had had seven years of experience as an actor in three different plays where farcical comedy combined with music were the chief ingredients. He had won increasing acclaim for his comedic abilities. He knew he could read an audience to see what appealed to it. Why not put all this experience to good use in his own play? It made sense to him to increase his versatility. The result was to be *A Green Goods Man*. The play would open in late 1894, but that date was still more than a year in the future. Now, once he had composed some songs, had begun the play, and had undoubtedly made commitments to Haviland and Howley, Dresser had to fulfill his contract with *The Danger Signal* for the 1893–94 season.

After a long and largely uneventful series of one-nighters during the fall and early winter, broken only by one-week stays in New York City, Boston, Baltimore, and Milwaukee, Dresser and the company traveled to St. Louis in late January 1894. There they played at Havlin's Theatre for a week, beginning on the twenty-eighth. Enthusiastic audiences welcomed the company, especially on Monday, the twenty-ninth, when a large crowd turned out for a benefit performance to honor the manager and doorkeeper of the theater. Theodore Dreiser, living in the city and writing for the local *Republic*, had seen the billboards with Dresser's face and name on them, announcing the coming of *The Danger Signal*. Now the ever insecure Dreiser could proudly show his friends that his family *did* amount to something, after all. He could prove to those who mattered to him that the Dreiser family could boast of success.

On Sunday, the twenty-eighth, Dreiser went over to Havlin's to greet his brother, finding him "stout, gross, sensual," "entirely surrounded by trunks and scenery of various kinds," on his arm "one of his passing flames." There was no missing Dresser's success. He was "dressed in the most engaging Broadway fashion: a suit of good cloth and smart cut, a fur coat, a high hat, and a gold-headed cane."[4] At twenty-two, Dreiser had gained an assertiveness that marked him as different from the diffident youth Dresser had seen at the time of their mother's death. Yet confident though he might be, Dreiser was still awestruck by the theater, that "world of claptrap melodrama, . . . [the] old smelly theatre, the juggernaut scenery of the play," and was even taken with his brother's ridiculous "engineer costume, an amazing suit of overalls, with the tufts of his red wig sticking out over his ears."[5] Now, however, it was the younger Dreiser's turn to impress his older brother with a dinner in his honor at Faust's, "then the leading restaurant of St. Louis, of a gay bohemian character."[6] After Dresser's evening performance on Saturday, 3 February, Dreiser, with eight of his *Republic* colleagues and brother in tow, led the way to Faust's for what he planned as a night of celebrating, with fine wines, food, and good conversation.

This was not to be, for, as Dreiser recalled, he had tried to combine too many disparate personalities at one gathering for the evening to be a success. Bohemianism shared the table with "stilted intellectual sufficiency" and "the utter innocence and naivete of Paul[,] . . . as barren of intellectual grip as a child." There were no topics in common that the entire group could discuss.[7] A couple of Dreiser's colleagues, however, were greatly impressed with—perhaps awed by—Dresser and referred to him as " 'Dreiser's brother Paul'—even 'dear old Paul.' "[8]

During the week leading up to the dinner, Dresser and Dreiser had had breakfast together daily; it was on one of those mornings that Dresser urged his younger brother to go to New York. Dresser described the city in "florid" detail and used himself as an example of the success one could win in New York. " 'My boy,' he exclaimed at one point one morning, 'you will never get it straight unless you come there and see for yourself. All these Western places are all right in their way, but there is only one New York, just one.' "[9] During this week Dresser also reinforced Dreiser's privately held reservations about marrying. Dresser thought Sara "Jug" Osborne White, Dreiser's fiancée, "charming," but he cautioned his young brother against marriage at that point in his life. Even after Dreiser and White *did* marry in 1898, Dresser was aloof toward this sister-in-law, showing a "persistent indifference to and private dislike of her," though he never openly expressed these feelings to Dreiser.[10]

Thus, Dreiser's emotions that week suffered the sweeping highs and lows of a roller-coaster ride. The disastrous dinner party that "was such a fizzle that [he] could have wept" marked the emotional valley for him.[11] During the same week, however, he had at least shown his beloved brother that he was successful as a newspaper reporter, and, awkward as he still was, he had gained a bit of self-assurance. Somewhere in the mix of all this were his feelings about Dresser's advice against marriage. Dreiser craved his brother's acceptance as an equal, if not an intellectual superior; he was jealous that one with so little appreciation of the life of the mind could be so popular with his own friends—these things ate at him. And then there was the New York business. That must have alternatively excited and terrified him, but when Dresser and *The Danger Signal* left St. Louis on Sunday, the fourth, "The idea of New York as a great and glowing center—better perhaps, as my brother had said, than any other place—had taken root . . . [and] caused me to think that there might be some opening for me. It wasn't like venturing into a strange and distant land without anyone to guide you."[12]

Once he left St. Louis, Dresser had only a few months remaining in the season. *The Danger Signal* cast spent part of that time winning audiences at Chicago's Haymarket Theater and playing in Montreal at the Theatre Royal. Shortly before the latter appearance, another Terre Haute native figured prominently in the news. By the 1890s Eugene V. Debs had achieved a degree of notoriety for his work on behalf of railroad workers. In 1893, more than two decades after he first began to work for the railroad, Debs founded the American Railway Union, an organization that worked for laborers in their efforts to be treated equitably by the railroad barons. Debs was born two and a half years before Dresser, and while the two never met, each knew of the work of the other. In the early 1920s, when there was serious effort to create a monument to Dresser in Terre Haute, Debs wrote to Dreiser, supporting the latter's efforts to have Dresser's body reburied in Terre Haute.

That was all in the future, however. May 1894 marked the beginning of the Pullman Strike. George Pullman had developed the idea of a sleeping car for railroads, patenting his idea in 1867 and establishing the Pullman Palace Car Company. In an effort to have his finger on the pulse of his company and his workers, Pullman founded the city of Pullman, Illinois, in 1880. Carved out of acres of land Pullman purchased on the western shore of Lake Calumet, thirteen miles south of Chicago, this unified community grew to a population of about fifteen thousand people—Pullman employees and their families—who lived in rental housing, attended church, shopped for goods at the town market, and attended the theater, school, and library in Pullman. At first the city was equated with cleanliness and concord and called an "American Utopia." Other utopian experiments existed at the time, but Pullman was different in the integration of the modern; as long as the nation's economy was good, even the most disaffected Pullman workers gave the paternalistic Pullman some credit.

When the causes of the panic of 1893 were not addressed and the economic depression continued to deepen and spread, the Pullman company ordered a drastic cut in employees' wages—an average of 33 percent between late summer 1893 and spring 1894 and even as much as half their pay in some cases.[13] At the same time the company maintained the price of goods, utilities, and housing rental rates in its "company town." Resentment among the Pullman employees rapidly grew, and the workers turned to Debs and his American Railway Union for help. In June, a month after the Pullman employees had called a strike, the American Railway Union threw its support to the workers. The work stoppage reached its peak on 4 July, but the movement was crushed shortly thereafter when the Grover Cleveland administration, having taken the side of management, sent federal troops to Pullman to enforce an injunction against the union and broke the strike. A jury found Debs guilty of contempt, and he spent six months in jail for his role in the strike.

The spring of 1894 saw a protest of another kind when Jacob Coxey's Army, four hundred strong, arrived in Washington, D.C., from Ohio to protest unemployment. The government was willing to pass legislation that favored corporate America, but it had ignored the plight of the working-class people, many who were suffering deprivations brought on by the continuing depression. Coxey's Army traveled to Washington to persuade Congress to change that deplorable situation. Coxey, a successful business entrepreneur from near Massillon, Ohio, and his "troops" started their journey on 25 March, Easter Day, and completed their trip in a little over a month, arriving in Washington in time to march on the Capitol on 1 May. Nearly fifty newspaper reporters began the march with Coxey and his army, reporting their every move to a news-hungry public. A crowd, estimated at twenty thousand people, waited at the Capitol for Coxey, anticipating his message.

Arriving at the Capitol grounds, Coxey was able to mount only the Capitol steps before security officers barred his way, refusing him permission to give a speech. The next day police arrested Coxey for trespassing on the grass and sent him to jail for twenty days. With the loss of their leader, the members of the army dispersed. In their efforts to secure equity for their workers, Debs and Coxey, in quite different ways, got the attention, if not the complete sympathies, of many Americans. For the time being, however, failure met these attempts to effect change for the working class.

The compassion and tireless work of Debs and Coxey on behalf of the economically dispossessed may have struck a chord with Dresser. Ever mindful of the plight of those less fortunate than he—a situation no doubt reinforced by the memories of his own family's poverty—and ever compassionate in his dealings with them, Dresser would later speak of the plight of the underclass and the cruel indifference of the wealthy, subjects of some of his songs. These events of 1894, as well as some of the things his brother Theodore would soon write about, surely had some impact on the sensitive, if naive, Dresser. The manifestation of these influences, however, lay in the future. For the time being, Dresser was enjoying the acclaim and financial rewards of his life, content to follow that life where it led without his conscience being bothered too much by the plague of introspection.

CHAPTER 15

Brothers in the City

In the summer of 1894, Paul Dresser wrote his young brother Theodore Dreiser, inviting him yet again to New York City. This time, after spending some frustrating days with his fiancée at her home in Missouri, Dreiser decided it was time to take his brother up on the offer. Traveling to New York by overnight train from Pittsburgh, Dreiser arrived at Jersey City at seven in the morning. He exited the train in pouring rain to find his "fat and smiling brother, as sweet-faced and gay and hopeful as a child" waiting for him at the end of the long train shed.[1] The two brothers boarded a ferry that took them over the Hudson River to New York City; then they journeyed by streetcar to sister Emma Dreiser Hopkins's house on Fifteenth Street, where Dresser was also living at the time. The shabbiness of the immediate surroundings during their trip, the uncollected garbage, and the horsecars—"this in the city of the elevated roads"—disappointed Dreiser, who had naturally expected much more.[2] He remarked to Dresser, "Well, you can't say this is very much," to which the brother responded, reassuringly, "My boy, you haven't seen anything yet. This is just an old part of New York. . . . But wait'll you see Broadway and Fifth Avenue."[3] At the Hopkins', Dreiser was reunited with his sister, whom he had not seen since their mother's death four years earlier; now, for the first time, he met her husband, George—the infamous Hopkins of Dreiser family stories.

During Dreiser's stay in New York, Dresser gave his brother a series of grand tours of the city, including an extended trip north on Broadway from Union Square to Forty-second Street, the theater district. They entered a horse-drawn cab, a vehicle that would soon be part of the past. In a short time electric streetcars would move people farther and faster, plying the miles and miles of rail lines more efficiently, if less romantically. Now, however, Dresser and Dreiser were content with their slow pace. With Dresser providing the narration, the younger brother marveled at the number of theaters one could see in such relatively short distance: the Fifth Avenue Theatre, Palmer's, Augustin Daly's, Koster and Bial's Music Hall, the Garrick, the Lyceum, the newly constructed Knickerbocker Theatre, and the Metropolitan Opera House. During his visit Dreiser saw wonders the likes of which he had only heard about until now: Altman's department store; the jewelry display in the windows of Tiffany's; Brentano's, filled with books, those precious tomes that took Dreiser away from the meanness of his youth; the studio of the famous photographer Sarony; the clothiers Lord and Taylor. At Madison Avenue and Twenty-sixth Street he viewed Madison Square Garden, where Augustus Saint-Gaudens's statue of the mythical Diana, still scandalous to some in her nudity, crowned the building. He saw the famous hotels of the times, including the Gilsey House on Twenty-ninth Street, where Dresser lived from time to time in a suite of rooms with his rosewood square grand piano—the instrument that Dreiser would later convert into a desk for his own use.

Dreiser was beside himself with wonder at such spectacles. He was far from being a country bumpkin, but he must have felt somewhat out of place dressed in clothing that was not cut after the latest New York fashion; too, he was conscious of not having enough money to buy those things he saw and desired. Some of the memories of what he saw and felt on those walks and rides with Dresser would surface in *Sister Carrie,* his first novel. For example, shortly after Carrie Meeber arrived in Chicago in August 1889, she found her way along State Street to the Fair store, one of the magnificent department stores that was thriving in a city only recently rebuilt. Carrie

> passed along the busy aisles, much affected by the remarkable displays of trinkets, dress goods, stationery, and jewelry. Each separate counter was a show place of dazzling interest

Van Pelt-Dietrich Library Center, Univ. of Pa.

Theodore Dreiser in his studio at 16 St. Luke's Place, New York City. In the back of the room is the desk Dreiser made from one of Paul Dresser's pianos.

> and attraction. She could not help feeling the claim of each trinket and valuable upon her personally, and yet she did not stop. There was nothing there which she could not have used—nothing which she did not long to own. . . . All touched her with individual desire, and she felt keenly the fact that not any of these things were in the range of her purchase.[4]

The walking tour that Dresser and Dreiser took another day could only have impressed the younger sibling even more. What an unlikely looking pair! Dresser wore a high hat, silk vest, trousers of the latest fashion, and a Prince Albert coat and bore an elegant walking stick (its parrot's head of green lacquer could be exchanged for the head of an alligator, a rooster, or a monkey); Dreiser wore mismatched clothing that betrayed a certain provincialism. Dresser carried nearly three hundred pounds yet moved with the elegance and grace of a dancer; Dreiser was thin and awkward. As they headed north, this odd couple stopped from time to time so that Dresser could introduce his brother to knots of admirers at street corners and in the numerous watering holes along the way.

Among their detours was the Hotel Metropole, whose bar attracted men whom New York, and the world, considered to be luminaries in their various vocations. Former western lawman Bat Masterson; boxers Battling Nelson, James J. ("Gentleman Jim") Corbett, Kid McCoy, and Terry McGovern; champion wrestler William Muldoon; and Tammany Hall leader Richard Croker were among this group, each a personal friend of Dresser. Dreiser recalled that "various high and mighties of the Roman Church, 'fathers' with fine parishes and good wine cellars, and judges of various municipal courts, were also of his peculiar world."[5] With his walks and his hobnobbing, Dresser "shone like a star when only one is in the sky."[6] Dreiser, trying to effect a certain air of casualness, wrote that his beloved brother

> was in his way a public favorite, a shining light in the theatre managers' offices, hotel bars and lobbies and where-ever those passing celebrities of the sporting, theatrical, newspaper and other worlds are wont to gather.[7]

The colorful Dresser was in his element, where hangers-on cried out his name, fawned over him, offered him drinks and asked him about his newest songs or latest conquest. Dresser told them his latest bawdy jokes, then made his male companions envious when bold women approached to touch him and coo over him, those beautiful, sensuous women whose forwardness both excited and repelled Dreiser—women he had only imagined in his fantasies. With his inordinate love of and obsession with women, with "his bravado and bluster and his innate good nature and sympathy," Dresser suggested Sir John Falstaff to Dreiser.[8]

This was, however, a Falstaffian figure who could not be counted on to look out for the best interests of his sibling. On the second night of Dreiser's visit, Dresser and some friends introduced him to the city's "'sinks' of so-called 'iniquity.'"[9] Watching from a corner as some women passed by, both repelling and inviting in their brazen manner, Dreiser heard a man remark that the women looked as if they were French. In his naïveté, Dreiser responded that the women looked American to him. Much laughter and teasing erupted over Dreiser's innocence. Dresser explained to his brother that "French" meant that these prostitutes had a "different way of doing it. . . . They go down on you—blow the pipe—play the flute."[10] Dresser insisted that his hesitant young brother accompany him to a brothel in the tenderloin district—"Satan's Circus"—to experience the delightful pleasures of fellatio with such a woman. There, an attractive prostitute with dark curly hair chose Dreiser, initiating him into a sexual act new to him.

After the liaison Dreiser was consumed with two thoughts: how "delicious" and "blissful beyond words" the experience was, and that God would surely punish him, perhaps with eternal fire, for such a deed. Paying the prostitute five dollars, Dreiser went out, "meeting my laughing, jesting brother" who began to tease him yet again.[11] On their way back to their sister's, Dresser took Dreiser to another brothel—the House of All Nations—one of the more infamous houses in the city. Once inside, Dreiser knew at once that this was unlike anything he had seen before. Here, in the parlor, a small orchestra entertained waiting guests. Upstairs were mirrored assignation rooms where girls of various nationalities and races "entertained" their customers. This time, Dreiser and Dresser were merely observers, but what young Dreiser saw merely increased his heated imagination. The House of All Nations was one of the city brothels that enjoyed the protection of Tammany Hall; this was a house that Rev. Charles Parkhurst, the sworn enemy of Tammany Hall and the president of the Society for the Prevention of Crime, had repeatedly denounced. He knew of what he spoke, for he had visited such brothels to gain firsthand knowledge of the "disgusting depths of this Tammany-debauched town"![12]

During their peregrinations, Dresser also took Dreiser to his publishing firm, then located at 4 East Twentieth Street. As the two trudged up the stairs to the office on the third floor, Dreiser took in the surroundings. When they arrived at the third floor, young Dreiser found that a single room, spartan in the extreme, housed the entire company. A piano that the Wing and Sons Piano Company had lent the publishers stood in one corner close by wooden racks displaying the few pieces Howley, Haviland and Company had published thus far. Dresser introduced his brother to the first of his partners. Twenty-two-year-old Patrick J. Howley, a bit younger than Dreiser, would, it was obvious, stand out in any crowd, for he was a "small, gargoylish hunchback with a mouthful of large, protruding, yellow teeth, and hair and eyes as black as those of a crow—the eyes as piercing," who spoke with a thick Scottish accent.[13] Later, at a nearby restaurant, Dreiser met Dresser's other partner. Frederick Benjamin Haviland was about twenty-four, "very quick and alert in manner, very short of speech, avid and handsome as to face and figure, a most attractive and clean-looking young person. He talked so rapidly as to give one the impression of words tumbling over each other or coming out abreast, and he shot questions and replies as one might bullets out of a gun."[14] What a trio they and Dresser made: the short Howley with his physical deformity; Haviland, tall and thin with a certain elegance to him; and the extravagantly corpulent Dresser. Dreiser was impressed by the three men and felt that each complemented his partners.

On Dreiser's first Sunday in the city, his brother took him by ferry and train to Manhattan Beach, a magic wonderland. There he saw the Manhattan and the Oriental, magnificent and exclusive hotels where the rich and the celebrated vacationed. Guests and transients alike were frequently treated to spectacular displays of fireworks, and one could count on hearing Anton Seidl's symphony orchestra and John Philip Sousa's band playing at the great circular pavilion during summer evenings. As the brothers strolled the paths near the Manhattan Hotel that night, they could hear the strains of Sousa's "Washington Post March."

The clothing of these lucky New York men who walked the same paths fascinated the small-town Dreiser and made him somewhat embarrassed with his own homely appearance. Their imported worsted three- or four-button cutaway suits made his own clothing appear shabby in his eyes. Their suits advertised all the fashionable colors. They featured electric blues, grays, browns, and dark and light tans, and many were topped with overcoats lined in silk. Oh, the magnificence of it all: "The straw hat with its blue or striped ribbon, the flannel suit with its accompanying

Theodore Dreiser in 1894, the year he first visited Paul Dresser in New York City.

white shoes, light cane and saw-toothed straw, the pearl-gray derby, the check suit, the diamond and pearl pin in necktie, the silk shirt."[15] And Paul! Was there no one of importance his beloved brother did not know? Dreiser recalled that his "good brother seemed to encounter a moderate proportion of all the more popular actors and actresses of whom I had ever heard. . . . By dusk or late night it seemed to me as though he had nodded or spoken to a thousand."[16]

One of the stops Dresser and Dreiser made on the first day of their outing was at the Church of St. Francis Xavier at 30 West Sixteenth Street, one of the wealthiest parishes in the city. Capable of seating more than twelve hundred with standing room for a thousand more, the church was relatively new, having been built only twelve years before. The high altar was "constructed of blue-veined Italian marble and dotted with Mexican onyx. . . . Above the high altar, in the chancel apse, [were] statues of the Sacred Heart, the Blessed Virgin, St. Joseph, St. Francis Xavier and St. Ignatius." The sound of a Hook and Hastings pipe organ of 80 ranks and 4,390 pipes, claimed to have been "by far the largest organ in New York City," could easily fill the reverberant space of the interior. The undercroft held another church, as large as the upper one, which had its own Hook and Hastings organ.[17] This was Dresser's church, one to which he came to find sanctuary and one to which his good friend, Father Henry Van Rensselaer, the pastor, welcomed him and his good works. Dresser told Dreiser that Van Rensselaer was "most comfortably berthed [at the church] and 'a good sport in the bargain.' "[18] Dreiser would return to St. Francis Xavier a little more than a decade later as one of the mourners for his beloved brother. The awe he felt at his first visit would be replaced by the bittersweet memories he kept of his and Dresser's time together this summer.

The wonders of New York City that Dreiser experienced during his short stay—the smells, the sights, the sounds, the size—threatened to overpower his senses. Too, his brother's life and style of living—things he witnessed for the first time—overwhelmed him in a different way. Dresser alternately awed and repelled Dreiser. The younger brother admired and envied Dresser's fame and ease with the rich and powerful; at the same time Dreiser realized that Dresser's celebrity and wealth came from his ability to write songs that appealed to the vast middle class—a kind of utterance contemptible, he thought, in its lack of intellect. Dreiser, the admirer, wrote that his brother's songs "bespoke . . . a wistful, seeking, uncertain temperament, tender and illusioned, . . . full of a true poetic feeling for the mystery and pathos of life and death, the wonder of the waters, the stars, the flowers, accidents of life, success, failure." In Dreiser's next breath, such songs were "pale little things . . . , mere bits and scraps of sentiment and melodrama in story form, most asinine sighings over home and mother and lost sweethearts and dead heroes such as never were in real life."[19]

The Dreiser who left New York City was the same young man who had arrived in Jersey City in the pouring rain. Inwardly, however, the young reporter had changed. His feelings about his brother were a jumble of contradictions, but he realized one thing unequivocally: New York City was the place he had to be. Success meant little if he could not achieve it there.

CHAPTER 16

A Green Goods Man

Convinced that he had to move to New York and work on one of the great newspapers of that city, Theodore Dreiser returned to Pittsburgh "in what a reduced mood," with a plan to save money for a return to New York and to "take one of [the] very frowning editorial offices by storm."[1] Paul Dresser must have felt quite satisfied with himself for having shown his brother a wider world of existence, but once Dreiser returned to Pittburgh, it was time for Dresser to get back to work, composing and preparing for another season with *The Danger Signal.*

By the opening of his fourth season with Henry DeMille's play, Dresser could be forgiven if he had become a bit bored playing Cpl. Heinrich Yost night after night in city after city. Performing that role had become so routine that Dresser probably could have done it in his sleep; the forthcoming season promised to be little different from his past three years. With few exceptions, one city would blur into another, one theater would become all theaters. The company's stop in Louisville in November, however, was one Dresser looked forward to. There he renewed a friendship that had begun during his Evansville days. Phil Hacker, traveling with a circus, was in the city at the same time, and he and Dresser got together to relive old times. While they were together, Dresser asked his friend to write down a couple of songs for him. Lacking the skill to write out all the music he carried in his head, Dresser had to turn to friends to do that job for him. As Dresser hummed the melodies to his newest creations, plunking out some of the notes on the theater piano, Hacker dutifully recorded them. Howley, Haviland and Company published them the next year as "The Battery" and "Jean."[2]

The Danger Signal company left the road in early December to take a long break until early March, but Dresser could not afford that luxury. Although exhausted by the rigors of the four months that lay behind him, he was exhilarated by what the immediate future held for him—touring and starring in his own play. On Thursday, 20 December 1894, only twelve days after concluding his tour with *The Danger Signal*, Dresser opened in *A Green Goods Man* at the Soldiers' Home Theatre in Dayton, Ohio. Trying out his work in various smaller cities was not only practical but a financial necessity as well since Dresser was a newcomer to writing plays and since the cost of a trial matinee in a New York City theater was more than a thousand dollars, a prohibitive expense even for him. In the Daytons, Decaturs, Altons, and Quincys, Dresser could tighten up the play, revising it here and there, making certain that everything worked before taking it to Boston, Pittsburgh, Philadelphia, Brooklyn, and finally to New York City.

Writing about the Dayton performance, a reviewer noted: "The star part is taken by [Dresser]. It is a musical comedy in three acts, interspersed with specialties." Then, with a comment that could have been addressed to any number of farce-comedies, the writer continued, "There is no plot to speak of, but the characters are all well taken by clever people."[3] Dresser's play was a satire on some of the things he knew of New York City from firsthand experience: its police and the graft that dominated the Tammany Hall machinery. Dresser played Herman Blatz, a bartender who was appointed a judge even though he had no legal experience. The skeptics were told not to worry about this minor oversight, for Blatz "is learning fast and it won't be long before he is hustling the best of Politicians. He'll soon be a member of Tammany Hall after he has served a term or two."[4]

The play was peopled with characters whose names could have been taken from almost any other farce-comedy: Blatz, who was in the "beer line," was joined by Rob A. Till, Dead Easy, Con Fidence, Willie Plug, and Olive Branch. Malaprops and stereotypical German dialect, straight from the variety show and from Dresser's more immediate role of Heinrich Yost, prevailed throughout—"If you get locked up in jail, come und led me know, und I get you oud."[5] Irish brogue came in and out. A number of topical allusions, including a bit of dialogue about the World's Columbian Exposition, were part of a feeble effort to provide the play with some currency. Numerous songs, including "After the Ball" and "The Bowery," were included, together with indications for other music to be interpolated in each of the acts. That the details of the play certainly changed, perhaps from performance to performance, is clear in the instructions Dresser gave that Act II "finishes with a medley to be arranged in the future."[6] *A Green Goods Man* concluded the year 1894 by traveling to three states and playing in seven theaters, including the Grand Opera House in Springfield, Ohio, where it "drew large business" on Christmas Day.[7] New Year's Day 1895 saw the company in Dresser's old hometown of Terre Haute. Unfortunately, the local newspapers said nothing about his visit this time.

The remainder of *A Green Goods Man*'s shortened 1894–95 season was thrilling for the thirty-six-year-old Dresser. Not only was he starring in his own play that critics reviewed favorably, but audiences were generally large and appreciative. At Havlin's in St. Louis, where Dresser had played with *The Danger Signal* only a year ago, the audience was "top heavy." In a theatrical juxtaposition that speaks volumes about the diversity of entertainment audiences could choose from, Dresser's offering appeared at Havlin's a week before boxer Bob Fitzsimmons's Specialty Company went there. (Later that spring *A Green Goods Man* found itself sandwiched between Fitzsimmons and a troupe led by John L. Sullivan, the former heavyweight boxing champion.)[8]

Frigid temperatures—the coldest of that winter—moved into the Midwest just in time to greet Dresser and his colleagues as they arrived in Kansas City, where the play drew fairly well in spite of the cold.[9] After a northward swing to Minneapolis, the troupe started an eastern journey that took it to Milwaukee, Chicago, and Washington, D.C., and then north up the eastern seaboard. Reports were glowing: "An audience [in Milwaukee] completely fill[ed] the Bijou and all S.R.O. admissions sold was the extent of the patronage bestowed upon Paul Dresser in 'A Green Goods Man,' "[10] while "Dresser . . . drew a large audience in Rapley's

Academy of Music [in Washington, D.C.]. Both play and players made a substantial success."[11] The play "was presented for the first time in this city [Boston], and the house management must have been satisfied at the business of the evening, for there was scarcely a vacant seat in the theatre. The company is a good one, and with the specialties introduced the show is excellent."[12] A Brooklyn reviewer wrote that the play was

> a very amusing farce seen for the first time by an audience that filled the house. As a provoker of uproarious laughter it is undoubtedly a success. It is evident that it was built for pure entertainment. It is well filled with songs, dances and travesties of a pleasing character. The people in it appear to have been carefully selected for the purpose of carrying the fun making idea out to the extreme limit. There are a number of specialties, which were cleverly executed and liberally applauded. Taken as a whole, the performance amply attains its object, that of amusing its auditors.[13]

On 23 March 1895, as *A Green Goods Man* concluded its week in Chicago, New Yorkers witnessed the closing of a landmark theater. Niblo's Garden, a mainstay in New York theatrical life for nearly seven decades, shut its doors, the building soon to be razed to make way for an office building. William Niblo established his Garden in 1828 in a building at the corner of Broadway and Prince Street, a location that quickly attracted the upper classes, "its status sustained by high entrance fees, expensive food, and urbane entertainments."[14] Here blackface minstrel troupes entertained countless numbers of people, and J. Cheever Goodwin and E. E. Rice's *Evangeline*, based on Longfellow's narrative poem, won fame as an early musical play.

It was the spectacular five-and-a-half-hour production of *The Black Crook*, however, that won for Niblo's its lasting renown as the house that launched American musical theater. Opening on Wednesday, 12 September 1866, the show ran for 475 consecutive performances. While some called it "rubbish" and "trashy," the *New York Times* remarked that "no similar exhibition had been made in an American stage that we remember, certainly none where such a combination of youth, grace, beauty and *elan* was found . . . [it was] decidedly the event of this spectacular age."[15] Beautiful young women, some clad in flesh-colored tights, were the sensation of the show. Their appearance established a standard for later lavish stage productions in which scantily clad young beauties prevailed over the dramatic element. When Dreiser first visited his brother in New York, Dresser had reminisced about seeing Niblo's when he arrived in the city. Then the Garden was in the center of the old theater district. Now the northward move of that district and bad economic times had taken their toll on Niblo's.

Buoyed by the success of his farce-comedy, Dresser copyrighted the title of a new play that he called *A Howling Success*. Although he did this in April 1895, before the close of *A Green Goods Man*, he never finished the play, undoubtedly another farce-comedy. For the rest of his life Dresser habitually copyrighted the titles of many plays he never finished. In each case he planned to base the plays on one or another of his songs, but perhaps in the end he felt that the dramatic contents of the songs were too lightweight to carry a fully developed play. On the last day of May 1895, only a month after Dresser had done so, brother Dreiser applied to the Library of Congress for a copyright of his own. Like Dresser, he probably never wrote, let alone finished, the intended play, but the title of the comedy drama has considerable bearing on a song Dresser wrote three years later.

On Saturday, 1 June, the day *A Green Goods Man* closed its season in New York City, Howley, Haviland and Company announced "The Return Of Their Partner, Paul Dresser, Who Will Be At The Office, 4 E. 20th Street, Every day during the Summer, where he will be pleased to receive old friends and welcome new ones."[16] During those months, Dresser recommenced his perambulations around the theater district, promoting Howley, Haviland and Company and its new songs, looking for performers for the company's music, seeking out new titles, and writing some fresh ones himself. What a welcome relief such activities brought to him. Except for the period of his "illness in the south," Dresser had been on the road for nearly two decades, often traveling the better part of nine months out of the year. He began thinking about leaving his performer's life behind him, but he knew he could not make that break quite yet.

Something happened that summer, however, that made Dresser decide to leave his own play. The 27 July issue of the *New York*

Clipper informed its readers that Frank R. Jackson, who had played the role of the sheriff in *Old Jed Prouty* for five years, would assume the lead in *A Green Goods Man* during the forthcoming season—a "part played last season by Paul Dresser, as a German, and the play is now being rewritten to admit of the change in characters."[17] Dresser told the public a week later: "I, Paul Dresser, for personal reasons, have withdrawn from 'A Green Goods Man' Co. and will not be connected with same the coming season. [I] [a]m open for engagement with any first class attraction."[18] Before long Dresser was traveling once again with the cast of *The Two Johns.*

Any number of questions arise about this situation. Why would Dresser leave the company of a play he had written and was starring in? Were there artistic differences between him and the director? Was he having financial problems? Dreiser wrote that shortly before the outstanding success of Dresser's 1895 song "Just Tell Them That You Saw Me," "there had been a slight slump in [Howley, Haviland and Company's] business and in my brother's finances."[19] Perhaps Fattie Stewart, creator of *The Two Johns,* had offered Dresser a salary he could not refuse at that point in his life, a salary that was sufficiently higher than what he was making with his own play. As the author of *A Green Goods Man,* Dresser presumably continued to benefit financially from his play's continued performances. If so, he would have been making this money, as well as receiving a salary for his work in Stewart's play. Additionally, he was realizing the benefits of his partnership in Howley, Haviland and Company, and before long he would begin to reap the financial rewards of his first big song success. *If* these suppositions are correct, his move, though perhaps born from desperation, proved to be an astute one from a business point of view.

CHAPTER 17

"Just Tell Them That You Saw Me"

In late August 1895, four weeks after Paul Dresser advertised his acting services in the *New York Clipper*, the paper announced the early success of his new song, "Just Tell Them That You Saw Me," as sung by George Evans (the "Honey Boy") at Holmes's Star Theatre in Brooklyn.[1] Three weeks later Howley, Haviland and Company took out yet another advertisement, this one naming ten performers, Meyer Cohen and Emma Carus—a promising new star—among them, who were featuring this song in their routines and shows, all of them "pronounc[ing] it a big hit."[2] At the end of October there appeared yet another ad boasting that "Just Tell Them That You Saw Me" was

> receiving more encores nightly than any song before the public today, and is more universally used by the leading vocalists in all branches of the profession than any other new song ever published. They are unanimous in its use. Always taking encores; in fact, a perfect whirlwind of success all along the line. No exceptions.

The names of at least thirty-four artists were included.[3]

An increasing number of people were hearing of Dresser's work as a composer. For nearly a decade he and his colleagues had regularly included his songs among their musical interpolations in *The Two Johns, A Tin Soldier*, *The Danger Signal,* and *A Green Goods Man*. Others had performed his songs in their own acts and shows. California baritone Cohen, traveling the West and Northwest with the Reilly and Woods show, for example, repeatedly sang Dresser's "Take a Seat, Old Lady," accompanied by a series of visual aids, entitled "Pictures from Life." Projected through a metal magic lantern, as the device was known, such "pictures" were single slides, or an endless belt of them, that provided a visual interpretation of the story being told in the words. Music, words, and visual technology were thus wedded to complement the singer's performance while adding to the listeners' enjoyment of the song, involving the audience vicariously in the unfolding of the story. Now with "Just Tell Them That You Saw Me," Dresser's name was about to become one of the most famous in the world of entertainment. This single song would do more for Dresser's reputation as a composer than any other of the five dozen or so songs he had written.

Besides promoting Dresser's songs, Howley, Haviland and Company bragged of its role in publishing "some of the BEST SONGS in America."[4] The firm was still very young, but Frederick Benjamin Haviland, Patrick J. Howley, and Dresser worked exceedingly hard to realize their dream of taking the business to the top of music publishing. The company already included important songwriters on its staff. Percy Gaunt, the composer of "The Bowery," a hit of 1892; Eduard Holst, known primarily for his musicals; and the up-and-coming Julian Holmes and George Evans were all under contract to Howley, Haviland. Evans, a former minstrel, later became the sensation of 1902 with "In the Good Old Summer Time." Charles B. Lawlor and James W. Blake, composers of the 1894 hit "The Sidewalks of New York"; Will T. Carleton; and Theodore F. Morse, the staff composer and plugger, were part of the team as well.[5]

There was always room for others with talent, and finding those people was part of Dresser's job. As the outside man in the firm, he was responsible for attracting singers to perform the company's songs and for convincing good songwriters to join the Howley, Haviland stable. In working with the public, Dresser was in his natural element, for he loved this part of the job—talking with people on his walks through the city, stopping in at the major hotels, watering holes, and theaters to buttonhole that new singer or composer who just might be the one Howley, Haviland was looking for. And the reverse was equally true. People loved the gregarious Dresser, this Falstaff of the entertainment world; they wanted to talk with him, be seen with him, hear his jokes, and just be included in his circle of acquaintances and friends.

Summer was Dresser's time of year. That was his creative time, the period when he could escape from the monotony of touring, which confined him for the other nine months of the year. In spite of the applause and adulation—and what performer could exist without that?—his audiences were largely anonymous, the routine sometimes numbing in the extreme. During June, July, and part of August, Dresser met his admirers face to face. He was not just another performer among thousands—he was out among his colleagues, a first among equals in that world of large egos and talents, instantly recognized and sought out. In a way, summers were what Dresser worked for the other three quarters of the year.

Those halcyon days of summer could not last forever, much as Dresser might like. Inevitably, fall and a new theater season beckoned him back to the road. As he traveled to the Academy of Music in Kalamazoo for the 20 September 1895 opening of *The Two Johns*, life must have seemed very good to the thirty-seven year old. "Just Tell Them That You Saw Me" was on its way to becoming not only *the* song to sing, but the catch phrase everyone would soon be uttering and seeing on such things as advertising buttons; although he was not appearing in it, *A Green Goods Man* continued to receive favorable reviews and large audiences; and *his* firm was in the process of establishing itself as an important player in the music-publishing business. As Dresser left New York City, life must have seemed very good, indeed.

Fattie Stewart's troupe spent October in a series of one-night performances in smaller cities in Illinois, Indiana, Ohio, and Pennsylvania with two weeks of breaks that helped ease the burden of constant travel. The schedules for November and December were light, with the company closing 1895 in a three-nighter at the Paterson Opera House in New Jersey. Such a moderate schedule was advantageous to Dresser, for with several breaks of five days or more during October through December, and with touring restricted to areas reasonably close to New York City, he would have been able to make trips back to help his partners with the business as the front man for the company and, perhaps, to offer encouragement to his younger brother Theodore Dreiser as he got his feet wet as the fledgling editor of a new publication for Howley, Haviland and Company.

After his visit with his brother in New York City during the summer of 1894, Dreiser had become depressed with his situation in Pittsburgh. Granted, he was a reporter for the *Pittsburgh Dispatch*, but he found little challenge in his work. He longed for the New York his brother had introduced him to and the opportunities that might be there for him. Finally, in November 1894, with money saved for the new adventure, Dreiser returned to New York, where he stayed for the time being with sister Emma Hopkins and her husband. He did not, however, find a warm welcome in that eastern Shangri-la and located no steady job. If Dresser had been aware of his brother's plight, he would undoubtedly have offered help, but Dreiser wanted to make it on his own and did not want to ask his brother for favors —yet. At that time Dresser had a two-week break from *The Danger Signal*, but if he was able to return to New York, it would have been for only a brief time, for he was then also involved with last-minute preparations for his own *A Green Goods Man*. Dreiser, however, suggested that he and Dresser were together on a November Sunday afternoon when Dresser played and sang a new song for his younger brother.

When Dreiser went job hunting, he rapidly found that he was merely one of many reporters trying to hook on with a paper in the city. Additionally, the bad economic times did not help Dreiser's chances. The diffidence he felt as an outsider hindered him in his search; he was "overawed and frightened" by the "air of assurance and righteousness and authority and superiority as well as general condescension toward all" of the New York newspapers.[6] He finally found a job at the *New York World* and languished there, writing mostly filler material and, on the occasions he was sent to cover a story, proving to be not very successful as a reporter. He resigned from the *World* and left the Hopkins' home because he could not contribute his share of expenses to their household budget.

Dresser was nowhere nearby to help his brother, and Dreiser moved into a succession of ever cheaper rooms and even pawned some of his belongings when he was close to being broke. Lasting until May 1895 in such a depressive state, he finally swallowed his pride and went to the office of Howley, Haviland and Company to inquire about Dresser. His older brother was still on the road with *A Green Goods Man* and would not return until he closed his season in New York on 1 June.

Music publishers were constantly thinking of new ways to promote their songs. Tried-and-true methods included paying singers to perform newly published songs in their acts in and out of the city; planting claques in the audiences to yell out the names of songs they wanted to hear or to sing along with the stage performers; paying organ-grinders on the street corners to play the latest tunes; and paying orchestra leaders in the better hotels to play new songs repeatedly. Long before the term "payola" was coined, its practice was rampant. Howley, Haviland and Company was no different from the other publishers in the methods it used to promote its songs, but in developing the idea of a literature magazine in which recent song publications would be printed and others touted, the company entered a territory in music promotion that had not been explored to any great extent and one that held promise as another way to reach more people.

Ev'ry Month, the brainchild of the firm, became a monthly publication directed primarily at women. Dreiser proposed to Howley and Haviland that he be the editor of *Ev'ry Month.* With Dresser's undoubted support, the two publishers acquiesced, offering the job to Dreiser at a salary of ten dollars a week until the first issue was published, after which Dreiser would be paid fifteen dollars a week. Dreiser's job was to provide the monthly with short stories, articles, and editorials, much of which he would write. "The Prophet," one of his columns, became a regular feature. Additionally, he sought articles from other writers.

Ev'ry Month proved to be an eclectic mixture of advertisements, photographs, and promotional material for new Howley, Haviland and Company songs, as well as an outlet for Dreiser's wonderfully diverse interests, including education, the sciences, philosophy, economics, and any number of other subjects. The October 1895 inaugural issue of the magazine was replete with articles about yachting: the United States yacht *Defender* had recently defeated

England's *Valkyrie III* in the America's Cup races. Appropriately, "The Defender March" was one of the featured pieces of music for that month. Other music included Dresser's "I Was Looking for My Boy, She Said; or, Decoration Day." Dreiser made his position clear about theater in the 1895–96 season and in doing so undoubtedly provided Dresser with some uncomfortable moments. In his undisguised sarcasm, Dreiser was biting the hands that fed him:

> Once more the dramatic season is on. . . . I . . . predict this season will not see one sterling gem from an author's reticule. . . . There are men with ideas enough—men unheard of—who could write us comedy-dramas, and they would not need to pander to vice, nor resort to machine-made humor at that. But we have jockey managers and sporty agents who know about prize-fights and punching mills, and only about prize-fights and punching mills. They wear four-pound diamonds and duck pants and stroll up and down Broadway endeavoring to induce popular saloon-keepers to write successes for them. They associate with sportsmen, and sportsmen only, and draw their ideas of popular sentiment from orphan asylums and Tenderloin institutions. Their idea of humor has an exquisite barrel-house flavor to it, and anything smacking otherwise is looked upon with but ill-concealed aversion. They put out Thrilbies and Hamlet Seconds, just as their less-ambitious but more business like competitors star the Corbetts and Brodies. They look only to the Bowery for material, while sterling authors are wearied out in attempting to communicate with them.[7]

Around this time Dresser began to express a longing to return to his roots in Indiana, perhaps having grown weary of traveling, tired, even if only for the moment, of his new celebrity. Dresser wrote to his old friend Emma Rector Flanagan, who had written to congratulate him on *Ev'ry Month*.

> I am still traveling with the 2 Johns Co. But dont know half the time where we are to be, so I always give my permanent address No 4 East 20th St [New York City]. Yes I am going to try & spend a few days with you this coming spring & only hope that nothing happens to prevent me from so

doing. Tell your Papa & Mama that I will make an extra effort to pay the visit.[8]

With "Just Tell Them That You Saw Me," Dresser had his first hit song. In these early days of Tin Pan Alley, the hit was a new phenomenon in American popular music, and Dresser now had a song

Indiana State Library

Twentieth-century sheet music for "Just Tell Them That You Saw Me."

that stood with "After the Ball" and "The Sidewalks of New York" as one of the first songs that enjoyed tremendous public and financial success. Dreiser remembered that on a "gray November Sunday afternoon" in 1894 Dresser went into the Howley, Haviland and Company offices, sat at the piano in one of the try-out rooms, and began playing a tune, repeating it over and over. After a while, Dresser said to his brother, "Listen to this, will you, Thee?" He performed the verse of the new song he had worked through only a short time before, but he had to stop as he was singing and playing the chorus, for he had broken into tears, moved by the sentiment that he had expressed in words and melody.[9] He steeled himself and finally got through the new song in its entirety. In the song, Dresser's narrator comes upon Madge, a former schoolmate from home; embarrassed to tell him what has befallen her—"[her] cheeks are pale, [her] face is thin"—Madge's message to the "old folks" is: "Just tell them that you saw me, . . . they'll know the rest, / Just tell them I was looking well you know. / Just whisper if you get a chance to mother dear, and say, / I love her as I did long, long ago."[10]

The following spring, when "it suddenly began to sell, thousands upon thousands of copies . . . [were] wrapped in great bundles under my very eyes and shipped express or freight to various parts of the country." Now "hand-organs, the bands and theater orchestras everywhere were using it." A button manufacturer created buttons with "Just Tell Them That You Saw Me" imprinted on them.[11]

Stories abounded about the immense popularity of the song and its catchy title. A man stole a coat with the song button on its lapel. When the owner of the coat saw the thief wearing the stolen garment with its identifying button, he called the police, who arrested the crook for the theft *and* as a fugitive from justice. Cartoonists frequently used the song for subject matter, even late in William McKinley's presidency. In one such cartoon, the president, top hat in hand, sits on a bench with Li Hung-chang of China. The Chinese gentleman holds a scroll upon which is printed Chinese characters and their translation: "Just Tell Them That You Saw Me." In another, the annoyed president peeks out of a White House window, "sueing for peace" from an organ-grinder's repeated playing of "Just Tell Them That You Saw Me." In a third, a proud Uncle Sam, victorious in the Spanish-

American War, waves good-bye to a ship whose flag reads, "Free Ride to Spain at Uncle Sam's Expense." Uncle Sam shouts to the departing boat, "Just tell them that you saw me—And that I was looking well!" The title was often used for send-ups: a vagrant sawed some wood in return for his breakfast. Before he returned to the road, he wrote a message across the saw—"Just tell them that you saw me, but you didn't see me saw." What did the double bass say to its player? "Just tell them that you saw me." And on and on.[12] Dresser had written one of the major hit songs of the early 1890s. He would soon compose the biggest song success of the late 1890s as well.

Free publicity from cartoonists and newspaper writers was enormously helpful in keeping a song in front of the public, but that came only after the song or its title had already caught the fancy of the public. A major part of a publisher's task was to bring a song to that point. Companies were ever looking for the novel idea for promotion. The February 1897 issue of *Ev'ry Month*, for example, described a promotion for Dresser's latest song—"A beautiful linen handkerchief containing the words of . . . ["Don't Tell Her That You Love Her"] with drawings in 5 colors depicting the story of the song."[13] Howley, Haviland and Company also gave packets of flower and vegetable seeds free to readers who wrote in to buy a song and soon used the Yellow Kid to plug their songs. R. F. Outcault, a good friend of Dresser and the creator of the "Yellow Kid," a satirical comic strip appearing in both Joseph Pulitzer's *New York World* and William Randolph Hearst's *New York Journal*, was the most famous cartoonist of the 1890s and early 1900s. The same February issue of *Ev'ry Month* ran an ad for *The Yellow Kid Catalogue* promising "a complete piece of New Music in each one, and reproductions of the first pages of over forty pieces of the latest and most popular vocal and instrumental music published by Howley, Haviland and Company."[14] The company would do almost anything to sell more songs.

At the end of April 1896 Dresser wrote again to his old friend Flanagan, this time about the forthcoming presidential campaign:

> Things are dull at present in trade circles. The *money plank* in the coming conventions of both parties is the cause of it all. It

> is the uncertainty. McKinley seems to be the man of the hour & the people want him. I am a Democrat still, but it looks as though McKinley would sweep things if nominated.[15]

Meeting in St. Louis in June, the Republicans chose Ohio governor McKinley as their candidate for president. The campaigns of McKinley and his powerful promoter, Mark Hanna, would both benefit shortly from the popularity of Dresser songs. In Chicago in July the Democrats nominated William Jennings Bryan, a son of Illinois, to be their standard-bearer. It was gold versus silver, the pleasant, somewhat unassuming McKinley, to whom Dresser bore a remarkable resemblance, versus the imposing, handsome Bryan, he of the mellifluous, golden voice.

In spite of his preference for Bryan, Dresser allowed the Republican campaign to draw on the immense popularity of "Just Tell Them That You Saw Me." Outfitted with new words, it became the official song of the campaign, "Endorsed by the Republican National Committee."[16] A sure sign of the popularity of something is when it becomes the basis for parody; by early summer 1896, a broad range of the American public was singing, humming, whistling, and playing Dresser's song, so much so that even with new words it was easily recognized. Monroe H. Rosenfeld, the composer of many popular songs, including "Take Back Your Gold" in 1897, wrote the new words that emphasized the need to maintain a strong, gold-based dollar, the platform upon which McKinley stood:

> Let others sing of silver bright and laud it to the sky,
> The honest little dollar give to me,
> No matter where you go lads, its value you can buy,
> In ev'ry town and land from sea to sea
> It has the good old sterling ring, like music to the ear
> In ev'ry age its worth has stood the test,
> And tho' some would condemn it, and others at it jeer
> The honest little dollar is the best!
> We do not want a dollar, lads, a dollar that will shrink,
> For honest labor let's give honest pay,
> And to uphold its credit, my boys, we'll float or sink,
> The honest dollar's sure to win the day
> So let them argue as they may, there is but one that's sound,
> And that with us shall ever have the call,

To pay our honest debts with and to pass the whole world 'round,
The honest little dollar beats them all!

Chorus
The honest little dollar the dollar of our day
The honest little dollar's come to stay
And when in next November McKinley gets the chair,
You'll find the little honest dollar there![17]

With the popularity of "Just Tell Them That You Saw Me," Dresser became a figure celebrated as never before. People on Broadway wanted to know him, wanted to be known *by* him. Gone were any feelings of failure and depression, for Dresser now enjoyed the rewards of songwriting as never before; "once more . . . [he] was his most engaging self," "a revivified figure on Broadway," who walked about "smiling and secure, his bank account large, his friends numerous, in the pink of health, and gloating over the fact that he was a success, well known, a genuine creator of popular songs."[18] One writer calculated the sales of the song at four hundred thousand; a reporter for the *Terre Haute Express* set the figure higher, at over a half million copies.[19] Based on a rather standard figure of four cents for every piece of music sold, Dresser's royalties amounted to sixteen thousand to twenty thousand dollars as the author and composer.[20] This was in addition to the salary he drew as a silent partner in Howley, Haviland and Company. By the summer of 1896 Dresser was richer than he had ever dared to dream.

The limited playing schedule of *The Two Johns* allowed Dresser time to carry out his continuing responsibilities for Howley, Haviland and Company. In the month before he wrote to Flanagan, he had penned a short note to her sister, Jeannette Rector, and told her he was "traveling all through the east . . . & it keeps me jumping to see all the music dealers & do business with them." He added that Howley, Haviland and Company's increased business had forced it to expand. The company originally rented a single floor in a building at 4 East Twentieth Street for six hundred dollars a month, but since then it had added the floor below and the basement of that building, and the rent was now fifteen hundred dollars a month. Dresser's excitement about the growth and the future of the company was apparent throughout the letter; he continued, "It will pay us as we are going to furnish our new floor with elegant plush parlor furniture, Moquette carpets, Persian rugs etc, & it will be second to none in N.Y." Additionally, the firm was "spending a great deal of money advertising 'Ev'ry Month,' " and Dresser expected that "business should be on the increase rapidly by '97."[21] Dreiser's observations enlarged poetically on the atmosphere of these establishments:

> There is an office and a reception-room; a music-chamber, where songs are tried, and a stock room. Perhaps, in the case of the larger publishers, the music-rooms are two or three, but the air of each is much the same. Rugs, divans, imitation palms make this publishing house more bower than office. Three or four pianos give to each chamber, a parlor-like appearance. The walls are hung with the photos of celebrities, neatly framed. . . . In the private music-rooms, rocking-chairs. A boy or two waits to bring *professional copies* at a word. A salaried pianist or two wait to run over pieces which the singer may desire to hear. Arrangers wait to make orchestrations or take down newly schemed out melodies which the popular composer himself cannot play. He has evolved the melody by a process of whistling and must have its fleeting beauty registered before it escapes him forever. Hence the salaried arranger.[22]

Any good publisher had to offer such physical amenities. More important to the success of the enterprise were those " 'peerless singers of popular ballads,' as their programs announce them, men and women whose pictures you will see upon every song-sheet, their physiognomy underscored with their own 'Yours Sincerely' " in their own handwriting. "Every day they are here, arriving and departing, carrying the latest songs to all parts of the land." These were the ones the publisher had to win over. These were the

> individuals who in their own estimation "make" the songs the successes they are. In all justice, they have some claim to the distinction. One such, raising his or her voice nightly in a

> melodic interpretation of a new ballad, may, if the music be sufficiently catchy, bring it so thoroughly to the public ear as to cause it to begin to sell. These individuals are not unaware of their services in the matter, nor slow to voice their claims. In flocks and droves they come, whenever good fortune brings "the company" to New York or the end of the season causes them to return, to tell of their success and pick new songs for the ensuing season. Also to collect certain prearranged bonuses.[23]

Dresser exulted in the success and celebrity that "Just Tell Them That You Saw Me" brought him. While he enjoyed the summer in New York City, with the relief that time of year brought from the wearisome travel from theater to theater, the summer of 1896 was more special than others, for he, the composer of the latest song sensation, was the talk of the city. As he traversed Broadway, stopping in his favorite hotels and bars along the way to rest his excessive frame and to tell, in his inimitable fashion, his stories or the latest jokes, he could always count on his adoring hangers-on to cling to his every word. They fawned over him, perhaps wanting an approving nod from him or merely to shake his meaty hand—just to be close to such celebrity—or hoping he might look with favor on their own song. Here he was in his "high hat and smooth Prince Albert coat . . . in his coat lapel . . . a ruddy boutonniere . . . in his hand a novel walking-stick. His vest [was] . . . a gorgeous and affluent pattern; his shoes [were] shining new and topped with pearl-gray spats."[24]

One night during that special summer, Dresser, brothers Ed and Theodore Dreiser, Haviland, Howley, Morse, the cartoonist Outcault, and other friends spent a convivial time together, feasting on a ten-course dinner. During the festivities, which lasted from seven in the evening until the next morning, waiters brought the party eight kinds of wine. Ah, Dresser may have thought, the rewards of such celebrity![25]

Buoyed by the success of "Just Tell Them That You Saw Me" and hoping to reach an even larger audience, Dresser tried his hand at composing piano music. In 1896 Howley, Haviland and Company published some short piano pieces to which Dresser

Van Pelt-Dietrich Library Center, Univ. of Pa.

Paul Dresser, the loving brother.

gave the title "After the Storm." A short introduction announces the storm in stereotypical musical fashion, replete with tremolo chords in both hands; a left-hand theme, marked fortissimo, intended to depict the angry procession of the storm, follows; finally, the storm's cessation is described as the music slows and quiets. Then follow four waltzes and a concluding finale, also in waltz meter and containing repetitions of music heard in the first and third waltzes. The music is naive in the extreme and simply not up to late-nineteenth-century standards found in thousands of other piano pieces that American composers wrote. "After the Storm" betrays Dresser's limited piano study and his lack of pianistic technique. One can almost see an unidentified hand writing this music down *for* Dresser, based on his musical ideas. These pieces appear to be Dresser's single attempt to extend his musical creativity beyond popular song. If Dresser had entertained hopes of becoming a composer of concert music, these pieces, and the limited reception they probably had, would have dashed those aspirations.[26]

The world of popular music was already changing rapidly, although this is more evident in retrospect, as things often are. If Dresser was ever content to rest on his laurels, this was not the time to do so. His position as one of the preeminent American song composers was constantly being challenged. In 1896 alone, three songs vied with one another for top sales. Maude Nugent's "Sweet Rosie O'Grady," published by Joseph W. Stern, and Gussie Davis's "In the Baggage Coach Ahead," published by Howley, Haviland and Company, captured the hearts of listeners and singers who were not yet tired of the waltz song. In "Sweet Rosie O'Grady," Nugent's words reflected the happy lot of a man in love with his "steady lady," "the sweetest little Rose the garden ever grew."[27] In the latter song, though, Davis, at one time the stage manager for C. V. Moore's Colored Minstrels, created what the trade called a "sobber": A family travels by train late at night. A bereft widower attempts to comfort his crying daughter. The beloved wife and mother is making the journey with them, but her body lies in a coffin in the baggage coach. Despite the song's success, Davis never enjoyed the financial rewards it brought because he sold it outright to Howley, Haviland and Company. Such transactions, however, were common in the relationship between composer and publisher. Davis's bad business decision and his death at age thirty-six seem to be an equally poignant counterpoint to the story he told. The third big hit of 1896, Joe Hayden and Theodore Metz's "A Hot Time in the Old Town," published by Willis Woodward and Company, was altogether a different type of song—it was part of the "coon" genre that captivated the public with jaunty marchlike rhythms. All three songs brought great financial reward to their respective publishers.

Continued success in the fickle world of popular entertainment lay with those who could adapt their styles to answer the demands of the marketplace. Those demands were determined by an often ineffable mixture of elements, few of them having much to do with music. Publishers, anxious to sell their wares, sought songs that would capitalize on the demonstrated success of a song or topic that had already caught the public's fancy. We have already seen this illustrated in the numerous songs about the World's Columbian Exposition. Similarly, publishers picked up on the rage for waltzes and the later fad of "coon" songs and ran those styles into the ground with hundreds of imitations.

Experimentation was not rewarded. Perhaps it might be better to say that publishers encouraged the imitation of success, so much so that many composers, including Dresser, found themselves trapped in a particular style that they used repeatedly because it had proven to sell well. That is not to say that composers of mother-and-home songs or waltzes were not sincere in their work, but they did find it difficult, if not impossible, to break away from their mold. As we shall see, Dresser later complained that he wrote the "junk" that the public wanted because his songs that were "too good to be published" would not win an audience.[28]

That performers had a part in shaping the tastes of the marketplace is certainly true. The cult of celebrity had, and has, a large role to play in the public's acceptance of something. Upon hearing a favored singer perform a new song, for example, many would want to own the sheet music for it, the cover of which often bore a picture of that artist. Individual stars could have considerable power at both the publisher and audience levels. The success of Dresser's "My Gal Sal," a song he wrote in 1905 after the public had lost its taste for his style, is a case in point. Dresser's "sister," Louise Kerlin Dresser, somewhat reluctantly added "Sal" to her repertoire, reluctantly perhaps because she thought it might be too old-fashioned for her audience. Louise Dresser's large following adored almost anything she sang. As a result, her fans embraced

"Sal," which she performed night after night, and made it a hit, albeit too late for Paul Dresser.

Then there is the public. Why will it embrace some things and reject others? Because of publishers' cleverness in advertising? Because of a composer's track record? Because of the singer with whom a piece is associated? Because it tires of a particular style, its imagination captured by something quite different from the ordinary (witness, for example, the popularity of ragtime music, which swept out the old, genteel musical utterances)? Why? The answer is for any, all, or none of those reasons. There is, of course, no magic formula for creating a hit. The process by which it is done and why it works is one of those wonderful, if exasperating, mysteries.

Dresser wrote seventeen songs between the beginning of 1895 and the end of 1896, more than he had composed in two years since 1889 and 1890, but none of his new efforts came close to competing with "Sweet Rosie O'Grady," "In the Baggage Coach Ahead," or "A Hot Time in the Old Town." And they certainly did not measure up to his own "Just Tell Them That You Saw Me"—at least in terms of commercial success. He had not yet been able to regain that touch that made the difference between just an ordinary song and one that would cause the nation to take it to its heart, singing and playing it repeatedly. At thirty-eight, the veteran composer of two decades still had good songs in him, and in the coming year he would write his song of songs—the one that would ensure his position as one of the great composers of American popular song. But for the time being he was trying too hard with little to reward his efforts.

In April 1896 Dresser corresponded with Flanagan, telling her that he was planning to visit Linton, Indiana, in the spring or summer once the season for *The Two Johns* had finished. Waxing nostalgically, he told her, "I would love to see that little *Brown School House* once more & also that little church. And in fact the old farm & all."[29] Dresser's new celebrity brought him conflicting emotions. He clearly loved being in the spotlight, loved the attention he now drew, enjoyed counting the well-known among his friends and acquaintances, positively exulted in his strolls through the entertainment district of New York as the "king of the hill," and loved being in the position to aid those less fortunate than he, but he also looked forward to getting away from that very fame he had won. Renewing old friendships, returning to old familiar spots he had known as a youngster, rebuilding family ties, and coming and going without an attendant fuss became increasingly important to Dresser. This is attested to in letters he wrote to boyhood friends, in interviews he gave, and increasingly in the words of some of his songs. Dresser had never been given much to introspection or reflection, but for the remaining decade of his life a more serious, thoughtful man gradually emerged, one who from time to time cherished the freedom that anonymity could bring.

PART 4

Celebrity to Obscurity: 1897–1906

CHAPTER 18

"On the Banks of the Wabash, Far Away"

The year 1897 was the most momentous of Paul Dresser's life. He left the stage after more than two decades of entertaining, became a full-time song composer, and wrote *the* song of his life, one that brought him not only celebrity but great affection from the public. In the same year, however, Dresser's enjoyment of his success was tempered by the tragic death of one of his sisters.

At some point in 1896 Dresser left the cast of *The Two Johns*. Late that year or early in 1897 he signed on with the company that was producing *Lost, Strayed or Stolen*. Described on its gaudy posters as "Three Hours in Paris," this was a musical farce that J. Cheever Goodwin and Woolson Morse had fashioned out of the play *Le Baptême du Petit Oscar*. Dresser's commitment was for only fifteen weeks, all of them spent at the Fifth Avenue Theatre in New York City. In August he wrote to Mary South in Terre Haute, "I am out of theatricals now having really all I can do to attend to my business interests here [in New York]. . . . I am tired of the theatre, as it is a Dog's life at that."[1] After more than twenty years of travel throughout the United States as medicine-wagon showman, blackface minstrel, and actor and singer in farce comedies, Dresser had had enough. Active participation on the stage as an actor held little interest for him for the rest of his life, although his past experiences and the creative side of him would inspire him to write at least two more full-length plays.

Theodore Dreiser viewed his brother's hit songs and involvement with musical farces with mixed emotions. On one hand there was familial pride, even envy, with Dresser's celebrity. At the same time, Dreiser could be disdainful of the work that had won that very prominence for his brother. The kinds of plays Dresser starred in and the popular songs—the "sobbers"—he composed all lacked the sort of class Dreiser pretended to: "[Paul] was in [no] way fitted intellectually or otherwise to enjoy high forms of art and learning . . . he was entirely full of simple, middle-class romance, middle-class humor, middle-class tenderness and middle-class grossness."[2]

As editor of *Ev'ry Month,* Dreiser contracted various authors to write articles for the magazine. In April 1897 Arthur Henry, Dreiser's friend and former employer as editor of the *Toledo Blade,* contributed "It Is to Laugh: A Little Talk on How to Write a Comic Opera." A tongue-in-cheek, yet savage, attack on the kind of entertainment Dresser excelled in, Henry's article certainly had the approval of Dreiser. Henry wrote, in part:

> You must have a certain number of choruses, solos, and duets, and specialties separated by bits of dialogue, and opportunities for falling down.
>
> You must give opportunities for a variety in the music also. There must be marches, waltz songs, eccentric songs, and ballads.
>
> Your dialogue must be short and bold, and must lead directly to the next act. Above all things avoid anything subtle. Your sarcasm must have large teeth. Rapier thrusts at social or political conditions are lost. Use a club, and be sure and land on the old wounds.

If Henry's words were not enough, his piece was accompanied by six photographs illustrating this sort of low-brow entertainment. A picture of Dresser and his colleagues bore the caption:

> Lewis Harrison and Paul Dresser, In "Lost, Strayed or Stolen." Here is presented the delicate humor of three gentlemen, in search of a lost infant, inquiring in the wrong home. A jealous Cuban lover's sudden return causes them to assume strange roles and mirthfully smash furniture in imitation of laborers. Uproarious applause.[3]

Dresser was shown as a hairdresser, clothed in a dark cutaway coat, lighter colored trousers, and spats and wearing a ridiculous wig.

The appearance of the article, however humorous its intent, in his own magazine, coupled with the knowledge that his brother had countenanced such a writing, must have caused Dresser discomfort if not outright pain. Henry had taken a broad ax to Dresser's brand of humor, the very kind in which he excelled. Musical interpolation, heavy-handed comedy, and lack of subtlety were, after all, the gist of Dresser's *A Green Goods Man* and hundreds of other farce-comedies. Dresser had taken his younger brother under his wing, brought him to New York, supported him with a job at *Ev'ry Month*, and sometimes acted as a surrogate, if misguided, parent. Now, through Henry, Dreiser had betrayed him. Dreiser apparently felt no remorse and perhaps dismissed his brother's feelings—if Dresser ever expressed them directly to him—as whining or inconsequential. Dreiser's concerns at the moment were centered on his own needs. He felt he deserved more money, and he certainly wanted more editorial freedom.

During the next months, quarrels undoubtedly ensued when Dreiser pressed these issues. The upshot was that Pat Howley and Fred Haviland, certainly with Dresser's knowledge, fired Dreiser, telling him the September 1897 issue would be his last. They were right to do so. Given his intellectual bent, Dreiser was ill suited for this publication. He had loftier literary ambitions, and he continually pressed them in his own writing and in those articles he commissioned. Such goals threatened to turn *Ev'ry Month* into something quite different from what Howley, Haviland, and Dresser had intended the magazine to be.[4] Thus, the parting of the ways was good for all four, although Dreiser could not comprehend that at the time. The resulting rift between the brothers was not healed for some time.

Dresser began working on a new song the month Henry's article appeared in *Ev'ry Month*. In the interval between then and the time Dreiser left the magazine, Dresser finished "On the Banks of the Wabash, Far Away," and it was on its way to becoming one of the most famous songs of the last decade of the nineteenth century, one that Americans would sing well into the twentieth century. With "Wabash," Dresser regained that ineffable touch, the musical magic that brought his celebrity to its zenith. It brought him fame as a figure in American popular culture, rivaled only by major players in the theatrical or sporting worlds.

In April, Dresser and Dreiser were undoubtedly ill at ease with each other, the Henry article due to come out during the month. According to Dreiser, the brothers were together at the Howley, Haviland office one Sunday morning when Dresser (perhaps in a moment of small talk to help ease the breach that existed between the two), asked Dreiser, "What do you suppose would make a good song these days?"[5] Dreiser remembered responding condescendingly to his older brother:

> Why don't you write something about a State or a river? Look at "My Old Kentucky Home," "Dixie," "Old Black Joe"—why don't you do something like that, something that suggests a part of America? People like that. Take Indiana—what's the matter with it—the Wabash River? It's as good as any other river, and you were "raised" beside it.[6]

Responding enthusiastically to the suggestion, Dresser said, "Why don't you write the words and let me put the music to them? We'll do it together!" Dreiser recalled that his protests were futile, for Dresser urged him to write down some words, and finally, "I took a piece of paper and after meditating a while scribbled in the most tentative manner imaginable the first verse and chorus of that song almost as it was published." Somewhat embarrassed by his efforts, since he felt that he "was rather loftily and cynically attempting what my good brother would do in all faith and feeling," Dreiser gave the lyrics to Dresser, who read them and encouraged Dreiser to "do a second verse, something with a story in it, a girl perhaps." Dreiser refused, and Dresser completed the song.[7] With this account, Dreiser takes full credit for having written the words to the first verse and the chorus of "On the Banks of the Wabash, Far Away." It was a claim he repeated in a letter to his fiancée, Sara Osborne White, a year later after "Wabash" fever had begun to sweep the country, but it seems to have been something he did not want to lay claim to in the larger world—yet. Undoubtedly, *if* he did write the words, he

IHS C9069

Fragment of the music for "On the Banks of the Wabash, Far Away," signed by Paul Dresser.

may have felt that such poetic utterances were far too sentimental and beneath him as a serious author.

Almost two years before that Sunday in April 1897, Dreiser wrote to the Library of Congress and included a check for the copyright of the title "Along the Wabash," a "Comedy Drama by Theodore Dreisser [*sic*], [indicating that] two copies of the above will be sent later."[8] Donald Pizer has made a case connecting Dreiser's title with his claim of having written the chorus and first verse to "On the Banks of the Wabash, Far Away." Dreiser's title and some initial words of the song's chorus are identical: "Oh, the moonlight's fair tonight along the Wabash."

> Although Dreiser's Indiana play was never written, its title and perhaps some of its sentiments seem to have stuck in his mind. That they emerged in a great popular success which was in a form analogous to a comic opera and which materially benefited someone else were ironies that Dreiser no doubt appreciated more in retrospect than at the time.[9]

On 23 January 1898, Dreiser wrote to White, telling her about the popularity of "Wabash" and confessing to her:

> I'll tell you something, but you musn't [*sic*] tell it to anyone. I wrote the words, and gave them to him outright, insisting that he should take all the credit as song writing is his field, not mine. I smile sometimes to think. It seems strange to hear

> people singing the words everywhere. I wrote the words in an hour, and although no one will ever know, it is a rediculous [*sic*] touch of satisfaction I get out of hearing it.[10]

Early that spring Dreiser heard a quartet singing a "plaintive and compelling" melody; it was "Wabash." "They were my words!" Dreiser later wrote. "It was Paul's song!"[11] Later that summer, not having seen his brother for some time, Dreiser ran into Dresser on Broadway, Dresser with "gold-headed cane, silk shirt, a smart summer suit, a gay straw hat"—his appearance bearing witness to the success of his new song.[12] "You turned the trick for me, Thee. . . . A part of ['Wabash'] is really yours." Dreiser countered "most savagely": "Cut that! . . . I couldn't write a song like that in a million years. You know I couldn't. The words are nothing." Dresser: "Oh, all right. It's true, though, you know."[13]

Sometime after that April day in 1897, but before late May or early June, Dresser traveled to the Chicago branch office of Howley, Haviland and Company and took a side trip to the Indiana health resort at West Baden Springs. Richard Dowell suggests that there Dresser continued to refine the song "and brought the music to near its final form."[14] Dresser, however, told a different story, claiming that he wrote the song in the heat of inspiration while he was a guest at that resort. He mentioned nothing about "refining" it there.[15] Returning to Chicago, Dresser met with Max Hoffman, his Chicago arranger. Hoffman remembered going to the Auditorium Hotel one evening to help Dresser polish the song. The arranger claimed that while he repeatedly played Dresser's melody on a camp organ "for at least two or three hours, [Dresser] was writing down words, changing a line here and a phrase there until at last the lyric suited him."[16] Satisfied at last with the results of melody and words, Dresser asked Hoffman "to make a piano part for publication," which he did the same evening, sending it in that form to Howley, Haviland and Company in New York.[17] Hoffman further stated that "during the whole evening we spent together, Paul made no mention of anyone's having helped him with the song."[18]

Once that business was concluded and Dresser had finished the song, he arranged for a tryout of "Wabash" in Milwaukee, where his good friend Charles K. Harris had his publishing office. Harris recalled that "no man in the country, I imagine, was closer to him than I was, for we were the only two composers who wrote both words and music to a song."[19] When he arrived in Milwaukee sometime in June, Dresser asked Harris

> to go with him to the Alhambra Theater, where Joe Natus was to sing a new song of his for the first time. He wanted my opinion of it. We went, and after its rendition he turned to me and asked: "What do you think of it?" I told him I would stake everything I possessed that this number was a sure-fire hit. Tears came to his eyes. We went to a telegraph office, where he wired his associates: "Harris says 'On the Banks of the Wabash' looks like a great big hit. Get song out immediately."[20]

Amid these conflicting accounts, one must remember that the events that unfolded over spring and summer 1897 occurred during the very time when the relationship between Dresser and Dreiser was at its lowest ebb. Dreiser, through the Henry article, must have hurt his brother considerably. The stress between the two brothers undoubtedly was palpable. *If* this was so, would Dresser have asked Dreiser to collaborate with him on a song, when Dresser proudly claimed that he *always* wrote his own words and music? If he *did* ask for Dreiser's suggestions for a song, was he attempting to assuage any guilt he might have felt, suspecting, or knowing, that Dreiser was going to lose his job? But then *if* Dreiser had nothing to do with the creation of "Wabash," why would he deliberately lie to his fiancée and tell her that he wrote the lyrics?

The directness of poetic expression in "Wabash" points more to Dresser at the peak of his craft than to Dreiser—Dreiser's typically convoluted style of writing would not make for good song lyrics. If Dreiser indeed was the author of most of the words to "Wabash," he had been an astute observer of his brother's craft and an unusually quick study in writing song lyrics. It is likely that Dreiser offered his brother the idea of a song based on the Wabash River (perhaps incorporating an idea or two from his comedy drama "Along the Wabash"), some thoughts as to sentiments to be included, and perhaps ideas for general word pictures for the first verse and chorus. Dresser probably then took his brother's ideas and crafted them into the words as they appeared in final form. If these assumptions are accurate, the song was the result of collaboration between the two brothers, but Dresser was mainly responsible for taking Dreiser's raw material, honing it to song poetry, and then wedding his unforgettable melody to the words.

During the second week in July, Dr. Thomas Moorhead, a Terre Haute friend, visited Dresser in New York. When Moorhead asked who the Mary was to whom Dresser referred in the second verse of "Wabash," the composer explained that "this personage was fictitious in the extreme . . . and was written merely for rhythmical purposes." But in reading it over to his friend, Dresser wondered, "Now, who in thunder is this unknown Mary to be to whom I have made allusion?" As they continued to puff on their Havana cigars, Moorhead interrupted the silence. "I have it," he said. "I know a young lady who is as pretty as a dream and who sings delightfully. Her name is Mary. Why not dedicate the piece to her?" Upon the revelation that this Mary was the fourteen-year-old daughter of Col. E. E. South, general agent of the Big Four Railroad in Terre Haute, Dresser exclaimed, "Why, the deuce you say. I know Colonel South very well, although I've never met his daughter and nothing would give me greater pleasure than to dedicate the piece to her."[21] By the middle of July, Howley, Haviland and Company was issuing professional copies of the song; on the twenty-fourth, Dresser, responding to a letter from Mary South, wrote, "I am glad to note the dedication proved agreeable to you." He promised to "mail a few copies on to [you] . . . When the song is issued in regular trade form."[22]

Sometime before "Wabash" was printed on good paper stock, performers in New York began including the song in their acts. For one of the early performances, Dresser devised a stage setting in which Terre Haute's Fort Harrison and the Wabash River formed the background for a group of soldiers gathered around a campfire. Although this was undoubtedly effective, the song rapidly proved that it could be sung to great success without such visual trappings.

In early August, Dresser wrote to Mary South to tell her he might try to visit Terre Haute in October when he would be nearby in West

Baden Springs, but he told her that he would "quietly slide [in] . . . for a day or so, but I wont [*sic*] say when I will be there, as I do not care for notoriety, so will just drop in, take a rig & ride around a few hours looking at the old place, & then away again."[23] If Dresser was sincere in his comment about not caring for notoriety—and there is no reason not to believe him—he would not be able to escape the tremendous acclaim waiting for him just around the corner.

A month later Dresser wrote yet again to Mary South, this time in an avuncular sort of way, telling her to enjoy herself with her friends: "Have a good time while you can, for there comes a day when we can look back & those little remembrances help brighten the years to come." Additionally, he reported that "the 'Wabash' is going fine. I have sold over five thousand to date. Had an order for 300 from Lyon & Healey [i.e., Lyon and Healy], Chicago, in this morning's mail."[24] Clearly, "On the Banks of the Wabash, Far Away" was on its way to attaining the degree of popularity that few songs from the nineteenth century had ever had. Dresser frequently shared the good news about "Wabash" with South, keeping her current with sales figures and with its reception all over the world. For her part, South was immensely pleased that Dresser had chosen to dedicate the song to her. At one point she sent him her picture, to which Dresser responded, "I received the exquisite photo of yourself many moons ago, & it holds a most prominent position on my desk, I can assure you."[25]

Although Howley, Haviland and Company did not have to do much to promote its new hit, it did so, nevertheless, by advertising in trade papers and through other ways. One promotion came in the form of a play check, drawn on the "Banks of the Wabash" in "Faraway, Ind.," with one thousand dollars payable to "anyone who has not heard the song." Signed by Paul Dresser, "Author & Composer," it was dated 1 April 1897. Does this tell us the date on which Dresser began writing the song, or is it mere happenstance?[26]

On 22 October, Dresser's jubilation at his success and growing fame was tempered by the tragic death of his sister Mary Theresa Dreiser Davis, who lived in Chicago. Crossing the Lake Shore tracks at Sixty-eighth Street and South Park Avenue, attempting to beat an oncoming train, thirty-one-year-old Davis dropped the bicycle she was pushing. As she stopped to pick it up, a Park

Paul Dresser's sister Mary Theresa Dreiser.

Manor suburban passenger train struck and killed her.[27] Writing to brother Theodore, Sylvia Dreiser mourned "Poor Theresa," whose "life was not a sunshiny one."[28] From the time of the accident until 5 November, Dresser wrote to Mary South twice. First, he told her about his sister's death and burial, and then on 5 November he wrote at length about a rewarding experience he had had at West Baden Springs:

> I enclose you a programme of last evening's entertainment given by the colored waiters of the hotel & it was first rate too. The young fellow who sang my two songs was backed up by a quartette & they rendered them very sweetly. The audience applauded wildly & then after it was all over, they began applauding again & some crank yelled Dresser & that settled it. I was compelled to stand up & bow my acknowledgements & then sat down. Then they went at it again & they began to yell speech & I had to get up & make a speech. It affected me very much as it all seemed so honest & felt that there was still a little heart in some of the people. I thanked them for the outburst of enthusiasm caused & brought about by a little sentiment & stated that as long as the world rolled around there would come up little pathetic incidents that would for the moment "make us all kin."
>
> You should have heard the sound of applause. It was deafening.[29]

"There was still a little heart in some of the people" is a telling, defensive comment, for Dresser's songs, which tugged at the heartstrings, certainly won little praise from the critics of popular song, the ones who made repeated calls for "better" music. The conclusion of Dresser's letter hit on his touchiness about such criticism, for he continued:

> While cynics might refer to the little simple melodies as trash, & the words as maudlin sentiment, still to me with apologies to none, the grandest word in English or any other language is *Mother*.[30]

When asked what led him to compose "Wabash," Dresser responded, "The same sweet memory that inspired that other Hoosier, James Whitcomb Riley, to sing of the 'Old Swimmin'

Hole.' I was born on the banks of the Wabash at Terre Haute. . . . My fondest recollections are of my mother and of my early days along this stream."[31] The song rapidly became a sensation, the *Chicago Record* reporting that on a single day one department store sold 1,471 copies of the song and that "Wabash" "has reached the most enormous sale of any popular song. Its author has received already from $30,000 to $50,000 in royalties upon his production which has given the Wabash a place in the world of song like that given the Swanee river by Stephen Foster's 'Down on the Swanee River.' "[32] Given the continued popularity of "Swanee River," it was inevitable that many writers compared "Wabash" to Foster's hymn to a river. On 5 August 1897, only three weeks after professional copies were sent out, a writer for a newspaper in Lagrange, Indiana, stated:

> Mr. Dresser . . . has endeavored to perpetuate the beauties of the Wabash as did Stephen Foster that of the Suwanee River, and certainly no song since the latter has awakened so much interest among lovers of a good song, nor has any other American author seemed as capable of filling the void left vacant by Foster. The song is a gem and a welcome relief from some of the so-called popular songs sprung on the public from time to time.[33]

Another wrote, " 'On the Banks of the Wabash Far Away' is the title of the prettiest and latest piece of music out, written by Paul Dresser. . . . The advance copy which has been sent us shows that the piece promises to become as famous as Foster's 'Way Down on the Swanee River.' "[34]

Within a year, Dresser reported that "Wabash" had broken all sales records and that the million mark would soon be passed, adding:

> I can't tell you just how much I have cleared off of the song, but the $50,000 estimate I have seen in some papers is very modest. You see I am a publisher as well as a composer and have a big printing house of my own in New York. I also write the words for all my songs, dictate the circumstances

> and stage settings for their public introductions, write my own ads, and sometimes sing my own songs. Now what do you think of that for a monopoly. Eh?[35]

The words of the song speak of a past made bittersweet by the realization that such place and time are irrecoverable and can only be conjured up in the heart's memory. Millions in the nation who had never seen the Wabash River embraced it as their own and thought of it as a place of idyllic beauty. It became a metaphor for the innocence of yesteryear now forever lost. The first verse is given over to beauties of nature—the cornfields swaying gently in the breeze and the delightfully cool woods, a place of respite from the stifling heat of summer—and to beloved Mother, no longer alive but still the one thing above all the narrator would give anything to see. Only in the second of the two verses is the river mentioned. While only alluded to in passing, it looms large in the story as the spot where the narrator proposed to "sweetheart Mary," his other beloved. Mary, the lovely young girl to whom the narrator professed his love, now lies buried in the churchyard. Regretting that he never convinced Mary of his feelings for her, the lover utters in anguish, "I'd give my future were she only here." Nowhere in the chorus is there mention of beloved Mary or mother. Instead, nature returns in the visual images of moonlight, of the luminosity of candles twinkling through the leaves of stately sycamore trees and in the "breath of new-mown hay"—all of this seen and breathed from the banks of the river. Adding to the poignancy of this past, the narrator concludes the song with the words "far away." "Far away" was the yesterdays of millions of Americans—the "far away" of life and times of a seemingly simpler existence in the village, the "far away" of kin and loved ones now gone, the forever "far away" of lost innocence, the "far away" now retrievable only through the heart. "Wabash" captured for Dresser and the nation the bittersweetness of place and time, a beloved river, and youth.[36]

To enhance the sentiments expressed in the words, Dresser created a memorable tune that nearly anyone can hum, whistle, or sing. Truly superior melodies possess a magical combination of repetition and contrast; the first helps one to remember easily the tune, while the latter offers a foil to ward off the possibility of monotony. Recurrence and dissimilarity work hand in hand in the best songs to create music that somehow seems delightfully fresh at each hearing. While composers of popular song in the last half of the nineteenth century commonly brought back to the refrain a melody they had already used in the verse, Dresser avoided this in "Wabash." The melody that ties the verse together and the tune unifying the chorus are different from each other, but the whole works.

Melody and words possess an unexplainable spellbinding logic all their own as they flow, like the river itself, unimpeded and inexorably from the verse to the end of the chorus. This analysis, of course, is a retrospective one suggesting a process in which spontaneity has little or no place. It is unlikely that Dresser, untutored in the theory of music, went through such a laborious and calculated process when he composed. Dreiser remarked that, unlike the extroverted brother who constantly needed people around him in his role as performer, Dresser the composer tended to be a solitary, slow composer, preferring the twilight hours to do his work, refining his songs by playing a tune over and over, changing it here, altering the contour there, getting it into his fingers and voice, brooding about it, worrying over it, committing some of it to paper, and at long last, when he had the tune to his satisfaction, often dissolving in tears over its sad and wistful qualities.[37]

The result in Dresser's finest songs is a marriage of words and music in which nothing seems contrived, where the tune has a naturalness to it, the words tell a mesmerizing story in serial fashion, and the whole suggests a contradictory combination of simplicity and elegance. Writing *about* a formula and putting that scheme into practice to create an unforgettable song are, of course, two different matters. The list of composers who succeeded in accomplishing the latter is short; Dresser, at his best, belongs to that select group. "On the Banks of the Wabash, Far Away" is a gift of time and place remembered.

The most famous of America's popular entertainers around the turn of the century included the song in their routines in music halls and on vaudeville stages; male quartets sang it repeatedly as a regular part of their programs; organ-grinders—some out of personal conviction, more because publishers paid them to plug new songs—wheezed out its lilting melody on their instruments; restaurant orchestras featured it as part of their repertoire; and people hummed it on streetcars, played and sang it in parlors, and whistled it along sidewalks.

The popularity of "Wabash" prompted numerous cartoons. A drawing in the *Chicago Record* on 15 April 1898 shows a group of cyclists bursting through the front page of the paper, accompanied by:

> Oh the moonlight's fair to-night along the Midway,
> From the parks the stream of joyous bikers steals;
> Through the darkness we can see their faces gleaming,
> Through the "WANT ADS" of THE RECORD came their wheels.[38]

Another cartoon has "Citycus" asking "Sububs," "Have you any music in the country?" An old, bearded gentleman replies, "Oh, yes. Our mosquitoes learned last summer to hum 'Banks of the Wabash.' "[39] Dresser's friend R. F. Outcault drew a cartoon panel that shows a parrot singing "Wabash" while a monkey, seated beneath the bird, reads a book about Charles Darwin. Fed up with the parrot's repetitions of the song, the monkey throws the book at the parrot, knocking it off its perch. The caption: "A little incident showing that even monkeys can't stand everything, and are really human."[40]

The list of anecdotes about "Wabash" is long, but a few examples will suffice to show how popular it was from the days shortly after Dresser composed it until well into the first half of the twentieth century. The *New York World* reported about an event that temporarily overshadowed the prizefight between featherweight boxers Terry McGovern and Tommy White at Coney Island in June 1900. When a lighting failure pitched the arena into total darkness and few knew the location of the exits, Frank Conlin quieted the panicking crowd of five thousand by whistling, in a penetrating sound that carried throughout the space, a tune known to nearly all who were there. After officials repaired the lights, the boxing match continued, but not until McGovern acknowledged Conlin's efforts as the crowd roared its appreciation. The tune Conlin whistled? "On the Banks of the Wabash, Far Away."[41]

Dresser remarked that he had received letters from all over the world about the song, including one from a Catholic priest who

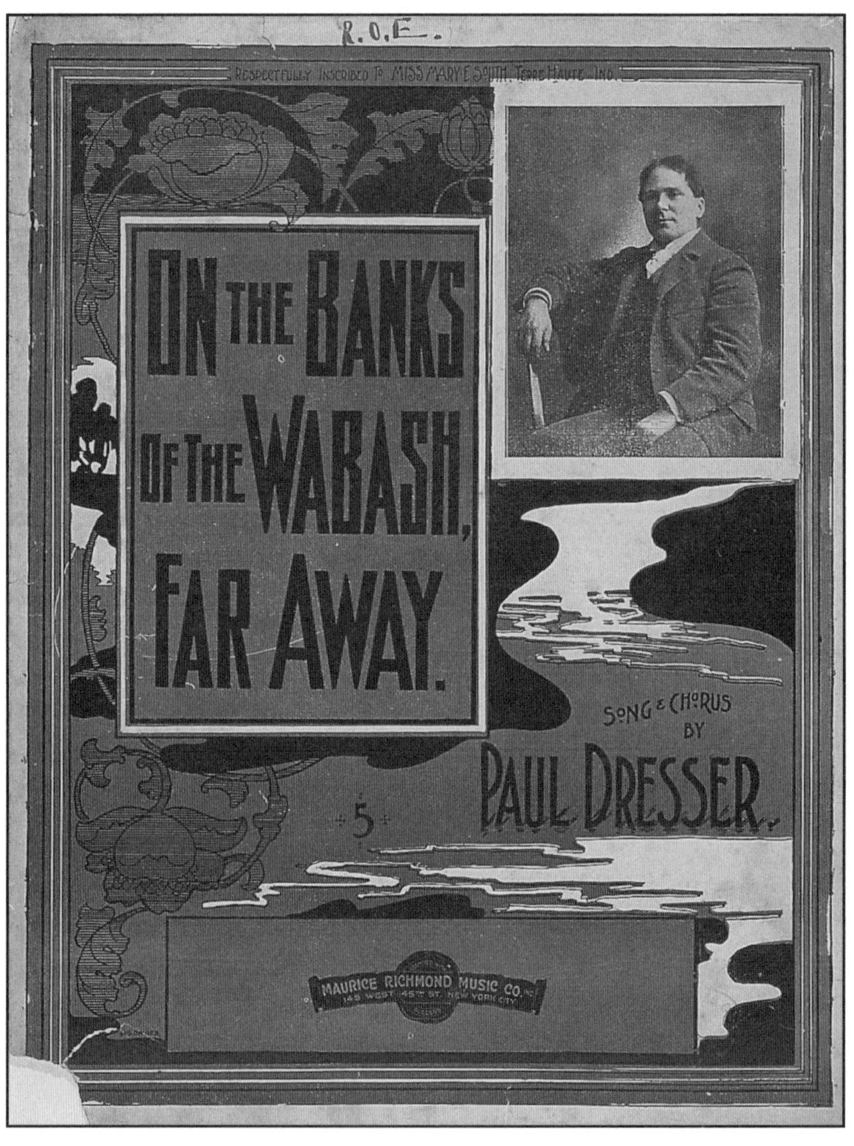

IHS

"On the Banks of the Wabash, Far Away," one of the biggest hits of the 1890s and Indiana's official state song.

had written from aboard a ship off the Australian coast. The traveling priest told Dresser that he had heard "Wabash" being sung and played as a regular part of the musical program in a hotel in Yokohama, Japan, and had seen the song for sale in every place he had visited.[42] A writer for the *New York Sun* told of the effect the song had on Edward Marshall, a correspondent for the *New York Herald* who was crippled for life in the Spanish-American War. After his injury, as a rescue party was carrying him to safety,

> Marshall was sleeping under the effect of another opiate, but as we changed off at the litter he woke and had another terrible spasm. When he was quieted he began to sing "The Banks of the Wabash." For nearly an hour, as we dragged the litter along, Marshall kept repeating the chorus of this song over and over.[43]

Four years later a columnist for the *New York Dramatic Mirror* wrote of the impact the singing of "Wabash" had on discontented, wet, weary, homesick, and just plain disaffected soldiers who were quartered at Montauk Point, Long Island, following their duty in helping quell the Philippine Insurrection. As the song began,

> A silence fell over the camp, and the sick men turned their heads and hid their faces on the pillows. . . .
>
> And soon from that whole wet, bedraggled, miserable camp of men went up a strange chorus. . . . Many a hundred husky, quavering voices, with an under note of sobs—sobs of brave fellows and good fighters—but with enough of the boy still in them to break down when the thought came to them of their homes through all the lonesomeness and damp. . . .
>
> ["Wabash" speaks] a language—not in words, but like Wagner, . . . with such clearness that it will make your heart grow deaf to everything else.[44]

Shortly after Dresser died, a Sullivan friend wrote to Louise Dresser:

> When we were in the Phillippine [*sic*] Islands, marching and fighting our way through the swamps and jungles, we had his songs to sing, and when we marched into the city of Pekin [*sic*], China we sang "The Blue and the Gray" and "On the Banks of the Wabash." It made us think of home and

> friends, and it seemed that the march was not so hard, when the boys struck up Paul's good songs. They cheered us up and enabled us to carry our Country's flag in triumph and crown the American soldiers with victory.[45]

An Indiana paper reported that "twenty thousand copies [of 'Wabash'] have been distributed to the school teachers of Indiana, and it has been listed as one of the songs to be taught in all the teachers' training schools of the state. . . . Recently . . . the Indiana State Normal school printed the song in its catalogue, of which more than 30,000 have gone out."[46] A member of the committee that was considering a fitting monument to the composer in the 1920s remarked ecstatically that Dresser's song had taken on the wings of immortality and filled all loyal Hoosier hearts "with the most poignant homesickness and longings for Riley's green fields and running brooks—Aunt Mary at the door, the frost on the punkin and the fodder in the shock! The Wabash is everywhere identified with the state name; it is a part of American history." Recognizing its practical value as well, the member saw the song as a "great advertisement of the state."[47]

In 1923 at the ground-breaking ceremonies for Dresser Drive in Terre Haute, the attorney for the county commissioners told how "Wabash" had united former Civil War enemies as they sang the song together, unifying America in the Spanish-American War. In a fireworks of hyperbole, he continued:

> ["Wabash"] inspired Indiana's sons on the muddy fields of Flanders—on the plains of Picardy—and in the shell shocked forest of Argonne where it seemed aid would never come—there it equalled a brigade of soldiers with bayonets. . . .
>
> May this single song be the chief cause of the rise of Terre Haute. That song is now our chief asset. . . . It is so fine, so high, so pure, it stamps our character—it is our soul—it is an exemplary sentiment worthy to be copied and imitated by the less fortunate and less favored.[48]

Also in 1923 the *Terre Haute Tribune* remarked that Indiana governor Warren T. McCray's forthcoming proclamation confirming that a Dresser memorial was to be erected in Terre Haute would be published "in every leading paper in the country and a country-wide demonstration will be held on that day including the singing of 'On the Banks of the Wabash,' " by then the state song.[49] A year later the Paul Dresser Memorial Association scheduled a national appeal to raise money for a Dresser memorial, a solicitation that would be made during the Indiana observance of State Song fortnight.

In February 1897, a month before William McKinley was inaugurated as the twenty-fifth president, the Ohio General Assembly elected Mark Hanna, the Cleveland industrialist, to the United States Senate, replacing John Sherman, who was to become McKinley's secretary of state. Hanna had been the president-elect's astute political manager and had also been largely responsible for getting McKinley elected governor of Ohio in 1891. Hanna was known for his own wealth, his close relationships with corporate America, and his abilities to raise large sums of money for the Republican party, and a bitter Democratic press often parodied him as the enemy of national interest and suggested that he would pay anything for a Senate seat. Shortly after Hanna received the general assembly's blessing, some wag wrote a parody of "Wabash," telling the story of the expense of Hanna's bid for the seat:

In my Indiana homestead full of Indians,
Here the wood there to be chopped gave me a pain,
It was there I'd count my money by the millions,
Then smoke my cigarette—and guess again.
I used to get a draft or two each day then,
Also a bunch of letters on your life,
They thought I corresponded with McKinley
But I'd just be advertising for a wife.

Chorus
Oh, I'd open wide the door, and then the window,
As patiently I waited there each day,
But I'd always get the draft I was expecting,
On the Banks of the Wabash far away.

What a high old time they had up in Columbus,
Up on High St., where the votes came pretty high,
It was there they tried to keep Mark from the Senate,

But lucky Mark was there to do or die.
Because he was a Mark, they thought him easy,
But they didn't even hurt Mark's appetite,
For Mark ate everything they sell in market,
And so Marcus and his boodle won the fight.

Chorus
Oh, Mark Hanna landed safely in the Senate,
But big money Marcus ponied up they say,
He was backed by all the banks—of course excepting—
The Banks of the Wabash far away.[50]

In 1940 the Paull-Pioneer Music Corporation, then owners of the copyright to the song, issued a new edition of "Wabash" with special choruses praising Republican presidential candidate and Hoosier native Wendell Willkie. With John W. Bratton's new words it became the song for the Willkie campaign. As one might expect, Franklin D. Roosevelt's policies were attacked:

Farmers will be glad to plow the New Deal under
When they vote November, North, South, East and West,
Farmer Willkie then will shout, "Let's get together;
All dig in and in happiness invest."

In the final chorus, Republicans optimistically sang:

When a harvest moon shines over the Potomac
Next November down in Washington, D.C.,
Uncle Sam will hang this sign up in the White House:
"Welcome Home, Willkie, and Prosperity."[51]

Today one only rarely hears "On the Banks of the Wabash, Far Away," composed by the man many consider to be the only true successor to Stephen Foster in the writing of sentimental home songs. Based on the musical merits alone, it is difficult to know why Foster's "My Old Kentucky Home, Good Night!" has endured while Dresser's has largely been forgotten. With their bittersweet memories of the past in words colored by the halcyon days of youth, both represent the grand tradition of the sentimental song. The music of each, relatively simple, speaks directly to the heart and possesses that ineffable magic that makes for a superior song.

CHAPTER 19

Patriotic Fervor and New Musical Directions

While "On the Banks of the Wabash, Far Away" continued to enjoy excellent sales all during 1898, and although many song composers kept the air filled with the sounds of waltzes, changes in the nation's tastes in popular music were becoming more pronounced. The black-dialect "coon" song, an outgrowth of late minstrelsy, with some rhythmic hints of ragtime thrown in, had already become a public favorite. "Coon shouters" such as May Irwin and Fay Templeton had created substantial reputations singing this music, as had the renowned minstrel Lew Dockstader. Audiences especially clamored for Irwin's rendition of Charles E. Trevathan's "The Bully Song," which she interpolated in *The Widow Jones*. In that show, which opened at New York's Bijou Theatre in September 1895, Irwin strutted around the stage to the immense delight of audiences and sang about her search for "dat nigger dat treated folks so free."[1]

The musical utterance, however, that was truly to alter the path of American popular song was ragtime, the jaunty rhythms of which, combined with a breeziness of verbal expression, were embraced increasingly by the public. Paul Dresser was not interested in the newer style. In John Jakes's novel *Homeland*, Dresser is asked to "play . . . some of that fast new stuff." His response, undocumented and through the words of Jakes: "That raggedy-time coon crap out of St. Louis? Not me. I know what the public wants. The heart ballad. The home song."[2] He did, however, try his hand at writing ragtime once: a solo piano piece, "Darktown after

Dark: A Bunch of Niggerism," that Howley, Haviland and Company published in 1899.[3] It is difficult to know how much of the music beyond the tunes is Dresser and how much can be credited to an arranger. The finished piece, no matter, is not convincing and does not go beyond a fairly rudimentary exploration of the surface of the new style. Dresser could not have been pleased with such tepid results. Indeed, such an unsatisfactory experiment probably convinced him that he had no future in writing that sort of music.

The changes in the popular culture of the time paled in comparison to what was going on in the nation at large. America's position in the world was forever altered on Tuesday, 15 February 1898, when the U.S. battleship *Maine* blew up in Havana harbor with the loss of 266 lives. Those who favored the retaliation of war immediately branded Spain and Cuban loyalists as the ones behind this heinous act; a little more than two months later Congress declared that a state of war with Spain had existed since 21 April, the day that Spain had broken off diplomatic relations with the United States. On the twenty-third, two days before Congress made its declaration, President William McKinley called for 125,000 volunteers and got them handily.

This was to be America's first war against a foreign power in fifty years, and how well or poorly the United States did now would have tremendous influence on how the rest of the world viewed its strength. If the nation could lay claim to any degree of innocence—and one would be hard pressed to make such a statement for a country that had only recently survived the cataclysmic years of civil strife—it moved aggressively beyond that innocence and its barrier of self-protective isolation to defend its interests and to assert itself in an acquisitive stance, the scope of which was previously unknown to America. The patriotic outcry that followed the *Maine* tragedy and the subsequent Spanish-American War became grist for the song composers' mill.

If Dresser's musical style was not changing, his personal political outlook and attitude certainly were, albeit gradually. Dresser, along with many other Americans, slowly came to realize that, while many were enjoying the rewards of the Gay Nineties, a vast underclass of human beings, mostly immigrants, was living in the most deplorable of conditions, especially on New York's Lower East Side. Jacob Riis had dramatically documented the plight of these people in his 1890 publication *How the Other Half Lives*.[4] While the patriotism stirred up by America's war activities had an immediate impact on Dresser's creativity, promising considerable financial reward from a public hungry for music and words to commemorate the nation's victories, the kind of situations that Riis and others exposed did not lend themselves easily to expression in music, even if composers were interested in attempting to do so. Additionally, commercial success and fighting on behalf of the dispossessed were antithetical to each other. Dresser had always shown compassion for those less fortunate than he by giving generously to tramps, to hangers-on, and to those who were simply down on their luck. In "My Brother Paul," Theodore Dreiser wrote that Dresser

> was a victim of many . . . importunities. If it was not the widow of a deceased friend who needed a ton of coal or a sack of flour, or the reckless, headstrong boy of parents too poor to save him from a term in jail or the reformatory and who asked for fine-money or an appeal to higher powers for clemency, or a wastrel actor or actress "down and out" and unable to "get back to New York" and requiring his or her railroad fare wired prepaid, it was the dead wastrel actor or actress who needed a coffin and a decent form of burial.[5]

When Dreiser chided his brother for such acts, suggesting that these people should have saved their money, Dresser responded:

> Well, you know how it is, Thee. . . . When you're young and healthy like that you don't think. I know how it is; I'm that way myself. We all have a little of it in us. I have; you have. And anyhow youth's the time to spend money if you're to get any good of it, isn't it? Of course when you're old you can't expect much, but still I always feel as though I'd like to help some of these old people. . . . [W]hat's the use being so hard on people? We're all likely to get that way.[6]

Dresser could help individuals, but the sheer numbers of the dispossessed were numbing to contemplate. The development of a social conscience reflected in music was not something he thought about until he became aware of the massive scale of the problems the underprivileged faced. As he did, the memories of his own family's poverty certainly surfaced; at that point he began to question America's unwillingness to come to grips with the dreadful situation so close to home, far removed from the exotic scenes of wartime. The words and music he wrote on the subject of the Spanish-American War, with its shouting, blatant patriotism, had brought Dresser considerable public acclaim and financial reward. Soon he would realize that a growing social conscience reflected in music would make many listeners uneasy and possibly turn them against him. Such introspection, however, lay in the near future. For the time being, Dresser was content to enjoy the celebrity that the success of "Wabash" brought him and the traveling he was doing for his company.

One of these trips took him to Chicago in mid-March 1898 to the midwestern branch of Howley, Haviland and Company. Scheduled for an early morning appointment on the sixteenth at the Ayer building on Wabash Avenue, Dresser overslept and luckily missed his appointment. Shortly before eleven o'clock that morning, a gas jet came into contact with a roll of wallpaper in a third-floor storeroom of the Ayer building; a devastating fire rapidly followed, destroying the building. At least six people were killed, and nineteen others were still missing and presumed dead in the rubble of the seven-story building when Dresser wrote to Mary South recounting his close call. It is not known precisely with whom Dresser had his appointment, but piano and organ firms rented space on the first two floors of the Ayer building, and the National Music Company had offices on the fourth floor; it may have been with one of these companies that he had business.[7]

A short two weeks later Dresser was in Indiana vacationing at Mudlavia, a health resort located in the idyllically named Peaceful Valley, near Attica. Indiana was rich in its more than 150 mineral wells and springs, the waters of which were touted as possessing healing qualities. Mudlavia, French Lick, and West Baden Springs, the largest and most magnificent of the state's health resorts, attracted thousands of affluent guests each year from throughout the United States and beyond its borders. These spas provided their wealthy visitors with amenities that met their every need.

If one's goal was to unwind from the stress and tension of everyday life, then soaking in the warm waters, being covered and massaged with "health-restoring" mud, or just being idle offered marvelously restorative powers. At Mudlavia, Dresser joined other guests in relaxing, exercising, drinking the pure springwater, and soaking in the resort's mud, which was fed by lithium springs and touted as the "greatest cure ever discovered for rheumatism, gout, stomach troubles & all diseases of the blood, nerves & skin."[8] Mudlavia's origins dated from 1884 when Samuel Story, a local worker who had been hired to dig some drainage ditches, discovered that the black mud in which he was working, combined with the springwater he drank to slake his thirst, "cured" his rheumatism. From that simple serendipitous discovery, the entire industry of the Mudlavia sanitarium grew, and it joined other Indiana health spas such as French Lick and West Baden Springs as resorts to which the wealthy class flocked. On 1 May 1891 the Indiana Springs Company opened an elegant new Mudlavia hotel, for which no expense was spared.

> Each room . . . was elegantly furnished in antique oak, heated by steam, and protected from fire by a fire alarm and waterworks system. A generating plant supplied the power for thousands of incandescent lights. In the hotel dining room, waiters and waitresses in starched outfits served meals prepared from food raised on the four-hundred-acre farm on the grounds of the hotel. Telegraph and telephone lines connected Mudlavia to the outside world.[9]

Guests could play tennis and croquet, participate in or listen to musical entertainments, attend chapel services, and merely forget about the outside world if they wished. Of course, the chief reason people came to Indiana's spas was to "cure" themselves of some ailment; the seemingly medicinal properties of the black mud and of the springwater, it was hoped, would accomplish that. To that end the sanitarium contained a "bathhouse that included bathing facilities with marble and onyx partitions, silver curtain rods from Germany, a mosaic floor of marble, and Tiffany windows. A blast furnace heated the . . . bathhouse, and the directors advertised that the air was exchanged in the whole building every five minutes."[10] Upon finishing their breakfast, some guests went to prepare themselves for their mud treatment. After disrobing in dressing rooms, they were taken into the men's or women's mud rooms "where attendants assisted them into a cot filled with four inches of hot mud infused with lithia water from the nearby mud lake and springs."[11]

Dresser, now weighing at least three hundred pounds, had traveled to Mudlavia to relax and to lose some weight through a combination of mud treatments and exercise. Approaching his destination in Warren County, southwest of Lafayette and close to his beloved Wabash River, he must have felt a sense of relief, knowing he could, for the moment, get away from the turmoil—no matter how rewarding—that celebrity had brought him. Leaving the Chicago and Indiana Coal Railway train at Attica, he had climbed into the Tally-ho, Mudlavia's stagecoach, while uniformed attendants took

Doug's Studio, Attica, Ind.

The Tally-ho, Mudlavia's stagecoach, in front of the hotel.

his luggage. Once he and his fellow guests had settled in the elegant carriage, the Tally-ho had taken them the four miles to Mudlavia.

Writing to South about his stay at the resort, Dresser exclaimed, "It takes two cart loads of mud to cover me. So you can imagine the excitement I am causing in this vicinity."[12] For the mud treatment,

> the attendant covered the guest completely with the hot mud until he or she was "simply a big and unsymmetrical bolus of black mud, with a head sticking out of one end of it." A rubber sheet topped the mud. For thirty to forty minutes the mummified guest rested and perspired, visited occasionally by a "sweat wiper." When the mud treatment ended, a warm shower washed away all traces of mud. Finally, a water massage in a private lithia bath followed by a stint in the cooling room left the guest with soft, glowing skin and, hopefully, fewer arthritic pains.[13]

In his letter to South, Dresser also wrote, "I walked four miles today & begin to think that I am a wonder indeed."[14] On one occasion he became a spokesman for the resort, quoted in a lengthy advertisement for it:

> After I've been in New York or Chicago for a while, I become soiled with a different kind of soil, and I long for mud, and become purified and strengthened and encouraged and gather new hope and new faith and new love for my fellowmen. Mudlavia is to my mind the gem of the Hoosier State. . . . When I am at Mudlavia, I wander out among the hills, I visit old rocky, rushing Pine Creek, and Buzzard's Roost and the Swimming Hole. . . . I cut sycamore canes on the Wabash to send to my friends on the Rialto. Mudlavia makes me young again and I think will bring out all that's good in a man, or a woman either, besides bringing out everything that's bad in a physical sense.[15]

The pleasures of Mudlavia, however, were short lived. During the middle of April Dresser traveled to Terre Haute for other pleasures. There the local-boy-made-good visited the Elks Club minstrel show at the Grand Opera House. In town the night before the show opened, Dresser "was in good humor" at an impromptu sing at the Elks Club, where he sat at the piano, his huge derriere hanging over the dainty piano stool. Accompanying himself, he "sang song after song while the Elks stood about him chewing tough ham sandwiches and enjoying his music."[16] "The Path That Leads the Other Way" and "Our Country, May She Always Be Right but Our Country Right or Wrong" were the new songs among those Dresser sang for his informal audience.[17]

A reporter for the *Terre Haute Evening Gazette* commented, "Mr. Dresser has not much of a voice, but he is such a man that his genial personality obviates entirely the necessity of a good voice to make his songs pleasing."[18] A reporter for the rival *Terre Haute Express* wrote about the same Elks Club impromptu affair, where Dresser "deposited his wealth of adipose tissue in one of the luxurious chairs" and "sang songs as touching as music could express and branched off into a rollicking 'coon' song [probably "You'se Just a Little Nigger, Still You'se Mine, All Mine"] which set all feet to stamping and faces smiling."[19] During that night, Dresser told reporters a bit about how he wrote songs, saying, "Yes, the power to write a sentimental song comes by spells. I must be in the right mood, or it is no use. I have tried and tried to study one out, but whenever I attempt and want to write a song, it is impossible. But when the humor seizes me I have not the least trouble, and it takes but a very short time to do it."[20]

Encouraging readers to get tickets for the minstrel show, the *Gazette* reporter added, "The costumes and stage settings will be gaudy and there is not much danger of any seats in the audience being left vacant."[21] The show was indeed an outstanding success, and both nights large crowds applauded wildly at its patriotic nature. The first act ended in an especially dramatic fashion, with curtains parting to reveal an image of the *Maine* as a chorus sang "The Stars and Stripes Forever." One paper reported that "the stars and stripes were waved from the stage while thousands of miniature flags were thrown from the gallery and went sailing through the house in all directions." Dresser, in attendance for the first night's performance, "occupied a seat in one of the boxes and applauded as lustily as any of the rest."[22]

During the late spring and early summer months, Dresser continued his travels, drumming up business for Howley, Haviland and Company's recent publications, recruiting professional singers to perform the songs, and, in general, looking out for the welfare of the firm. "Wabash" continued to sell extremely well. From New York City Dresser wrote to South: "The 'Wabash' is still the great hit of the day. Our sales this week up to date [11 August 1898] have reached nearly 10,000 copies. So you see that as much of [a] chestnut as it really is, the song is selling just the same."[23]

Meanwhile, sometime during this year, Howley, Haviland and Company moved to larger quarters at 1260–66 Broadway (at Thirty-second Street), where it remained until 1900. The firm's need for more space, and for newer, up-to-date furnishings that would reflect its increasing success, anticipated moves other publishers would make during the first decade of the new century. The industry would continue a gradual northward move "to follow the center of the theatre district."[24]

On 28 December 1898, after a courtship of six years, twenty-seven-year-old Theodore Dreiser finally married Sara Osborne White, affectionately nicknamed "Jug." They remained married for forty-three years, although Dreiser left his wife on a number of occasions, and the two were permanently separated by around 1914. What Dresser thought about the marriage is unknown. In 1894 he had expressed reservations about his brother's thoughts of marrying. Then, of course, Dreiser had been younger and only beginning to make a mark for himself. It is not known if the passing of four years made a difference in Dresser's estimation of Jug, although Dreiser felt his brother never really cared for her. Dresser was too much the gentleman to ever openly express any negative feelings he may have harbored about this sister-in-law, though. The correspondence that survives between the brothers shows that Dresser was always an exemplar of courtesy where Jug was concerned. If Dreiser's perception that Jug was "rather amused by [Dresser, but didn't understand] the least thing in connection with his life or the character of the stage" is correct, perhaps Dresser, too, intuitively felt that lack of understanding and ultimately decided that the two would always have a polite but wary relationship.[25]

During January 1899 Dresser heard that his youngest sister, Claire "Tillie" Dreiser Gormley, who had moved to Arizona to improve her health, was in financial straits and wanted to return to the East Coast. Writing her on 31 January, Dresser told her he was in "bad shape. Have had two attacks of the 'grippe' & feel bad." Typically, though, he was more concerned about his sister's well-being than he was with his own health and sent her twenty-five dollars, adding "as soon as you are able to travel I will bring you to Rochester [where father Johann Paul Dreiser was then living] unless you improve so much that it will be better to remain [in Phoenix]. . . . I am ready to send you a ticket to come on the moment you say the word."[26] Dresser's siblings knew they could call on him for help; at times their readiness to do so amounted to taking advantage of his generous nature.

CHAPTER 20

A "Sister" Discovered, More Fame, and Hints of Change

During the summer of 1899, Louise Kerlin, a twenty-year-old singer from Evansville, Indiana, traveled with her husband to Chicago to the branch office of Howley, Haviland and Company, then located in the Masonic Temple. She had been a professional singer for about two years and was looking for new material for her performances. Raymond Hubbell, a song plugger for the firm, took her to a practice room and played for her two new Paul Dresser songs—"In Good Old New York Town" and "There's Where My Heart Is Tonight." Impressed with Kerlin's rendition of them, Hubbell suggested she talk with Dresser, who was in Chicago that day. Kerlin, of course, knew of Dresser from the celebrity of "On the Banks of the Wabash, Far Away" and had sung one of his "coon" songs in her performances, but she had never met him. Entering Dresser's office, Kerlin remembered "thinking at the time that I had never seen such a fat man."[1] Hubbell made the introductions and remarked that Kerlin had just tried out some of Dresser's songs.

Dresser had met any number of singers who had performed his music and long ago lost count of the bright-eyed ingenues who hoped to become stars through their contacts with important people like himself. Nevertheless, he engaged Kerlin in small talk, planning to usher her out of his office shortly, claiming busyness. When he found out she was from Evansville, however, his ears perked up. What memories he still had about his days there! He pressed her for more information: "Any relation to 'Billy' Kerlin, who ran an engine

Univ. of Southern Indiana Special Collections and University Archives, Tom Mueller Collection.

Jack Gardner, Louise Kerlin Dresser, and Jack Lait in Evansville, 1909.

on the [Evansville and Terre Haute] Railroad?" Louise: "He was my father."[2] Astounded at meeting the daughter of one of his childhood heroes, Dresser gave her his full attention. He had, he told her, worked aboard one of Billy Kerlin's trains a long time ago as a candy butcher, selling candy, smokes, and newspapers. Her father had befriended him, showing him great kindness—something he had scarcely ever gotten from his own father—and he had never forgotten Billy Kerlin. Now it was too late to repay that kindness directly, for Billy Kerlin had been killed in a railroad accident six years earlier.

By this time Dresser's attitude toward Louise Kerlin had changed from one of polite indifference to attentive interest. She represented a reconnection to that wonderful time of his early maturity. But did she have any real sort of singing voice? "Will you sing the 'Wabash'?" Dresser asked.[3] Hubbell sat down at the piano to accompany the nervous youngster. As Hubbell played the brief introduction, Kerlin took a deep breath and then began, " 'Round my Indiana homestead wave the cornfields." Not only did she sing "Wabash," but she added the two new songs she had tried out in the practice room. Hearing Kerlin sing convinced Dresser that she had real abilities as a performer. She did not just sing the music but became one with the sentiment and word of what he had written. There was certainly no superficiality in her interpretations. Not a good poker player, Dresser could not hide the fact that he was deeply moved. When Kerlin finished singing, "Paul's face was wet with tears and he got out of his chair, crossed over to the piano, and took me in his arms." The emotion of the moment spread to all those in the room—Kerlin, her husband, and Hubbell; before long, all were in tears. Kerlin and Dresser began an animated conversation, with Dresser asking "a million questions" about Kerlin's life.[4]

"Suddenly [Dresser] wheeled around in his chair and called a number on the telephone." Speaking with the drama editor of the *Chicago Tribune*, Dresser told him, "I just want you to know that my kid sister, Louise Dresser, is here in Chicago and is opening on the 'Masonic Roof' in a few weeks. I didn't want her to go on the stage, but she went anyway. She's been calling herself Louise Kerlin, but from now on she is Louise Dresser."[5] What Dresser had told the *Tribune* reporter about Kerlin's appearance onstage in Chicago was not true, but Dresser then called the Masonic Roof Garden, a fine vaudeville theater in the city, talked with John J. Murdock, a personal friend, and told him he "wanted an opening for his sister—and he got it."[6] Turning back to Kerlin, Dresser exclaimed, "Your father was an idol of mine when I was a boy. If there is anything I can do for his girl to help her make a name for herself, it's done right now."[7]

Kerlin was absolutely flabbergasted because "[Dresser] hadn't asked my consent, how I felt about it, and the two men in the room were completely ignored. It was his idea, his way of thanking my father and none of us had anything to do with it."[8] Dresser swore everyone in the room to secrecy about what he had done. Edward Dreiser, Dresser's youngest brother, who was in Chicago at that time attempting to make a career for himself in the theater, was let in on the secret and approved of Dresser's actions. From that point Louise Dresser became a stellar performer, and by the time she left vaudeville for motion pictures she was a headliner, making more than seventeen hundred dollars a week.

* * *

On 21 July 1899, just around the time Louise Kerlin became Louise Dresser, Robert Ingersoll, the outspoken, passionate orator and political leader, died. Paul Dresser had first heard Ingersoll speak at the Evansville Opera House in the early 1880s, at some point had met him, and had become friends with him. Upon hearing of Ingersoll's death, Dresser moved to the piano, intending to write a musical tribute to his friend. Dresser told a reporter, "I started in like this:

> 'Good-by, Bob, I knew you well;
> For men like you there'll be no hell'

Then I intended to run in something to the effect that I didn't believe as he did, but I skipped that just for the time and drummed out:

> 'The God you scorned so everywhere,
> Was good to you here—he'll be good to you there.' "

Dresser was interrupted, then could not finish his tribute. This song was going to be so different from his mother, home, and love effusions that he was not certain how to continue.[9]

In the meantime, people continued to embrace "Wabash" as a musical sensation, a phenomenon that was now going into its third year.

> All the hand organs in the country had taken it up, and at the same time all the young women who could sing and many of them who couldn't sing were pounding the life out of it on the pianos and the melodeons, and the concert hall people were bawling themselves hoarse with it on the stage. Men were whistling it, and so were boys, and for a while it was the only air one heard from morning till night. It was catchy, and it kept running in the heads of the people. At the Indianapolis opera house Sousa's band played it one evening. Former President [Benjamin] Harrison, who was in a box, arose and sang the words of the chorus, and the entire audience joined in with him. William Jennings Bryan got a cold dinner on one occasion by waiting to hear the author play it for him nine consecutive times. It has been played and replayed, and sung and resung, but the pathos is in it still.[10]

Even allowing for more than a little exaggeration in this account, the fact of the matter is that "Wabash" *was* immensely popular throughout the nation. Its success sometimes brought to Dresser unwanted attention and requests from people who were convinced they had a winning poem that, if set to the proper music, would guarantee them a fortune. Dresser received one bit of doggerel that dealt with a mother who had abandoned her starving baby. Food was available but beyond the tot's reach. The attempted rhyme of "message" with "sausage" was but one of the poet's failings:

> On the shelf there lay life's message—
> A sandwich made of sausage—A savior for this tiny little elf;
> But the baby slipped and fell—There is little else to tell—
> She was dead all through; the sandwich on the shelf.[11]

Another offering was from a temperance advocate who sent Dresser thirteen poems on the subject of drinking. Dresser claimed that he responded, "Dear Madam—Your poem received and contents carefully noted. I was just getting over a beautiful spree, but your verses have driven me to drink again. I am drunk and glad of it."[12] This sounds more than a bit fanciful, as if Dresser wished that he had written such a response.

Even as Dresser was enjoying his time in the sun, he and many others were not prescient enough to realize that nostalgic utterances, such as those seen in "Wabash," would soon be considered out of fashion. Not yet in the song limelight, but making steady progress toward it, was ragtime, a new kind of music that piano players had introduced to mass audiences for the first time six years earlier at the World's Columbian Exposition in Chicago. In 1899 John Stark published Scott Joplin's "Maple Leaf Rag" in Sedalia, Missouri. While Joplin's was not the first ragtime music to be published, the piano piece attracted a large audience. In the same year Joseph E. Howard wrote the first truly successful ragtime-like song, "Hello! Ma Baby." With the catchy, syncopated rhythms of ragtime, coupled with the breezy slang of Ida Emerson's "Hello! ma baby, Hello! ma honey, Hello! ma ragtime gal," the song titillated the ears of a wide public and began the fad for this new kind of song.[13] Yet the year 1899 also saw M. Witmark and Son's publication of the waltz "My Wild Irish Rose," a sedate song that achieved substantial success. For the moment, both styles, so opposite from each other, could attain popularity side by side. Before long, however, the sentiments and rhythmic sounds of ragtime would prevail, sweeping away the musical outpourings of Dresser and so many others, making their utterances sound quaint and old-fashioned.

Meanwhile, the year 1900, the last year of the nineteenth century, witnessed turmoil in the entertainment industry. The 1900–1901 theater season was marked by "the outbreak of labor hostilities between vaudeville actors and theater managers."[14] In mid-March 1900 a dozen vaudeville managers met for three days in Benjamin Franklin Keith's private office in Boston. During these secret meetings the managers discussed the escalating salaries of vaudeville performers and decided to form an alliance "for mutual protection and to regulate the dates and salaries of performers."[15] Continuing their discussions throughout the spring, and growing in strength to about sixty managers who controlled more than sixty vaudeville houses, the group, led by Keith and Edward F. "Ned" Albee, formed the Association of Vaudeville Managers (AVM).

The major bone of contention between the AVM and the actors was the 5 percent fee that the AVM proposed to charge as a commission for booking performers into its chain of theaters. Already paying their own agents 10 percent in commissions and tipping other workers in the theater, actors were outraged with the AVM's proposal, considering another commission to be nothing but a kickback. At the same time, they knew they would be frozen out of some of the best theaters in the country if they failed to pay the charge. In mid-June eight actors, led by George Fuller Golden, formed their own group that, they hoped, would offer members protection from the demands of the AVM. Golden and his colleagues chose the name White Rats for their union, modeling it after the Water Rats and Terriers in England and pointing out the somewhat obvious fact that rats was the word "star" spelled backward—an indication of the personal qualities and talents of its members. A *New York Dramatic Mirror* article stated:

> The Water Rats of England, to which all the prominent performers belong, is a very influential body, and the White Rats of America hope to become like them in time. Just now the Rats have no intention of worrying the big vaudeville cat, but it is barely possible that if she catches a few of them the others may make arrangements to trim her claws.[16]

In a mere month and a half the White Rats grew to include more than 150 entertainers—Dresser, George M. Cohan, Eddie Foy, and minstrels Lew Dockstader and George Thatcher among the best known of the members. Even former heavyweight boxing champion Gentleman Jim Corbett, who had frequently toured in vaudeville acts, was a member. By midwinter 1901 the club numbered more than five hundred and had admitted women to its membership: Lillian Russell and May Irwin were among the first Ratlambs, an awkward appellation soon changed to White Stars. The White Rats, through the power of its numbers, and in its decision that no member could accept an engagement unless it had been made through the White Rats Vaudeville Agency, became a major bargaining force for actors. Hostilities between the White Rats and the AVM continued to grow as the White Rats became an ever bigger, ever more influential union.

CHAPTER 21

Masses, Classes, and Asses

In early 1900 Paul Dresser contributed his thoughts about composing songs to the book *Hits and Hitters*, published in New York by Herbert H. Taylor. Subtitled *Secrets of the Music Publishing Business*, the book consisted of interviews with the "March King" John Philip Sousa and songwriters Harry Von Tilzer, Charles K. Harris, and Dresser, among others. The interviews, however, were largely self-promotion pieces, leading a disappointed reviewer to write, "If there are secrets given away in the writings of these ladies and gentlemen they are so unimportant as to be almost imperceptible."[1]

At some point this year Howley, Haviland and Company became Howley, Haviland and Dresser, a wise move on the part of Pat Howley and Fred Haviland.[2] While they knew that Dresser possessed little business acumen, both recognized the value of having his name on the masthead. Now Howley and Haviland boasted for all to see that their firm had one of the greatest composers of popular song in their stable as a partner and writer.

To say that Dresser and his songs were the darlings of the popular-music world is certainly accurate. But members of the classical-music establishment have nearly always been antipathetic, if not downright hostile, toward popular music and its ready acceptance by the masses. The critic John Sullivan Dwight long ago took to task the "monster" concerts of Patrick S. Gilmore, railing against the massed orchestra and chorus at the 1869 Peace Jubilee as "a plan so vain-glorious in the conception, so unscrupulously advertised and glorified before it had begun, and having so much claptrap mixed up with what there was good in its program."[3] Then in Dresser's day the *New York Times* music critic W. J. Henderson argued that the one way to raise the standards of music in America was to

> abolish the music halls in which vulgar tunes set to still more vulgar words provide the musical milk upon which the young of the masses are reared. Abolish the diabolical street pianos and hand organs which disseminate these vile tunes in all directions and which reduce the musical taste of the children in the residence streets to the level of that of the Australian bushman, who thinks noise and rhythm are music. Abolish the genuine American brand of burlesque . . . and the genuine American "comic opera." . . . Abolish the theatre orchestra which plays the music hall stuff. . . . Abolish those newspapers which degrade art by filling their columns with free advertising of so-called musical performers who are of the genus freak.[4]

Sometime during 1900 Dresser gave an interview to a reporter from *Metropolitan Magazine*. In the ensuing article, "Making Songs for the Million," the writer mentioned that Dresser had boasted of having taken piano lessons for only six months, had talked of teaching himself about the "science of music," and had joked that his piano teacher had entered a convent, probably in dismay at the kind of music he composed. In the interview, Dresser admitted that his songs

> are in no way wonderful creations, viewed from the standpoint of high-class music. But they seem to please the masses, and the classes don't bother me much. I suppose it's a nice thing to write high-class music, but this idea of starving to death and then having a monument put over your grave as a kind of offering to your genius don't [*sic*] take my fancy. A nice broiled steak with plenty of bread and butter and coffee makes the most substantial monument to a starving genius.[5]

Annoyed to no end with Dresser's comments, a writer responded vituperatively:

> What can be done to advance musical appreciation in America when we have Mr. Dresser and others like him to contend with? The problem is indeed grave. . . . While Mr. [Henry Lee] Higginson is slowly raising up on golden foundations a love for the divine art [with the Boston Symphony Orchestra], the author of the "Blue and the Gray" and scores of other song writers of his type are flooding this country with their "yellow back" music. While such serious composers as Horatio Parker, Edward MacDowell, Arthur Foote, Dudley Buck, . . . and others, musicians who have devoted years of conscientious study at home and abroad to their art; who never stoop to write trash for the sake of making a hit, are slowly educating musical taste, so called musicians who can perhaps, play a little from ear on the piano, have audaciously intruded into the field of composition where they are as much out of place as a "bull in a china shop" and are piling up the counters of our music stores with "topical songs" and Sousaesque "two-steps." They are doing all they possibly can to retard musical culture. . . . We can sympathize with Mr. Dresser's music teacher. Can nothing be done to counteract the effect of these topical songs which are debauching our musical taste? They go from one side of this broad country to the other, so quickly do Americans follow the crowd in their eagerness to hum whistle and sing "the latest." In a few weeks the song is dead and another in its place, but in those few weeks the sale of some trashy "coon song" has exceeded that of Franz or Schubert in a lifetime.[6]

One can imagine Dresser's own annoyance at such criticism. After all, he had on a number of occasions admitted that his compositions were not of the finer sort, that he wrote what the public wanted to hear. Nevertheless, this sort of criticism rankled him, for deep within his being he wanted to be accepted as a legitimate composer in spite of his technical limitations.

Dresser's annoyance turned to anger in October when a writer for the *Syracuse (N.Y.) Post Standard* took him and other composers to task for their sentimental, nostalgic songs. The article was only one of many that pleaded for the education of the public toward a better class of music. With his response to the paper, Dresser sent the editor "two or three songs of mine that are considered by musicians 'higher grade music.' " Not mentioning the titles of these songs, he continued angrily:

> Why write them when so many high class musicians are out of work and out of funds at the same time? . . . Bread and butter is what we are all after and it must be bitter consolation to the spirit of a dead one to see a grand monument of granite towering towards the sky over its rotten remains and at the same time to know that death perhaps was brought about through lack of the necessaries of life and in many cases, starvation and all because he would write high class music.[7]

Dresser went on bitterly: "Go home and try to sing your babies (if you have any) to sleep with 'The Palms,' 'The Holy City,' Gounod's 'Ave Maria' or the Toreador song from 'Carmen' and see if your little babies don't wish their high class editorial papa in Haides [*sic*]." Concluding his long diatribe, Dresser admonished the editor, "I write for the masses, not the classes and at no time for asses."[8]

Clearly, Dresser was infuriated by the criticism, but such judgment was growing louder and more frequent in the comments and writings of those in the world of "high" culture as they tried to come to grips with the phenomenon of a rapidly growing popular culture—a culture that was already swamping the "better" class of the arts in its wake. Dresser's slightly older fellow Hoosier, James Whitcomb Riley, faced a dilemma similar to Dresser's. He wanted to be judged a great writer beyond his dialect poetry. Yet that is precisely the sort of writing his audiences clamored for. In his acceptance of the kind of expression he knew to be his strength, Riley was clearly more temperate than Dresser when he was quoted shortly before Dresser's interview:

> I would rather have the assurance that I had pleased the rank and file of the people, the common run, than to please all the erudites in the world. The good Father of us all made the

> world for the generality of mankind, for the great consensus, and not for the few.[9]

On Tuesday, 8 November 1900, Doubleday and Page published Theodore Dreiser's first novel, *Sister Carrie*. Certainly Dreiser had eagerly anticipated this major event. The protracted negotiations that surrounded *Carrie*, however, could only have left him with a

Van Pelt-Dietrich Library Center, Univ. of Pa.

Emma Dreiser, Paul Dresser's second eldest sister and a model for Carrie Meeber in Theodore Dreiser's *Sister Carrie*.

bitter taste in his mouth. Dreiser had had to force his publisher to honor its original contract with him. Novelist Frank Norris, a reader for Doubleday and Page, wrote to Dreiser in late May that *Carrie* "was the best novel I have read in M.S. since I have been reading for the firm, and . . . it pleased me as well as any novel I have read in any form, published or otherwise."[10] After reading the novel, however, publisher Walter Page had other ideas, writing to Dreiser, "We are sure that the publication of *Sister Carrie* as your first book would be a mistake. It would identify you in the minds of the public with the use of this sort of material; and we think it would require years and a long list of other different books by you to remove the impression."[11] In part, "this sort of material" referred to Carrie's rise to success in spite of having been the mistress of two men. In not punishing his heroine for her immorality, Dreiser had rebuffed the views of the genteel tradition and had in his realism rebelled against the artificial, but literarily accepted, mores expressed in the majority of novels written before *Sister Carrie*. Although Dreiser succeeded in forcing Doubleday and Page to publish his first novel, the toll of that effort and its meager rewards were great on his psyche, forcing him ever deeper into despondency, a depression from which he would not recover until late spring 1903, thanks largely to Dresser's intervention.

In late November 1900 Charles Hoyt, whose *A Tin Soldier* provided Dresser with the opportunity to test his abilities as a singer and an actor, died at his home in Charlestown, New Hampshire, at the age of forty. Bereft over the death of his second wife in childbirth two years earlier and manifesting increasing mental instability, Hoyt was committed to a private asylum in July 1900 but had recently been released so that he could recuperate at his home. A writer stated that Hoyt "contrived to combine the best features of vaudeville, a pleasing element of opera, a hint of burlesque, and a wonderful display of the knowledge of human nature."[12] More recently, another said, "No American played a more important role in turning farce-comedy into musical comedy."[13] In November 1891 Hoyt's *A Trip to Chinatown* reached the New York stage, where it played for 657 performances, a record not broken for nearly twenty-five years. One of the most popular stage entertainments of the decade, it is said to have made a half million dollars in its first five years.[14] The popularity of Hoyt's work was astounding. In the year he died, fourteen of his plays were performed, and most were touring throughout the United States. In their appeal to many Americans, Hoyt's plays constituted a theatrical equivalent of Dresser's songs. Soon, however, the public's appetite would turn to new sorts of theatrical and musical expression, leaving the Hoyts and the Dressers behind.

On Christmas Day, Johann Paul Dreiser died in Rochester, New York, at age seventy-nine. Some of the Dreiser children fondly remembered their father as a deeply religious man. Theodore Dreiser's view of his father's faith, however, was less than charitable; agreeing that his father was a religious man, he felt nonetheless that Johann Paul had followed his faith so fanatically, so unquestioningly, that his family had suffered as a consequence. At the same time, he also had tender memories of his father, with his frail, "grasshopper" appearance, "his peculiarly German hair and beard combed and brushed as much like those of Rembrandt's old men as may be," wearing a derby hat that belonged to Dresser as well as some of Dresser's clothing that had been altered to fit his thin frame.[15] Dresser, never really close to his father since the end of the Sullivan days, wrote simply to Jesse Rector the day after Christmas: "Just a line to say that father died Christmas morning at the age of almost 80 years."[16] After his trials by fire in Sullivan, old Johann Paul's life and thoughts had turned increasingly inward. God came to preoccupy his daily existence, removing him in thought, if not in deed, from Sarah and the children's lives so often that at times they were scarcely aware of his presence. Johann Paul was with them physically, but he could not give his large tribe the emotional succor they needed.

What hopes, what dreams had young Johann Paul and an even younger Sarah shared in their early lives together, only to abandon them? In some ways Johann Paul Dreiser and Sarah Mary Schänäb had become more separate from each other by staying together in their marriage. Johann Paul was clearly more comfortable with life as it *had* been, never accepting or understanding his children's ways or their cavalier attitudes toward the faith. While Sarah took an amoral stance toward her children's faults, *her* emotional attachment to them sometimes foisted upon them feelings of guilt or unworthiness if they failed her. As in all families, the Dreiser children carried some of the baggage of their parents and in turn handed some of it down to their own issue. Now the protective shield was gone for the Dreiser sisters and brothers as Johann Paul, a widower for a decade, joined his wife Sarah in eternal life, buried beside her in Chicago's St. Boniface Cemetery.

Sometime in 1901 Dresser wrote a poem about his father's death and reunion with Sarah. Although he never composed music for the words, the text expressed Dresser's love for both parents and their feelings for each other:

I stood beside the grave
Of my dear old angel mother,
For ten long years in silence,
Had she waited for another.
Silent, silent, and alone.
Beneath the watchful eye
Of God, she knew her mate was coming,
In the bye and bye.

I saw him lowered tenderly,
Inched close down by her side,
It seemed that they were starting out,
Again as groom and bride.
I shed no tears but almost smiled
I seemed again a boy.
And felt, that with the grave began
Their everlasting joy.[17]

With their parents gone, Dresser and his siblings represented the generation of Dreisers on the front lines of mortality.

The new year began with continued hostilities between the Association of Vaudeville Managers (AVM) and the White Rats. The AVM held to its position of demanding a commission from the players, while "Big Chief Rat" George Fuller Golden succinctly summed up the Rats' philosophy: "Why should a man pay for the privilege of working?"[18] Reaching an impasse in negotiations for a satisfactory resolution of their differences, the vaudeville union staged a walkout at matinees in eastern theaters the AVM controlled. The first day of the strike—Thursday, 21 February—closed or curtailed the operations of Benjamin Franklin Keith's houses in

New York, Boston, Philadelphia, and Providence, Rhode Island. The effect of the strike was instantaneous. No White Rat appeared on any of those stages, and the theater managers scurried about trying to cobble together something that might substitute for the regularly scheduled show. Even though the best acts were not onstage, thus depriving audiences of the finest in popular entertainment, the sympathies of many lay with the Rats. In spite of their superior numbers, they were the Davids, out to defeat the Goliath theater circuits. The vaudevillians were about to win the initial battle between the two groups, but they would lose the war in the end. Acts of protest continued sporadically until the middle of March, when the AVM finally rescinded its policy of exacting booking commissions from the vaudevillians. The *New York Dramatic Mirror* held that combinations of any kind were an anathema to theater, but it also said, "If there be any combination to be commended it is that of the actors or performers in self defense against the aggressions of those wholly concerned in the theatre's material interests."[19]

During the strike, Edward F. "Ned" Albee of the AVM suggested to the newspapers that "the strikers were mostly inferior acts who had trouble getting regular bookings, and that the leaders were political agitators."[20] Keith echoed Albee's sentiment: "All this trouble has been caused by agitators, irresponsible persons who are unable to get good work to do themselves, and who have stirred the other up to attempt a display of strength."[21] This was a common charge that management often leveled at dissenters in times of unrest. Still fresh in the memories of many Americans were recollections of the psychological and physical wounds caused by the violence in the Haymarket Riot of 1886 and the Homestead Strike of 1892. The Pullman Strike of 1894 was even more vivid. All were events for which anarchists and political agitators were blamed. Were actors less likely to have similar troublemakers in their midst? In coupling the act of dissent with anarchy, Albee hoped the public would take management's side. The Rats countered that their organization was "not controlled by Anarchists nor agitators, but by level-headed, God-fearing men."[22]

Although Dresser was no longer active on the stage, he was a White Rat, in sympathy with the demands of the group. He supported its cause in the best way he could—by performing his own songs in White Rat benefit programs. Such programs greatly aided the Rats, providing them with money they could use to pay expenses. And that cache could be sizable. During the week of 16 March 1901, for example, benefit programs brought more than twenty thousand dollars into the Rats' treasury.[23] Having already sent a couple of companies on the road, the Rats entertained even more ambitious plans, such as sending a White Rat Minstrel Show on tour with the backing of Dresser, George Thatcher, and other important entertainers. By May the Rats were financially able to honor their esteemed leader, Golden. Golden's Golden Jubilee, a gala evening with performances and presentations by more than fifty members, including Dresser, Marie Dressler, Tony Pastor, and Gentleman Jim Corbett, realized more than nine thousand dollars for Golden. The financial euphoria the vaudeville union enjoyed probably made it less vigilant than it should have been, for the uneasy truce between the AVM and the White Rats that had been declared in mid-March proved to be short lived. "By the end of the season, Albee's crafty behind-the-scenes maneuvering reduced the White Rats to token opposition."[24]

In late March Dresser was grieved to hear of the death of Margaret Catherine Rector, the young daughter of Julia and Jesse Rector. As Dresser's surrogate family, the Rectors had always been generous with their affection for him; they were down-to-earth people and gentle reminders of the world Dresser had come from, so different from the many hangers-on, the would-be friends who inhabited his world of celebrity. He could always count on them to keep him grounded. Responding to the tragic news, Dresser wrote movingly to his "Dear friends Jesse & Julia" back in Linton, Indiana:

> Of course you know & I know that every reference to the terrible ordeal you have gone through brings a heart ache & each heart ache a tear—Cut down in the flowerhood of life. . . . I can appreciate fully your sorrow & your grief—The home will be more lonely—for a face is missing, one of your own flesh & blood—One that you nursed for many years. . . . Every turn will remind you of the fact that she has gone. . . . Be brave—for God knows who to take & when to take them.[25]

Tragedy of a national kind struck that summer. For the third time in only three and a half decades, an assassin's bullet killed a president. Although Dresser was nearly seven when John Wilkes Booth shot Abraham Lincoln in 1865, the youngster recalled only seeing pictures of, or hearing people talk about, the railway funeral cars enshrouded with black crepe. James A. Garfield's assassination was a different matter. Shot on 2 July 1881, the president lingered for two and a half months before succumbing to his wounds. During that period newsprint vultures kept their deathwatch ever before the public. Dresser would certainly have followed these accounts as he traveled as a comic singer in Chicago, Louisville, and New York during that summer.

When Garfield finally died on Monday, 19 September, the entertainment world expected it. Now, on this Friday, 6 September 1901, the news was more shocking. Less than two weeks before the twentieth anniversary of Garfield's death and for the third time in Dresser's life, a president had been assassinated. Leon Czolgosz had gunned down William McKinley as he was welcoming visitors to the Pan-American Exposition in Buffalo, New York.

CHAPTER 22

Jimmy Bulger

In November 1901 Paul Dresser received news of a boyhood acquaintance's troubles, which must have prompted vivid memories of his own childhood and youthful indiscretions—indiscretions that if not checked would have taken him down the wrong path. Little more than thirty years before, Johann Paul and Sarah Dreiser and their clan had counted James and Mary Bulger and their children among their friends in Sullivan, Indiana. Both families had bought provisions at William Griffith's general store, had attended the little Catholic church in town, and had shared poverty at one time or another; fathers of both families had little patience with children who got out of line and had sons who would soon get into serious trouble.

The Bulgers had come to Sarah's aid when she and three of her children returned to Sullivan in 1879. Now the Bulgers' second-oldest son, thirty-four-year-old Jimmy, was in Dannemora Prison in New York State, convicted of murder and sentenced to be executed on 8 December. When Jimmy Bulger's plight came to the attention of Dresser, he wrote to other members of the Dreiser family about the case. Bulger was now using the name Whitey Sullivan, perhaps in an effort to keep from his parents news of his life of crime. His first name was a wry contradiction of his flaming red hair, his new surname a likely nod to the town of his youth. Bulger received a stay of execution, and for nearly the next year and a half Dresser involved himself in the case, proposing a commutation of the death sentence to life in prison if new evidence warranted that action.

Three years earlier, perhaps with some knowledge of a previous incident of crime in Bulger's life, or possibly as a kind of reflection on his own past, Dresser had written a song recounting the story of a young man who, ignoring motherly advice, "wandered down the path that leads the other way. / He simply drifted from the fold, poor lad and went astray." The hopeful narrator of the song—perhaps Dresser himself—continues, "The Shepherd tho' may find him yet and bring him back some day."[1] Dresser had been blessed with a number of shepherds—his mother and Father Herman Alerding among them—who had rescued him at various times. Was it too late for a shepherd to rescue Jimmy Bulger?

The next year, 1902, began with acclaim from those whose approbation meant a great deal to Dresser. On 10 January Dresser was in Terre Haute for a guest appearance with the Vandalia-Pennsylvania Minstrels at the Grand Opera House. At noon on the day of the performance, and in spite of the cold, a big street parade "headed by a guard of Company B. and the V.-P. band" wound its way through the streets of downtown Terre Haute. After the dress rehearsal "to acquaint the boys with the costumes and with the plan of how the big show is to come off," the cast was free to relax for a couple of hours before curtain time.[2] As the curtains parted at eight o'clock, a sizable chorus entered, all of its members dressed in Vandalia-Pennsylvania uniforms and each carrying red and green railroad signal lights. Once the chorus members had taken their seats and the applause for them had died down, the end men began their routine, telling the latest outrageous minstrel jokes and funny stories about the city and people of Terre Haute. The audience howled with laughter, especially when locals were selected for the end men's skewering. Nostalgic melodies, "coon" songs, instrumental solos, duets, buck-and-wings, skits, and many more jokes kept the crowd in good humor. A Pan-American prize drill by Company B, under command of a Captain Thomas, concluded the entertainment.

While the audience members loved the evening, greeting the cast "with frequent and repeated applause and encores," most of them were there to see and hear Dresser, and they were not disappointed. "Coming before the audience Mr. Dresser told of his birth in Terre Haute and spoke of his visit to the old homestead during his stay in the city. He said that he always had a kind feeling for Terre Haute and there was no place that gave him more pleasure to visit."[3] The beaming and ample Dresser then delighted the crowd by singing three of his most recent songs. The newest of these was "Way Down in Old Indiana," a song that Richard Jose, an acclaimed countertenor and foremost Dresser interpreter, had premiered at Keith's Theatre in Boston only a week before. Many in the Terre Haute audience certainly were moved by Dresser's recollection of "The scenes of a lifetime the best; / [The place] when I am gone it is there I would rest; / Way down in old Indiana."[4] Dresser followed this bit of nostalgia with his generic war song "Mr. Volunteer," for whom "Many a mother's heart will ache," and to whom "Uncle Sam will take off his hat."[5]

Ever the consummate performer, the greatly loved Terre Haute boy saved his best and most sentimental song for last. In "I Just Want to Go Back and Start the Whole Thing Over," Dresser sang of his desire to return to the homely roots of his youth, to "the old rail fence," "to the old red barn . . . all covered o'er with clinging vine," to be "back among the nodding fields of timothy and clover," "to the golden days of June," "to the resting place of mother on the hill."[6] The forty-three-year-old little boy, housed in the extravagant frame of a three-hundred-pound, elegantly attired man, led many in the audience to tears. A cynic might accuse Dresser of milking his audience with bathetic emotionalism, and to be sure, he knew what appealed to listeners. But the sincerity of his musical sentiments were mirrored in his personal letters often enough to make one believe that his words were heartfelt and genuine. One can easily imagine both the thrill of the Terre Haute audience at Dresser's performance and how much he was moved by the repeated ovations he won. He had, after all, spoken directly to the hearts and feelings of his own people, his own Hoosiers, his own Terre Hauteans.

When he left the next morning to return to business in Chicago, Dresser praised the Vandalia-Pennsylvania "boys" and expressed his gratification for the acceptance of his new songs. A month later he sent a copy of "Way Down in Old Indiana" to the *Terre Haute Evening Gazette* together with a note expressing the sentiments that "my love for the State where I was born, and for the people who have been ever kind to me, gave me inspiration. Indiana to me is always a tender memory, because it means the home of my childhood." His optimistic disposition was as bright as the day star he mentioned as he continued his nostalgic and effusive review:

> The sun always seemed to shine brighter, the grass seemed more green and the people seemed more affectionate and loyal in the old fashioned way. While I have been away for many years, my heart was ever there, "Way Down in Old Indiana," where the tall sycamores grow, where the Wabash river flows[,] the place that gave to a nation such great men as Harrison, Hendricks, Voorhees, Martin, McDonald, Dick Thompson, Gen. Lew Wallace and James Whitcomb Ril[e]y, Maurice Thompson.[7]

Now, however, Dresser had other things to do. In addition to songwriting and his continuing work for Howley, Haviland and Dresser, he took on a new challenge. Musical pirates, breaking copyright laws, were making large sums of money, cheating publishers, composers, and authors out of their rightful share of profits from music sales. Dresser entered the fight against these thieves. Early April 1902 saw him traveling to Washington, D.C., to meet with Ohio senator Mark Hanna, Indiana senator Albert Beveridge, and Secretary of State John Hay. Dresser and other artists were seeking their support for copyright protection of American music beyond the nation's borders, especially in Canada and England, where breaches of American copyrights had been particularly blatant, and Dresser filed papers of record with the Department of State.[8] Two months later, at its annual meeting, the Music Publishers Association appointed Dresser a "committee of one to have in charge the subject of violation of American copyright music in London, England."[9] Dresser's specific charge was

> to represent the Association before the Secretary of State and such other Government Officials as to him seems appropriate for the purpose of securing such action as will relieve the Music Publishers of the United States from loss and annoyance occasioned by the unauthorized publication and sale of their copyright music in London, England.[10]

Records are silent regarding any outcome of Dresser's work here.

After the century turned, Dresser felt increasing pressure from his competitors and their new approaches to writing popular song. This was not the time for complacency. One of his rivals had for a long time won enthusiastic acclaim as part of a family act and was becoming well known in the early part of this new century as a song composer. His creations exuded the very jauntiness and breeziness that were becoming an important ingredient in a successful song. For the 1900–1901 season, George M. Cohan had expanded his family sketches and routines into *The Governor's Son,* a stage musical that played for two years. One of the songs in the musical was "Yankee Doodle Doings," a forerunner of the exuberant patriotic pieces for which Cohan would become famous.

Cohan had been in show business from the time he was a child, and now, already well known, he had rapidly climbed to the top of the entertainment world. In August 1902 an advertisement screamed out the news that Cohan and his family were being paid three thousand dollars for playing a one-week vaudeville engagement at the Masonic Temple Theatre in Chicago—the "Largest Weekly Salary Ever Paid to Any Act in the World."[11] Eight months later the Four Cohans opened at New York's Fourteenth Street Theatre in George's *Running for Office*. Both *The Governor's Son* and *Running for Office* were somewhat weak as musicals, betraying their origins as vaudeville routines, but Cohan, the composer, was giving voice to an exciting style of music, a language that would soon burst forth in "Give My Regards to Broadway" and "The Yankee Doodle Boy" (both in *Little Johnny Jones*, 1904).

Other serious competition in 1902 came from the song "Under the Bamboo Tree," which singers repeatedly interpolated into *The Wild Rose, Sally in Our Alley*, and *Alphonse and Gaston*, all top shows then playing in New York City. Bob Cole and John Rosamond Johnson's song became the darling of New York audiences. With its ragtime rhythms, its gentle but persuasive jaunty style, and its playful words, "Bamboo Tree" joined "At a Georgia Camp Meeting" and "Bill Bailey, Won't You Please Come Home?" as an important addition to the new kind of song that audiences were beginning to love.

Dresser's style of song, while rapidly becoming passé, was still an important staple in many performers' routines. During the fall of 1902, for example, Jose, who built a substantial career singing with minstrel troupes led by Lew Dockstader, with George Primrose and William West, and with George Thatcher, featured Dresser's new ballad "In Dear Old Illinois" in his performances on the East Coast. Throughout his long career Jose was an enthusiastic supporter and interpreter of Dresser songs, popularizing many of them, including "Your Mother Wants You Home, Boy (And She Wants You Mighty Bad)," "Calling to Her Boy Just Once Again," "Every Night There's a Light," "He Fought for the Cause He Thought Was Right," "I Wonder Where She Is Tonight," and "I'd Still Believe You True." His wife claimed that Jose "received a special salute from Teddy Roosevelt in 1898 as his Rough Riders, riding down Broadway on the way to Cuba, stopped to hear Jose sing Dresser's 'Goodbye, Dolly Gray' from an elevated platform." Grace M. Wilkinson, the author of a biography of Jose, *"Silver Threads among the Gold,"* wrote that this incident occurred in Tampa, Florida.[12] Whatever song Therese Jose and Grace Wilkinson were recalling, Dresser never wrote "Goodbye, Dolly Gray." The only Dresser song bearing "Goodbye" in the title was "Good Bye for All Eternity," written in 1899, a year after the Roosevelt incident supposedly happened.

Dresser spent some of his time during the early part of 1903 following the case of his old acquaintance Bulger, who was now back in the news. Bulger and four others had been convicted of breaking into the First National Bank of Cobleskill, New York, on 27 November 1900. During the attempted robbery, a night watchman had discovered the five thieves, and they had shot and killed him. Bulger, the first man to be placed on trial, had been convicted of murder and sentenced to death. The courts had stayed Bulger's original execution date, but it had since been rescheduled for 25 February 1903. Now there was talk of new evidence that would appear to provide Bulger with an alibi for the night of the murder.

On 2 February Dresser wrote to Senator Beveridge, his friend, on Bulger's behalf. Without passing judgment on Bulger—"I don't know just how guilty or how innocent he may be"—Dresser suggested to Beveridge that Bulger's sentence be commuted to life imprisonment: "He got into bad company . . . & his companions made him the scape goat—& from what I can learn the people of Schoharie [County, where the crime had taken place] would not object to a changing of the death sentence to life imprisonment."[13]

In the letter Dresser recalled that Bulger had been a schoolmate, a claim that doesn't hold up in the face of the evidence. Bulger, born around 1867, was some nine years younger than Dresser and would have been only about four when the Dreiser family left Sullivan in 1871 to return to Terre Haute. That Dresser knew the family is certain, but Bulger could not have been a schoolmate of his. Dresser added that Bulger's "father & mother were good people of the soil who lived up to the laws of God & Man.—The boy left home 19 years ago—They never saw him since tho Mother knows nothing of his trouble. His father & an oldest sister know of it: & the family today is very poor."[14] Theodore Dreiser recalled that Bulger "was occasionally horribly beaten by his father, who considered a heavy horsehide whip to be of more significance argumentatively than words."[15] Because Theodore was born after the Dreisers moved from Sullivan the first time in 1871, he would have been recalling this from their second stay in Sullivan when Dresser was no longer with the family—or perhaps his parents told him about such beatings. Apparently Dresser knew nothing about the elder Bulger's savagery.

Responding to Dresser's letter, Beveridge said he would "confer with the New York Senators about it right away."[16] Whether these actions had anything to do with the immediate deliberations on Bulger's fate is unknown, but the day before the scheduled execution, the governor of New York granted Bulger a stay for two weeks. Gov. Benjamin B. Odell, Jr., based his action on the claim of Rev. James B. Curry, pastor of St. James Roman Catholic Church in New York City, and others that "fourteen witnesses have been discovered . . . who, it is alleged, can swear to having seen Sullivan [i.e., Bulger] on the night of the murder . . . at a point too far from the scene of the crime to have made it possible for him to have been there."[17] Then on 10 March the governor continued the stay of execution for two weeks in order for the New York Supreme Court to act on an application for a new trial.[18]

All of this was to no avail; having heard the purported new evidence, the judges reaffirmed the death sentence, and Bulger was "executed with electricity" at Dannemora Prison at 11:38 A.M. on 24 March.[19] Upon hearing the news of Bulger's death, Dresser undoubtedly reflected on their two lives. Their fathers had been abusive in different ways. Bulger's father had administered savage beatings to his son, but Dresser's father was not given to such violence. Instead, Johann Paul Dreiser's abuse was of an emotional and psychological kind. Johann Paul had expected much from his eldest son, perhaps holding him to a higher standard than he did the younger children. Young Paul had disappointed the old man any number of times, perhaps out of sheer willfulness or perchance as a perverse way of seeking the affection and approbation old Johann Paul withheld from him. As he thought about Bulger's life and death, Dresser may have reviewed his own troubles with the law in the past: his arrest after the incident with Charley Kelley, his extended stay in jail after police arrested him for theft in 1876, and the arrest during his conflict with St. George Hussey in Montana.

As Dresser ruminated on these incidents and contemplated Bulger's fate, he may well have uttered, "There but for the grace of God go I." Dresser had indeed chosen the path that took him from the one Bulger had taken. Sometime after writing to Beveridge, Dresser took an extended trip to the Midwest, possibly dropping in quietly at Terre Haute. As had become his custom, he may have spent a few days at one of Indiana's health spas—perhaps at the brand-new West Baden Springs Hotel; if so, the refreshing healthful waters of the spa might have been an unconscious act of ablution following his involvement in the Bulger affair.

CHAPTER 23

Dreiser's Troubles

On 9 April 1903 Paul Dresser copyrighted the title "The Voice of the Hudson," which he planned to develop into a "spectacular melodrama" based on the song of the same title he had already written. As he had in the past, Dresser failed to follow through with a finished dramatic work, but Howley, Haviland and Dresser did issue the song, referring to it as "The Best Ballad Written during the Last Decade."[1] At the end of April, Dresser took out an ad in the *New York Dramatic Mirror*, reprinting a glowing review of "The Voice of the Hudson." The uplifting quality of the words and music, it said, were welcome "when the ragtime contortions distress the majority of the people"; the song placed Dresser "in a class far ahead of the vendors and mongers of the stuff now erroneously styled popular songs."[2]

An anonymous reviewer in the *New York Record* belonged to that group of people who thought that such "ragtime contortions" were bound to be short lived, that they were merely a temporary vogue, that the pubic would regain its senses and return to the genteel, nostalgic song once it had its fill of such music. Of course they were wrong. Songs about mother and home had had their place in the sun for a long time. Now they were to be replaced by newer styles that, to the ear of the listener, more accurately reflected contemporary life. Any number of composers now lauded the exciting technologies of the telephone, the automobile, and the airplane. There was still place for mother, it was true, but now she would have to share space with those technologies, those protestations of love—some made in racy double entendres—those very ragtime contortions that would soon lead to the jazz age. Wearing one's love of mother on the sleeve, as millions had done in the past, was a bit embarrassing to many. The newer styles of poetry, and the music which bore them, were welcome arrivals. Howley, Haviland and Dresser worked hard to keep up with the competition.

These were times of expansion, of constructing new buildings for the established music publishers as they gradually moved uptown. Charles K. Harris, Harry Von Tilzer, William H. Anstead, the Peerless Publishing Company, Sol Bloom, and Leo Feist all relocated their firms. The Feist building, a five-story brownstone at 134 West Thirty-seventh Street, boasted a subbasement with fireproof vaults for holding publishing plates. Hundreds of thousands of copies of sheet music were stored in the basement. Business offices were located on the first floor, while the band and orchestra department and the Feist inventory of stereopticon slides took up the entire second floor. Reception rooms and teaching studios were on the third floor, and on the fourth, one found the advertising department.

Not to be outdone by the competition, M. Witmark and Sons built an even grander house. Only ten years earlier Witmark had occupied a "little one-room office in a ramshackle wooden building at Broadway and Thirteenth Street."[3] Since then the company had moved twice, and now it was preparing to relocate to an eight-story structure (two of the floors underground and six above) at 144–46 West Thirty-seventh Street just below the old Marlborough Hotel. In addition to music and plate storage in the two stories underground, the building had on the second floor "nine studios for the convenience of the profession, with as many pianos and pianists in attendance" and on the fifth and sixth floors a library and booking agency.[4] Howley, Haviland and Dresser joined this northward exodus in June 1903, moving to 1440 Broadway, where "extensive alterations have been made and the floor transformed into a model publishing house with spacious stock rooms, light and airy offices, cozy reception rooms and a large number of music rooms all supplied with new pianos."[5]

In some cases self-promotion among the publishers was even more blatant than usual. Songwriting partners Will A. Heelan and J. Fred Helf pretentiously referred to themselves as the "Real

Writers" of songs.[6] Competition to secure that next hit song, the song that would guarantee temporary financial well-being, became increasingly cutthroat. Anxious to duplicate the success of its hit "In the Good Old Summer Time," Howley, Haviland and Dresser was rumored to have paid five thousand dollars for "Tell Tale Eyes," a new waltz.[7] In a contest to lure songwriters to its firm, the American Advance Music Company offered a cash prize of a thousand dollars to whichever of its composers had the best-selling song during a given three-month period. American promised to give the composer the money in addition to a four-cent royalty for every copy of sheet music sold. The *Dramatic Mirror* complained that the "slow starter" would be penalized under the rules of the contest, but rumor had it that another publisher was prepared to offer a fifteen-hundred-dollar prize on the same conditions.[8] Earlier, the *Dramatic Mirror* protested:

> The competition is so keen in the music business that publishers will go to any extreme to push their wares. Diamond rings and pins, handsome stage costumes, and even a weekly remittance of solid cash are some of the inducements held out to popular singers by publishers, in order that their music may be used by those who have caught the fancy of the public.[9]

A "prominent publisher," exasperated with the situation, stated that far too many songs were being written and that firms were buying and publishing nearly any and all songs offered them in the hope of staying ahead of competitors. He proposed that the current copyright fee of a dollar be increased to twenty-five to discourage publishers from this practice. Such a charge, he thought, might force publishers to seek out real quality in their songs.[10]

Dresser's responsibilities to his firm included working with performers to entice them to sing his firm's recent offerings. In an effort to stay in the forefront of the competition, Howley, Haviland and Dresser expanded its personnel in this area in the summer of 1903. The company hired Sam Gross, whose job was to link a singer with his or her ideal song. Neither a writer nor composer, Gross added a new dimension to song publishing—that of the specialist, attempting to find the magical combination of singer and song that would result in the much-desired hit. Perhaps Howley, Haviland and Dresser moved in this direction for reasons that were justified at the time. On the other hand, the trio may have been experiencing financial difficulty already and may have made this decision out of desperation. Whatever the case, if Dresser was worried about the firm, he never mentioned it in his letters that have survived. Perhaps he was not aware one way or the other, as the needs of his own family were such that he had to neglect the business, turning most of his chores over to his partners.

Much of the remainder of Dresser's year was taken up in his role of family helper, as he was now the eldest child of a clan without parents. Following the Indiana trip he made after writing to Albert Beveridge on Jimmy Bulger's behalf, Dresser returned to New York City. There his beloved brother Theodore Dreiser needed help. The stress of the negotiations over *Sister Carrie,* the reluctance of the publisher to promote it as it had other novels, the printing of only about a thousand copies, its general lackluster reception by the public, and the scathing criticism of the unpunished and unredeemed Carrie had been devastating to Dreiser, and he had gradually withdrawn from society over a long period of time. Too proud to ask his siblings for help (he had deliberately lost contact with Dresser, and the others were not in any position to help in any event), away from Jug, and unable to find work, Dreiser sank into the darker depths of depression even more. Perhaps he was nearly ready to relive the fate he had bestowed on the hapless George Hurstwood, Carrie's former lover:

> Now he began leisurely to take off his clothes, but stopped first with his coat and tucked it along the crack under the door. His vest he arranged in the same place. His old wet, cracked hat he laid softly upon the table. Then he pulled off his shoes and lay down.
>
> It seemed as if he thought awhile for now he arose and turned the gas out, standing calmly in the blackness, hidden from view. After a few moments in which he reviewed nothing, but merely hesitated, he turned the gas on again, but applying no match. Even then he stood there, hidden wholly

> in that kindness which is night, while the uprising fumes filled the room. When the odor reached his nostrils he quit his attitude and fumbled for the bed.
>
> "What's the use," he said wearily, as he stretched himself to rest.[11]

Hurstwood's fate, however, was not to be Dreiser's, for at long last Dreiser was able to overcome his ghostly double and reverse his long psychological descent. In early 1903, with the promise of a job at the New York Central Railroad, Dreiser felt utter despair loosen its grip on him. Though armed with this good news, he was still penniless, so he pawned his watch for twenty-five dollars at the Provident Loan Association. Having money was the euphoric tonic he needed at that point in his desperate circumstance. After he treated himself to a good dinner, he decided to buy a new hat to replace the old, battered, embarrassing one he had been forced to wear. Feeling sanguine about life for the first time in ages, he proceeded up Broadway and, as he got to the twelve hundred block, he saw Dresser leaving the Imperial Hotel, yet another of the latter's residences. Dresser was on his way out of town. The brothers had been estranged since the blowup at *Ev'ry Month*, and Dreiser was determined not to be the one to make the first step toward reconciliation. He had steadfastly avoided any contact with Dresser, but now it was too late; his brother saw him. Dresser had worried about Dreiser but had not known for some time where his younger brother was living. As Dreiser later recalled, Dresser "looked at me with his big soft blue eyes—the eyes of my mother. He pressed the lips of his big jolly mouth together in a way that I knew meant pain."[12] Again, he was "like a distrait mother with a sick child."[13] As envy and jealousy raised their ugly heads within him, Dreiser steeled himself for the inevitable offer of help. "Instinctively I felt a revulsion of feeling—a kind of hatred of his prosperity and of him." Engulfed in self-pity, Dreiser continued:

> How could he be so prosperous when I was so hard up? How could he go on in his merry, comfortable way and have me slipping along in the side streets comparatively hungry. And now he was going to offer me sympathy—me, who had always walked so proudly alone. I drew defiantly aside.[14]

Ever the ebullient and generous brother, Dresser ignored his brother's icy demeanor and pressed a roll of bills into Dreiser's hand. Meeting his brother's refusal of aid, the maternal Dresser, his eyes filling with tears, told his brother not to let his pride come between them:

> I know you're bright. I know you are able. You can get along, but don't let me go away worrying about you. Take it [the money] and you can pay me when you choose. You can give it all back to me when I come back if you wish. Only take it now.[15]

As Dresser got into his cab, Dreiser promised to come see him. The "good brother," the "best of sons," the "only man I ever knew who was wholly and absolutely swayed by the tenderest of sentiments" had won his brother over yet again.[16] Sarah Dreiser lived on in the gentleness and generosity of her eldest son. With Dreiser's promise to let Dresser help him, the two parted, Dreiser going on his way, with the feeling that he was on his way back. He had conquered Hurstwood, and whether he wanted to admit it, Dresser had played a crucial part in destroying this demon.

Dresser was naturally concerned at seeing Dreiser in such a desperate state. When Dreiser kept his promise to see his brother, Dresser brooked no nonsense from him. He took Dreiser to a department store and bought him a suit, other clothing, and shoes to replace the rumpled, torn, and soiled garments Dreiser had been wearing. Dresser then announced that he had made plans for Dreiser to be a guest at a health sanitarium one of his celebrity friends operated in Port Chester, Westchester County, New York. A tough regimen of diet and strenuous exercise would surely restore Dreiser's health. "I've got it all arranged and you go tomorrow. . . . There's nothing left now but to bow your head and receive the paternal—I mean the fraternal blessing."[17] The Olympia Hygienic Institute, run by the tyrannical William Muldoon, was not for the faint of heart. Muldoon had been, by turns, the undefeated world wrestling champion, a trainer of John L. Sullivan, and a sometime actor, having toured with Helena Modjeska and with his own William Muldoon's Athletic Stars a decade earlier. One writer generously described him as a "gentle giant" with a certain helpless-

Van Pelt-Dietrich Library Center, Univ. of Pa.

William Muldoon's Olympia Hygienic Institute in Port Chester, New York, where Theodore Dreiser spent six weeks in 1903.

ness to him that made women take to him, a man with a "light, springing step."[18] Dreiser, on the other hand, wrote of an earthier Muldoon with a long laundry list of occupations, including:

> a scullion in a ship's kitchen . . . , a "beef slinger" for a packing company, a cooks' assistant and waiter in a Bowery restaurant, a bouncer in a saloon, a rubber down at prize fights, a policeman, a private in the army during the Civil War, a ticket-taker, . . . [a] "short-change man" with a minstrel company, later a circus.[19]

In addition to working with Modjeska in *As You Like It*, he had performed with a variety of other partners, including Jake Kilrain, in the farce comedy, *A Winning Hand*, featuring "Athletic Sports, Sparkling Melodies, [and the] Latest Dances."[20]

Austin Brennan, Mame Dreiser's husband, had been a guest at Muldoon's a couple of years earlier and described in fearsome terms the place and the routines the patients underwent: "I think I endured more pain during the three weeks I spent [at Muldoon's] than at any like period of my life . . . it was a sort of premonition of *Dante's Inferno*."[21] The sixty-year-old Muldoon—a "savage and yet gentlemanly-looking animal in clothes," "a tiger or a very ferocious and yet at times purring cat, beautifully dressed, . . . a kind of tiger in collar and boots," "lithe, silent, cat-like in his tread"—was also a martinet.[22]

The regimen that all Muldoon's guests followed was strenuous in the extreme. Days began at 5:30 when someone knocked loudly on the door. The guests were expected at the gymnasium for calisthenics at 6:00; exercises with medicine balls followed, with Muldoon goading his guests, through hearty, earthy language and dripping sarcasm, to go faster, to go farther, to simply endure. Then came the cold shower—ten seconds to get wet (as if anyone wanted more than that), twenty seconds to soap one's self, ten seconds to rinse, and twenty seconds to towel dry—a one-minute routine that Muldoon himself supervised, again screaming directions to the cowed and thoroughly intimidated guests. Following a light breakfast, guests were free for a little more than two hours to do what they chose. At 11:00 or 11:30, more exercise: horseback riding or walking and running a four- or seven-mile trail. Then came another light meal. Guests spent the afternoons doing a variety of things gauged to improve their health and well-being. After the evening meal, lights were extinguished at 9:00. Perhaps the last thought many guests had as they dropped, exhausted, into sleep was that another identical day was only hours away. But of course this rugged routine worked. For many it was the first time since they were young that they had exercised and followed a somewhat reasonable diet. Most important was that they had little or no time for self-pity—Muldoon and his staff saw to that.

On 21 April 1903 Dresser and Dreiser boarded a train at the Forty-second Street depot and traveled to White Plains, where they disembarked and hired a carriage for the remainder of the trip to Muldoon's, all the while Dresser singing bits of his new songs and boosting Dreiser's spirits with motherly praise and encouragement. Dreiser spent six weeks at Muldoon's, and when he left on 2 June, his spirits and body were revived. If he was not exactly a new man, he was at least able to think about his future and put his recent depression behind him. He went to the New York Central Railroad, where he worked first piling lumber and then as a pile-driving inspector. Dresser paid the $256.75 it cost Dreiser to stay at Muldoon's, feeling that anything was worth seeing his younger brother in such good spirits.

PURCHASE, N. Y., May 30th 1903

Mr Theodore Dreiser

To WILLIAM MULDOON, Dr.

TERMS $35 per week FROM April 21st to June 2d 1903

Six weeks Board and treatment	$210
Cleaning shoes	2
3 prs socks	2 55
2 suits underwear	6
1 blue shirt	3
2 Bath towels	1
Gym suit	6
Gym shoes	4
Leggins	2
1 blue shirt	[illegible]
Telephones N.Y.	80
2 prs socks .85	[illegible]
2 Bath towels	[illegible]
1 suit underwear	[illegible]
1 blue shirt	[illegible]
Gloves	1 50
6 stamps	12
"	17
Expressage	1 50
Laundry	48
2 N.Y. telephones	80
2 — telephones	80
trip to Tarrytown	1 25
Laundry	.88
N P telephone	20
	$256.75
Received by cheque	100
Balance due	156.75

Received payment in full by cheque June 13 1903 Wm. Muldoon per L. With thanks

Van Pelt-Dietrich Library Center, Univ. of Pa.

Receipt of Paul Dresser's payment for Theodore Dreiser's stay at Muldoon's.

CHAPTER 24

The Good Son, the Loving Brother

The day after he delivered Theodore Dreiser to the sanitarium, Paul Dresser celebrated his forty-fifth birthday, one he observed by stage-managing a show in Schnaben Hall at the Vaudeville Club of Brooklyn. This single event, together with the rehearsals for it, undoubtedly provided Dresser with a few moments of relief from the psychological and emotional rigors of his year. First there was the work at Howley, Haviland and Dresser; then the episode with Jimmy Bulger; and now the troubles of his brother. That one day, that Wednesday, 22 April, belonged to him; he was in his element once again—working in the theater.

But this respite was exceedingly brief. There was family to care for, especially Dreiser. Dresser represented the last line of defense for his family, and he took his responsibilities seriously even if his siblings did not always appreciate his aid. While Dreiser was a resident at Muldoon's, Dresser became his brother's cheerleader, calling and writing to him; even after Dreiser left the sanitarium in June, Dresser continued to provide his younger brother with emotional and financial support through frequent calls and letters, the latter often filled with Dresser's corny brand of humor. Dresser fretted over Dreiser, reassuring him he would get a better job, scolding him when he took too much time away from his own writing, and often sending his "Tedarino" money even when it was unsolicited.

Except for the vaudevillian sort of humor he used to lighten the tone of his letters, Dresser's concern for his younger brother was almost maternal. Dreiser remarked that Dresser's "voice and manner . . . [were] largely those of mother, the same wonder, the same wistfulness and sweetness, the same bubbling charity and tenderness of heart."[1] Many times Dresser's concern and compassion deeply moved Dreiser. Years after Dresser had helped the family move from Sullivan to Evansville, for example, Dreiser wrote touchingly, "Blessed are the merciful, for, verily, they have their reward! Paul, the good son, the loving brother: write his name high among those who have wrought for affection's sake. Jailbird,

IHS C4781

Paul Dresser at the height of his career.

writer of pointless ballads, singer of trivial songs—even so, write his name large as one who loved his fellowmen!"[2]

Dresser's lack of introspection and reflection, on the other hand, annoyed his younger, more intellectual brother to no end. Even more troublesome to Dreiser were Dresser's lack of refinement, his middle- or lower-class qualities, and his coarseness and downright sexual vulgarity. When Dresser, Dreiser, and their brother Edward were living together, Dresser would sometimes walk around in front of the other two, naked save for a towel draped over his telling erection. Although Dreiser was himself an "unregenerate sex enthusiast," to use the same words with which he described Dresser, his brother's unseemly display of manhood disgusted him, and he soon found another place to live.[3]

Dresser wrote to Tillie Dreiser Gormley two weeks after their brother left Muldoon's: "Theodore has gotten through with his course at Muldoons & is now up the NY Central RR. He looked fine when I saw him last Sunday."[4] To his brother he wrote playfully:

> Dear Tedarino. Your long looked for & muchly expected letter came Dooley to hand this am. . . . Now that depressed *gagerino* . . . must be cut out. Remember the future of the great NY Central system must not weaken. . . . I hope to hear of your advancement as general all around Supt. of the tie lifting gang of Gorillas. So long Theo, Tend to your knitting & don't worry. with love I am ever the same old brother. Paul. "the pen is mightier than the sword," bigosh.[5]

Four days later: " 'The *wicket flue* when none pursue' 'Coffee doesn't settle anything' 'Woman like tea, sometimes is weak' 'The Hen layeth, while the sluggard playeth' Oh Yes—and tomorrow a m I leave in a *Closed Carriage with a double veil* closely drawn over my face. Yes—How be ye."[6] Dresser enclosed five dollars with this missive. The stream of cheerful but unsophisticated letters continued. Shortly after Dreiser became a pile-driving inspector, Dresser wrote from a steamy Chicago, "Well—this is H——l. Hot, awful simply awful. Suppose you have those spikes driven so d——d deep that in the ages to come, they will be dug & looked upon as the great sticks of Macaroni used by the monsters who lived in 1903."[7]

Dresser's self-censorship is surprising. Given his penchant for the bawdy joke, his refusal to spell out swearwords seems quite prim.

Soon Dresser was back in New York where his new song, "Lincoln, Grant and Lee," was nearing the final stages for publication. He had asked Dreiser for pictures of the three presidents for his title page, but in a subsequent letter he informed Dreiser that he had changed his mind: "I don't think I'll use any of them or any pictures over the title page." In closing, he reminded Dreiser that he would see him at dinner on Sunday, 16 August: "chicken *Pot Pie—Wow.*"[8]

Still feeling financially pinched in spite of his steady job, Dreiser asked Dresser for money three months after he left Muldoon's; the indulgent brother responded generously with a check for fifty dollars.[9] Dresser encouraged Dreiser to dig in, to not get sidetracked, and to do some serious writing, and he sent him other brotherly and motherly advice:

> Now you cut out giving opinions & views to every rube who writes & wishes to know something about God, Jeff Davis & Roosevelt—You have been working long & hard to get yourself in condition to write so when you do write let it be on your book. Don't waste grey matter on anything but your lifes ambition.[10]

On 18 October, in a letter addressed to "Mr. Theodore Dreiser, Supt. Vice Prest. Master Mechanic, Pile Driving Overseer—& Associate of Guineas," Dresser again wrote to reassure his brother: "Do not think for a moment old man that I am thinking any the less of you. Not at all. . . . Any one causing to think any the less of you, that is out of the question."[11] Yet despite Dresser's attempts to encourage him—and the improvements brought about from his stay at Muldoon's—Dreiser still struggled. He despised his job with the New York Central, and if he had thought *Ev'ry Month* was beneath him in terms of his intellectual ambitions, one can only imagine his discontent with the menial tasks he had to perform at the railroad. Additionally, from time to time he had had to ask Dresser for money to make ends meet, certainly an act that only added to his feelings of shame and resentment—shame that he was reduced to begging, resentment at his brother's good fortunes. After all, he must have thought, he was in his thirties; he should be independent and not have to rely on his brother for money. When Dresser had sent him the fifty dollars, he had also offered him clothing—new articles as well as Dresser's cast-off suits that would have to be drastically altered for Dreiser's much slighter frame. To Dreiser, 1903 was a miserable year in which, to his dismay, Dresser really had become his brother's keeper.

In a letter, Dresser told Dreiser about his own personal struggle. Dresser was a large man whose fatness bore testimony to an enormous appetite that he readily indulged. Eating well, if not always healthily, was a sign of his prosperity, a rejection of the poverty and want of his youth. By 1898 he weighed 290 pounds, something that, as he put it, gave him "more anxiety, . . . than the disposition of his money." Some had joked that he had to put "two pennies in the slot machines to get weighed."[12] Over the years his self-indulgence, coupled with a lifestyle that had recently become less than energetic now that he was away from performing, had added an immense amount of weight to his frame. By 1903 he weighed more than 300 pounds. Various diet regimens that he tried from time to time occasionally brought him to a slightly lower weight and size, but those victories were partial and temporary at best. The pounds always came back and, in their perversity, always in greater number than those he had lost. Now, in the middle of his forties, he began to worry about his health and the risks associated with his obesity.

Although Dresser never mentioned it, women may have begun to be repelled by his enormous size. This would have been devastating to him, far more of a concern to him than the state of his health. Whatever the reason, he was obviously sensitive to his size, for he recounted his reducing schemes in his letters for the rest of his life. His eating regimens often approached the level of starvation: "Liquor and I are strangers since Sept. 20th—just one month the day this reaches you—I have been living on milk alone, for over two weeks & am losing flesh fast—Have not eaten even a cracker—Will keep it up for awhile longer—want to get off a good bunch of fleshliness."[13] In the same month Dresser noted, "I am feeling fine—Been living on milk now for eleven days—& feel like a *prince*—Not even a cracker have I eaten. Nothing at all—Losing flesh, clear eye, good color—lots of ambition—& a strong heart."[14]

The *New York Telegraph* ran the following story from around the same time.

> Paul Dresser Starving
>
> Paul Dresser, song-writer and ex-actor, has lived for seventeen days without food, although he is ordinarily a very hearty eater, as may be surmised from his size. He weighed 328 pounds when he began to starve himself, nearly three weeks ago. Yesterday Mr. Dresser weighed 275 pounds, having lost fifty-eight [*sic*] pounds by reason of his self-denial.
>
> "I propose to get down to 250 pounds before I again partake of solid food," said Mr. Dresser. . . . "During the past few days I've been loosing [*sic*] only a little more than a couple of pounds per day. All the nourishment I have taken since I began fasting has been the juice of oranges and some natural spring water."[15]

If the story is close to being accurate, Dresser had lost almost twenty pounds a week—nearly three pounds a day—for a three-week period! Of course he was soon suffering the ill effects of his injudicious eating regimen:

> Paul Dresser Quite Ill. Made Up for His Recent Fast and His Stomach Collapsed.
>
> Paul Dresser is seriously ill at the Marlborough Hotel. The songwriter's latest ailment, his physicians say, is directly traceable to the abuse of his stomach after his voluntary fast of thirty-five days.
>
> Early this Spring Dresser weighed 326 pounds, and was gaining nearly a pound a day. He was warned by physicians that he would have to undergo heroic treatment, and he resolved to starve himself. For thirty-five days he lived on only orange juice and water, and he lost sixty-six pounds in weight. Since then, however, he has been making up for the meals he missed.[16]

The last part of this article is missing, but it probably suggested that Dresser had been overeating again, or at least that his stomach would not take the sudden change from starvation to a return to regular eating.

While Dresser wanted to reduce the size of his immense body, he also took advantage of his prodigious frame, boasting about it in an advertisement for "Harris, The $4 Shoe Man [at] 520 Pine":

> Paul Dresser Weighs 285. . . .
>
> He's the fattest, richest, jolliest song-writer in the world. Lives in New York. He wrote "On the Banks of the Wabash"; he also wrote a letter to HARRIS the other day. This is it: My dear Mr. Harris—The pair of shoes you sold me some time ago have given me perfect satisfaction; in fact, they are the easiest and best walking shoes I have had in years, and you can readily understand what this means, coming from a man who weighs nearly 300 pounds. Sincerely yours, PAUL DRESSER.[17]

In his 18 October letter to Dreiser, Dresser also mentioned that his colleague Bob Davis "has been with me all the afternoon & we have been fitting a big ad for the Clipper."[18] The ad would announce a new play titled *After Many Years*, the fruition of Dresser and Davis's collaboration. Dresser was probably hoping to carve out yet another career for himself as a playwright. After all, he was a seasoned performer, and he had already written one play, *A Green Goods Man*. As a well-known songwriter, he thought, his name on a play would certainly give it some luster, wouldn't it? Dresser and Davis sent the play to Wesley Rosenquest, proprietor of the Fourteenth Street Theatre and a successful producer. Rosenquest had been involved in the world of theater for nearly three decades. Certainly he would be able to assess the merits of this new play.

At the same time, however, Dresser and Davis hedged their bets by sending *After Many Years* to Harry Powers, proprietor of the Powers Theatre in Chicago. Dresser remarked that "we are hustling—you can bet on that."[19] Hustling they were, indeed, but this new play, a melodrama in four acts, was never to be produced during Dresser's life, and Davis's attempts to have it mounted after Dresser's death were to no avail. If acted in a truly melodramatic style, the play's effusive dialogue, plot of deceit, disguised identity, threatened maiden, last-minute rescue, and ultimate triumph of good over evil might have won it a modest following, but much of the play would have struck many as rather quaint. *After Many Years* was to have featured one of Dresser's standard mother-and-home songs. As written, the second act, set in a Colorado mining town, included a scene in the bar of the Eagle Rest Hotel. There, one by one, a group of hard-bitten faro players would break into tears as the "notes of the organ come creeping into the room. . . . [The] music . . . sad and low, [full] of pathos and tenderness with grand burst[s] of chords."[20] The song? "Would I were a child again / Back in the long ago, / Just one voice to banish all pain, / Whispering soft and low, / There in her sheltering arms, / Safe from the wind and rain, / The world could not tempt with its charms, / Were I a child again."[21]

Finally, Dresser wrote Dreiser late in the year from Chicago, after a monstrous snowstorm: "I would have sent you a telegram yesterday but this *willage* had a *bliz* on & I felt that the *bliz* might blow the wires down & then the delay might make you feel most wretched. . . . I am feeling fairly well today but *have eaten a lot of stuff that should have [been] fed to the animals at the menaginary*—10 below zero old sport today—*Reg Chicawgy weath*. How be ye." Then getting to the point of his letter—which was to help Dreiser find another job—he continued, "Had a letter from Bob Davis [Dresser's collaborator]—He says he will do something for you after Jan. 1st. . . . Remember after Jan 1st the chances are better than at any other time. But up to the 1st nothing can be done."[22]

Throughout all his efforts to boost Dreiser's confidence and spirits, Dresser had other things to deal with, not the least of which were his business matters. He found the time, however, to answer correspondence from his old friends. In November 1903, feeling quite nostalgic, Dresser wrote to Mamie Coffman, whom he had known in Sullivan more than three decades before:

> Many times I have thot of the old red brick seminary, the childish joys and heartaches, and, after all that I have gone through, what would I not give to once again return to them. There is one song that I wrote, the theme of which is "That's Where My Heart Is Tonight." When I wrote it, in my mind

was the old swimming place at Morrison Creek, out beyond your father's farm. I am sending you a copy of the song, in every line you will find some spot around dear old Sullivan that I love.[23]

CHAPTER 25

Parting of the Ways

Throughout 1903 things were not quite right for Howley, Haviland and Dresser. Certainly there was pressure to find a new hit song, the stress of keeping up with other music publishers. But there must have been some difficulties among the three partners as well, for by year's end Fred Haviland left and went his own way. On 12 December, in one of the last letters he wrote to Theodore Dreiser in 1903, Paul Dresser mentioned, almost as an afterthought, that "Pat [Howley] & I bought Mr. Haviland out yesterday—So the new firm is Howley-Dresser Company."[1] Howley, Haviland and Dresser had enjoyed unusual success for slightly more than a decade and had recently published "In the Good Old Summer Time," by George Evans and Ren Shields, and Hughie Cannon's "Bill Bailey, Won't You Please Come Home?," both tremendous hits. A year before, its publication "Blooming Lize" had been interpolated in Isadore Witmark's comedy *Chaperones*, much to the great delight of critics and audiences. Witmark, however, was less than happy about the intrusion of this Ben M. Jerome and Matt C. Woodward tune. He wanted only his music to appear in his play.

Lacking evidence, it is impossible to reconstruct what precipitated the split among the three partners after more than ten years of collaboration. With three recent hit songs from the firm, the decision is even more puzzling. Perhaps they found it increasingly difficult to agree on business matters. Maybe Haviland merely wanted to try his own wings, for upon leaving his partners he immediately established F. B. Haviland Publishing.

The partnership with Howley began a new chapter in Dresser's life, but the company suffered financial troubles from the outset, and its life proved to be extremely short. Whatever thoughts Dreiser might have had about this development are unknown, for we do not know if he responded to Dresser's news about the new firm. He was probably so self-involved with ordering his own life at this point that he did not give Dresser's plight too much thought. After all, Dresser had been the successful one all his life. There was little to make Dreiser believe that such would not be the case with the new firm.

The year 1903 ended with a horrific tragedy, the news of which spread rapidly throughout the world. On Wednesday, 30 December, more than sixteen hundred people, in a post-Christmas celebratory mood, attended a special holiday matinee performance of *Mr. Bluebeard* at the Iroquois Theater in Chicago. As "eight dashing chorus girls and eight stalwart men in showy costume" came onstage to sing "The Pale Moonlight," fire broke out when a flame from an overloaded electrical circuit ignited some stage curtains. Eddie Foy, the vaudevillian and Dresser's close friend, rushed to the stage apron and urged the audience not to panic. Dressed in "tights, a loose upper garment, and . . . face . . . one-half made up," he kept his head through the turmoil and encouraged those members of the orchestra who had remained on the stage to continue playing in an effort to restore some degree of calm. After doing what he could, Foy fled the conflagration at virtually the last minute—as if in some terrible melodrama suddenly and tragically made horribly real.[2] In spite of Foy's efforts, sheer terror and panic prevailed in the audience. In the smoke and confusion it was difficult at best for the crowd to egress because many exits were not clearly marked. The doors opened on to Dearborn and Randolph Streets, but when people groped and trampled their way to some of them, they found them bolted shut.[3]

More than one-third of the audience—602 people—died, most of them women and children. Cries for investigations into criminal negligence and demands for justice were shouted in the newspapers and on the streets even before officials determined the final death toll. Foy was one of the few heroes in this disaster; the same man was to help carry Dresser's coffin on the day of the songwriter's funeral only a short two years later.

After the new year began, Dresser wrote a letter to Bob—most likely his friend and collaborator, Bob Davis: "Ask Theo to look these over and fix up words so we can publish."[4] Dresser was probably referring to *After Many Years*, the play he and Davis had written in 1903. The letter raises a number of questions. Why did Dresser rely on Davis as an intermediary? Why didn't he ask his brother himself? Is this in any way some evidence that Dresser and Dreiser had collaborated in the past, or was Dresser merely recognizing his brother's abilities as a writer? Did Dreiser really contribute the words to the first verse and chorus of "On the Banks of the Wabash, Far Away"? Since Dresser never acknowledged his brother's help—indeed, he always said that he wrote both words and music to his songs—is this why Dresser was reluctant to personally ask his brother to "look these over and fix up [the] words"?

Dresser had much to keep him busy. He had to work like a dog to get the new firm moving, to convince songwriters that the Howley-Dresser Company was the right publisher for them. He and Howley had to work hard just to keep their heads above water. Securing a hit song would show other firms and the staff members who had deserted Dresser and Howley that they were still contenders, a team to be reckoned with. At just the time Howley-Dresser was making itself known as a new firm, the houses of Shapiro, Bernstein and Company and the Whitney-Warner Publishing Company announced their consolidation as Shapiro, Remick and Company. In advertisements for the merger, the new firm crowed that it was the "strongest and most complete music publishing business in the world."[5] The competition had just become more fierce. If Howley-Dresser had its work cut out for it before, this consolidation would make that work even more difficult.

By the middle of February 1904 Howley-Dresser, retaining its old offices in the Holland Building at Fortieth Street and Broadway, had published a dozen instrumental pieces and songs, including Dresser's offering "Your Mother Wants You Home, Boy (And She Wants You Mighty Bad)." The team hoped this new effort, which Richard Jose sang repeatedly, would be a hit, marking the company as a success and enticing composers to work with it. Jose, ever Dresser's friend and avid supporter, introduced "When I'm Away from You, Dear," yet another new Dresser song, in early

March. When it published "On a Good Old Trolley Ride," Howley-Dresser, constantly on the lookout for a new twist to help sell a song, issued an advertising novelty. In the shape of a trolley transfer, the card read: "This transfer not good at the intersection of Misery Street and Cholera Morbus Avenue. If the conductor refuses to take this transfer, give it to the motorman; if he will not take it up, stand on the corner and whistle the chorus and a policeman will take you up."[6]

By the end of February things were looking reasonably good for Haviland. He had already announced ten publications, including "Havana," a Cuban-American intermezzo Theodore Morse composed. In the not-so-distant past, Morse had been especially close to Dresser at Howley, Haviland and Dresser; in 1898 Dresser had dedicated "Come, Tell Me What's Your Answer, Yes or No" to Morse, and the two of them had even collaborated on the innocuous and somewhat insipid "Coontown Capers," but Morse had jumped ship earlier and was now with Haviland. Over the next two years Morse turned out nearly twenty songs and toured as a singer with his own vocal trio. Long after Dresser died, Morse turned out "M-O-T-H-E-R," the impressive hit song of 1915, and two years later he crafted an Arthur Sullivan tune into "Hail! Hail! The Gang's All Here."

Although neither Howley-Dresser nor Haviland lacked material to publish, neither firm had yet found the one song that would bring them outstanding financial success. And the competitors were always there. Every week Charles K. Harris published his "Charles K. Harris Herald" as an advertisement in the pages of the *New York Dramatic Mirror*, and Leo Feist also regularly appeared in the same pages, plugging his songs with clever little stories about them. A single example, used to promote "Mary Ann," and the veracity of it vouched for by the publisher himself, will suffice to illustrate Feist's approach:

> A little hamlet up on the N.Y., N.H. and H. Railroad, just one station beyond Noroton, Conn., is known on the map as Darien. Every one who has traveled over this road has no doubt been attracted by the pretty little village. The other afternoon the coaches were filled with theatre parties who

> were just returning from New York, where they had attended the various matinees, all lively, all jolly, and singing bits of the up-to-date hits. When the train pulled into the little village above named, attendants at each end of the coach opened the doors simultaneously and shouted "Darien." Of course, we all know how hard it is to understand the average attendant who calls the stations, but, to make this little press story short, the moment the attendants shouted "Darien," the theatre party took up the cue and immediately began to sing the chorus of "Mary Ann," which is to-day the biggest popular song hit on the market.

Lest the reader did not get it, Feist's ad provided the obvious:

> This press story may not be quite clear to you, but if you will consider just about how the train attendants shouted "Darien," and draw upon your imagination a little, you can readily see why the theatre party understood them to shout "Mary Ann" instead of "Darien."[7]

On 26 March the astute Feist took out a large ad in the *Dramatic Mirror*, thanking Louise Dresser for singing his company's song—the same "Mary Ann"—at the Circle Theatre. Feist expressed "his thanks and appreciation . . . for her clever rendition . . . and the agreeable surprise afforded him."[8] We do not know what Paul Dresser's feelings about Louise were at that point. If he felt that she, too, had deserted him, he never let on in his letters. Louise certainly had not abandoned her "brother," but in establishing her own career she had to make professional connections with rising composers and to perform those songs she believed would enhance her reputation as an important singer. Paul Dresser had not contributed any new material to her repertoire for quite some time. In fact, Louise would introduce just one more Dresser song, "My Gal Sal," and that was still to come. It was clear that more than ever Howley-Dresser needed a stable of established singers to perform the songs it published. Only Jose could be counted on to fill that bill well.

A week after Feist's tribute to Louise Dresser, the *Dramatic Mirror* carried a three-quarter-length picture of Paul Dresser.

Obviously near his maximum heft of more than three hundred pounds, he nevertheless gives the impression of grace and elegance. Dressed in an excellent suit of clothing, his left hand resting gracefully in the pocket of his fine trousers, he gazes off into the distance. Prosperous and businesslike though he looks, the softness of his face, with the slight smile playing on his lips, suggests the maternal tenderness that Dreiser so often mentioned when writing about his brother.[9]

CHAPTER 26

"The People Are Marching By"

By the middle of May 1904, scarcely six months after Pat Howley and Paul Dresser started the Howley-Dresser Company, the firm was in serious financial difficulty. Attempting to mollify brother-in-law Austin Brennan, who had lent him money for the new company, Dresser wrote assuredly to him on the nineteenth: "Your various letters & telegrams have been received. Rest easy your note (the second one) will not be used, & the other will not be pressed against you, for I saw the bank people." In one of the few instances where Dresser expressed bitterness, he added "I've been getting the snotty end of the stick for a long time, so I am going to use it on some of the others."[1]

This bitterness surfaced ten days later in his rambling and angry response to a newspaper reporter. He began his comments calmly enough. On his methods of songwriting, he wrote: "Some of the doggerel of which I am guilty I write anywhere. . . ; but the real songs seem to come to me all at once, in a flash, an inspiration. I have a big organ in my place . . . and sometimes I get up at night and play softly on it when I have thought of a melody." Suggesting the spontaneity he felt was necessary, he continued: "I have never taken lessons in song writing. I don't think the natural song writers ever take lessons. I do not see how they could. They would lose all the inspiration in studying technique." Expressing his love for the songs of Stephen Foster that "still touch the heart," of the poetry of Heinrich Heine that had been set to music, and of his favorite song, Arthur Sullivan's "The Lost Chord," Dresser offered his formula for success: "Song writing is like everything else; you study your public, and you study the trend of the times and you usually strike the right note." The tone of his answers then suddenly became dark:

> I want to tell you that I am not a sentimentalist. It is true that I write Home-and-Mother songs, but if you lived most of your day, as I do, on the road between Thirty-fourth street and Fifty-ninth street on Broadway, right in the heart of the Rialto, you would soon cease, as I have, being a sentimentalist. There are the greatest lot of grafters and cutthroats in this place that could be. . . .
>
> Oh, sentiment is a great thing! You just try writing sentimental songs and make a success of it, and see what you think then. Sentiment is all rot! Don't I believe there is such a thing as true sentiment? Plenty of it, but there is not much of it here—right in New York. Everybody is trying to get the best of everyone else, and they have little time for real sentiment.[2]

Dresser, obviously fed up with criticisms of his sentimental songs, but realizing that he had become trapped in this style, remarked:

> What the public wants is junk, and they get it. They won't be satisfied unless they do. You can sell a thousand of [the junk songs] where you would not be able to sell a hundred of the other. Why do people prefer the bad? I suppose because they don't want to think—they don't want anything but the mere surface touched. It is the same way with plays and with literature. Give them the worst that is in you and turn out plenty of it and you'll get on, but don't shut yourself up in your study and work and work and work, for the public won't have the result of all those hours. They want junk . . . the junk of your mind, and if they are satisfied with that, why should you trouble to give them the solid silver?
>
> My desk is filled with songs that I have written when the inspiration came to me—genuine songs of feeling that ought to stir the heart, but I am so sure that they will simply go over

> the heads of those to whom they are sung that I have not the heart to publish them.
>
> You think it is enough, perhaps, to be successful in the financial sense, that a man should be satisfied to sell his songs and let it go at that. But the true artist is never satisfied unless he knows that he is doing his best work, and this is just as true of the man who writes popular songs as the man who paints pictures or writes books.[3]

A new Dresser surfaces in the next, concluding, portion of the interview. Here is a man deeply moved by the plight of the dispossessed, one who wants to respond in some way to what he has seen, one with an emerging social conscience. There was no single thing that shaped these new attitudes. Perhaps Dresser had recalled Terre Hautean Eugene Debs's fights for the ordinary worker and the dispossessed. Certainly Dresser's walks through the tenement slums of New York's Lower East Side unnerved him as the slums had Jacob Riis more than a decade before. Riis's photographs and narrative in *How the Other Half Lives* told graphic stories of rodent- and filth-infested tenements; of dirty ragamuffins playing in the streets; of the unbelievable stenches of grease, food, body odors, urine, and human excrement emanating from the buildings and streets; of the dark, miserable hallways where fresh air was a luxury; of the unbelievable numbers of human beings crammed into tiny spaces. Although Dresser had always been generous with individuals less fortunate than he, the horrors of what he saw in the Lower East Side brought that sort of social conscience to a different level. While his own youth had been marked by periods of abject poverty and want, it was nothing compared to what he now saw. Conversations with his brother Theodore Dreiser and Dreiser's writings about the downtrodden may also have triggered an introspection new to him, the kind of introspection and thoughtfulness that propelled the Progressive reformers who wanted to redress the blights that urbanization, business, industry, greed, and attendant corruption had created.

Where did Dresser fit in all this? At some point he may have realized that he had been part of the problem. Because of his celebrity, he had, after all, enjoyed the friendship of some political high and mighties, one of them Richard Croker, a successor to William "Boss" Tweed of the Tammany Hall political machine. Although thousands of poor supported Croker because of the largesse he had bestowed on them to ensure their political loyalty, such generosity did little to get to the root of the problems of the destitute and dispossessed. Was Dresser being a hypocrite in enjoying the heady company of these people who were in a position to effect change but did little? The helplessness he felt was overwhelming. All this was so new to him. At some level he must have felt a certain satisfaction with his many acts of kindness and generosity over the years. But was that enough? Was there nothing he could do for these poor, miserable people? Could his music, in any way, be a vehicle for his social conscience? More mother-and-home songs would not be a solution. Perhaps he was just irritated at constantly being taken as a mere sentimentalist, that he wanted his public to see that there was honest emotion behind him and his music. Whatever the mix was, it was expressed in his heated words that continued:

> I want to tell you something that impresses me very seriously. It may seem strange that I, a writer of sentimental ballads, whose name is associated with Wandering Boys and Home and Mother and all that, should talk about *anarchy and socialism*, and I don't want you to mistake and think that I am an Anarchist. I am nothing of the kind, but a thinking man when he sees what I have seen must be impressed.
>
> I spend a great deal of time wandering about the East Side, in the poorest quarters of the city, and I have friends all over. I go to those places and I talk to the people, and I visit their eating places and their shops and cafes, and I hear them talk and I watch them.
>
> Some time there is going to be a great social war—a commune; and it will be just as dreadful as the French commune. The streets of this city will run with blood. You will see it, and I will see it. It is a great big cloud that is slowly creeping over the horizon; and just as the French people went on gaily, ignorant of the danger, so we go on. Every day the rich of this country are getting richer and richer, and the poor are getting poorer and poorer.[4]

Dresser then suggested a direction he was considering taking, one he knew his public would not receive favorably:

> I am invited to sing at the American Theatre this Sunday night and I am thinking quite seriously of singing a song of mine, just completed, that has not yet been printed. I know the kind of audience that I shall sing before there, and I judge that it will not go. . . . It is a song that if it ever does become popular will, I am afraid, bring me into some sort of disfavor. It begins:
>
> The People, the People are marching by.
> The crowd of the downtrodden, far and nigh.
> Is heard in the homes where the weary sigh—
> The People, the People are marching by.[5]

What Dresser quoted is the chorus to the song. The verses of the song are:

> Hark, somewhere don't you hear a cry,
> Soft and subdued like a summer sigh,
> Rising in volume while drawing nigh,
> Until re-echoing in the sky,
> It comes thundering back, bidding all awake,
> Right must be right, let the wrong-doer quake,
> Throw off the fetters with one mighty shake,
> For the People are marching by.
>
> In every corner of this great land,
> Slowly but surely there gathers a band,
> Ready to strike at the word of command,
> Hark to the warning on every hand.
> Read ye the handwriting on the wall,
> Beware! Oh Beware! ere there comes a fall,
> Crushing the good, the bad and all,
> For the people are marching by.[6]

This song has survived in three versions, none of them ever published. A single sheet of music paper contains the words to the first verse and chorus. Part of a second verse, different from the one quoted above, appears on the same page. There are also two pieces of music on that page. The first is a "dummy" tune with the words to the first verse and chorus placed under a melody; the rhythms, predominantly quarter-notes, in no way fit the scansion of the words. The second tune, nearly identical to the first in its contour, is marchlike with rhythms that *do,* for the most part, fit the rhythms of the text. Neither the handwriting nor the music manuscript is Dresser's, but the resemblances between the cursive letters and Dreiser's script are quite close. Because the page is undated, one cannot tell if it is contemporaneous with Dresser. If it is later, could Dreiser have attempted, however crudely, to write a tune that would fit the words Dresser had penned earlier? The tune on the upper half of the page betrays a certain ignorance of the niceties of music notation, while the melody written on the bottom half follows standard notational practice. It appears that someone semiliterate in music wrote down a melodic contour, perhaps copying it as he sang it or as it was sung to him. Then perhaps another individual, more versed in music, refined the song and gave it a distinctive rhythmic shape, a more finished quality. A finished copy of the music also exists. Obviously prepared by a professional copyist, the manuscript bears a tune somewhat different from the two versions that appear on the single page; a full piano accompaniment is also included. Only one thing is missing to prevent this from being typeset as a song: the words. There is no text on any of the three pages of finished music.

Dresser must have written the words to "Ye Wolves of Finance" and "See Them on the Avenue" around the same time that he penned "The People Are Marching By." The sentiments he expressed in the words of each song are similar. There is no evidence, however, that he ever wrote music for these other two songs.

"Ye Wolves of Finance"

Is there no one in this land
Of 80 million, great and grand,
To take the people by the hand,
A Savior of the Nation?
A man who hears the people's cry
Of warning as they march on by;
Some one that money cannot buy,
Columbia's degradation.

If such there be, let him stand out
And hear the mighty welcome shout
Of millions as he looks about
Upon the scene of sorrow.
The money changer has no care;
Like Shylock, he must have his share.
Columbia, beware! beware!
There may be hell tomorrow.

In some little household nook,
Perhaps in tin can or in book,
There's something hid; don't overlook
The savings of the years.
A mother now grown old and gray
Just saved up for a rainy day;
Go, get it, Wolves; then on your way
Don't mind her falling tears.

Ye wolves of finance, whet your knives
Upon the hearts of babes and wives
Of those who toil; go, take their lives,
For are they not your debtors?
Awful, then, the judgment day,
When ye shall cringe and shriek and pray
And baby hands shall point the way
Halt! you money-getters.[7]

"See Them on the Avenue"
See them on the avenue,
Their silken skirts a-trailing
While down among the poor and lowly
Babes for sustenance are wailing.
With every sob a heart is broken;
Would that I could ease your sorrow,
But cry away you little dears,
The price of food goes up to-morrow.

In the fields of God Almighty,
Nourished by the sun and rain,
Overburdened stalks are bending,
Loaded down with ripening grain
Then the gleaner comes a-gathering—
Comes the money-changer, too.
Says, "you take the husks and leavings,
God intended them for you."[8]

This is strong material, bitter in its black-and-white character and unlike anything Dresser ever wrote before. The unrelentingly serious and damning tone of each of the songs is more than a little unnerving when one places them in the context of all of Dresser's music. While there is no way of knowing the order in which Dresser composed these three songs, the words of "The People Are Marching By" seem to be a logical continuation, and consequence, of the expressions of the other two songs. The deeds of the "wolves of finance" and the "money-changers" will cause the "downtrodden" to "throw off the fetters with one mighty shake" and to march on the land, "crushing the good, the bad and all." One wonders what Dreiser would have thought of his brother now. If he knew of these songs, would he have been proud of his older brother's introspection and militancy?

Concluding the long interview with the reporter, Dresser remarked:

> Do I intend to go on writing lyrical songs? No, I suppose all of us have higher ambitions than the work we are engaged in. I am anxious to write a musical comedy or something of that kind.
>
> The future of song writing? I see no great future for it, unless people wake up and demand good work and appreciate it. We can't stand still in that profession any more than in any other, and unless the songs get better they must deteriorate. I have, as I told you, my desk filled with songs that I know are too good to be published, and I go on and write junk—because that will sell and we must live and do the work that will help us live; that is all.[9]

What were the songs "too good to be published"? There exist in various states of completeness fifteen songs that never saw publication. Perhaps these are the ones to which Dresser was referring; perhaps not. If they *are* the ones Dresser was describing, he was deceiving himself, for none of them approaches the standards of "On the Banks of the Wabash, Far Away," for example. None of the fifteen is extraordinary in any sense.

What was Dresser to do? He was obviously caught in a terrible snare. As it stood, he would have to decide whether to make a living writing his traditional sentimental songs or instead to compose what he thought would be a "better" class of song that would reflect his seriousness and his growing social consciousness—the type of song that obviously would not sell.

CHAPTER 27

More Problems and Decline

At the end of May 1904, Paul Dresser participated in a benefit performance for the White Rats at New York's Grand Opera House, sharing the stage with George Evans and Ren Shields, among others.[1] Evans had established himself as a very successful vaudevillian, having left his earlier career in minstrelsy behind him. A friend of Dresser since the days when he featured some of Dresser's songs in his performances, Evans had become famous for an old-fashioned waltz he and Shields had written. Howley, Haviland and Dresser had published "In the Good Old Summer Time" in 1902, and it had since become the hit song that all publishers sought. Now, on this Sunday evening in May, Dresser, Evans, Shields, and other stars were "paying their dues" yet again, entertaining a large audience for the benefit of the organization that had supported them during their struggles at the turn of the century. Although the White Rats had lost its war with the Association of Vaudeville Managers, the group remained together, providing a collegiality that its members welcomed.

A horrendous disaster occurred only a few days later and prompted another series of benefit concerts by entertainers. On 15 June, the *General Slocum*, an excursion steamer plying New York's East River, exploded and burned, killing more than a thousand of its passengers. The outpouring of financial help from members of the entertainment community was instantaneous, as it had been on the occasion of the Johnstown Flood back in 1889. Benefit upon benefit was held with the proceeds used to alleviate the suffering of the survivors. Although accounts do not mention Dresser appearing in these benefits, it would not be surprising if he did, given his appearances at benefits for the White Rats and his demonstrated compassion for those in trouble and those less fortunate than he. Commemorated in articles and poetry of the time, the disaster also found its way into an unfinished orchestral composition by Charles Ives. Ives wrote, "This awful catastrophe got on everybody's nerves. I can give no other reason for attempting to put it to music."[2] To give his own music some of the flavor of a fun-filled afternoon aboard a steamboat, Ives quoted from the melodies of a few popular songs the *General Slocum*'s orchestra may well have played for the crowd. "Little Annie Rooney," "Ma Blushin' Rosie," "Violets," and "The Sidewalks of New York," a Howley, Haviland favorite of 1894, were among them. In order to convey the tragic turn of events following the explosion, Ives then turned to the hymns "Bethany" ("Nearer, My God, to Thee") and "Throw Out the Life-Line" for inspiration.

Bad news was unyielding. On 28 June, less than two weeks after the *General Slocum* tragedy, the fraternity of entertainers was saddened when Daniel Decatur Emmett died. On hearing the news, many recalled the times they had heard Ol' Dan. If the youngsters in the profession had never heard him in performance, at least they, and a nation, knew "Dixie." In his thoughts about Emmett, Dresser revisited that October evening more than two decades ago when he made his break into the big time. What a heady experience that Chicago benefit concert for Ol' Dan had been! There he was, young Dresser on the stage of the Grand Opera House with some of the biggest names in show business. A sense of nostalgia probably swept over Dresser as he relived that night. He knew that moment was forever gone, that he would never again know the purity of that experience—that instant of unadulterated terror combined with exhilaration.

Perhaps, in a reflective moment prompted by Emmett's death, Dresser wondered if his own time was past, if he and his music had become part of a yesteryear that could never be recaptured. Emmett had had his moment in the sun and then had become something of a living relic when his adoring fans turned their attention to newer kinds of entertainment. Was this to be Dresser's fate as well? Certainly he had exulted in the glorious, warming sun of his own adoring public; was that moment gone? Had he and his music become living ghosts, the very stuff of the nostalgia about which he wrote so well? Dresser's moment seemed to him to have been deliciously long and leisurely yet frightfully and painfully brief.

Dresser became increasingly depressed during the remainder of the year, complaining at times of vague illness: "I am not feeling any too well these days, *cause* I know not, but think it comes through not wearing an overcoat. I will take better care in the future."[3] It was naive for him to think that wearing an overcoat would ward off illness. The cause of his problems was instead a combination of physical and psychological demons. Dresser's morbid obesity and his near-starvation regimens, the fact that he was no longer a celebrated figure on Broadway, and the precipitous decline in the fortunes of the Howley-Dresser Company all took an enormous toll on him. Before December, Dresser and Pat Howley filed for bankruptcy. One can sense Dresser's emotional and psychological heaviness in a letter he wrote to his sister Mame Dreiser Brennan:

> If I have a flat over my head Jan 1st & after I will be only too glad to let Austin [Brennan's husband] share it with me. I am feeling pretty fair these days & hope that things will soon be all right with me. I hope to be out of the bankruptcy courts before very long. I go down to Ed & Mai's [Dresser's brother and sister-in-law] quite often & they are & have been very kind to me & will of course repay when things are coming my way.[4]

Slightly more than a month later, on 10 January 1905, Dresser wrote yet again to Brennan and her husband: "Dear Austin & Mame, Howley and I were discharged in bankrup[t]cy yesterday. Thank God. That's some good news."[5] Howley-Dresser had survived approximately a year. While the bankruptcy could not have come as a complete surprise to the partners, given their difficulty in staying even with their competition, this turn of events, nevertheless, could only have added to Dresser's despondency, even as he tried to put a positive face on the situation.

Still optimistic that he could rejoin the leaders in song publishing, Dresser, with his brother Ed Dreiser, immediately formed the Paul Dresser Publishing Company at 51 West Twenty-eighth Street, introducing the new company only four days after Dresser's announcement of the court's action on his bankruptcy petition. Lacking any capital of his own to start the business, Dresser had to borrow money from Ed's wife and her mother.[6]

After the bankruptcy, Howley started P. J. Howley at 41 West Twenty-eighth Street. By March the firm advertised its "coon" song "What's the Matter with the Mail?" in the pages of the *New York Dramatic Mirror* and soon announced other "new hits."[7] Howley had taken the old Howley-Dresser catalog, so the Paul Dresser Publishing Company had to start from scratch, establishing its own inventory. This was no doubt an overwhelming task, especially when other companies had expanded and now that the market was primarily for the newer kind of song style that was an anathema to Dresser.

If Dresser did not realize his ineptness in business matters, others certainly did, but they still felt the name Dresser would attract composers and performers. For his name, Dresser was paid $25 a week, but Ed Dreiser kept him out of the business end of the firm.[8] In the early days of the new company, it did seem as if Dresser might still have some of his former appeal. On 7 January 1905 the *Dramatic Mirror* advertised "The Paul Dresser Publishing Company: Old Friends but New Firm; New Ideas and New Songs."[9] A positive note was sounded in the same paper in early February when the company announced it had placed two songs with George Primrose's Minstrels:

> Mr. Primrose is singing "Evalyne" [*sic*] which Paul Dresser wrote expressly for him. The feature song, which is produced with spectacular effects, and the entire chorus, is "She Fought On By His Side." Everybody thinks this song will attain the popularity achieved by Dresser's "The Blue and the Grey."[10]

Another brief paragraph followed, stating that "R. I. [*sic*] Jose sent a telegram to Paul Dresser from Keith's, Boston, which said that 'She Fought On By His Side' and 'Mary Mine,' were the two biggest song hits he has ever had."[11]

This news may have given Dresser hope. Nearly thirty years before, at the beginning of his career, twenty-year-old Dresser had performed his "Where the Orange Blossoms Grow" for Primrose. Could Primrose's performances of these songs earn the forty-six-year-old composer the public's affection again? In the end, the answer was no. Nostalgic song and old-fashioned minstrelsy would not return to favor, and Dresser and Primrose simply were not part of the future.

Dresser, or some other composer under contract to his firm, had to write a blockbuster hit if this new company held any hopes of competing with the other publishers. In a sense, the Paul Dresser Publishing Company bore a certain resemblance to mom-and-pop operations when compared to the huge music-publishing operations to the north of it. Seen from the vantage point of history, the new firm seemed marked for oblivion from the start. It immediately lost money and lacked the funds to conduct its business properly. It did not, for instance, have the money to advertise in the trade papers the way Howley, Haviland and Dresser had, and very few ads appeared after January 1905. It had become a day-to-day operation, and the atmosphere surrounding it must have been oppressive. The Paul Dresser Publishing Company certainly could not compete with the likes of Charles K. Harris or with Leo Feist, financially secure and notorious in their self-promotion. Harris, for example, boasted that his songs were being performed by seventy-one different singers, including May Irwin, Pat Rooney, George Evans, Joseph Howard, and Marie Dressler.[12]

Of the seven songs Dresser published in 1905, only "My Gal Sal" ultimately became a hit, but it was slow to start, achieving that status neither in time to save the company nor to save Dresser from dying in poverty. Nine months after Dresser died, Ed Dreiser wrote to brother Theodore Dreiser about his dilemma with the company: "The business . . . was a failure from the start, and when I got out of there, I was $2500.00 to the bad, which was not all my own." He had borrowed fifteen hundred dollars from his wife, Mai, and her mother, Margaret Skelly, "which I have not been able to repay, and at the present time cannot even make the promise to repay any part of it."[13]

Dresser tried to keep up a brave front, showing continued interest in his songs. On 11 March he wrote to the Brennans, then living in St. Louis, and sent them a complimentary pass to a performance of the Primrose Minstrels, who were appearing at the Century Theatre there. "Now you go & see the show & you will hear 'She fought on by his side,' & also 'Evalyne' [*sic*] which is sung by Mr. Primrose & I think they are singing 'My Gal Sal' which is my new one."[14]

From Boston in May, where he was probably representing his company, Dresser wrote to Theodore, who was obviously upset. Dresser had arrived very late for an engagement with the Dreisers, and Theodore, perhaps feeling that Dresser's tardiness reflected his indifference to his sister-in-law, had taken his brother to task. Dresser wrote:

> Do not feel sore. A couple of hours waiting for a meal is not the worst thing that can overtake a man. I am sorry that a man of fame (ahem) like myself should have kept you and Juggie waiting that Sunday morn.[15]

And, concluding in an enigmatic manner that might have, in retrospect, been seen as prophetic, he added, "But remember that fame in many cases is but the last few throbs of a broken heart."[16]

The very end of May brought some more sad news to Dresser. On Tuesday, the thirtieth, Fattie Stewart—John Stewart Crossy—died in St. Louis at the age of seventy-one. Stewart had given Dresser his first starring role in *The Two Johns* in 1886. Born in Dublin, Stewart had been, in his own words, a seafarer, but he left that to become a comic singer in New York beginning in 1848. Then followed a succession of appearances at Barnum's Museum in New York and in various minstrel troupes, including the Sable Harmonists and Buckley's Minstrels, as well as much traveling as a singer and clown with a number of different circuses. Stewart started a couple of his own minstrel companies and in 1882 wrote the one-act farce *The Two Johns*, as an afterpiece for a benefit show at Hyde and Behman's Theatre in Brooklyn. The farce proved to be so popular that Stewart expanded it into three acts and began touring the country with it.[17] Dresser would be forever grateful to

Stewart, for Stewart had been one of Dresser's teachers and through *The Two Johns* had given him the opportunity to try out many of his early songs. The experience had been invaluable, the camaraderie wonderful. Within a short year, two figures important to the early part of Dresser's career had died. First was Emmett, forever part of the history of American popular culture, and now Stewart, his first mentor, was gone.

Perhaps using his corny sense of humor as a form of relief from all this recent dark news, Dresser wrote a letter in doggerel verse to brother Theodore Dreiser late in June. Dreiser had recently become editor of *Smith's Magazine*, and Dresser congratulated him on his work: "Dear Broth. Just been looking over 'Smiths Mag' for *June*—Great—*fine—exstatic—imperishable Genius art thou*

ode
On the shores of the Jersey Central Rale Road
Scented by the marshes sweetund breze
I see a littul tender footed maden
Whare the tranes go flying thru like Rokefurt chese

The balance follows later on a freight train—Yours *Broth*"[18]

In August Dresser wrote optimistically to his brother-in-law Austin Brennan: "Things are running about the same with me. Prospects better anyway." But the letter ended on a sour note about one of his former partners. "By the way,—A man by the name of Couchois was arrested for pirating & printing spurious Editions of music & was arrested. Howley is mixed up in it & is a big a crook as [Fred] Haviland."[19] The *Dramatic Mirror* reported on a hearing "in the case against Garrett J. Couchois, . . . a music dealer, and Louis Eggers, proprietor of the Calumet Press." The charge against the two was violation of the "trademark law in printing and disposing of copies of certain musical compositions." Couchois had been doing business out of a building at 41 West Twenty-eighth Street, the very location of Howley's publishing firm.[20] In late October Couchois was found guilty of violating the trademark law, specifically by affixing a fraudulent trademark to "Hearts and Flowers," published by Carl Fischer. If the verdict pleased Dresser, and it undoubtedly did, given his intense past interest in the copyright laws, he probably received little solace by the thought that one of his former trusted friends might have been mixed up in this business, although there is no evidence to prove Howley was.

In September hope probably returned to Dresser's heart, for on the eighth he and Michael Carmichael copyrighted *Timothy and Clover*, "a play of Indiana in 4 acts." Here the deceitful and hypocritical Rev. Laban Snepp and Jeptha Moss do battle against goodness, as personified by Bill Moss and the unlikely but predictably named Timothy and Clover Hay. The play's locale is Lickskillet, Indiana, with frequent references to spots dear to Dresser—Merom, Switz City, and Linton. Indianapolis is the great metropolis that holds out the promise of sophistication and experience to all who visit there, but it is a city that can equip poseurs with considerable pretension. The true hero of the piece is Bill Moss, whose goal in life is to provide comfort and help to the disadvantaged. He is truly a good person, the very picture of a well-lived Christian life. Bill is obviously patterned on Dresser. Bill espouses ideals of social consciousness, also a common theme in Dresser's work in later years. It is not coincidental that Moss is an immense man, weighing more than three hundred pounds. The most odious of the characters in the play is Snepp, who unctuously spouts religious pieties as he tries to deny the "fatherless and widows" their rightful inheritances. Through Snepp, Dresser wreaked a sort of personal vengeance on those in his mother's family who had long ago disowned her for her marriage to Johann Paul Dreiser. (The name Snepp, by which some of Sarah's family was known, was a corruption of Schänäb.) As a child, Dresser certainly heard stories of conflicts between the Schänäb and Dreiser families. Some of the Schänäbs were forever convinced that Sarah had married beneath her station—and had wed a Catholic to boot! Now came Dresser's chance to turn the tables. Dresser's revenge occurred only on paper, though, for *Timothy and Clover* was never produced.

During December 1905 Dresser reported dejectedly to his sister Mame Brennan: "I am still on Earth & things are running along slowly.—Music business is bad on account of it being just before Xmas. No music (or at least very little sold this time of the year on account of books, toys etc.)."[21] The Paul Dresser Publishing Company was in trouble. If Dresser really knew that fact in his heart of hearts, he was not about to let on. Besides, he and the firm would triumph. It was only a matter of time, wasn't it? The truth of the matter was that after the big advertisement for the Paul Dresser Publishing Company appeared in the *Dramatic Mirror* nearly twelve months earlier, little else was heard about the firm. Composers were not about to sell their songs to a firm whose namesake had had a recent history of bankruptcy and division.

The world that Dresser had known, the one in which he had played an important part, was collapsing around him. He undoubtedly realized this in those increasing moments of cold reckoning. To many in the profession his publishing company was synonymous with an older style of song, the kind that was not as popular as it once had been. Many felt that the Howley-Dresser and Dresser firms had not kept up with the times. The larger firms, ensconced in their up-to-date offices, had more with which to entice new composers. Whether those blandishments amounted to better distribution of the music, fancier equipment, a larger staff to handle their needs, or sumptuously decorated showrooms, the Paul Dresser Publishing Company just could not compete at the same level. The larger firms had the wherewithal to reward handsomely those selected performers who sang their latest publications. The Paul Dresser Publishing Company was not in the position to do that. The company simply did not have the money needed for promoting its songs. None of the people Dresser had helped in the past stepped forward to repay money he had given them. His friend Charles K. Harris remembered that "Paul had a little memorandum book in which he kept a record of those who owed him money; and when I inquired why he did not collect now that he was in need, he told me that he had been turned down in every instance."[22]

And then there was Dresser's music. Although Dresser's firms had published a variety of songs in the past, they had excelled in and built their reputations on old nostalgic mother-and-home songs. Now those certainly sounded quaint to younger listeners, who had had the sounds of ragtime in their ears for more than a decade. But Dresser was determined that he would not, or could not, write that kind of music. After all, ragged music was only a passing fancy, wasn't it? Still, many who once adored his style of music were turning to the newer kinds of popular song expression. Not only was his public abandoning him, but friends seemed to be deserting him at all turns. Theodore Morse had gone. Haviland and Dresser had long since ceased being friends; Howley had left as soon as bankruptcy was approved. As Louise Dresser became increasingly popular, she had naturally turned to a variety of composers for music that she could feature in her performances. Although Dresser had been one of those favored writers in the past, Louise had not sought him out in a while.

That, however, changed when Louise sang "My Gal Sal." Dresser published "Sal" in 1905, when troubles surrounded him from so many sides. In her memoirs, Louise recounted her initial connection with the song. She was in New York City, playing Keith's Union Square Theatre. Dresser asked her to come to his offices, showed her a new song he had recently composed, and insisted she sing it in place of Vincent Bryan's "That's How I Love You Mame," a song she was then performing to great audience acclaim. Louise refused, Dresser insisted, and he sang it for her. As she later recalled, "Paul was not a great musician; he strummed a few chords and melodies on a little white organ he had carried about with him for years. He had no great voice . . . but oh! how he could sing!" Louise relented and promised Dresser she would sing his new song the next day at the matinee, but first she made him promise he would not come to the theater that day since she would be very nervous, not having had sufficient time to rehearse. Dresser agreed but went back on his word. The sight of Dresser in the audience flustered Louise, her nerves got the better of her, and she sang poorly. Dresser stormed into her dressing room and gave Louise "hell for being so weak-kneed and such a quitter," but he soon relented, admitting he had been wrong to come to the theater. After Dresser left, Louise rehearsed the new song at length with the orchestra leader and sang it successfully at the evening performance. Dresser returned to the theater that night *after* Louise had sung, "his arms full and overflowing with violets he had bought from a flower vendor." Louise's rendition of "Sal" helped begin an interest in it, but the song's true success was not to come until shortly after Dresser died. At the moment he heard Louise singing his song, however, Dresser's life was made a little happier. His "sister" had not deserted him.[23]

Indiana State Library

"My Gal Sal," Paul Dresser's last hit. This sheet music was published after the release of the 1942 movie *My Gal Sal*, starring Rita Hayworth and Victor Mature.

CHAPTER 28

Final Days

In his December 1905 letter to his sister, Paul Dresser told Mame Dreiser Brennan that he had "been a little ill recently, but nothing to amount to anything."[1] Some of Dresser's siblings, not fully aware of his business reversals or the state of his health, beleaguered him; ever the generous soul, he could not help but aid them. His sister Tillie Dreiser Gormley had moved to Phoenix, Arizona, hoping that the hot, dry weather would cure her tuberculosis, but by December 1905 she had returned to New York. Dresser wearily wrote to brother Theodore Dreiser, "Did you know that Tillie had returned from Arizona? . . . I received a letter from her this morning & she has had a severe hemorrhage of the lungs & it almost killed her. I am going to send her back to Phoenix Ariz." He added a note about sister Sylvia Dreiser's illegitimate son, Carl, whom Sylvia had abandoned years before: "Another letter apprizes me of the fact that little Carl is in rags in Chicago. So I am going to place him in a school. Same old tale of woe—woe—"[2] In the next seven weeks, depression embraced Dresser ever more, and his physical health continued to decline. Theodore wrote perceptively:

> His was one of those simple, confiding, non-hardy dispositions, warm and colorful but intensely sensitive, easily and even fatally chilled by the icy blasts of human difficulty, however slight. You have no doubt seen some animals . . . of an especially affectionate nature, which when translated to a

> strange or unfriendly climate soon droop and die. They have no spiritual resources wherewith to contemplate what they do not understand or know.[3]

Deaths of former colleagues, business disaster, the loss of his musical catalog to his former partner, the knowledge that he was probably being cheated by his former colleagues and others, failure to produce *Timothy and Clover*, the unwillingness or inability of his debtors to repay him, bouts of illness, his repeated failures to lose the excessive weight he carried, and the inordinate demands of the more dysfunctional members of his family only added to Dresser's anxiety and depressive state. Always one to enjoy raising a glass with his friends, Dresser now began to drink heavily, and Theodore felt that his beloved brother "emanated a kind of fear. Depression and even despair seemed to hang about him like a cloak. He could not shake it off."[4] As early as a full two years before, Theodore had noticed his brother was being "shut out from that bright world of which he deemed himself an essential figure."[5] He was no longer a bon vivant on Broadway. More hurtful than all of that, however, was the desertion of his friends, "like winter-frightened birds."[6] In 1903 Dresser's song spoke tellingly about that abandonment:

> Where are the friends of other days,
> Friends that I used to know;
> Friends that were ever by my side,
> Friends of the long ago?
> Vainly I turn, but find them not
> Somehow it seems to me,
> They do not seek me as they once did,
> What can the matter be?[7]

In late 1905, his mental, physical, and financial declines now accelerated, Dresser resigned himself to the fact that he could no longer afford to live in a hotel. For a while now he had not had the money to eat out often and so had accepted the invitation to take his meals with an aunt of brother Ed Dreiser's wife.[8] Now he was about to lose even more of his independence, but he had no other choice. He moved in with his sister Emma Dreiser Nelson—now remarried after divorcing her first husband—at 203 West 106th Street, an act of resignation that only exacerbated the precarious state of his mind and body. His move was but another step in his decline, and he began to see premonitions of death all around him. Superstitious like his mother, now gone from him for more than fifteen years, Dresser saw "broken horse-shoes," "cross-eyed women," and the number thirteen as omens of a bleak future that awaited him.[9] The darkness of such omens was confirmed when he found a hat laying on his bed: death was unquestionably near!

Throughout the first four weeks of January 1906 Dresser's condition continued its course, the outcome of which seemed inevitable. A doctor took Theodore aside and told him, " 'Paul cannot live. He has pernicious anæmia. He is breaking down inside and doesn't know it. He can't last long. He's too depressed.' " Theodore continued, "I knew it was so and what the remedy was—money and success once more, the petty pettings and flattery of that little world of which he had been a part but which now was no more for him."[10] No longer able to summon up even the energy to do much writing and escaping into troubled sleep and drinking more, Dresser languished at his sister's home, only a short remove from the Broadway strolls of his glory days. That time of celebrity, of hangers-on, of well-wishers, of glamour were never to be his again. "Of all those who had been so lavish in their greetings and companionship earlier in his life," Theodore wrote, "scarcely one, so far as I could make out, found him in that retired world to which he was forced."[11] Ironically, Dresser had now become as one with the pathetic lost creatures he repeatedly wrote about in his songs. He was broke, ignored, and all but forgotten. With remarkable foresight, Theodore had written in 1900 about just such a figure:

> Then the wane.
>
> Of all the tragedies, this is perhaps the bitterest, because of the long-drawn memory of the thing. Organs continue to play [the song], but the sale ceases. . . . Other songwriters displace him for the time being in the public eye. His publishers have a new hit. A new author is being bowed to and taken out to dinner. A new title-crowned celebrity is strolling up his favorite Broadway path.

> At last, after a dozen attempts and failures, there is no hurry to publish his songs . . . he may even be neglected. More and more, celebrities crowd in between him and that delightful period when he was greatest. At last, chagrined by the contrast of things, he changes . . . his haunts, and, bitterest of all, his style of living. Soon it is the old grief again, and then, if thoughtless spending has been his failing, shabby clothing and want. You may see the doubles of these in any publisher's sanctum at any time—the sarcastically referred to *has been*.[12]

Dresser's realization that he had become that has-been must have been the last of a long series of cruel blows that were gradually undermining his physical and emotional well-being. The world of popular music had moved on without him, and new composers and styles of songs had already replaced him and his. Although Dresser was probably unaware of it, young upstart George M. Cohan, the darling of the entertainment world, was enjoying the success of his new musical, which opened in Springfield, Massachusetts, on 24 January. *George Washington, Jr.* would move to the Herald Square Theater on Broadway less than two weeks after Dresser died. Dresser's death marked the close of one era of song, while Cohan's success illustrated the remarkable capacity for change that popular song had and has. "You're a Grand Old Flag," Cohan's new hit, extended the style of "The Yankee Doodle Boy" and "Give My Regards to Broadway," two of his earlier successes. The exuberant character and driving rhythms of these march songs were just what audiences wanted in the early years of the new century. That high-spirited quality was more in keeping with the general mood of the country than were the gentle, nostalgic musical portraits of mother and home.

At Emma's, Dresser spent some of his interminably long days reminiscing for Theodore—remembrances that Theodore drafted into a sketch of Dresser's life.[13] Dresser rallied his spirits and energies for a short time to compose "The Judgment Is at Hand." The song would soon be heard in public for the first time as Dresser's own requiem.

THE WESTERN UNION TELEGRAPH COMPANY.
INCORPORATED
23,000 OFFICES IN AMERICA. CABLE SERVICE TO ALL THE WORLD.
ROBERT C. CLOWRY, President and General Manager.
RECEIVED at 2610-3rd AV Jan 30 1906
To Mr. Theodore Dreiser,
399 three ninety nine Mott av ny
Paul is dying. Ed

Van Pelt-Dietrich Library Center, Univ. of Pa.

Ed Dreiser's telegram to Theodore Dreiser, 30 January 1906, notifying him that brother Paul Dresser is dying.

On Tuesday, 30 January, the east already settling into darkness, Dresser's sister-in-law Mai Dreiser went to Western Union and at 5:14 P.M. sent a terse message to Mame Dreiser Brennan at 4706 South Broadway, St. Louis: "Paul is dying." Dresser clung to life for little more than another hour, his will unconsciously fighting a physical body that strove to surrender. One can never know if bits of melody, of words, flitted through his mind, but if they did, they were forever turned aside when his brain hemorrhaged and he died at 6:23.[14]

Theodore was not present at Dresser's death, but a call from Emma brought him to the brother who had "shone like a star when only one is in the sky."[15] By the time Theodore arrived, Dresser was "already cold in death, his soft hands folded over his chest, his face turned to one side on the pillow, that indescribable sweetness of expression about the eyes and mouth—the empty shell of the beetle."[16] His beloved brother was dead. Although Theodore felt his brother lacked the aesthetic and intellectual capacity to appreciate the finer writers and thinkers, he knew, without a doubt, that Dresser excelled in his own middle-class way. More important was his tenderness and sympathy that "gave him a very definite (beautiful indeed) force and charm."[17]

Obituaries were many. *The Music Trades* said:

> There was, perhaps, no song-writer in this country who was better known or who enjoyed a larger circle of friends than Paul Dresser. The exceptionally large number of successful songs that he had written, coupled with an attractive personality, made him a popular figure from one end of the country to the other. . . .
>
> ["On the Banks of the Wabash, Far Away"] has been published in eight or nine languages.
>
> Mr. Dresser has made several fortunes out of the sale of his songs, the greater amount of which was given away to his friends as fast as he made it.[18]

Another obituary reported: "His body was none too large to carry that great heart that was large as life itself, and which always beat warmly and loyally for his friends. . . . [He] was the greatest of them all as a song writer of the people."[19]

More objective was the obituary that said that while Dresser's songs won little or no attention from the classical world, they did "possess an undeniable melodious quality." The same notice called attention to two sacred songs, "Bethlehem" and "In the Great Somewhere" as examples of music that "give him some claim to critical consideration."[20]

Finally, the *New York Dramatic Mirror* dwelled on the kind of songs Dresser had composed, declaring, "Among the song-writers there are men who touch human nature closely, and many of their efforts have sentiment that reaches beyond the commonplace that the mass delights in." Offering Dresser's treatment of the sentimental in life as an example for some playwrights to emulate, the article continued:

> The success of men like Dresser has its lesson to those who write plays intended to appeal to the multitude. If there were less of the vulgarly sensational and more of human nature, and even of the simpler sentiment that seems hackneyed, in the melodrama that is now current, the results would be better all around.[21]

American popular culture and its audience had changed, however, and Dresser's method of touching a common chord of sentiment in the multitudes no longer resonated with many of the makers of that culture or with much of the public.

Yet Broadway would certainly remember one of its illustrious own. With that in mind, a memorial testimonial was planned in order to raise the funds for a permanent grave for Dresser. This would take place in March "at a Broadway theater, yet to be selected" and would feature a review of his famous song hits.[22]

CHAPTER 29

Memorials

While Broadway undoubtedly was sincere in its desire to honor Paul Dresser's memory with some sort of benefit performance, March came and went. April arrived and with it the cataclysmic earthquake and fire that destroyed much of San Francisco on the eighteenth and nineteenth. Understandably the entertainment community put most of its extra energies into benefit programs for the relief of the victims of this monumental disaster. This is not to say that benefit performances for individuals did not occur during the spring. On 15 May some twelve thousand people attended a concert at Madison Square Garden to honor Patrick S. Gilmore, the famed bandleader. Gilmore had died fourteen years earlier, and his widow and children were now destitute. Bands and orchestras of John Philip Sousa, Victor Herbert, and Frank and Walter Damrosch and a chorus of twelve hundred honored his memory that evening, and the proceeds were given to the Gilmores. Nine days before the Gilmore affair, the White Rats held their annual benefit in New York. George M. Cohan, now the star of Broadway, was the featured performer.

Although the Rats had planned to help pay for Dresser's funeral, it does not appear that any receipts from the annual benefit were used for that purpose. A month later friends of George Fuller Golden, founder and former president of the White Rats, gave him a benefit at the New York Theatre. Performers included Lillian Russell and Cohan. The Rats contributed a large floral piece and five hundred dollars to the beneficiary, now in ill health, while the concert realized four thousand dollars for him.[1] Any plans the entertainment fraternity may have had to honor Dresser were never again mentioned in the papers, and consideration of a fitting memorial for him waxed and waned for another decade or more.

Almost as soon as Dresser was buried, members of the Dreiser family started—or continued—their bickering with one another. The underlying leitmotiv of the quarrels was money. Some of his brothers and sisters found it impossible to believe Dresser had not left a sizable estate at his death and were suspicious that they might be cheated out of the portion they felt due them. After all, he had made immense amounts of money from his songs, hadn't he? Before the acrimony over Dresser's financial estate really surfaced, however, a bizarre incident occurred that further separated a family already divided.

On 19 March, a month and a half after his funeral, officials at Calvary Cemetery on Long Island sent Dresser's remains to Chicago, where they were placed in a vault in St. Boniface Cemetery, the cemetery where his parents lay. The document authorizing the removal had been signed by "Mrs. Austin D. [Mame Dreiser] Brennan and Maggie Skelly."[2] Vera Dreiser, daughter of Ed Dreiser and granddaughter of Skelly, wrote that the authorization "had been a forgery. . . . My grandmother was Margaret Skelly, never Maggie."[3] Whatever the truth is about Skelly, Mame was certainly a party to this, as most likely was Theodore Dreiser. When the deed was accomplished, or only shortly afterward, Mame wrote to Theodore: "Arrived [Chicago] last evening. . . . We layed dear Paul in the vault this morning. Leave for home at 9:15 this evening. All looked at Paul and all is well."[4]

These actions came as a complete surprise to other Dreisers, who were understandably angry at not being consulted and who probably began to harbor suspicions about being left out of other decisions as well. Dresser's body remained in that Chicago vault for the next twenty months, until, all bills paid, he was finally laid to rest beside his good father and the best of mothers on Saturday, 23 November 1907.[5] Almost a year later, Carl Dreiser Kishima, son of Sylvia Dreiser, wrote to his Uncle Theodore, "Was out to see Uncle Paul's grave last week, and found it to be covered with geraniums and wild flowers. Uncle Paul hasn't any tombstone over his grave."[6] Dresser's grave was to remain unmarked until a rainy Sunday afternoon in November 1922, when the Indiana Society of Chicago dedicated a monument over his resting place. The unusual but fitting memorial is a huge boulder brought to St. Boniface from the banks of the Wabash River and now inscribed:

Paul Dresser
1859 [*sic*] Author 1906
State Song of Indiana
"On the Banks of the Wabash, Far Away"
Erected By
Indiana Society of Chicago
Nov. 1922
Rededicated Nov. 1974

At the moment, however, Mame wanted to recover her family's share of the funeral expenses. Her husband, Austin Brennan, wrote to Judson Wells, the attorney for the White Rats, inquiring about the benefit the group had talked about giving, the proceeds of which would be used for the cost of Dresser's funeral. Wells did not respond. Mame wrote to Theodore asking him to inform her about the status of Dresser's affairs. Theodore had not yet replied when Austin fired off a letter to him:

> I am now writing you, presuming that you consider it none of my business to question your stewardship. I wish, however, to impress upon your mind one thing; that I consider your attitude a questionable one, as it must be plain to you that if it were not for the care and expense exercised by me, that the remains of your brother, Paul, would rest in the Potter's Field.

Austin informed Theodore that he "would consider it an honor to bury him if I could afford to." At the time, Dresser's remains still had not been committed to the earth. "The atmosphere of rottenness that seems to have impregnated the whole sad and deplorable affair will right itself anon, you may rest assured," he continued. "Have you anything to say?"[7]

Photograph by the author

Paul Dresser's gravestone in St. Boniface Cemetery, Chicago; inscribed "Paul Dresser / 1859 [*sic*] Author 1906 / State Song of Indiana / "On the Banks of the Wabash, Far Away" / Erected by / Indiana Society of Chicago / Nov. 1922 / Rededicated Nov. 1974." To the right of Dresser's stone is the grave marker for John [Johann] Paul Dresser [*sic*] and Sarah Mary Dresser [*sic*] with the inscription: "A Good Father & the Best of Mothers."

In the same month Theodore wrote to the members of the family, explaining his attempts to secure bondsmen or bond money to enable him to act as the administrator of Dresser's estate. In the letter Theodore complained that Wells, whom he had asked to review Dresser's estate and business dealings, enormously complicated by the bankruptcy of the Howley-Dresser Company and the numerous financial problems of the Paul Dresser Publishing Company, had been less than honorable:

> Personally, I think Judson G. Wells is like all the rest of Paul's friends—a Large Fake. Why he does not want me to act, I cannot understand except probably that he feels that anything he would do during my administratorship would have to be thoroughly known of and appreciated by me.

Van Pelt-Dietrich Library Center, Univ. of Pa.

Theodore Dreiser, ca. 1907, around the time he became the executor of Paul Dresser's estate.

> If I had money and was able to hire a lawyer of my own accord, I would not ask Wells to do anything at all. I would prosecute an inquiry on my own hook.
>
> In regard to the general expenses which were involved at the time of the funeral, I am willing to stand my share, or even more than my share.[8]

A week later Mame wrote to Theodore to remind him that when she was in New York she had been appointed temporary administratrix of Dresser's estate, an appointment ratified by Theodore, Ed, and Emma. The gist of Mame's letter expressed her considerable bitterness to those who were impeding progress in dealing with the estate. Slapping at Theodore, Mame told him that Wells had offered to waive his contingency fee and expenses for *her*, which suggested to her that Wells must have had some prospect of realizing something from work on the estate. Continuing with her long litany of complaints, she wrote:

> The disgraceful burial bills are unpaid, which I am sure I could have arranged for long before this, and will now, later on, whether one, two three or four respond or not.
>
> The only real lively act was committed by Ed over the phone to Huhna [Anthony Huhna, undertaker at 91 Sixth Avenue, New York City] wishing to know how much money had been paid him from the white rats.
>
> When I consider the expense to me, of necessity incurred by Paul's death and those which have been added to it more recently, then of the waste of time and opportunity through lack of foresight, or, worse than all, the contemptible and narrow-minded judgment of some members of our family of which I have been made a victim, especially when I know that both of the parties heretofore mentioned [sisters Sylvia Dreiser and Tillie Dreiser Gormley] were the most distant ones from Paul in his heart's affections[9]

Mame added: "I do not agree with you that all of Paul's friends are fakes and imposters; he was made the victim of a generous, sympathetic and noble nature, I will admit,—too refined in temperament to cope with his cold-blooded critics, who profited by his generous bounty only to receive his reward—their condemnation." In a bitter conclusion, Mame asked Theodore rhetorically: "Do you need to go outside of his family circle to find strong evidences of graft and ingratitude? The facts have been apparent, and known to many of his friends. He suffered in want, alone, uncomplainingly, weeks before he died, with no one in whom he could confide or cheer him excepting Emma."[10]

Shortly after this, Ed reminded Theodore that Ed had borrowed money from his mother-in-law to get the Paul Dresser Publishing Company started and that he had his own financial problems, beholden as he was to Skelly and her generosity. Additionally, Skelly "gave the plot to bury Paul in, which under the circumstances, considering I have lost every dollar I could get my hands on, should stand for my part of the burial."[11]

In the meantime, Theodore explored the possibilities of having Dresser's last play, *After Many Years*, performed in hopes of realizing some financial profit for the family. Bob Davis, of *Munsey's Magazine* and coauthor of the play, offered to try to get it produced, with the Dresser estate to get 25 percent of the profits and Davis the remainder. Writing to Mame, Theodore said, "[Davis] holds from Paul a full release of interest which Paul gave at the time of the Howley-Haviland smash-up. If he wanted to, he wouldn't need to make any division whatsoever. He does it because he thinks it is the only honest thing to do."[12]

And the familial vultures continued to circle. A month later Al Dreiser added his criticism to that of Mame and Ed. Writing from Chicago, he asked Theodore:

> Who is getting the royalties [from Dresser's songs]? I have a feeling that all is not right in this matter. I wish to know something about it. There ought to be a lot of money in Paul's songs and I would like to see some of it coming my way, or at least know where it's going to.
>
> I hear different kinds of news from friends and acquaintances but nothing from my own people.[13]

Theodore responded to Al that "the matter of investigating Paul's affairs is in the hands of Judson G. Wells." Wells was to review the books of Howley, Haviland and Company and the more recent accounts of Pat Howley and Fred Haviland as individuals as well as to "communicate with the men who published Paul's songs in London, and find out just what has been sold since the last statement was rendered to Paul during his life. Paul left no personal property, as you perhaps know."[14]

Theodore then hired Thomas McKee to sort out Dresser's business affairs—more specifically, to determine who held the copyrights to Dresser's songs. It was an exasperating experience for McKee, who at one time had been a lawyer for Doubleday publishers. In September 1907, more than a year and a half after Dresser died, McKee reported to Dreiser that "that gang that has the songs come pretty close to the line of highwaymen, and I have grave doubts of your getting satisfaction, let alone money."[15] Yet Theodore persisted, even though it was some time before Dresser's confusing affairs were placed in reasonable order and before Theodore could give a financial accounting to his brothers and sisters. Given the family quarrels and jealousies, it must have seemed a thankless task to Theodore. Still, Theodore most often handled his responsibilities creditably and attempted to mollify his brothers and sisters with accounts of monies coming to them from the sale of Dresser's songs. It is most probable that even wayward brother Rome Dreiser shared in the royalties from Dresser's music. In the 1920s Rome lived at the Rufus S. Dawes Hotel in Chicago, watched over by John Hanson, superintendent of the hotel. While never contacting Rome directly, Theodore sent him money for his living expenses through an intermediary. All return correspondence always came from Hanson and never from Rome.[16]

Even after Theodore's death in 1945, expenses related to Dresser's affairs and funeral resurfaced. Mai Dreiser wrote to Theodore's widow, Helen, reminding her of the money Mai and Ed had spent helping Dresser shortly before his death.[17] She did not ask for payment of this old debt, but one suspects that if Helen, feeling sorry for Mai, had sent her money, Mai would have accepted it gladly. Mai wrote:

> We started Paul in business [and] made it possible for him to publish "My Gal Sal." Through that transaction we were out

> . . . four thousand dollars. Paid Paul a salary of $25 a week. . . . Ed . . . left his salary in the treasury. I opened a charge account . . . and furnished the rooms to the tune of $2000. I don't think Theo knew this part of our life: poor Paul[;] while he was at Emma's, [he] told them there would be enough for every one when he passed on.
>
> The truth was he didn't have a quarter to buy a meal—ate all his meals at my Aunt Kate's. . . . He told Emma that story so they wouldn't put him out in the street. I wonder if you know I had to pay Paul's funeral expenses. I heard the White Rats society sent Mary [Mame] Brennan $250[;] she spent that check to have the body removed out west. [F]orged my mother['] s name and had the grave opened. Mame asked me to forgive her for this before she died—of course I did. So you see Helen we never sent a bill for all this to the Estate of P.D.
>
> It galled me to see statements giving some royalties to people that were sent to Ed. People that wouldn't give Paul a cup of tea when he was down & out and he certainly was down & out when we picked him up. I told this to Mame many times and wrote out statements for her to send to Theo, but I guess they never reached him. I have the receipt for Paul's funeral and the letter sent with it. I had to pay it in order to get our deed back for the grave [in New York] in which Paul was buried.[18]

One will never know with certainty the veracity of some of Mai's claims, but there is no doubt that she and Ed were a great help to Dresser during his most difficult days.

Shortly after Dresser's death, people across the nation, especially in Indiana and Terre Haute, began to plan various ways they could memorialize him. With few exceptions, most of the plans fell by the wayside, some because they were too grandiose and unrealistic, some because of the interference of Theodore, some because America changed dramatically after 1940, and some because of a combination of these and other reasons. The following catalog is meant to be illustrative rather than exhaustive.

As discussed, neither the White Rats nor other members of the entertainment community ever held a benefit for Dresser.

Indifference or the press of more worthy causes attended the first attempts to pay tribute to him.

At one time Terre Haute had a Dresser post office and a Dresser power plant. U.S. 41, a major north-south highway that covers the entire length of western Indiana, was once known as the Paul Dresser Memorial Highway. Dresser Aviation Field, important to the development of new airmail routes in the late 1920s, attracted barnstorming pilots and visiting celebrities. By 1928 newspapers announced the beginning of passenger service from Chicago to Atlanta with Dresser Field as one of the intervening stops.[19] Only five years later, though, the Board of Aviation Commissioners changed the name of Dresser Field to Paul Cox Field, honoring a Terre Haute pilot killed in an air crash the previous year. The Dresser telephone exchange was also a short-lived tribute, adopted in 1922 to "give impetus to the [proposed] Paul Dresser Memorial . . . about the time there was agitation . . . [by] citizens of Lafayette to have the . . . Dresser memorial located [there]."[20] The village of Dresser, Indiana, also known as Taylorville, still exists, an eyesore of small homes and trailers that abuts on what remains of the Paul Dresser Memorial.

In 1913 the Indiana legislature designated "On the Banks of the Wabash, Far Away" as the state song. Sung at most public events in Indiana well into the 1930s, "Wabash" has been replaced in the minds and hearts of Hoosiers by "(Back Home Again in) Indiana." When Theodore Dreiser was making plans for a nationwide celebration of Paul Dresser Day, to coincide with the release of the movie *My Gal Sal* in 1942, he became aware of an earlier film that had starred Barbara Stanwyck and Fred MacMurray and had included "Indiana" in its musical score.[21] Dreiser viewed this music as a plagiarism of "Wabash." Written in 1917 with music by James Hanley to words by Ballard MacDonald, the song borrows admiringly—and shamelessly—from Dresser. Using the refrain to "Wabash," where Dresser wrote, "Through the sycamores the candle lights are gleaming," MacDonald penned, "The gleaming candlelight still shining bright / Thru the sycamores"; Dresser's "Oh, the moonlight's fair tonight along the Wabash" became "When I dream about the moonlight on the Wabash"; and Dresser's "From the fields there comes the breath of new-mown hay" were changed to "The new mown hay sends all its fragrance." Hanley took the melody from those measures of Dresser's song where the words "Through the sycamores the candle lights are gleaming" appear and, with but the change of a single note, took all of that tune to fit MacDonald's words "When I dream about the moonlight on the Wabash." By using note values of long, followed by short, durations throughout his song—precisely those note lengths that pervade Dresser's song—Hanley simulated the entire musical mood of "Wabash." The complicated state of Dresser's business affairs, including the numerous questions about copyright ownership of his songs, and Dreiser's own developing career had not left Dreiser a great deal of time, as his brother's executor, to deal with all the intricacies of Dresser's estate; thus he was probably unaware until 1940 that others had expropriated some music and words from "Wabash" for their own use.[22]

If Dreiser had *really* collaborated in the creation of "Wabash," such musical and textual borrowing would be a blow to his own artistic pride. Too, Dreiser could have felt that the popularity of "Indiana" might overshadow his brother's state song and possibly temper the recognition Dreiser hoped the movie *My Gal Sal* would bring Paul. In any event Dreiser wrote to the Paull-Pioneer Music Corporation, then the owners of the copyright to "Wabash," alleging copyright violation against Hanley and MacDonald. The president of Paull-Pioneer informed Dreiser that the Maurice Richmond Music Company, owners of the copyright to "Wabash" in 1917, had granted permission to Hanley and MacDonald to use two bars of music from "Wabash" with some change in the lyrics. Not content with this explanation, Dreiser continued with increasing acrimony to attempt to make his case against Hanley and MacDonald for the next six months, even after attorneys told Dreiser that he had no control over what the Maurice Richmond Music Company had done in 1917. Offered two hundred dollars to settle the matter, Dreiser angrily refused the money, at which time the president of Paull-Pioneer accepted the money on Dreiser's behalf, sending him a check for that amount.[23]

While Dresser's state song was sung at all sorts of gatherings in Indiana well into the 1940s, "Indiana" has gradually replaced "Wabash" in the minds, hearts, and ears of many younger

Hoosiers. Indeed, many people—Hoosier and non-Indianan alike—mistakenly believe that Hanley's is the state song and have never heard "Wabash." While Stephen Foster's "My Old Kentucky Home, Good Night!" is sung before the running of the Kentucky Derby and identified as the state song by those gathered there and by others who watch the event on television, the preliminaries to the Indianapolis 500 race, a mass event much larger than the Kentucky Derby, and one that represents and identifies Indiana to many outsiders, features the singing of "Indiana," not the state song. Today one only rarely hears "On the Banks of the Wabash, Far Away," composed by the man many consider to be the only true successor to Foster in the writing of sentimental home songs. Based on musical merits alone, it is difficult to know why Foster's song has endured while Dresser's has largely been forgotten. With their bittersweet memories of the past in words colored by the halcyon days of youth, both represent the grand tradition of the sentimental song. The music of each, relatively simple, speaks directly to the heart and possesses that ineffable magic that makes for a superior song.

It is also puzzling why "Indiana" has supplanted "Wabash" as *the* favorite song about Indiana. Hanley's song, as it is usually performed, has a jauntiness, a sprightliness that gives it a certain appeal to the ear, but "Wabash" possesses that same buoyant quality when it is sung at a tempo slightly faster than is customary today, but one at which it was often sung at the turn of the century. Perhaps without realizing it, some *do* hear "Wabash" as it is imbedded in its shadow twin. Nonetheless, its loss from collective memory diminishes the musical treasure of yesteryear. While writings of George Ade, Booth Tarkington, and James Whitcomb Riley, Hoosiers all, still help many people fondly recall a time and place past, albeit through memory's mist, most have forgotten, or do not know, Dresser's state song.

In July 1923 Terre Haute mayor Ora Davis broke ground for the Paul Dresser Drive. The *Terre Haute Tribune* reported that when completed it would "encircle the city with a beautiful forty-mile drive, placing Terre Haute among the foremost cities of its size in the matter of park and boulevard systems." Davis referred to Dresser Drive and a proposed Dresser monument as "the dawning of a new era in the territory along the length of the Wabash river at this point."[24] Before long, however, city fathers reduced the extravagant boulevard to six miles and finally settled for the completion of a one-mile Paul Dresser Drive, which was opened on 28 May 1932 with a Paul Dresser Day and Wabash River Festival.

In the late 1930s Theodore Dreiser began negotiations with several movie studios for a film about his brother. *My Gal Sal* opened in 1942 with Rita Hayworth portraying Sal. Victor Mature, a screen matinee idol of the 1940s and 1950s who later played Samson in *Samson and Delilah*, the Cecil B. DeMille epic of 1949, starred as Dresser. Casting the athletically built Mature in the part of the three-hundred-pound Dresser was certainly artistic license and called for the willing suspension of disbelief from those who had known Dresser personally. While its costumes and some of its songs captured some of the flavor of the 1890s, the movie was more fantasy than biography and did little to revive interest in Dresser's music.

In 1961, upon learning that Dresser's birthplace was in an area to be taken over by the city of Terre Haute for an urban-renewal project, the Vigo County Historical Society formed the Paul Dresser Birthplace Preservation Committee, whose goal was to restore and relocate the house to Fairbanks Park close to the Wabash River. Successful in its efforts, the historical society opened the home to the public in July 1966. A year later the Indiana General Assembly designated Dresser's home as a state shrine and memorial, and in 1973 the house was included in the National Register of Historic Places. In 2002 the historical society renovated and rededicated it.

In March 1971 Johnny Mercer, then president of the Songwriters Hall of Fame, signed a certificate stating that Dresser had been elected to that prestigious group of composers "in recognition of outstanding contribution to American Popular Music."[25]

Among the ideas that it reviewed for a tribute, the Paul Dresser Memorial Association, founded in 1922, considered an extensive Paul Dresser park and lake system and a monument similar to the Arc de Triomphe, whose legs would span U.S. 40. The group ultimately agreed upon the construction of two memorial circles, one on either side of U.S. 40, with sycamores to be planted on the perimeters of both circles. Huge electric candles placed in the center of each circle were to symbolize the words "through the sycamores the candle lights are gleaming." Plans and construction proceeded in fits and starts, and during the Great Depression the WPA contributed eighty-eight thousand dollars toward the building of this impressive monument. The entire plan, however, was never realized.

In September 1994 only a few fragments of concrete below grass level and an encircling dirt roadway gave any hint that the northern circle ever existed. While the southern ring remained, a twenty-seven-foot-wide dirt road encircling it, the site was overgrown with weeds, the starts of young trees, and unrestrained growths of bushes. Crumbling brickwork outlined the perimeter of a raised inner circle seventy-six feet in circumference, with broad ascending steps on both the east and west sides. Within the circle was a concrete pedestal three and a half feet high with three electrical conduits protruding from its top, all that remained of the foundation for the southern candle. Just inside the dirt road nine mature sycamores survived, undoubtedly those planted in 1930. An auto graveyard, a field for church-league softball games, a playground with broken and rusting equipment, and a building for the Kerman Grotto, a fraternal lodge, bordered the site. The majestic sycamores, sentinels guarding the circle, contributed the sole dignity and beauty to the sorry area. Less than half a mile away Dresser's lovely Wabash flowed serenely on, unmindful of the turn of events that prevented the realization of an enduring monument. In 1998, just four years later, the southern memorial circle was nearly obliterated.

Even after Dresser's body had been spirited away from New York and shipped to Chicago, the Dreiser family and Indiana politicians argued among and between themselves over the most appropriate place to bury Dresser yet again, with Theodore Dreiser feeling that St. Boniface was "a cheap, 10th rate Catholic cemetery."[26] Disagreements over the appropriate location for Dresser's final resting place and a monument by which to mark it continued for the next decade and a half. The various plans for a suitable monument to identify Dresser's grave came to naught, and to this day he remains in St. Boniface, protected by the immense boulder from the Wabash. His beloved mother and his father lie beside him.

In 1992 the city of Terre Haute and the state of Indiana paid tribute to Dresser and his brother Theodore by naming a bridge after

Photograph by the author

What remains of the unfinished memorial to Paul Dresser in Terre Haute.

Photograph by the author

One of the proposed monuments to Paul Dresser—an arch modeled on the Arc de Triomphe.

each. These bland, utilitarian monuments, typical of how America often honors its famous, are not without a certain irony that was probably unintentional but that would, nevertheless, have irritated Dreiser and amused Dresser: The one-way bridge coming eastward into Terre Haute is named for Dreiser. In name, at least, he is forever being returned to the city and state he always wanted to leave. In spite of Dresser's celebrity nationwide and beyond, he always wanted to return to the scenes of his childhood, hallowed in his memory. Now his journey is pointed *out* of Terre Haute via the west-bound Paul Dresser Memorial Bridge.

For nearly nine decades, those who hoped to honor Dresser found precarious footing on the slippery banks of the Wabash. While they executed some plans successfully, more often they failed. Dresser's most lasting monument may ultimately rest in the memories and thoughts of those who are ineffably moved by his words and melodies, which recall and yearn for—sometimes with great heartbreak—the simpler times and the innocence of youth.

Through his songs Dresser succeeded in capturing an American past of carefree days, small-town pleasures, and idealized motherhood, all images that served Americans well, whether they chose to remain in rural villages or move to the larger cities. Yet even before Dresser's death, Americans were ready to move on, to leave behind his effusions as reminders of a quaint but no longer relevant time. As America changed from a relatively isolated nation to an increasingly powerful player on a global scale, so, too, did its popular songs change. Rarely again did they conjure up a past with the same wistfulness and poignancy that Dresser brought to many of his songs. Those looking for clues to illuminate some of this late-nineteenth-century sentimentality could scarcely do better than to listen to and sing some of the songs of Dresser.

Dresser's finest songs are those that speak and sing of times remembered, that touch on the irrecoverable past that reminds us of the evanescence of life. Through his songs we can return, if only for a moment, to what we recall, however imperfectly, as the simpler life. For a few brief moments, Dresser's magic can inexplicably touch us as little else can. This is perhaps his greatest gift to the American people, and our remembrances and emotional response to his songs may well serve as the best memorial to him.

PART 5

The Songs

CHAPTER 30

The Creative Process and the Dissemination of Popular Songs

Early on, Paul Dresser lacked the technical skill to write down his melodies in all but the most rudimentary shape. It would not have been unusual for him to hum to a colleague a tune whose melody he had in his head; someone, perhaps the piano player, then might hastily write it down in musical shorthand that he could decipher—in enough substance so one could accompany Dresser when he sang the resulting "song." At that stage, the song was more of an improvisation than a refined, finished product. In the early days, when Dresser was in Terre Haute and Evansville, the press of time—or perhaps a number of other factors—likely kept him from recording a final version on paper for publication. We have to wait until the summer or fall of 1886 for evidence of his first published song.

Before he began to compose in earnest, Dresser frequently used musical and poetic ideas of others as models. In 1902 a reporter wrote that Dresser "drifted into song writing from taking old songs and changing the melody. Many believed that the tunes were original, and he never considered it necessary to change [a]nyone's belief on that subject."[1] Although Dresser never mentioned specific sources, we have already seen that "Where the Orange Blossoms Grow" reminded listeners of Stephen Foster's "Old Folks at Home." It would not be surprising if Dresser emulated Foster and that generation of composers more than once in his early efforts. After all, this was the music closest to him in spirit and in fact. Some of the popular songs from the decades of the

1850s through the 1870s, including Civil War tunes, minstrel songs, and a large portion of Foster's works, constituted a body of music Dresser and countless other Americans would have known, sung, and played. This was the core of popular vocal music Dresser would have carried in his mind and on his lips as he began his career as an entertainer.

In spite of the difficulties he had had in 1886 with Max Sturm over the ownership of "The Letter That Never Came," its popular success certainly encouraged Dresser as a composer. Buoyed by the knowledge that he could compose music the public enjoyed, he added "composer" to the list of his credentials and in 1887 began his real start in this area, writing nine songs in that year alone. From the beginning his was an intuitive art, and he always freely admitted that he knew little about the "science" of music, having studied piano for only a short time as a teenager. As he put it, "I have never taken lessons in song writing. I don't think the natural song writers ever take lessons. I do not see how they could. They would lose all the inspiration in studying technique."[2] Among the popular-song composers of the day, Dresser was not alone in his lack of music education. A critic wrote, "It is soberly maintained by a large number, possibly a majority, of successful popular song writers that a knowledge of music—that is, of composition and harmony—is a distinct handicap. It educates a man's taste beyond that of those whom he is striving to reach."[3]

Dresser always maintained that he was self-taught and could write his sentimental songs only when he was in the right mood. "When the humor seizes me I have not the least trouble, and it takes but a very short time to do it."[4] In addition to the "right mood," Dresser had to have the proper motivation:

> Personally, I don't think that one can write a song in a sentimental strain—one that can catch the popular fancy—without some sort of inspiration. I have frequently been offered large and tempting sums of money for a song to be written in a hurry—made to order. I have needed the money in such cases, but I couldn't write the songs in that way.[5]

In another interview Dresser stated:

> How do I write a song? It depends on what you call songs. Some of the doggerel of which I am guilty I write anywhere—here in the office on a writing pad sometimes; but the real songs seem to come to me all at once, in a flash, an inspiration. I have a big organ in my place at the Gerard and sometimes I get up at night and play softly on it when I have thought of a melody.[6]

In an undated interview in the *Junior Munsey*, Dresser stated that he always strove to speak to some elemental human emotion in his songs—the old themes of "filial, parental, or romantic love, or love of country." Then he sought to freshen his subject in some new way, either in the way he related the story or in a new melodic approach.[7]

The creative process for Dresser most frequently began with his humming a tune or a melodic fragment that almost seemed to haunt him. Sometimes, however, it was the other way around, with words or a mental picture prompting a tune. Theodore Dreiser tellingly remarked that "he was constantly attempting to work [his ideas] out of himself."[8] Going to a piano or to a portable organ, his preferred instrument, Dresser played his tune, or the fragments, over and over, jotting his ideas down in crude form on a piece of music paper, changing notes here, a note there. Dreiser felt his brother's mood was one of depression during such times. Rather than being despondent, however, Dresser was probably lost in intense concentration, a focus that allowed him to shut out all distractions while he was composing. Contrary to Dresser's comment about writing the good songs rapidly once he was in the proper humor and was inspired, Dreiser witnessed his brother working out the tunes slowly, brooding over them,

> thrum[ming] a melody by the hour, especially toward evening or at night. He seemed to have a peculiar fondness for the twilight hour, and at this time might thrum over one strain and another until over some particular one, a new song usually, he would be in tears![9]

Then, released from his long absorption, his mood and countenance changed to one of "marked elation or satisfaction."[10] Dreiser recalled that Dresser's great hit of 1895, "Just Tell Them That You Saw Me," was the result of just such a process. Improvising, then working out the tune on a piano in a room at Howley, Haviland and Company, Dresser later came out to his younger brother and "played and sang the first verse and chorus. In the middle of the latter, so moved was he by the sentiment of it, his voice broke and he had to stop. Tears stood in his eyes and he wiped them away. A moment or two later he was able to go through it without wavering."[11]

Whether the process was long or took but a short time, once Dresser had decided on just the right fit of words and music, he gave them to someone else to arrange the piano part and make a clean copy of the completed song, after which it was ready to be engraved. The initial step in publication was to issue "professional copies" printed on thin newsprint. The publishers gave these free to professional singers; orchestral arrangements were made to accompany the more prominent artists. Well-known singers cut deals with publishers, promising to feature the publishers' songs in their performances in return for weekly payments. If, in the opinion of these singers, a particular song showed promise, its publisher then printed regular copies of the song, distributing them to stores that sold sheet music. If the song began to sell reasonably well, the publisher then advertised it in the company's own publications and in trade papers such as the *New York Clipper* and the *New York Dramatic Mirror*. If the song showed promise of being a hit,

> Canvassers are often sent about to the music halls where a song is being sung for the week, to distribute hand-bills upon which the words are printed, to the end that the music-hall frequenters may become familiar with it and the sooner hum and whistle it on the streets. Boy singers are often hired to sit in the gallery and take up the chorus with singer, thus exciting attention. Friends and hirelings are sent to applaud uproariously, and other small tricks common to every trade are employed to foster any early indication of public interest in the piece.

> . . . very few know of the important part played by the hand and street organ and by the phonograph in familiarizing the masses with the merits of a song.
>
> With the organ-master-general the up-to-date publisher is in close communication, and between them the song is made a mutual beneficiary arrangement.[12]

Singers promoted songs as they traveled to opera houses and theaters, performing night upon night—with matinees thrown in—in town after town, city after city, throughout the nation. With but a little delay, audiences in Nebraska villages, or in frontier towns in the territories of Arizona and New Mexico, could listen to the same songs that people in large eastern cities were hearing. While some in a community—whether in New York City or in Keokuk, Iowa—might not deign to be seen at popular entertainment shows, audiences tended to represent the makeup of the location. In a sense, democracy was in action in the theater as it was in a sports venue. Figuratively speaking—and excluding racial mixing—wealthy and poor, men and women, people from different ethnic groups and of various religious persuasions—or none at all—rubbed shoulders as they would have at a baseball field.

Some in the audience, enchanted by a Richard Jose's or a Julia Mackey's singing of a recent ballad, would go to a local store, purchase the sheet music (sometimes for the cover itself), take the song home, and share it with the family. What was the kind of music promoted and sung in halls and on stages that would persuade the listener to buy it for his or her own use? More often than not it was the sentimental song of mother and home that had the greatest impact on an audience. Certainly other kinds of songs must have had good sales, but in an age when gentility and sentimental expression were still important, music recalling mother's attributes would have sold well. It is virtually impossible, however, to determine precisely sales figures for nineteenth-century popular songs.

As the century wore on, specific singers were increasingly identified with particular songs, their reputations used to help sell sheet music. The cover of the music carried attractive illustrations or pictures of handsome or beautiful singers or saucy soubrettes whose renditions of the song had become famous. To many in the public, these glamorous people became models for admiration and emulation. By buying music with one of these images on the cover, the amateur would possess his or her own picture of the star—and he or she could sing the very music that had brought celebrity to that star. Dreiser wrote of these " 'peerless singers of popular ballads,' as their programs announce them, men and women whose pictures you will see upon every song-sheet, their physiognomy underscored with their own 'Yours Sincerely' in their own handwriting."[13]

And what lay ahead for the successful composer!

> Before, he was commonplace, hungry, envious, wretchedly clothed. After it he is the extreme of the reverse. Do not talk to him of other authors who have struck it once, had their little day, and gone down again, never to rise. He is for the sunlight and the bright places. No clothing too showy or too expensive. No jewelry too rare. Broadway is the place for him—the fine cafes and rich hotel lobbies.
>
> He is a great man and the world knows it. The whole country is making acclaim over that which he had done.[14]

The sad truth was that there were far more one-hit composers than those who had repeated successes.

Dresser would be one of the rare ones who succeeded time and time again, but it took some time to establish himself. The lightning bolt of "The Letter That Never Came" was not to strike again for some time. Dresser continued to hone his skills as a songwriter, turning out some sixty compositions before his next hit, "Just Tell Them That You Saw Me," came in 1895. In the meantime he learned much from listening carefully to what the public liked. As he put it later, "song writing is like everything else; you study your public, and you study the trend of the times and you usually strike the right note."[15]

CHAPTER 31

The Elements

Today, when music is anywhere and everywhere at the push of a button or the turn of a switch, it is difficult to imagine a time when, to hear music, one had to actually sing, hum, whistle, or play it or listen to someone else perform it live. In the days before recorded performances, popular songs became known to many through oral tradition. Others could learn the music from the printed music page. Regardless of how one came to know a song, it involved making live music of some sort, an important part of nineteenth-century American culture. Those who had the ability to read music could, if they were able to afford it, buy the sheet music for songs and learn the music that way. They then possessed an item for their personal collection that they could bind in a volume together with their other favorites. If they chose to do so, they could tear off the covers and use them as decoration.

The musical style of nineteenth-century popular songs often reflected recycled music traditions from the past. Italian opera as well as Irish and Scottish forebears could be heard clearly in songs before American composers fashioned their own styles out of an eclectic synthesis of the musical past. The harmonium, also known as the parlor or pump organ, had once been the instrument of choice for accompanying these songs, but the piano gradually became the favored instrument for that purpose. Keyboard accompaniments tended toward the uncomplicated, with chords in block or arpeggiated figurations in the left hand and the right hand often duplicating the singer's melody. All this made it possible for even a person with elementary pianistic skills to play many of the accompaniments. For countless numbers of people, music making was a major form of recreation: Family members would gather in the parlor with one of them at the keyboard. Others could join in, singing their favorite songs of the past and some of the new ones they had recently heard and bought. They would treasure forever the memories of those moments—the hilarity of the silly songs, the sentimental words that brought a lump to the throat or tears to the eyes, and the closeness that the music brought to them. Such moments became part of a nation's individual—and collective—past. Years later a song, or merely a snippet of its melody, might trigger those memories and transport one back to those golden days.

Even though there is no account of the Dreiser family, or many other poor families for that matter, having owned a piano, that did not preclude music making in the form of singing. A voice, after all—whether sweet or raucous—belonged to all. Dresser's generation, and the one before it, would have known and sung "Just before the Battle, Mother," "The Battle-Cry of Freedom," "The Battle Hymn of the Republic," "Tenting on the Old Camp Ground," and "When Johnny Comes Marching Home"—some of the great songs the dreadful Civil War inspired. Then there was the ubiquitous "Dixie," appropriated, in a sense, by southerners but sung throughout the nation. That same group of people would also have sung Stephen Foster favorites ("Oh! Susanna," "Old Folks at Home," "Jeanie with the Light Brown Hair," "My Old Kentucky Home, Good Night!," "Massa's in de Cold Ground," and "De Camptown Races" among them), tunes they might first have heard when minstrel shows or medicine-wagon shows came to town. Septimus Winner's "Listen to the Mocking Bird" of 1855 had long been another favorite. "Grandfather's Clock," "I'll Take You Home Again, Kathleen," "Silver Threads among the Gold," "Carry Me Back to Old Virginny," and "Put Me in My Little Bed," all from the 1870s, became part of the treasury of nineteenth-century song.

Composers from one to two generations before Dresser, some who wrote songs during all of Dresser's creative years, included George Frederick Root (1820–1895), Stephen Foster (1826–1864), Septimus Winner (1827–1902), Charles A. White (1830–1892), Henry Clay Work (1832–1884), Hart Pease Danks (1834–1903), William Shakespeare

Hays (1837–1907), David Braham (1838–1905), and Edward Harrigan (1845–1911). Among the composers born within ten years of Dresser were Thomas Paine Westendorf (1848–1923), James Bland (1854–1911), Charles K. Harris (1867–1930), and Joseph E. Howard (1867–1961). Harry Von Tilzer (1872–1946) and George M. Cohan (1878–1942) represent part of yet another generation. Composers from this span of four generations wrote songs that remained part of the American consciousness well into the twentieth century.

Put simply, nineteenth-century songs told stories. With the tale beginning, unfolding, and concluding in a series of verses and a chorus, a song was a miniature musical drama, an operatic scene without the acting, but one that was often interpreted through visual aids as the singer performed it onstage. Storytelling through popular song is customarily straightforward in content and intent. Rarely does one find poetic devices, such as metaphor or simile, that one might observe in nineteenth-century hymnody or in songs intended for the concert stage. Many popular songs, verse, and hymns, however, are filled with the genteel verbal expression typical of the nineteenth century, a language that can seem somewhat convoluted, quaint, or even affected to later ears; Dresser's poetry is no exception. "And then the chasm it grew wide, / Between the husband and fair bride,"[1] "Give me again my childhood,"[2] "A mother on a winter's eve, sat by the firelight,"[3] and "List to my plaint,"[4] along with the numerous "thees" and "thous," all sound rather high-flown—sometimes, it seems, at odds with the lightness of the music that accompanies this material. But convolutions of expression and dialect can capture and preserve a distinctive moment in time. From the distance of a century, most of the dialect poetry of Hoosier writer James Whitcomb Riley sounds as old-fashioned as Dresser's effusive language:

> I got to *thinkin'* of her; and a-wundern what *she* done
> That all *her sisters* kep' a-gittin' married, one by one.[5]

As does the earlier music of Foster:

> Way down upon de Swanee ribber,
> Far, far away,
> Dere's wha my heart is turning ebber,
> Dere's wha de old folks stay.[6]

On the other hand, both Dresser and Riley *did* write poetry that doesn't encumber the ear in such ways:

> When my dreams come true! when my dreams come true!
> True love in all simplicity is fresh and pure as dew;—
> The blossom in the blackest mold is kindlier to the eye
> Than any lily born of pride that looms against the sky.[7]

or

> Oh, the moonlight's fair tonight along the Wabash,
> From the fields there comes the breath of new-mown hay,
> Through the sycamores the candle lights are gleaming,
> On the banks of the Wabash, far away.[8]

Quite often, however, it was the dialect type in poetry and in song that won the greater popular acclaim both then and continuing to the present day.

For much of the nineteenth century, numerous verses were needed to create and elaborate the story. One singer usually performed this narrative. Then a chorus, also called a refrain, followed every verse. Here a group, often joining in harmony, sang the never-changing words and music, the latter almost always a repetition of something one had already heard in the verse. By the end of the century, however, composers reduced the number of verses to two or three. The music of the chorus became independent of that found in the verse, was sung by only a soloist, and over time became the most important part of the song.

Because of these changes, the composer now has a short space in which to convey a musical message. Within the few measures of music for the verse and chorus, he or she tries to create a tune that will become memorable, one that many will want to sing or play repeatedly. To that end the composer must invent a melody that combines repetition and variety in an ineffable magical mix. While there are no definite formulas to guarantee success, the composer's possession of a melodic gift is of primary importance. At his best, Dresser wrote tunes that are gratifying to sing, melodies with interesting contours that move inexorably forward to the end of a section. Sometimes, but not always, Dresser's songs contain a musical hook that makes a particular melody memorable, a device that lends cohesion and unity to the music. The chorus to "On the Banks of the Wabash, Far Away" provides a splendid example of the hook. Here the melody and rhythm of the opening notes—"Oh, the moonlight's fair to[night]"—provide the musical material for the entire chorus. By repeating and slightly varying the rhythmic cell of a long duration followed by a short one and by manipulating the fragment of melody—now right side up, now upside down—Dresser draws listeners and singers into the song, capturing them for the moment and giving the ear an easy-to-remember melody and the voice gratifying music to sing. More important, this hook does not sound contrived; rather, it has a naturalness—an inevitability as to its ultimate destination—that makes it memorable.

Dresser, like many of his contemporaries as well as composers before his time, tended to concentrate his tunes around a five-note cell. This pentatonic scale becomes the melodic nucleus for sections of a song or, indeed, for the entire composition. To that melodic cell he judiciously added the coloring of diatonic or chromatic notes beyond those found in that nucleus.

Example 1: "I Believe It for My Mother Told Me So"[9]

Example 2: "I Long to Hear from Home"[10]

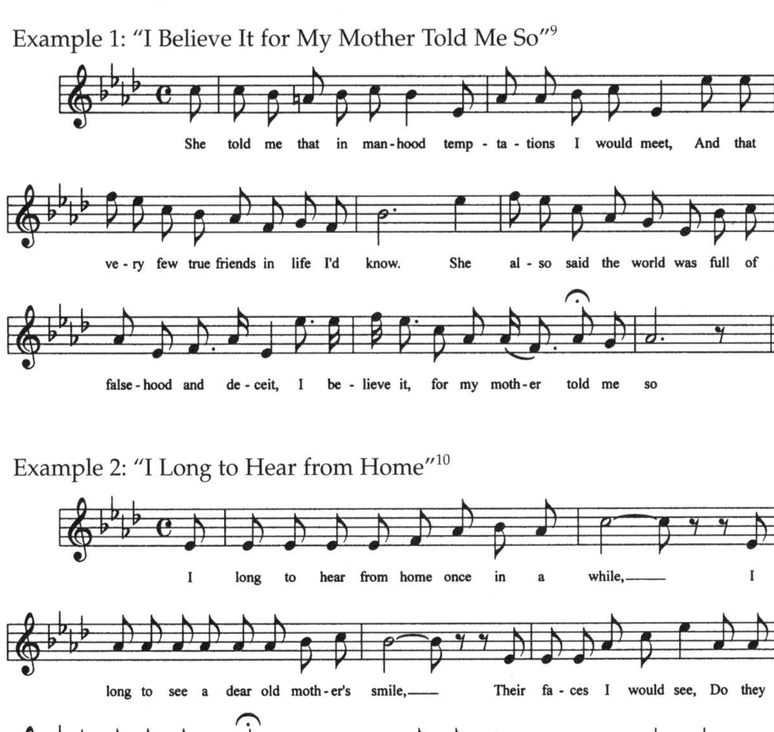

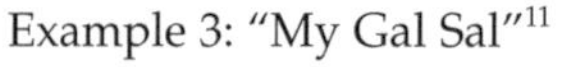
Example 3: "My Gal Sal"[11]

Example 4: "On the Banks of the Wabash, Far Away"[12]

Dresser's pentatonic-infused melodies add to a long list of songs his immediate predecessors and contemporaries wrote using the same device. Foster's "Old Folks at Home," "Jeanie with the Light Brown Hair," "Oh! Susanna," "Massa's in de Cold Ground," and "Nelly Bly" all illustrate pentatonicism to varying degrees, as do other well-known nineteenth-century songs, such as "Tramp! Tramp! Tramp! The Prisoner's Hope," "The Battle-Cry of Freedom," "The Battle Hymn of the Republic," and "Aura Lee" among them.

Example 5: "Tramp! Tramp! Tramp! The Prisoner's Hope"[13]

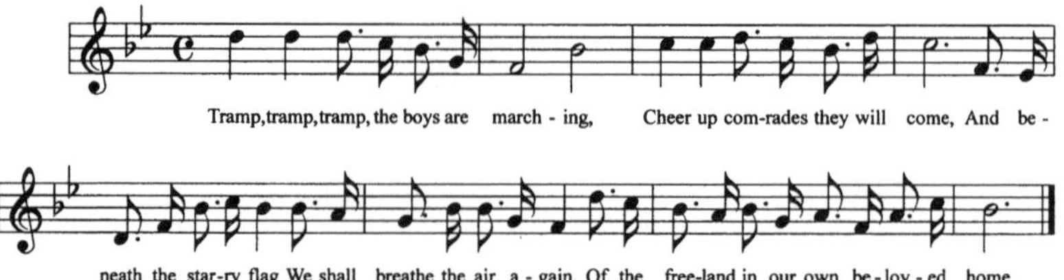

Example 6: "The Battle-Cry of Freedom"[14]

Example 7: "Old Folks at Home"[15]

Example 8: "Massa's in de Cold Ground"[16]

Dresser's choices of rhythm have much to do with the overall quality of the song. Sometimes a repeated rhythmic motive impedes that forward direction. "Show Me the Way," a sacred song of 1896, provides such an example. There, a long note followed by two short ones becomes the insistent rhythmic pattern that he uses in nearly every measure of the song; the result is an annoying sing-song quality.

Example 9: "Show Me the Way"[17]

On the other hand, Dresser often used a repeating rhythmic pattern to provide cohesion to a song and yet avoided monotony by incorporating flexibility within the repetitions of that pattern. No single rhythmic scheme dominates the verse to "On the Banks of the Wabash, Far Away." In the chorus, however, it is a different matter. There, the rhythmic cell mentioned above prevails. Dresser skillfully varied the pattern ever so slightly from time to time so that the flow of the melody's forward movement is not impeded. The entire song illustrates well the principles of rhythmic unity and variety. These standards, or the lack of them, however, do not guarantee a song's popularity or failure. The frequently repeated pitches of the melody of "Just Tell Them That You Saw Me," coupled with a rhythmic pattern consisting primarily of notes of equal value, would seem to argue against success. That, however, was not the case here, for Dresser combined music and words to create the magic of his first major hit. The formula for the success of a popular song is an ineffable one, indeed.

One often finds the "Scottish snap," the rhythmic pattern of a short note followed by a longer one, in instrumental and vocal music of the nineteenth century.

Example 10: "Kathleen, Mavourneen"[18]

Dresser's songs are no exception, but he always employed the device judiciously, reserving it for a brief instant. Two songs, written nearly two decades apart, provide good examples.

Example 11: "The Letter That Never Came"[19]

Example 12: "The Day That You Grew Colder"[20]

Musically, most of his songs seem of a piece, but the better ones contain inspired melodies that can still capture the ear of the singer and listener. In "Love's Promise," for example, the contour of the tune is quite appealing.

Example 13: "Love's Promise"[21]

Also appealing is the chorus to "I Wonder If There's Someone Who Loves Me," where the shape of the tune largely offsets the four repeated pitches at the beginning of the following example.

Example 14: "I Wonder If There's Someone Who Loves Me"[22]

In the chorus to Dresser's great hit "My Gal Sal," the melody has a naturalness to it, a tune that flows, unimpeded, to its final destination.

Example 15: "My Gal Sal"[23]

Dresser's songs are in major keys and employ the harmonic language his fellow songwriters, and those who preceded them, had come to rely on—major triads built on the first, fourth, and fifth scale steps. Thus the tonic, subdominant, and dominant chords provide nearly all the harmonic underpinning to the melody. Such songs join thousands of others for which such spare harmony is all that is required. The limited harmonic language is also helpful to the keyboard accompanist, who then must learn how to play only a few chords. Customarily, in a verse or chorus of sixteen measures, the seventh, eleventh, and fifteenth measures of a song signal a partial or full cadence to follow immediately. At that point the second or sixth scale step often assumes a prominent place in the melody and is predictably harmonized with the dominant chord of the dominant chord—a so-called secondary dominant. In other words, one can anticipate that this "color" chord might appear at least three times within a sixteen-measure span. That is the extent to which Dresser and his colleagues traditionally used it. In the chorus of "On the Banks of the Wabash, Far Away," on the other hand, Dresser delights the ear by shortening this predictable time span, using the secondary dominant of the dominant five times in only eight measures of music. Part of the enchantment of "Wabash" lays in that very telescoping of the distance between those "color" chords. In this musical sleight of hand, harmonic and melodic movement seem to propel the section forward, providing contrast to the verse where the more predictable harmonic rhythm is found.

As they moved toward the twentieth century, an increasing number of songwriters invested more melodic interest in the chorus, making it musically independent from the verses and the more important of the two sections. While the verse or verses became less important musically, they still continued to carry the story. In fact, one can easily miss the import of the story if the verse is not sung. Only in the verses to "My Gal Sal," for example, do we learn that "frivolous" Sal had died a fortnight before the narrator begins his tale. The chorus only describes Sal as having "a heart that was mellow"; as being a good listener; a girl with a wild streak.[24] Although Dresser used the past tense "was" in the chorus, the listener could believe the word merely indicates a relationship in the narrator's past. Similarly, only in the second verse of "On the Banks of the Wabash, Far Away" do we learn that the narrator's sweetheart, Mary, lies buried in the churchyard. The words of the chorus never refer to her or to the storyteller's mother, mentioned in the first verse.

With some exceptions, Dresser used the design of repetition-contrast-repetition for the melodies to his verses. He then followed this AABA pattern of sixteen measures with a chorus half, or equal, the length of the verse. On occasion, however, he ventured beyond his familiar ground to create longer songs. In attempting to extend his melodic and poetic thought over a longer span, his ambitions sometimes exceeded his abilities as a composer. In "The Curse of the Dreamer," Dresser abandoned his typical model to write a lengthy operatic scena of 137 measures—two to three times longer than his typical songs. Divided into two sections, the second merely a musical repetition of the first, and the whole concluding with a coda with a new melody, the song is pure melodrama and not very good melodrama at that. Described on the title page as a

"Descriptive Solo," the song begins with a brief recitative: " 'Tis ended she's gone / Forgive her no never, / Gone with another"; the abandoned male narrator pleads to "Angel's [*sic*] above [and] / Demon's [*sic*] below [to] / List to [his] plaint." Dresser then changed the key and meter to invoke "the curse of the ages [to] follow her on / In ev'ry land and clime." The concluding third portion of this initial section has the narrator singing in a new key: "Somewhere . . . a sad voice is crying / May the curse of the ages and misery follow her to the gates of eternity." All of this foregoing music is then repeated with new words. The song, however, concludes with a surprise: in the coda the narrator discovers he has merely been dreaming this terrible scene: "Here you are love by my side / 'Twas only a dream, not true. . . . / There is none my love like you."[25]

Not only was this a musical stretch for Dresser—one that is not convincing—but his poetic muse abandoned him, leading him to forced and trite rhymes: "And down in the earth shall she grovel. . . . / To the requiem clang of the shovel" and "With a fiendish incarnation, / Thro' the gates of perdition I'll follow her on to eternal and lasting damnation."[26] "A Baby Adrift at Sea," composed nearly a decade earlier in 1890, represents another of Dresser's attempts to compose a convincing lengthy dramatic ballad and is equally unconvincing. With these songs Dresser clearly was trying to extend himself musically, efforts perhaps made in an attempt to be taken seriously as a composer of something beyond the typical mother-and-home sentimental song. As much as he may have wished it, however, his success was not to be as the composer of music on a grand scale but as the creator of the miniature, working within the limitations of a somewhat predictable structure, manipulating it through repetition or slight variation in nearly 150 songs.

It is important to realize that Dresser and his contemporaries rarely attempted to write melodies that underscored or interpreted the sentiments of the words they were setting to music. Topics as disparate from one another as love, death, war, humor, or religion were nearly always served by the same sort of melody and structures discussed above—in a kind of neutral, interchangeable line and form. Having said that, however, the truly memorable song, working its magic upon the listener, bears witness to a composer's skill in transcending those very limitations.

CHAPTER 32

Love, Religious, and Comic Songs

Love Songs

The topic of love constitutes nearly a third of Paul Dresser's songs. Even though he won little success from his love songs, it was a genre to which he gave much time, thought, and creative energy for nearly two decades. Nearly a third of these songs are waltzes, as are many of the most acclaimed songs of the Gay Nineties, among them "Little Annie Rooney," "After the Ball," "A Bicycle Built for Two," "The Sidewalks of New York," "The Band Played On," "In the Baggage Coach Ahead," "Sweet Rosie O'Grady," and "My Wild Irish Rose."

The predominant subject of the songs is the loss of a loved one—through abandonment or death—and the faithfulness of the lover left behind:

> If her heart ached with pain, I'm sure that no one ever knew;
> It seemed tho' he were false to her, to him she still was true.[1]

In "He Brought Home Another," the lure of the city takes Nell's lover from her. Thinking that he will marry her, poor Nell waits patiently for him, only to find that, "He brought home another, / And called her [his] bride," and Nell died that night "In a humble sort o' cottage," her heart completely broken. Now, "He lives in the mansion, on yonder hill, / Nell, she still is sleeping, / Behind the mill."[2] "If You See My Sweetheart" provides an extreme example of the patience of the abandoned lover as she asks the friend of her beloved to seek Tom out as the friend travels across the sea. In the forty years that follow, the friend becomes "the master of an ocean steamer, great and grand, / [but] He never brought her tidings, / No news to dry her tears . . . / [and] The maid of yesterday, / Is now a woman bent with years, . . . feeble, old and gray."[3]

On occasion, Dresser's deserted one is a man:

> 'Tis just three years ago, since she went away, . . .
> She wandered out one evening, at closing of the day, . . .
> No word of anger in the past had we.
> She just went out, without good-bye,
> Since then I'm wondering,
> If she'll ever come back to me?[4]

The mythical Nell or Nellie appears in another song, this time as the one who causes the emotional injuries. In " 'Tis All That I Have to Remember Her By," angry words have caused Nellie to abandon her lover, whose "heart seem[s] to break as I [think] of the wildwood / Where we first made love 'neath the old willow tree." Now, after the passing of many years, the only thing the man has to recall his Nellie is her message in an old faded letter she wrote to him at their parting, "given to [him] with a tear and a sigh." Now faded and stained with his tear drops, the old man keeps this "dear little token" to remember his lost love.[5]

The titles of "The Day That You Grew Colder" and "My Heart Still Clings to the Old First Love" tell their entire stories. In the latter, the narrator's words, "I'm sure I heard her singing of an old familiar stream" give way to:

> Oh, the moonlight's fair tonight along the Wabash,
> From the fields there comes the breath of new-mown hay,
> But my heart still clings to the old first love,
> On the banks of the Wabash, far away.[6]

and sure enough—Dresser predictably repeats the melody of his major hit of four years earlier!

In the gentle "Gath'ring Roses for Her Hair," a loved one "sleeps without a care . . . In the churchyard on the hill, / Just beyond the crooning mill." Her lover, who in youth had gathered flowers to decorate her tresses, now wishes "that I were by her side, / To share her lot whate'er be tide."[7]

Lest one think Dresser's romantic love songs are all about relationships gone awry, he *did* compose a few in which lovers remain together and even marry, as in "I Told Her the Same Old Story," "In the Sweet Summer Time," "Come, Tell Me What's Your Answer, Yes or No," and "I'd Still Believe You True." "When I'm Away from You, Dear" tells the listener how poorer the world is when the lover is absent: "The skies that the poets dream of / Are anything but blue." "The flowers drop and die, . . . the days seem an endless misery. . . . / When I'm away from you."[8]

"Rosie, Sweet Rosabel," one of the first Dresser songs that his new partners Fred Haviland and Pat Howley published as the George T. Worth Company, is an unusual love story. A man discovers a baby girl abandoned on his doorstep. Bringing her in from the cold winter weather, he names her Rosabel, raises her to womanhood, falls in love with this "charming black eyed sweet Rosabel," proposes to her, and tells us that "soon I'll marry Sweet Rosabel" in spite of their obvious great difference in ages.[9]

Finally, two other songs should be singled out to illustrate that, like all composers, Dresser was capable of bad musical and poetic judgments, probably prompted by haste and lack of self-criticism. "Jean," a real "sobber," as such songs were known in the trade, relates the story of a man passionately in love with a woman he cannot live without. Jean, however, has other plans and leaves this lovesick poet. Song composers wrote endless numbers of such sad tales. Dresser, however, could not find his poetic muse for this one. His pathetic lover sings:

> Jean my love it is of thee!
> I sing in fondest ecstasy!
> And when on the land or sea,
> My sweetest dreams are all of thee!

Later, the forlorn and hapless man sings:

> Jean for thee my heart is aching,
> The time has come 'tis almost breaking,
> For me it seems there's no awak'ning.

and

> Jean my love I've ne'er deceived thee,
> Not for worlds love would I grieve thee;
> I swear it wilt thou not believe me?
> Tell me love would'st thou bereave me?[10]

If such sophomoric rhymes were not enough to ensure failure for this song, Dresser compounded the silliness of his verbal inadequacy by writing the music in a "Tempo di Bolero"! The combination of the seductiveness of bolero rhythm and bad rhyming give the song a comic cast—at least from the distance of a century after it was composed. This certainly was not Dresser's intent. Another example of the failure of his poetic sense is in the rhyming he used in "Little Fannie McIntyre." Here a young man, struck delirious by his love, sings:

> Little Fanny McIntyre.
> She's the one I most admire,
> She sets my heart strings on fire,
> Little Fanny McIntyre;
> She leads in our old church choir,
> She's the picture of her sire;
> Girls, they envy, boys admire,
> Little Fanny McIntyre![11]

One could predict that neither of these two songs would capture a large audience.

Many of Dresser's narrators are debilitated by the torments of their love for their partner—of love gone awry, of abandonment, of infidelity, and of death—the ultimate earthly divider. Their pleadings, cajolings, prayers—rarely threats—are to no avail. Nothing will bring the loved one back. In effect, life stops for these unfortunates. Their sole reason for being is gone, leaving them with but memories. These melodramatic vignettes had a certain appeal to a nineteenth-century audience, but Dresser (and so many of his colleagues) painted his narrators with such broad melodramatic strokes that to later ears they rarely seem other than cartoon figures. Dresser's love songs are, for the most part, rather predictable in content and in music, rarely showing the creative spark and imagination that set his mother-and-home songs on a higher plain.

Religious Songs

Included in Dresser's songs are seven that contain religious or quasi-religious texts. "When Mother First Taught Me to Pray" may be a version of the song an Evansville paper mentioned that

Dresser had composed in 1883. The song is a miniature anthology of references to family, with its memories "Of home, of father, mother, brother, sisters near and dear." Even "Rover . . . that dog we loved so well" has his place here. But the strongest memories for the narrator were of nestling by his mother's side as she recounted for her children some of Jesus' sayings: "O suffer little ones come unto me" [*sic*]; and "forgive your enemies." For the child, now grown to manhood, the "sweetest pray'r of all" was hearing his mother begin, " 'Our Father dear, in Heav'n.' " After Mother intoned those words, the children continued " 'Give us this day our daily bread.' "[12] "Show Me the Way," marketed as a "Sacred Song," is a plea to God for a better life free from sin. The penitent narrator, mindful that death is near, begs God to take pity on the sinful soul of His child: "Mercy, O mercy is all I ask, / Tho' the hour of eleven be come."[13]

Dresser followed the tried-and-true formulas in these two songs. Each has two verses followed by a chorus. Given its numerous Scottish snaps and pentatonic melody, "When Mother First Taught Me to Pray" sounds like an older song than its date suggests. "Show Me the Way," on the other hand, is more hymnlike in its restrained rhythm. There is a certain gentleness to the song that would enable it to hold its own with other religious songs of the day.

Dresser's musical prayer to the Virgin Mary asks her to intercede with her Son on behalf of "us, poor sinners, here."[14] In its thirty-two measures in an AABA design, "Ave Maria" is similar to Dresser's other songs, religious or not. Unlike those songs, however, this one avoids pentatonicism and has a single verse and no chorus. Dresser endowed this sole verse with a gently undulating melody, providing a mood quite appropriate to the subject of the music. In spite of its good qualities, however, "Ave Maria" never approaches the richness found in Ethelbert Nevin's "The Rosary," published a year earlier in 1898. Was Dresser hoping to capitalize on the tremendous success "The Rosary" enjoyed with the public? Even though Nevin's melody consists of three statements of an A section with some changes at the end of each and lacks the contrast of a B portion, it has that undefinable magic that made it a hit, whereas Dresser's song joined thousands of other religious or quasi-religious songs composed at the time that were performed for a short time and then forgotten.

The melodies of "In the Great Somewhere" and "Glory to God" share a prevailing pentatonicism. The former song lacks a chorus and has a sing-song quality, with the words "In the great somewhere" or "Of the great somewhere" sung twelve different times, creating a somewhat annoying insistent pattern.[15] "Glory to God" has a martial sound, consistent with the sentiments of the text praising and hailing God and His Son.

In "Bethlehem" the singer's part, with its wide melodic contour, is almost operatic; at times the piano accompaniment is quite difficult for the amateur pianist. The story runs an emotional gamut from the infant Christ lying in the manger to the two Marys weeping at the crucifixion of Jesus, replete with "thunders roaring" and "mighty rocks split" to Christ's resurrection when "All nations in God's name sing."[16] In sum, it is similar to an operatic scena, the drama of which is hampered only by the fact that the same music is used for all three verses. Dresser did not attempt to provide contrasting music for the variety of moods he expressed through the words. Thus, the music for the baby Jesus and for his crucifixion are of a single piece—there is no appropriate dramatic support.

Dresser's last song, "The Judgment Is at Hand," is refreshingly different from nearly every other song he composed. The melody fully uses all the notes of the diatonic scale; the verse is an unusual twenty-four measures in length rather than the customary sixteen or thirty-two; additionally, the verse does not end in the tonic key as one usually finds. Rather, the last note is harmonized with the dominant chord that anticipates the entrance of the chorus. Finally, the music of the chorus is independent of that of the verse. The words are an admonition to the living that at the Judgment Day, "The great trumpet blast of Jehovah [will be] heard," and the Lord will ask "what good have ye done . . . have ye clothed and fed the hungry or turned them from your sight, / Or have ye robbed the orphan and the widow of her mite[?]" Those "who have struggled so hard in my name then shall find peace and rest, / The Masters arms are opened wide come to the throne with the blest!" "As ye have sown, so shall ye reap, . . . Judgment is at Hand."[17] Given the increasing social consciousness of Dresser's later years, such words assume a significance beyond their typical religious sentiments. They can be viewed as the composer's indictment of the self-centered wealthy and the prediction of *their* fate at that last dreadful day. Dresser invested the music of the chorus with a certain grandeur appropriate for the text of final judgment—a music not dissimilar to that found in other religious songs of the times. All in all, it is a very successful musical essay.

Most of these songs, however, are marked with a sincerity that, in itself, does not do anything to raise them above the level of mediocrity. They add little to Dresser's reputation. The thoughts contained are common to much lackluster sacred music of the century, and the musical settings that Dresser provided for his words are virtually interchangeable with those he used for most of his other songs. Only the words are different, and even then the narrator's pleading for God's mercy seems to be little different from the forsaken lover entreating his loved one to return. There is little doubt that Father Herman Joseph Alerding, the good priest who was young Dresser's savior in times of trouble, would have been proud of his charge, and Johann Paul Dreiser certainly would have approved as well. But Dresser's sacred songs seem like curiosity pieces among his far more popular music about mother and home. Dresser, ever Sarah Dreiser's good son, was repeating his mother's secondhand pithy comments and religious sentiments in musical form. She, too, would have been pleased.

Comic Songs

For a man who spent nearly twenty years as a singer and comic performer, it is surprising that Dresser wrote comparatively few humorous songs. He composed "What a Wonderful World It Would Be!," his first effort in this genre, in 1889 at the time he was traveling with John Stewart Crossy in the Two Johns Company. With words by J. S. G. (certainly Crossy himself, despite the variation in the last initial), the song features a narrator who dreams of an ideal world "full of peace . . . where troubles and trials and quarrels should cease," where "streets of New York were respectably clean," and where "we never had dread of our mothers-in-law." The world would be perfect "if busts and if bustles were just as they seem," "If that sort of office which seeks out the man / Would insure he was built upon honesty's plan," "If boarding house keepers would buy better meat," and "If their chickens were fit for a mortal to eat."[18] The song, clearly in the minstrel tradition, was undoubtedly written for performance in *The Two Johns* and would have appealed to singer and listener alike with the serious alternating with a humorous series of "what ifs."

In 1890, while in the cast of *A Tin Soldier*, Dresser wrote four comic songs, some of them perhaps for interpolation within that comic farce. "The Band Played Annie Laurie; or, To Hear Them Tell It" would have had considerable appeal to the audience, which was encouraged to join in with a resounding "Yes!" at regular intervals following questions from the singer. The fourth verse asks:

> Does the man who stays out late at night come home without a head?
> Yes! to hear him tell it;
> When his wife calls him at daylight does he jump right out of bed?
> Yes! to hear him tell it.

Then follows a longer section:

> He sits down to his breakfast, tells his wife he's feeling great,
> And sends her to the cellar while he sneaks out through the gate,
> Does he stop to enter yon saloon, on account of cruel fate?
> Oh! yes, to hear him tell it![19]

Other verses tell of New York's "constant mirth" upon hearing the boasts of Chicago and St. Louis, and of John L. Sullivan's boxing superiority over James J. Corbett and other prizefighters. Seven verses continue this pattern, each ending with the chorus, whose words provide a strange non sequitur to the text of the verses: "And the band played Annie Laurie, and Annie Rooney too!"[20] At the mention of Annie Laurie, Dresser quotes the melody from the well-known song of that title. In "The Limit Was Fifty Cents," four verses tell the story of a poor soul who lost all his money in a poker game after his fellow players slipped him a "Mickey Finn." The last laugh, however, belongs to this seemingly hapless man, for he had been playing the game with counterfeit money and has turned the tables on *them*.[21]

Four years later Dresser wrote "Three Old Sports from Oklahoma." A decidedly silly song that Dresser and his cohorts featured in *A Green Goods Man*, it deals with the shenanigans of a trio of hard drinkers, three womanizers, three politicians, and even a trio of "Hebrews from Jerusalem," complete with comic dialect to make their point.[22] A gentler song from the same play is "The Battery," in which a young man longs for Friday nights when he can go to Battery Park. On those evenings he enjoys the children playing, the lovers promenading, the "great ships in the harbor," and the "steamboats speeding"; especially memorable to him is the band playing music that is grander, in its own way, than "opera with its tenors and sopranos" or of "Madame Patti, of Melba, Eames or Calvé."[23]

Among Dresser's comic songs are a few "coon" songs. "There'll Be Weeping, There'll Be Wailing," published in 1890, is the first song in which Dresser used that term. Rather than being an authentic "coon" song, however, it is similar to any number of other songs Dresser wrote and contains none of the rhythmic syncopations one finds in the typical "coon" style. Its subject is how blacks will pay for their earthly misdeeds when they meet the Lord on the Judgment Day. "Did You Ever Hear a Nigger Say Wow?" of the same year is similar in music and content, containing no syncopated rhythms but consisting of a short catalog of stereotypical attitudes, behaviors, and preferences of blacks, as seen by white bigots of the time. "I'se Your Nigger If You Wants Me Liza Jane" and "When de Moon Comes Up behind de Hill" both contain words that passed for black dialect, and each is filled with stereotypical images of blacks, but only in the first do we find any of the syncopated rhythms one finds in "coon" songs.

As early as 1898 a writer for the *New York Dramatic Mirror* complained that so many "coon" songs and "rag-time stuff" had been turned out that it seemed as if many composers could no longer write "the simple, straight melodies which used to charm a few years ago before this syncopated, double-note craze struck the country." Furthermore, the current lot of "coon" songs lacked any interest, being "only vulgar"; "when decomposition sets in death isn't far off." "An era of sentimental music is about due."[24] As late as 1905, when he was desperately trying to recapture his magic with the public, Dresser wrote yet another "coon" song, "Niggah Loves His Possum; or, Deed He Do, Do, Do," after the rage for such songs had passed. All of his "coon" songs are quite tame, all in a moderate tempo rather than in the more lively one typical of the style. Many include the rhythmic pattern of a short note followed by a long one, a device commonly found in "coon" songs, but not one that was new to music. As we have seen, one finds that Scottish snap in innumerable songs, regardless of tempo, from the last forty years of the century.

A year before he died, Dresser wrote his last comic song, "Jim Judson," recounting the deeds of a man thought to be fair game for the tricks of everyone. Instead, Judson is a wily, "street smart" man who steals "old pal" Henry Hawkins's rig, horse, and wife, the consequences of which put Henry in the insane asylum.[25]

Those comic songs in which Dresser includes black dialect and modest syncopations can hold a candle neither to the true "coon" songs of the time, such as "The Bully Song," nor to those songs with a more prominent ragtime influence. But then few syncopated songs of this period matched the high-spiritedness and acclaim of "A Hot Time in the Old Town," "Hello! Ma Baby," "Bill Bailey, Won't You Please Come Home?," or even the more gentle rhythmic undulations of "Under the Bamboo Tree." None of Dresser's songs have the rhythmic exuberance of a "Ta-Ra-Ra Boom-De-Ay!," which became immensely popular in 1892 and seemed to be everywhere. Mollie Thompson's "original acrobatic version" of the song made "Boston and Philadelphia crazy." At Philadelphia's Bijou Theatre, Thompson, the American "sprightly soubrette," sang and danced "with such decided chic as to win lavish plaudits. She was recalled again and again, and when she did her famous handspring the applause reached the proportions of a hurricane."[26]

None of Dresser's humorous songs attracted the attention of a Mollie Thompson or, indeed, of any of the major performers of his time. While the composer himself had earned a substantial reputation for his comedy routines, he turned to that material only occasionally for music. The humor contained in such music was funny at the time, but the songs did not win much appreciation beyond their use in the comic farces in which he starred. Comic song was not where Dresser's real interests lay. In its lack of mean-spiritedness and double entendre, and with its gentle fun-poking,

Dresser's humor must have seemed quite tame to some audiences. There is nothing in his comic songs to embarrass; rather, the music was a good-natured effort that reflected his background in family shows in family theaters. Dresser's competitors obviously had the upper hand in writing the sorts of comic and syncopated songs for which most audiences clamored.

CHAPTER 33

Patriotic Songs

In the 1890s, before America's war with Spain, Paul Dresser wrote a half dozen songs whose subjects were war and patriotism. "My Flag! My Flag!" and "He Was a Soldier," both from 1892, are generic, for Dresser was not writing with a specific battle in mind. Other songs recalled the Civil War. In one, the listener is asked not to judge the young Confederate soldier who lies buried far from his grieving mother because "He Fought for the Cause He Thought Was Right." In another, a young soldier lies buried near the Western and Atlantic Railroad tracks between Chattanooga and Atlanta: "What his colors, none able to tell; . . . And when he appears on the great Judgment Day, / Our Father'll not ask, 'Was your suit blue or gray'!" Dresser remarked in the printed upper margin, "Let this be an Olive Branch to the North and South to be again a united people."[1] Another song comments on the poignant day in May that Americans had set aside three decades earlier as a special time for remembrance. A mother, "most feeble and grey," finds her long-lost soldier son among the veterans marching to the cemetery to decorate the graves of their fallen Civil War comrades.[2]

Dresser lived at a propitious time for the rekindling of patriotic fervor in the nation. The sinking of the *Maine* in 1898 and its aftermath brought forth an efflorescence of visual art, poetry, literature, and popular song about that event and the ensuing Spanish-American War. Dresser created nine songs with reference to the Spanish-American War, five of them in 1898 alone. In "We Are Coming Cuba, Coming," the United States is sending "bullets, brains, and soldiers" to the beleaguered nation.[3] In another song, an all-sacrificing mother admonishes her son to

"Keep up your courage lad, . . .
I bid you go, fight for your Country's sake.
You're going to the war, my boy, and while you are away,
Remember that a mother's pray'rs are with you night and day,
In battle lad, remember there is no such word as fear,
Your God comes first, your country next, then mother dear."[4]

At the same time, another mother, in "We Fight Tomorrow Mother," begs her son not to go to war: "They took your father, brother, now they want the other one." Her pleas are unavailing, for her son steals away in the darkness, joins the army, and writes to his mother the night before a battle:

We fight tomorrow mother, tho' I've never fought before.
I'll be brave just like father was, on the battle fields of yore,
But I'll return home, mother, my angel one to you,
We fight tomorrow mother, for the Red, White and Blue.[5]

True to his word, at the conclusion of the war the son, astride "a coal black charger, [and now] a hero" returns safely to his mother. "Tho' he came home a Gen'ral, he was still her darling boy."[6] "On the Banks of the Wabash, Far Away" was still immensely popular when war with Spain broke out, and there are a number of accounts of it having been sung by American troops during the battles. Dresser may have had good intentions in allowing Andrew B. Sterling to write new topical words to the melody, but in retrospect, "On the Shores of Havana, Far Away" seems to be more of an attempt to capitalize on the popularity of "Wabash" than the expression of heartfelt sentiment.

Oh, the moon shines down tonight upon the waters,
Where the heroes of the Maine in silence lay,
May they rest in peace, the loved ones who are sleeping,
On the shores of Havana, far away.[7]

The year 1899 brought two more Dresser songs with reference to the Spanish-American War. The title of "In Good Old New York

Town" hides the fact that the song deals with a "soldier boy . . . left behind to die . . . In far off Santiago." The boy's last wish: "Take me back to New York town / If I'm going to die. / I've a longing to be there. . . . I feel that I could rest in peace / In good old New York town."[8] "Come Home, Dewey, We Won't Do a Thing to You" celebrates the deeds of Adm. George Dewey, the "Grand old hero of the Red, White and Blue" who, at the Battle of Manila, "changed the map and made us in the eyes of all the world / A nation great with friend as well as foe."[9] Dewey became America's first war hero since the days of the Civil War:

> The navy quickly promoted him to admiral, and his walrus-mustached face graced newspapers and magazines across America. Politicians devised all manner of schemes for being seen with him when he returned to the United States; sculptors carved his features in stone; parents named sons after him.[10]

In 1900 Dresser wrote yet three more songs dealing with the recent war. "Give Us Just Another Lincoln" evokes the spirits of the sixteenth president, in company with Thomas Jefferson, Andrew Jackson, Ulysses Grant, and George Washington, to rally the troops; "Wrap Me in the Stars and Stripes" relates the tale of a young American soldier rescued at the very last minute from execution by a Spanish firing squad; and "The Blue and the Gray" tells of a mother

Indiana State Library

IHS

"Give Us Just Another Lincoln" and "The Blue and the Gray," both published in 1900.

who loses her three sons in battle—the first at Appomattox, the second at Chickamauga, and the third in the Spanish-American War. (One wonders how long in the tooth this third son was!) The latter song enjoyed immense success, bringing at least sixty thousand dollars to Howley, Haviland and Company. "Our Country May She Always Be Right but Our Country, Right or Wrong" is a saber-rattling patriotic song in which Dresser mentions no specific conflict. Instead, he issues a rallying cry to stand up for America "And hurl defiance at our foes, / Who ever they may be."[11]

Feeling that patriotism was a subject he could continue to play with some success in 1901, Dresser featured mother and soldier son in "Mr. Volunteer; or, You Don't Belong to the Regulars, You're Just a Volunteer!": "You're only one of the rank and file, / But some one [mother] holds you dear!"[12] "There's No North or South To-Day" has a young boy asking why men in differing uniforms—blue and gray—are marching together, their eyes brimming with tears. The boy's father explains that these men were once enemies, "But all is forgot, they now march 'neath the flag. / The banner that makes us a kin . . .

> There is always a West,
> There is always an East,
> Where the sun shall rise, they say;
> But we're marching abreast,
> From East to the West,
> For there's no North or South to-day."[13]

A unified nation is also the subject of a later song, "Lincoln, Grant and Lee; or, The War Is Over Many Years."

"After the Battle" of 1905 is a generic war song. Dresser mentions no specific war or battle in his words, and one senses that he is merely trying to play his "war card" to a public that had once eagerly listened to his earlier songs about the Spanish-American War. "She Fought On by His Side" of a year earlier chronicles the story of Nell, the sweetheart of a fallen Union soldier. Suddenly appearing at his side, Nell tells her mortally wounded love that she will be his bride. When the call goes out for additional soldiers, Nell "donned a suit of blue, / She marched on beside her sweetheart, and yet he never knew; / 'Mid the cannon's roar and thunder her heart filled with pride, / She never flinched nor faltered, but fought on by his side."[14]

Dresser even mined the Boer War for subject matter, extolling the virtues of Irish soldiers fighting with England in "The Green above the Red," "not because they love their queen," but:

Fighting not for flag or country,
Fighting not because it's just,
Longing for Old Ireland's freedom,
They fight because they must . . .
When they come back from the Transvaal,
You'll see the Green above the Red.[15]

Two years later, in "The Army of Half-Starved Men," Dresser took the side of the outnumbered Boer army—"A hundred thousand [English] to . . . [the Boer's] ten"; " 'Tis might against the weak and weary." Opposing soldiers meet one another in battle, the gracious Englishman saying to his Boer counterpart, "All honor, sir, to you, / For you certainly deserve it, / After all that you've been through. . . . The maker sometime will reward you."[16]

A certain bitterness about the nation's short memory of the heroic deeds of its fighting men prevails in "When You Come Back They'll Wonder Who the ——— You Are" of 1902. Those same heroes seem "useless, until we're in a hole. . . . But after all is over, / And the battle has been won, / The friends that they have left are mighty few."

You may fight for the flag, fight for its stars,
Fight for the colors, you may fight for its bars!
Tho' crown'd with your vict'ries, and covered with scars,
When you come back they'll wonder who the ——— you are.[17]

The public was now abandoning its love of the old sentimental mother-and-home songs and embracing newer styles, and because of Dresser's gradual loss of popularity, he may have been identifying with these forgotten soldiers. Certainly this seems true in a poignant song of the very next year, a song having nothing to do with patriotism or war.

Where are the friends of other days,
Friends that I used to know;
Friends that were ever by my side,
Friends of the long ago?
Vainly I turn, but find them not
Somehow it seems to me,
They do not seek me as once they did, . . .
Vainly my heart cries out to them, . . .
I am alone![18]

Dresser could easily have written, "When I come back they'll wonder who the ——— I am!"

CHAPTER 34

Songs of Mother and Home

In nineteenth-century America as more and more fathers worked away from the home, mothers increasingly became its idealistic and ideological center. Those who moved from the village and found that the city was often cold and impersonal longed for home, the "old cot," the humble dwelling. In turn, they endowed the sense of place—of home and village—with special, near mystical, properties. Song lyrics increasingly coupled mother and home in the desire to return to the misremembered halcyon days of childhood, where one was protected by mother and was safe in the old homestead; mother *and* home become twin anchors of lost innocence, sharing space on a single, sacred pedestal.

Especially after the 1850s mother's new status was reflected, and tribute paid to her, in poems, magazine articles, advice pieces, and songs. One of the results of this adulation of mother, often intertwined with the longing for home, was a body of American popular song that enjoyed wide circulation and success in the last half of the century; another outcome was the creation of a misleading image of mother.

Septimus Winner, writing as Alice Hawthorne, spoke to many when he described the emotional pain mother's absence caused:

What is home without a mother?
What are all the joys we meet,
When her loving smile no longer
Greets the coming, coming of our feet?

The days seem long, the nights are drear,
And time rolls slowly on;
And oh! how few are childhood's pleasures,
When her gentle, gentle care is gone![1]

That mother and her love were considered to be irreplaceable is clear in another song Winner wrote:

Ah! never can another,
Her place in life supply, . . .
For there's no one like a mother,
And we dread to see her die.[2]

Songs about mother became so ubiquitous in the 1850s and early 1860s that "Mother on the Brain," a light-hearted verbal quodlibet of at least forty titles of mother songs, each verse ending with heavy-handed humor, must have seemed like a breath of fresh air to listeners besieged by songs about mothers who ministered to their dying sons, or of dying mothers who had already attained angelic status here on earth. Additionally, it was great fun to sing to the air "The Bonnie Blue Flag." Three verses are more than enough to illustrate the author's intentions:

As you look on the songs that you see now-a-days,
The gentle words of Mother will sure meet your gaze;
"Who will care for Mother now?" if I'm numbered with the slain;
"Oh! bless me, Mother, ere I die" with Mother on the brain. . . .

"What is home without a Mother?" "It was my Mother's voice;"
"Sing me to sleep, my Mother;" I feel I'm growing worse;
"Be quiet, do, I'll call my Mother;" Mother's coming in the rain;
"Let me kiss him for his Mother;" with Mother on the brain.

"It was my Mother's customs," "My gentle Mother dear;"
"I was my Mother's darling;" for, I loved my lager beer.
"Kiss me good-night, Mother," and bring me a Bourbon plain—
"Mother dear, I feel I'm dying," with Mother on the brain.[3]

American society had its share of abusive mothers, ethnic mothers, mothers involved with social issues, mothers of color, mothers of various social and economic classes, alcoholic mothers, unwed mothers—mothers who fit into any number of these categories. But such a variety of figures never appeared in song; in the few instances where one finds a different sort of female—for example, a woman involved in the temperance movement—she is almost always satirized. In the popular-song literature of the time, the particular fell victim to an invention that, over time, has become an accepted and venerated icon. The mother we meet in song after song represents a species of woman that existed only in the individual and collective imaginations of authors, composers, artists, publishers, and, to a lesser extent, performers.

With the exception of those Civil War songs in which she plays a role, mother exists in a space into which little of contemporary life ever intrudes; the consequences of history, of industry, and of technology are the unspeakable enemies from which the listener is protected, from which the listener is taken and returned to the haven of mother's love and protection, to the innocence of childhood. Such songs may have consoled countless numbers of listeners who were otherwise prisoners of their frenetic lives in the contemporary world. Icons of mother and home may have constituted universals in a pluralistic society where it was hard to find a common denominator. An idealized, illusory mother, often coupled with a misremembered picture of home, may have given the listener a mooring, an anchor for comfort and solace in a period when all the old rules, standards, lifestyles, and guidelines seemed to be crumbling before one's eyes.

But the mythology of strong, selfless, all-forgiving mother is often presented at the expense of a weak son. The male narrator typically betrays an arrested emotional development and is unable to face or accept the realities of adulthood. He betrays a near pathological obsession with, and attachment to, mother, pleading to be returned to her bosom far away from the realities of the present time:

> Backward, turn backward, oh, time in your flight,
> Make me a child again just for to night!
> Mother come back from the echoless shore,
> Take me again to your heart as of yore . . .
> Rock me to sleep, mother, rock me to sleep.[4]

One of the prevailing leitmotivs in these songs is parting or loss, very often the actual or impending death of a child seen through mother's eyes or the loss of mother told from the vantage point of a son. The prevalence of stories about death might have reflected, in part, a greater realization of one's mortality, especially following the cholera epidemics of 1832, 1849, and 1866. There can be little question that the unprecedented deaths of young males in the Civil War prompted the outpouring of words and music to comment on the nobility and tragedy of death, and the deaths of individual soldiers may have been fixed upon, in part, to heighten the singular human being in the context of such wholesale slaughter. Additionally, lower birth rates in the late part of the century, coupled with continued high mortality figures, might have made the immediate experience of death a more intolerable one than ever before.[5] Death and maternal grief are sometimes given specificity:

As some fond mother who bewails her child,
and vents her grief in mournful accents wild,
so look'd Columbia's Genius, when Stern Death,
Relentless Tyrant! snatch'd her favorite's breath.[6]

This is mother in the persona of the nation, mourning the loss of her son, George Washington, some three decades after his death.

Parting and death were usually afforded a more general treatment that lent a universality to the narrator's tale, enabling many listeners to claim the story as their own. Even though specific names are given, the fate of these children was common enough that most people could have related to the mother who talks to her dead son and daughter:

Long years have pass'd my Willie
Since I laid you by the side,
Of the gentle little Mary,
Her Mother's joy and pride.[7]

And the "fierce red fever [that] bound [Willie] in its chains" would have reminded many of how death had claimed *their* loved ones.[8]

A Union or Confederate soldier or, indeed, most anyone, could have identified with the sentiments of the dying soldier, whose last words expressed concern for his mother:

Soon with angels I'll be marching,
With bright laurels on my brow;
I have for my country fallen!
Who will care for Mother now?[9]

or with the one who wrote:

I lay thinking of you, mother,
And the loving ones at home,
Till to our dear cottage, mother,
Boy again I seem'd to come,

but whose journey will not be to his early home, but to his death.[10]

Children who had lost their mothers at an early age, if given a poetic inclination, might have written:

My mother died ere I could scarce
Breathe her beloved name,
And o'er my childhood's sunny path
Dark clouds of sorrow came[11]

And most listeners would have agreed that

There was silence in the homestead,
By the hearth and in the hall,
And our sorrow like a wintry cloud
Hung darkly over all
For the love that was to us far more,
Than all the world beside
Went down with mourning to the grave
The day our mother died.[12]

Another dominant subject in these songs is the celebration of mother's traits. Mother is gentle and faithful:

Sweetly a Mother's love shines like a star,
Brightest in darkness, when daylight's afar;
In clouds or in sunshine, pleasures or pain,
Mother's affection is ever the same.[13]

She is a loyal and devoted friend:

> So do what you can for her while she is here;
> Don't trust in your sister or your brother.
> Oh, the friend in my need was a friend to me indeed
> God bless her, my own dear mother![14]

And she is remembered after her death as a sainted, angelic figure:

> Now her spirit hovers near,
> A guardian angel pure and mild;
> She whispers love my heart to cheer,
> And guards the footsteps of her child[.][15]

Authors frequently took objects associated with mother and elevated them to the status of talismans, amulets that triggered the narrator's memories of mother and of his or her childhood. "Days Gone By," a song Paul Dresser wrote the year his mother died—although it is uncertain if he composed this before or after her death—is a catalog of objects made sacred by dint of their belonging to family in the old home: the cradle near the fireplace, a ball and bat that brother played with, playthings on the floor, a pair of worn-out spectacles, a paper left unread, father's old worn hat, and, of course, mother's armchair. The chorus ends with the narrator sobbing: "And when I see these relics, / They bring tears to mine eye, / They're only sweet remembrances / Of days gone by."[16]

Given mother's pure, angelic, kindly, gentle, understanding, omniscient, sacrificing, and all-forgiving attributes, it is not surprising that she often appeared on the cover of sheet music in Madonna-and-child poses. Mother projected a Christ-like image at times, too, and home became an earthly paradise. Indeed, some of the popular-song poetry honoring mother reflected an unmistakable religiosity similar in tone to that found in some nineteenth-century hymns. Many listeners would have found comfort in this, without ever analyzing why it was so. In an enterprise dominated by males—from the author to the composer, cover artist to publisher—songs about iconic mother may have constituted messages—both conscious and subliminal—to wives, sisters, and sweethearts that *this* mother should be the exemplar for *all* women. Mother was essentially a fabrication in which many nineteenth-century males *wanted* to believe. One can scarcely imagine the problems this must have presented for nineteenth-century women, for they would nearly always fall short of this ideal—in their eyes as well as those of their husbands, fathers, brothers, and sweethearts. In her own way, manufactured mother represents an antithesis of Mary Shelley's *Frankenstein*, but her benevolence is not always what it seems. Details may have changed somewhat during the century, but authors nearly always fixed mother on a pedestal as a kind of "marble queen and captive," to paraphrase the title of Joy Kasson's book.[17]

While the true simpler life in the old home was irretrievably lost, mythical mother, so ingrained in the nineteenth-century imagination by some of that century's most favorite music, continued, for better or for worse, to dominate attitudes toward mothers well into our own century. In many ways this mythology hovers over us yet today, suggesting, and often dictating, ideas and expectations of what a "good" mother is.

Long before the days of Tin Pan Alley dominance, music publishers played a major role in guiding the public's taste in popular song, and the bottom line was as important as it is today. A song that combined motherhood and temperance issues would have had some success as a vehicle for social protest, for example, or, if treated in a comic manner, would have been successful on the minstrel stage, but the financial return to the publisher probably would have been limited compared to the proceeds from a sentimental mother song that appealed to a wider audience.

Additionally, success held out the hope for continued good fortune: the initial commercial achievements of songs with comforting and protective mothers fed author, composer, and publisher interest in duplicating those accomplishments. Elizabeth Akers Allen's poem "Rock Me to Sleep" was so popular with the public that at least seven composers, George F. Root and John H. Hewitt among them, set the words to music. The success of these early mother-and-home songs prompted a number of "reply" or "answer" songs, including songs with mother speaking from the grave: "Call Me Not Back from the Echoless Shore," "The Mother's Reply to Rock Me to Sleep," and "Keep Me Awake Mother."

Successful Civil War songs that dealt with mother and her hero son led to imitation: "Just before the Battle, Mother" spawned "Tell Me of My Darling Boy; or, The Mother's Reply to Just before the Battle" and "Just after the Battle Mother." "Mother Is the Battle Over" gave birth to "Yes My Child the Battle's Over" and "Dear Mother the Battle Is Over." Capitalizing on commercial success, as in the common spin-off phenomenon found in so much of our current popular culture, obviously was not unique to the twentieth century.

There is a relative poverty of language in these songs; rarely does one find the rich kind of expression that metaphor and simile provide, for example. Such plain utterance, however, created an accessibility that allowed for diverse interpretations, so that listeners from different social, economic, or ethnic classes could interpret the words in a variety of ways, relating them to the unique experiences each brought to the music. Thus, generic expression lent itself to a multiplicity of interpretations.

It was in this very genre of sentimental songs about mother, often linked with home, that Dresser excelled. Mother offers her child advice about the ways of the world—how to treat other people—as the Golden Rule instructs—and always assures him of her unending love. She will always be at the door to welcome home and to forgive her prodigal son, her wayward boy—and Dresser certainly was often that. Between 1887 and 1905 Dresser composed at least forty-five mother or mother-and-home songs. In that period of nearly two decades, scarcely a year passed that Dresser did not explore these topics, and his poetic utterance was usually sensitive enough to prevent his songs from sinking into the swamp of banality that plagued hundreds of other mother-and-home songs.

Dresser's narrator, exhausted at the end of the workday, drifts off to sleep and dreams of returning to the idyllic scenes and times of childhood and to his ever loving mother:

I wander'd home from business cares,
And sat down by the fire,
I watched the fitful flames until
My eyes began to tire,
My thoughts went back into the past,
To days of long ago,
How long I sat I cannot tell,

The lights were burning low,
When my mother placed her arms around me,
And called me her darling boy,
My mother smiled as she always did,
On her first love, her only joy.
My mother pressed me to her breast, was kissing my tears away,
When I awoke and found t'was but
A dream of my boyhood days.[18]

At mother's knee, the child receives pithy advice that will serve him well in life:

A rolling stone would gather little moss. . . .
The Father watched o'er me from above,
She bade me pray to him with head bowed low,
She said if I'd take her advice, some day I'd be with him.
She told me never turn my back on sorrow or distress,
But give what e'er I could to help the poor. . . .
So try and love your neighbor as you always love yourself,
Your deed will make you known where e'er you go.
A man who's honest needs no monument when he is gone.[19]

Mother cautions him not to mislead girls about his feelings:

You're going to see your sweetheart now, be careful what you say,
Don't break her heart because she's fond of you,
Don't tell her that you love her if you don't.[20]

and reminds her son that "one man out of ten is seldom true."[21]

If nothing else, musical mother was a great solace to her child. In a song of 1900, a widow tells her little son about his daddy and tries to comfort his fears:

On a dark, dark day de Lordy took him away,
But I caint hardly b'live he went away to stay;
Like de bird in de nes' he's jes' takin' a res',
'Cause de Lordy thinks it bes'.
Honey, don't you cry, caint you understan',
Dere ain't such a thing as de boogeeman;
Dere's nothin' could touch you, if dey tried,
When Mammy's by yo' side.[22]

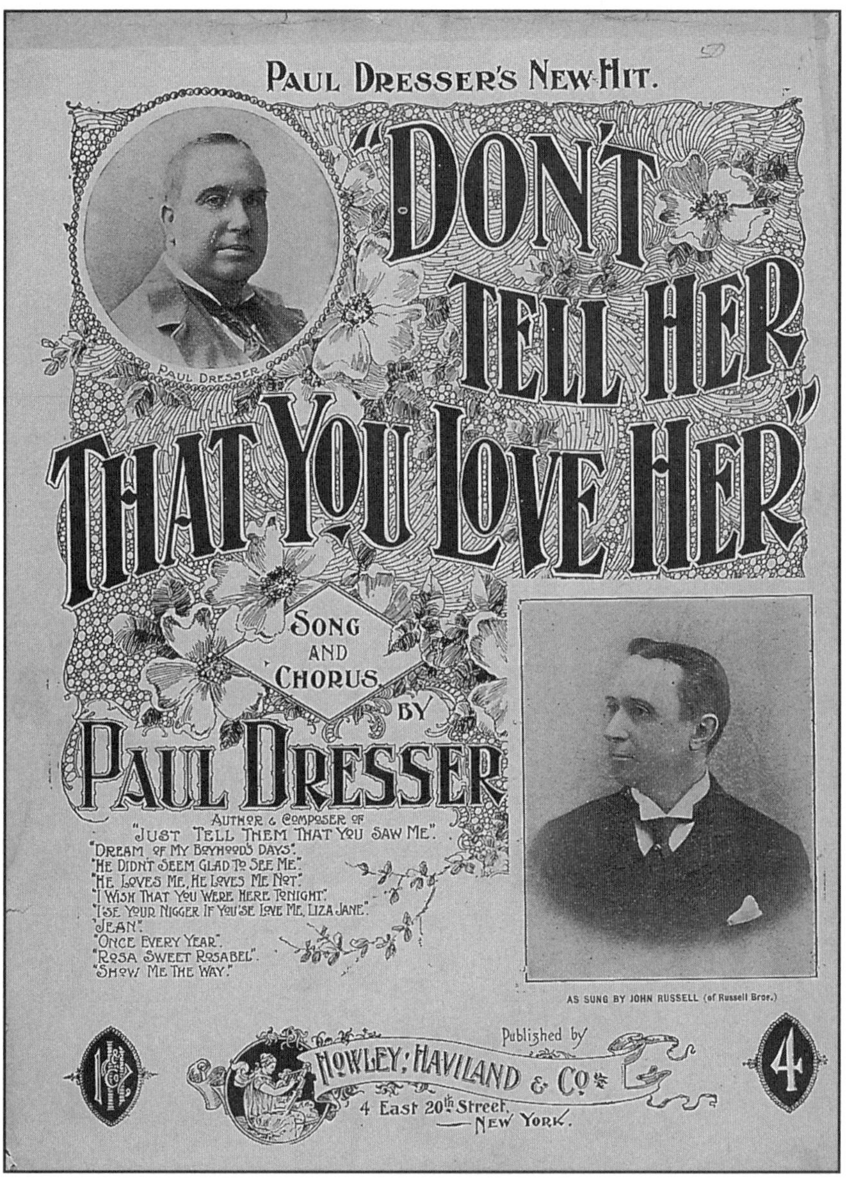

IHS

"Don't Tell Her That You Love Her," published in 1896.

Dresser's use of dialect here is sensitive in its touch, appropriate to the dignified and caring black mother's concern for her son. This is refreshing in an era when such dialect was more often used in "coon" songs in a demeaning and denigrating way.

In her attempt to prepare her son for the world, mother's advice could sound self-serving, as if mother were the only true friend in the world:

> She told me that in manhood temptations I would meet,
> And that very few true friends I'd know.
> She also said the world was full of falsehood and deceit,
> I believe it, for my mother told me so.[23]

Theodore Dreiser claimed that this song, "I Believe It for My Mother Told Me So," was

> one of those charming and babyish expressions of [Dresser's] inmost self as well as his unchanging adoration of his mother—an expression of affection which, since it was not only dedicated to her but expressed in very primary and yet effective language his profound love of her and so her emotional control of him, must have comforted her no little.[24]

On the other hand, and perhaps somewhat fancifully, Dresser said he had written the song after he had overheard an argument among "a gang of young toughs in New York City. I stopped to listen. 'How do you know that is true?' sneeringly demanded a burly lad. 'Why, bekase me mudder tole me so,' shouted a little fellow with mingled indignation and sincerity."[25]

Whatever the inspiration for the story, "I Believe It for My Mother Told Me So" had an immediate effect on listeners. An obituary claimed that Dresser earned about eight thousand dollars from this song alone.[26] However the song came about, there is little doubt that Sarah Dreiser was the mother who had told Dresser so. Although Johann Paul Dreiser might rail against the moral failings of his family, his harping must have seemed like just so much muttering. Sarah might placate her husband with a certain amount of bowing and scraping to him, but there was no doubt that she was the parent whom the children respected and feared. What she said was the gospel.

There is no doubt that Sarah was the parent with the true control over the family. On more than one occasion it was she who decided that it would be best, for economic reasons, to divide the family, leaving Johann Paul in Terre Haute with the older children while she returned to Sullivan or went to Evansville or Warsaw with the rest of her brood. As divisive as this might seem, Sarah was able, in this way, to keep her large family intact, except for her wayward Rome. Sarah's control over her children could verge on the cruel; she sometimes resorted to emotional blackmail to keep the children in line and in the process filled them with the dread of abandonment. Threatening to leave her children when they misbehaved, she would don her bonnet and shawl, and carrying a packed basket, would go out the door. The crying and terror this produced in the children is predictable. Long after she was dead, Theodore had dreams of Sarah "threatening to go off and leave me, and [I] would awake to find myself in tears."[27] Dreiser also remarked that Sarah "succeeded in drawing her children to her as with hooks of steel."[28] Johann Paul's zealous adherence to his Roman Catholicism repelled most of the children. Too, his inability to support his family weakened any position of parental authority he may have wanted to exercise. Little wonder that father appears but rarely in Dresser's songs. Sarah was the strong parent. But that strength lay not in moral uprightness. Her willingness—even readiness—to accept her children's indulgences of the flesh or of other kinds of scandalous behavior never provided them with a sense of right and wrong that would serve as their moral anchor. The hurtful, flesh-and-blood, amoral Sarah is a mother Dresser never wanted to admit existed—a kind of mother who never appeared in his songs or, indeed, in other mother songs of the period. But he believed her always, for as he said, "my mother told me so."

How does one reconcile the lusty and promiscuous Dresser with the man who wrote the lovely songs about ideal women—mother and chaste maiden? Dresser clearly was able to compartmentalize his thoughts and views about women, indeed his very life, into opposite sides of the same coin. On one hand, he turns his song mother into an icon of purity in thought and deed, into an omniscient, ever-forgiving woman. That innocence, coupled with the power of absolution that Dresser's women possess, marks them as unattainable ideals, beings removed from the real world. These women are endowed neither with sexuality nor sensuality.

Never is there the slightest suggestion of anything untoward in their behavior. They are not real but rather fit into the manufactured icon of what virtuous woman was supposed to be. Additionally, they belong not to the here and now but at a remove from the narrator. Because of their distance from the anguished male narrator, either through time or death (and often both), he can worship—and love—them without having to truly commit himself. Distance and death guarantee that their purity is protected forever. The mothers of Dresser's songs could easily have been his own mother, Sarah, sanitized of all her faults; most of the girls, his own sisters before they lost their innocence. In his heart of hearts, certainly Dresser knew that even his own mother did not meet those ideals that he and so many other composers described. He was perpetuating a myth that the marketplace had helped to create.

On the other hand, a sexually charged being inhabited the dark, underside of that coin—the sort of woman everyone knew existed but the type genteel society spoke of in hushed tones, if at all. The flesh-and-blood woman, of whom Dresser wrote but once, is the direct antithesis of the sanctified female. That sexually charged female is the one he felt worthy of his strategems of seduction, the one he numbered among his conquests. His "gal Sal" is different from his typical pasteboard, cut-out women. Sal, "a wild sort of devil," represents the sort of woman he lusted for in everyday life, the one he sought to seduce.

For Dresser—consciously or not—these two icons of womanhood were distinctly separate types whose characters and attributes never met. His song mother could never be related to his women of the street. His mothers could never have been fallen angels, or daughters of Baal. Conversely, it probably never entered Dresser's mind that a *nymphe du pavé* could ever attain the status of purity, of sainted motherhood. The two types were absolutely and forever separate to him. His brother reflected that while Dresser was

> always sighing over the beauty, innocence, sweetness, . . . of young maidenhood in his songs, . . . [he really] desire[d] and attract[ed] quite a different type—the young and beautiful, it is true, but also the old, the homely and the somewhat savage—a catholicity of taste I could never quite stomach. . . .

> I could see how completely dependent upon beauty in the flesh he was, how it made his life and world.[29]

Clearly, no one would publish songs that boasted about Dresser's conquests or of the women who fired his fleshly imaginings—even if he had ever wanted to compose such music. Even Sal, his "wild sort of devil," sounds somewhat virtuous, clothed, so to speak, in the lilting, genteel meter of a waltz.

Dresser often intertwines the themes of isolation and mother in the same song. As rural communities lost more and more of their citizens to the larger cities, separation from home, from rural roots, from parents, from the values of youth became a hard and poignant fact of nineteenth-century life. Any number of songs recounted that separation, told from the perspective of mother who remained behind or the son or daughter who went to the city and, for whatever reason, could not or would not return home. Those who transplanted themselves to the city often found the reality of their new lives at odds with the dreams they had harbored for their futures. Far from the rural communities and families that nurtured them, they learned all too soon that the city could be a shockingly impersonal place, where neighbor cared little for neighbor, where work in the stifling atmosphere of an ugly factory was much harder—and less satisfying—than hard work done outdoors in the countryside. Gone was the ready contact with family and its reassurance and support. The wrenching loneliness could be overwhelming.

Granted, there were countless attractions one could never find in the small village—enticing things, opportunities, and people beckoning seductively like so many sirens. Those who lacked a strong moral foundation could easily find themselves swept into the vortex of dissoluteness much as Carrie Meeber had in *Sister Carrie*. Everyone knew, or had heard of, someone who had succumbed to such temptation. Dresser may have been speaking from personal experience when he wrote "The Path That Leads the Other Way" in 1898. There, a callow youth "coldly listened [to his mother's advice] just because he tho't that he / Was far beyond advising." In anger, the boy left home for "cities far away" where "he wandered down the path that leads the other way, / He simply drifted from the fold, poor lad and went astray."[30] The youngster ended up languishing in a prison cell. Jimmy Bulger, the former Sullivan friend, may have been the subject of this song, but Dresser may also have been revisiting some of his own past and indulging in a bit of autobiography. Another wayward man was the subject of "The Convict and the Bird" of 1888. In that song, a bird becomes the saving grace for a prisoner "Doom'd all the days of his life." The convict, whom Dresser claimed he modeled after the outlaw Cole Younger, takes care of the sparrow, feeding it and listening to its song day after day. To the convict the bird represents freedom. Shortly after the bird finishes its last song and dies, the convict gains *his* freedom through his own death.[31] In another song, a man's beloved

> . . . went to the city . . . far, far away. . . .
> She grew kind of restless and wanted to go.
> Said she'd be back in a few weeks or so.
> She went to the city with a tear in her eye, but she never returned.[32]

The longing to return to the edenic times of youth in the small village, to somehow relive life before the fall from innocence and grace, could have been overwhelming. To "go back and start the whole thing over," as Dresser wrote in 1901, and to be able to shut out the noisy, frenetic life in the city—that was a dream of many.[33] Some, for one reason or another, could never bring themselves to return. In one of Dresser's songs, a narrator, unwilling to return home, sends his family his love through an acquaintance, asking him to

> Tell them that you saw me,
> That I had a start,
> Do not tell them stories,
> And break my mother's heart.[34]

In "Just Tell Them That You Saw Me," Dresser returned to the same theme and words. The song was inspired by fellow Terre Hautean Will Riley, who had gone to New York City, hoping to win acclaim as an actor. Failing, he became despondent, at which time Dresser ran into him on the street. Dresser was going back to Terre Haute soon and asked Riley if there were any message he might like to send his family back home. Riley's response: "Oh. I don't know, don't care. Just tell them that you saw me; they will know the rest."[35] Refusing Dresser's offer of help, Riley went his own way, but as Dresser walked to his hotel those words stuck in his mind. Soon afterward Dresser came upon a short article in the newspaper that told of Riley's suicide. Haunted by Riley's comment, Dresser wrote his song but changed the character to "Madge," his "schoolmate in a village far away." Now pale and ill, the girl longs to see her mother once again, but "pride alone [keeps her] away." She asks the narrator to

> Tell mother I am coming home some day.
> Just tell them that you saw me, . . .
> Just whisper if you get a chance to mother dear, and say,
> I love her as I did long, long ago.[36]

Dresser wrote several other songs in this same vein. In one, a sister pleads with her runaway brother, "a wild wayward lad, a mother's only joy," to

> Come home with me dear brother, . . .
> For if I go home without you,
> How mother will cry. . . .
> So come home, don't let her worry,
> You're breaking mother's heart![37]

In another, an "absent boy" far from home ponders if anyone at home misses and still loves him, "if a heart there is that's longing / My saddened face once more to see." He wonders if anyone there is angry with him for his childhood faults. In a reassuring turn of sentiment, the lad reminds himself that

> There's one I know who'll always love me
> At sight of me she'll bound with joy!
> I know that there's a Home where I am welcome,
> A mother, too, who loves her absent boy![38]

In still another, "A care-worn face has waited, and has watched for many a day / By the window for a fair hair'd boy, who long since went away." Mother keeps her vigil through the years, praying for her wayward boy to return to her. When he does come home, "She falls in his arms with a sharp cry of pain / In the arms of the boy that she'll ne'er see again." Angelic mother, "like all noble womankind, with hope unto the last" has gone blind.[39] Finally, in "The Outcast Unknown," Dresser writes of the poignancy of a child lost forever, of a mother never knowing the fate of her baby. Mother prays to God to be kind to her daughter "Who had sinned and no mercy was shown." Unknown to mother, daughter lies buried in an unmarked grave in the bleak countryside by an old ruined mill; only the drooping weeds weep over her.[40]

Two themes Dresser returns to time after time are the child, reared in the innocence of the small village but now removed to the city and under the spell of evils, and the all-forgiving angelic mother, who absolves but still reminds the child of duty and responsibility. The words in both kinds of songs had considerable resonance with those late-nineteenth-century listeners who felt a terrible dislocation, and perhaps a sense of guilt, in their move from rural communities to life in the cold, dispassionate, impersonal cities. Mother and home provided them with an anchor of stability, no matter how modest, and a link to the imagined Eden of their youth. Certainly these themes rang true for Dresser. He worked these streams often, not only for the financial rewards they brought him as composer and author, but because he believed in their sentiments—feelings he often included in letters he wrote to his friends back in Indiana.

In 1901, as the twentieth century began, with both parents dead, the forty-three-year-old Dresser wrote:

> I wander'd back in a dreamy way, to scenes of childish joy,
> And the strangest feeling o'er me came, as I thought myself a boy. . . .
> I wander'd to the resting place of mother on the hill, . . .
> I just want to go back and start the whole thing over, . . .
> To the golden days of June, . . .
> Back to the fields and start all over.[41]

In trying to describe a paradise to which the listener could go back, Dresser attempted to recapture the spirit of "Wabash," with its definite sense of place. Such efforts, however, always came up short in terms of public acclaim. "Way Down in Old Indiana," for example, is replete with trite and ineffective triple rhymes in the verse: "There lie the scenes of a lifetime the best, / There's where I watch'd the sun sink in the West, / And when I am gone it is there I would rest," and ordinary rhymes that sound somewhat comical: "With a heart full of longing, my thoughts turn tonight. . . . / The same wayward lad in the mellow moonlight."[42] The nostalgic sentiments, now sounding mawkish, are not aided by the sextuple-meter sing-song melody that accompanies them. "In Dear Old Illinois" is no better: "My heart is yearning, my thoughts are turning again I am a boy; / The sun shone brighter, my heart seemed lighter, in dear old Illinois." One could easily substitute the name of another state, rhyming it with the last word of the line, and achieve the same result. "Illinois" provides the only element of specificity to the words. The song is clearly a generic one, with the "perfumed clover blossoms," the "waving fields of corn," the "rolling prairies," the "old log cabin," the church, the "sweetheart, with the tenderest blue eye," and, of course, mother.[43] The words to "Sweet Savannah," with the "humble cottage," "mother old and gray," and "sweet magnolias," are somewhat better, but the song suffers from a static melody that lacks any forward drive.[44] In "The Town Where I Was Born," composed the year before he died, Dresser again wrote a generic song with references to the village choir, the church with its spire, the running brook, the friends, and "sweethearts tried and true seated beneath the sugar tree." The words of the chorus are somewhat better:

> There were no brown stone mansions there,
> No gilded halls of fame,
> There were no silks or laces rare, all tarnished o'er with shame,
> The smiles out there were genuine,
> And hearts were seldom torn,
> And friends tho' few, were staunch and true,
> In the town where I was born.[45]

The grandeur and sweep of the words to "Wabash" are nowhere found in these songs. In fact, in their frantic search for a sense of place, some of them become little more than parodies of the authentic feel of "Wabash."

For Dresser and others of the time, the Middle West was where innocence might still be found. The East, alluring as it may be, and in spite of Dresser's acclaim there, was not where his heart lay. As it was for James Whitcomb Riley, Dresser's slightly older contemporary, the middle of the country—especially Indiana—was not only the heartland of the nation but the place that still retained much of the untroubled past. As Riley "gave the state of Indiana pride of place" in his literature, Dresser dignified his native state through some of his music and words.[46] These two artists did much to bring the Middle West to the consciousness of the nation as the century turned.

At a time when America was being incorporated, to use Alan Trachtenberg's phrase, if one could but return to that Middle West, to breathe the air, to see old friends, to revisit old, cherished spots with their memories, then perhaps the loss of childhood innocence would be only temporary; as if with a magic wand, that air, those friends, and those locales might grant reentry, if only briefly, into that lost paradise.[47] That, of course, was impossible. Incorporation had already affected most of the country; the notion of escape in the Middle West, or in any other region of America, was an illusion, often a cruel one. Industry and business, in their hard-headed ways, recognized that, but those who dreamed with the heart clung to their fantasy. Mythical scenes of childhood became a sensory parallel to illusory, ideal mother. Dresser captured the poignancy of this yearning best in "On the Banks of the Wabash, Far Away." One smells the "breath of new-mown hay" from the fertile fields; one can see the waving cornfields and can feel and almost taste the "woodlands clear and cool." One sees not only Dresser's beloved river, but in those mirrored waters one beholds as well the lovely reflected vision of the sweet moonlight. Sight is also suffused with the magical luminosity of candlelights shimmering, flickering through the leaves of the sycamore trees. And to the heart's memories belong mother waiting in the doorway, "As she stood there years ago, her boy to greet" and the grave of sweetheart Mary.[48]

"On the Banks of the Wabash, Far Away" is Paul Dresser's gift of time and place, far away.

CHAPTER 35

A Gift of Time and Place

After the turn of the century, illusory Eden became a place younger composers of popular song cared less and less about visiting. In this they were joined by a growing number of listeners. Songs of yearning and nostalgia seemed quaint to those who moved to the syncopated rhythms of ragtime now incorporated into songs. Some composers would continue to turn out songs in the older musical style: "A Bird in a Gilded Cage," "In the Good Old Summer Time," "On a Sunday Afternoon," "Meet Me in St. Louis, Louis," "In My Merry Oldsmobile," "In the Shade of the Old Apple Tree," and Paul Dresser's own "My Gal Sal" all recalled an earlier era in the lilting quality of their waltz meters. Even some of these songs, however, marked a newer era in the breeziness of their words. A lover strolls with his "baby mine," his "tootsey wootsey"[1]; "Flossie," who has left her Louis for the fair in St. Louis, assures him that she'll be his "tootsie wootsie" as they dance the "Hoochee Koochee"[2]; the double entendre of "You can go as far as you like with me" and the more obvious "They love to spark in the dark old park" in "In My Merry Oldsmobile" were not lost on many listeners.[3]

More and more, however, the breeziness of word was matched with rhythmic exuberance, a kind of jauntiness one could never find in a waltz. With "Hello! Ma Baby," "Bill Bailey, Won't You Please Come Home?," "Under the Bamboo Tree," "Give My Regards to Broadway," and "Good Bye, My Lady Love," different types of expression sometimes replaced some of the old-fashioned, genteel words that dealt with love or the loved one. For a younger generation of Americans, "Hello! ma baby, Hello! ma honey, Hello! ma ragtime gal" said it all.[4] Even the silliness of "If you lak-a-me, lak I lak-a-you / And we lak-a-both the same, / I lak-a say, this very day, / I lak-a-change your name" in the chorus of Bob Cole and John Rosamond Johnson's immense hit "Under the Bamboo Tree" had greater appeal for some than did the stilted nineteenth-century language of love.[5] The musical speech and verbal expression of popular song were changing rapidly, even if the latter was expressing, albeit differently, the same emotions of an earlier era.

Once Dresser began to compose in earnest in 1886, there was a constant flow from his pen, resulting in more than 140 songs. Before 1901 Dresser wrote 116 of these. In three years—1890, 1896, and 1898—he published more than one-third of that total, with 14 in 1890 alone. During the decade from 1886 to 1896, when constant touring throughout the country made his life extremely busy, Dresser still found time to compose nearly 70 songs, most of which Willis Woodward and Company published.

As only the composer, Dresser did not share in the financial largesse his better-selling songs, such as "The Curse" and "The Pardon Came Too Late" brought to Woodward. By the time he left the stage for good, however, he had for three years taken a personal hand in publishing his songs. As a partner with Pat Howley and Fred Haviland, Dresser's financial status changed significantly, although it is difficult to know with any precision what his profits were. Eager to duplicate the success of "The Letter That Never Came," for which he claimed he received nothing, he turned out song after song, a number of them quite a bit below his customary standards—he admitted as much for most of the songs he composed between 1890 and 1894. It took almost a decade and some sixty more songs before he had another success, that with "Just Tell Them That You Saw Me" in 1895. From that year through the turn of the century, one or more of Dresser's songs enjoyed more than modest success.

Why was Dresser so successful as a song composer? In his best songs, his music evoked a poignancy of its own, combining appealing contours within the confines of a prevailing pentatonicism. His words conveyed a message that transcended the limitations of ethnicity, religion, economic status, gender, and region. In these songs, he was able to appeal to the listener's emotions without descending into the bathos that characterized thousands of other songs written in the last thirty years of the century. The honesty of the sentiment Dresser expressed was what struck a ready accord with so many listeners. He often drew upon experiences that were true to him, fashioning many songs after his own inner feelings and experiences, and, in the process, creating portions of an autobiography: the wayward child who was in danger of journeying "The Path That Leads the Other Way"; the child who sends the message "Just Tell Them That You Saw Me" to his family back home; the youngster, now grown to manhood, who longs for the village of his youth; that same adult who yearns for what he remembers as the carefree days of his boyhood, of those delicious days wandering "On the Banks of the Wabash, Far Away."

As we have seen, Dresser was unusually adept at compartmentalizing his life. The "unregenerate sexual enthusiast" side of Dresser conflicted regularly with "the good son," "the good Catholic" who wrote about the purity of womanhood. One can view his earthy, sensualistic life—his consorting with prostitutes, his urge toward seduction—as a metaphor for the ugliness and immorality that many Americans saw in nineteenth-century life: the evils of corporate America, of the rich getting richer and the poor getting poorer, life in large metropolitan areas where often little stock was placed in seemingly outdated standards of morality and integrity, and on and on.

At the same time, many longed for a state of innocence they sensed had been left behind. Yearning after lost innocence is a universal obsession, not exclusive to the 1800s, but that century witnessed an effusion of works dedicated to that theme. Thousands upon thousands wrote, sculpted, painted, and composed with that idée fixe in mind. Often a word or two suffices as a metaphor for that past, a time recalled as an idyllic period in one's life. "Far away" and "home" can conjure up scenes of that remembered paradise. Stephen Foster's narrator longs "for de old plantation, / And for de old folks at home" "Way down upon de Swanee ribber, / Far, far away."[6] Through his singer, Dresser's thoughts often "revert to scenes of childhood, / Where [he] first received [his] lessons Nature's school" "on the banks of the Wabash, far away."[7] "Far away" and "home" become metaphors for an irrecoverable place and for the innocence of our individual and collective pasts, both of which have now, in our maturity, attained the status of myth.

For Dresser, "far away" and "home" represented his life as an innocent in Terre Haute and Sullivan, Indiana. For many, mother can be an even more powerful metaphor of innocence, of the past. The thousands of mother-and-home songs in the nineteenth century extolled the past that was forever "far away." Those phrases were also metaphors for the nation's past, her lost innocence. At a time when rural America was being abandoned for the city, when advances in technology could lead to a confusing, impersonal sort of existence, many Americans could, and did, find immense comfort in far-away mother and home as recalled in poetry and music. While it is true that the marketplace drove much of the demand for such songs, and while it is equally true that much of that poetic and musical utterance was far from first-rate, a few composers, Dresser more than most, were able to invest that genre, that mold, with considerable grace and beauty.

In the words he wrote to his songs, Dresser was often able to walk the fine line between noble sentiment and maudlin sentimentalism. His music, simple in its harmonies and with melodies that are oftentimes memorable, provides an ideal support for those words. When he succeeded in wedding unpretentious yet poetic utterances with equally unassuming but flowing melodic lyricism, Dresser's songs became models worthy of emulation. In the words of Charles Hamm, his "songs, in their expressive content, are squarely in the tradition of Thomas Moore and Stephen Foster. He was the only worthy successor to these two."[8]

Theodore Dreiser's close friend, the acid-tongued H. L. Mencken, was not given to sentimental nostalgia, but Dresser's songs strangely moved him. He recalled some emotional moments that occurred at the 1920 Democratic National Convention in San Francisco following the placing of Al Smith's name into nomination. The band began to play "The Sidewalks of New York" and followed with song after song after song.

> In five minutes the convention had been transformed into a carnival. In 10 minutes all politics was completely forgotten. In 15 minutes every delegate was on his legs, his voice raised in sentimental song. In 20 minutes they were all dancing. In half an hour they were kissing the gals in the aisles. . . . It was a debauch of sentimentality, an orgy of mush. Absurd, God knows—but somehow lovely.

Mencken suddenly realized that nearly all the songs the delegates sang were Paul Dresser songs. "It was a stupendous demonstration in honor of Dresser—an extraordinarily dramatic proof of the horse-power of his peculiar genius." Mencken "was struck that '10,000 average Americans yearning to lift their voice in song' thought not of songs by Stephen Foster, not of patriotic pieces, but of the musical legacy of Dresser, 'an humble minstrel man.' "[9]

If these things are true, why have Dresser's songs not lasted in the memories and on the lips of people today? For one, his timing was not good. He composed his songs just a little too early to take full advantage of the new technology of recording. At least four singers *did* record Dresser songs during his lifetime: baritone J. W. Myers recorded "Just Tell Them That You Saw Me" in 1895; George J. Gaskin, an Irish tenor, recorded the same song in 1896 and "On the Banks of the Wabash, Far Away" in 1897; Steve Porter also recorded "Wabash" in the last part of 1897; Myers recorded "Way Down in Old Indiana" in 1902; and Richard Jose, a foremost interpreter of Dresser's songs, recorded "The Day That You Grew Colder" a year before the composer died.[10] Nonetheless, recording was in its infancy, and mass marketing of records was still in the future.

At least three other major occurrences in American culture seem to have militated against the popularity of much of American song from the last part of the nineteenth century. Community singing, which was an important and pleasurable way to disseminate a common body of song to a wide intergenerational population, largely fell out of favor shortly after World War II. School assemblies, grange meetings, and gatherings of social clubs all had afforded some time to singing songs, if only patriotic ones. Younger generations learned the very songs their elders knew and loved, songs that belonged to a core of popular music from the nineteenth century, tunes and words that both adults and young people could sing together. That has not been the case for nearly a half century. Now the only songs that span various age groups for community singing are those that find use for specific occasions. "Happy Birthday to You," "The Star-Spangled Banner," "Take Me Out to the Ballgame," and "Auld Lang Syne" seem to be the only songs that *everyone* knows.

When one couples the demise of community singing with the development of a distinct youth culture beginning in the 1950s, a youth culture that claimed its own music, different from that of adults, it is easy to understand the divide that has prevailed during the past fifty years. Additionally, the stilted, quaint language of many of the songs of the last four decades of the nineteenth century has seemed to work against the general acceptance of this music by an audience of any appreciable size today. Songs that avoid such verbal extravagances tend to have fared better in terms of public recognition. "My Wild Irish Rose," "The Band Played On," "The Sidewalks of New York," "Daisy Bell" ("A Bicycle Built for Two"), and possibly "When You Were Sweet Sixteen" come readily to mind. Between the efforts of Foster and some songs of the early twentieth century exists an immense body of popular song that few people sing today. While a number of songs from that very body were acclaimed at the time, they have fallen by the wayside.

Dresser's poetic and musical language belongs to that great golden age of popular song of the late nineteenth century, a time of genteel expression suffused with emotion and nostalgia about mother and home—emotion worn readily for everyone to see. Singing and listening to Dresser's songs provided one with a haven, a respite from everyday life and from the ominous presence of the modern world. Briefly, one could recall moments of innocence, now made all the more touching by their loss. Those halcyon days, never to be forgotten by those who had lived them, had become bittersweet memories as village life gradually disappeared and the United States began to extend its influence and power beyond its borders. But for those willing to listen then and now, Dresser's music was a gift, one of time and place, recalled lovingly and poignantly and captured forever as in musical amber.

APPENDIX 1

Alphabetical List of Published Compositions

Title	*Year*	*Publisher*
"After the Battle"	1905	Paul Dresser
"After the Storm" (Waltzes for Piano Solo)	1896	Howley, Haviland
"The Army of Half-Starved Men"	1902	Howley, Haviland & Dresser
"Ave Maria"	1899	Howley, Haviland
"A Baby Adrift at Sea"	1890	Willis Woodward
"Baby Slumbers"	1887	Balmer & Weber
"Baby's Tears"	1889	Willis Woodward
"The Band Played Annie Laurie; or, To Hear Them Tell It"	1890	Willis Woodward
"The Battery"	1895	Howley, Haviland
"The Blind Mother"	1889	Willis Woodward
"The Blue and the Gray; or, A Mother's Gift to Her Country"	1900	Howley, Haviland
"The Boys Are Coming Home Today"	1903	Howley, Haviland & Dresser
"Calling to Her Boy Just Once Again"	1900	Howley, Haviland
"Come Home, Dewey, We Won't Do a Thing to You"	1899	Howley, Haviland
"Come, Tell Me What's Your Answer, Yes or No"	1898	Howley, Haviland
"The Convict and the Bird"	1888	Willis Woodward
"Coontown Capers" (music by Theodore Morse)	1897	Howley, Haviland
"The Curse"	1887	Willis Woodward
"The Curse of the Dreamer"	1899	Howley, Haviland

Title	*Year*	*Publisher*
"Darktown after Dark" ("A Bunch of Niggerism" for piano solo)	1899	Howley, Haviland
"The Day That You Grew Colder"	1905	Paul Dresser
"Days Gone By"	1890	Willis Woodward
"Did You Ever Hear a Nigger Say Wow?"	1890	Willis Woodward
"Don't Forget Your Old Parents at Home" (Willis Woodward issued song in 1889)	1887	Lyon & Healy
"Don't Tell Her That You Love Her; or, Mankind Is Seldom True"	1896	Howley, Haviland
"A Dream of My Boyhood Days"	1896	Howley, Haviland
"Every Night There's a Light"	1898	Howley, Haviland
"Gath'ring Roses for Her Hair"	1899	Howley, Haviland
"Give Us Just Another Lincoln"	1900	Howley, Haviland
"Glory to God"	1902	Howley, Haviland & Dresser
"Good Bye for All Eternity"	1899	Howley, Haviland
"The Green above the Red"	1900	Howley, Haviland
"He Brought Home Another"	1896	Howley, Haviland
"He Didn't Seem Glad to See Me"	1893	George T. Worth
"He Fought for the Cause He Thought Was Right"	1896	Howley, Haviland
"He Loves Me, He Loves Me Not"	1893	George T. Worth
"He Was a Soldier"	1892	Willis Woodward
"Her Tears Drifted Out with the Tide"	1890	Willis Woodward
"Here Lies an Actor"	1888	Willis Woodward
"The Honest Little Dollar" (melody from "Just Tell Them That You Saw Me"; words by Monroe H. Rosenfeld for Republican national campaign)	1896	Howley, Haviland
"I Believe It for My Mother Told Me So"	1887	Lyon & Healy

Title	*Year*	*Publisher*
"I Can't Believe Her Faithless; or, Since Nellie Went Away" (cover has 1891, but first page has 1889)	1889	Willis Woodward
"I Just Want to Go Back and Start the Whole Thing Over"	1901	Howley, Haviland & Dresser
"I Long to Hear from Home"	1888	Willis Woodward
"I Send to Them My Love"	1888	Willis Woodward
"I Told Her the Same Old Story"	1893	Willis Woodward
"I Was Looking for My Boy, She Said; or, Decoration Day"	1895	Howley, Haviland
"I Wish That You Were Here Tonight"	1896	Howley, Haviland
"I Wonder If She'll Ever Come Back to Me"	1896	Howley, Haviland
"I Wonder If There's Someone Who Loves Me"	1890	Willis Woodward
"I Wonder Where She Is Tonight"	1899	Howley, Haviland
"I'd Still Believe You True"	1900	Howley, Haviland
"If You See My Sweetheart"	1897	Howley, Haviland
"I'll Keep These Letters for Her Sake" (words by Julian Holmes)	1891	T. B. Harms
"I'm Going Far Away, Love"	1892	Willis Woodward
"In Dear Old Illinois"	1902	Howley, Haviland & Dresser
"In Good Old New York Town"	1899	Howley, Haviland
"In the Great Somewhere"	1901	Howley, Haviland & Dresser
"In the Sweet Summer Time"	1897	Howley, Haviland
"I'se Your Nigger If You Wants Me Liza Jane"	1896	Howley, Haviland
"It All Seemed Strange to Her, Poor Thing" (words by George F. McCann)	1895	Howley, Haviland
"Jean"	1895	Howley, Haviland
"Jim Judson"	1905	Paul Dresser
"The Judgment Is at Hand"	1906	Paul Dresser
"Just Tell Them That You Saw Me"	1895	Howley, Haviland
"Just to See Mother's Face Once Again"	1891	Willis Woodward

Title	*Year*	*Publisher*
"The Letter Came at Last"	1887	T. B. Harms
"The Letter That Never Came" (Harms publication has words by Dresser, music by Max Sturm; *The Songs of Paul Dresser* gives Dresser as composer and author)	1886	T. B. Harms
"The Limit Was Fifty Cents"	1890	Willis Woodward
"Lincoln, Grant and Lee; or, The War Is Over Many Years"	1903	Howley, Haviland & Dresser
"Little Fannie McIntyre"	1890	Willis Woodward
"Little Jim"	1890	Willis Woodward
"The Lone Grave"	1890	Willis Woodward
"Love's Promise"	1887	Balmer & Weber
"Mary Mine"	1904	James H. Curtin
"Mother Will Stand by Me"	1889	Willis Woodward
"Mr. Volunteer; or, You Don't Belong to the Regulars, You're Just a Volunteer"	1901	Howley, Haviland & Dresser
"My Flag! My Flag!"	1892	Willis Woodward
"My Gal Sal; or, They Called Her Frivolous Sal"	1905	Paul Dresser
"My Heart Still Clings to the Old First Love"	1901	Howley, Haviland & Dresser
"My Sweetheart of Long, Long Ago"	1891	Willis Woodward
"Never Speak Again"	1887	Willis Woodward
"Niggah Loves His Possum; or, Deed He Do, Do, Do"	1905	Jerome H. Remick
"The Old Flame Flickers, and I Wonder Why"	1898	Howley, Haviland
"On the Banks of the Wabash, Far Away"	1897	Howley, Haviland
"On the Shores of Havana, Far Away" (words by Andrew B. Sterling)	1898	Howley, Haviland
"Once Ev'ry Year"	1894	Howley, Haviland
"Only a Dear Little Star"	1888	Willis Woodward

Title	*Year*	*Publisher*
"Our Country May She Always Be Right but Our Country, Right or Wrong"	1898	Howley, Haviland
"The Outcast Unknown"	1887	Willis Woodward
"The Pardon Came Too Late"	1891	Willis Woodward
"The Path That Leads the Other Way"	1898	Howley, Haviland
"Paul Dresser's Battle Hymn"	1903	Howley, Haviland & Dresser
"Perhaps You'll Regret Some Day" (music by Theodore F. Morse)	1898	Howley, Haviland
"Rosie, Sweet Rosabel"	1893	George T. Worth
"A Sailor's Grave by the Sea"	1897	Howley, Haviland
"Say Yes, Love"	1896	Howley, Haviland
"She Fought On by His Side"	1904	James H. Curtin
"She Went to the City"	1904	James H. Curtin
"Show Me the Way"	1896	Howley, Haviland
"The Song of Father Time"	1889	Willis Woodward
"The Songs We Loved, Dear Tom"	1888	Willis Woodward
"Sousa's Band Is on Parade Today"	1905	Paul Dresser
"A Stitch in Time Saves Nine"	1889	Willis Woodward
"The Story of the Winds"	1888	Willis Woodward
"Sweet Savannah"	1898	Howley, Haviland
"The Sweetheart That Never Came"	1894	Howley, Haviland
"Take a Seat, Old Lady"	1894	Howley, Haviland
"There'll Be Weeping, There'll Be Wailing"	1890	Willis Woodward
"There's a Ship"	1892	Willis Woodward
"There's No North or South To-Day"	1901	Howley, Haviland & Dresser
"There's Where My Heart Is Tonight"	1899	Howley, Haviland
"Three Old Sports from Oklahoma"	1894	Howley, Haviland
" 'Tis All That I Have to Remember Her By"	1895	Howley, Haviland

Title	*Year*	*Publisher*
"Tootsey and Wootsey"	1887	Balmer & Weber
"The Town Where I Was Born"	1905	Paul Dresser
"The Voice of the Hudson"	1903	Howley, Haviland & Dresser
"Way Down in Old Indiana"	1901	Howley, Haviland & Dresser
"We Are Coming Cuba, Coming"	1898	Howley, Haviland
"We Came from the Same Old State"	1899	Howley, Haviland
"We Fight Tomorrow Mother"	1898	Howley, Haviland
"We Were Sweethearts for Many Years"	1895	Howley, Haviland
"We've Not Met in Years"	1891	T. B. Harms
"What a Wonderful World It Would Be!" (words by J. S. G. [John Stewart Crossy?])	1889	Willis Woodward
"When de Moon Comes Up behind de Hill"	1900	Howley, Haviland
"When I'm Away from You, Dear"	1904	Howley-Dresser
"When Mammy's by Yo' Side"	1900	Howley, Haviland
"When Mother First Taught Me to Pray"	1892	Willis Woodward
"When the Birds Have Sung Themselves to Sleep"	1901	Howley, Haviland & Dresser
"When You Come Back They'll Wonder Who the ——— You Are"	1902	Howley, Haviland & Dresser
"When Zaza Sits on the Piazza"	1905	Paul Dresser
"Where Are the Friends of Other Days?"	1903	Howley, Haviland & Dresser
"White Apple Blossoms"	1891	Willis Woodward
"Wrap Me in the Stars and Stripes"	1900	Howley, Haviland & Dresser
"Yes! I'll Wait Awhile"	1896	Howley, Haviland
"You Spoke Unkindly to Your Mother, Jack"	1890	Willis Woodward
"You'll Be Mama's Big Boy By and By"	1889	Willis Woodward
"Your God Comes First, Your Country Next, Then Mother Dear"	1898	Howley, Haviland

Title	*Year*	*Publisher*
"Your Mother Wants You Home, Boy (And She Wants You Mighty Bad)"	1904	Howley-Dresser
"You're Breaking Mother's Heart"	1890	Willis Woodward
"You're Going Far Away Lad; or, I'm Still Your Mother, Dear"	1897	Howley, Haviland
"You'se Just a Little Nigger, Still You'se Mine, All Mine"	1898	Howley, Haviland
"Zulala Zula"	1890	Willis Woodward

APPENDIX 2

Chronological List of Published Compositions

Year	Title	Publisher	Dedicated To
1886	"The Letter That Never Came" (Harms publication has words by Dresser, music by Max Sturm; *The Songs of Paul Dresser* gives Dresser as composer and author)	T. B. Harms	
1887	"Baby Slumbers"	Balmer & Weber	
	"The Curse"	Willis Woodward	May Howard
	"Don't Forget Your Old Parents at Home" (Willis Woodward issued song in 1889)	Lyon & Healy	Hattie E. Martin
	"I Believe It for My Mother Told Me So"	Lyon & Healy	Hilda Thomas
	"The Letter Came at Last"	T. B. Harms	
	"Love's Promise"	Balmer & Weber	Tillie [Clara Clothilde] Dreiser
	"Never Speak Again"	Willis Woodward	Emma Sheehy
	"The Outcast Unknown"	Willis Woodward	Chauncey Olcott
	"Tootsey and Wootsey"	Balmer & Weber	
1888	"The Convict and the Bird"	Willis Woodward	
	"Here Lies an Actor"	Willis Woodward	The Actors' Fund of America
	"I Long to Hear from Home"	Willis Woodward	
	"I Send to Them My Love"	Willis Woodward	

Year	*Title*	*Publisher*	*Dedicated To*
	"Only a Dear Little Star"	Willis Woodward	John Stewart Crossy, Jr.
	"The Songs We Loved, Dear Tom"	Willis Woodward	
	"The Story of the Winds"	Willis Woodward	
1889	"Baby's Tears"	Willis Woodward	James Reilly
	"The Blind Mother"	Willis Woodward	Joseph Haworth
	"Don't Forget Your Old Parents"	Willis Woodward	
	"I Can't Believe Her Faithless; or, Since Nellie Went Away" (cover has 1891, but first page has 1889)	Willis Woodward	
	"Mother Will Stand by Me"	Willis Woodward	
	"The Song of Father Time"	Willis Woodward	Mr. and Mrs. Frank McKee
	"A Stitch in Time Saves Nine"	Willis Woodward	
	"What a Wonderful World It Would Be!" (words by J. S. G. [John Stewart Crossy?])	Willis Woodward	
	"You'll Be Mama's Big Boy By and By"	Willis Woodward	
1890	"A Baby Adrift at Sea"	Willis Woodward	Mrs. M. A. Roby
	"The Band Played Annie Laurie; or, To Hear Them Tell It"	Willis Woodward	
	"Days Gone By"	Willis Woodward	
	"Did You Ever Hear a Nigger Say Wow?"	Willis Woodward	Louis Wesley
	"Her Tears Drifted Out with the Tide"	Willis Woodward	
	"I Wonder If There's Someone Who Loves Me"	Willis Woodward	The memory of Florence
	"The Limit Was Fifty Cents"	Willis Woodward	
	"Little Fannie McIntyre"	Willis Woodward	

Year	*Title*	*Publisher*	*Dedicated To*
	"Little Jim"	Willis Woodward	
	"The Lone Grave"	Willis Woodward	
	"There'll Be Weeping, There'll Be Wailing"	Willis Woodward	
	"You Spoke Unkindly to Your Mother, Jack"	Willis Woodward	
	"You're Breaking Mother's Heart"	Willis Woodward	
	"Zulala Zula"	Willis Woodward	
1891	"I'll Keep These Letters for Her Sake" (words by Julian Holmes)	T. B. Harms	
	"Just to See Mother's Face Once Again"	Willis Woodward	
	"My Sweetheart of Long, Long Ago"	Willis Woodward	
	"The Pardon Came Too Late"	Willis Woodward	
	"We've Not Met in Years"	T. B. Harms	
	"White Apple Blossoms"	Willis Woodward	A. Jefferson (another copy to Lillian Wood)
1892	"He Was a Soldier"	Willis Woodward	James Wright
	"I'm Going Far Away, Love"	Willis Woodward	Harry Sigourney
	"My Flag! My Flag!"	Willis Woodward	Howard Barnes
	"There's a Ship"	Willis Woodward	Frank Coltman
	"When Mother First Taught Me to Pray"	Willis Woodward	Ed Gilman
1893	"He Didn't Seem Glad to See Me"	George T. Worth	
	"He Loves Me, He Loves Me Not"	George T. Worth	Mabel Morrison
	"I Told Her the Same Old Story"	Willis Woodward	Rosabel Morrison
	"Rosie, Sweet Rosabel"	George T. Worth	

Year	*Title*	*Publisher*	*Dedicated To*
1894	"Once Ev'ry Year"	Howley, Haviland	
	"The Sweetheart That Never Came"	Howley, Haviland	
	"Take a Seat, Old Lady"	Howley, Haviland	W. E. Gorman
	"Three Old Sports from Oklahoma"	Howley, Haviland	Edward J. Abram
1895	"The Battery"	Howley, Haviland	
	"I Was Looking for My Boy, She Said; or, Decoration Day"	Howley, Haviland	Veterans of the Late War
	"It All Seemed Strange to Her, Poor Thing" (words by George F. McCann)	Howley, Haviland	
	"Jean"	Howley, Haviland	Jean Kaufman
	"Just Tell Them That You Saw Me"	Howley, Haviland	Irene Stearns
	" 'Tis All That I Have to Remember Her By"	Howley, Haviland	
	"We Were Sweethearts for Many Years"	Howley, Haviland	Georgia A. Stirling
1896	"After the Storm" (waltzes for piano solo)	Howley, Haviland	
	"Don't Tell Her That You Love Her; or, Mankind Is Seldom True"	Howley, Haviland	
	"A Dream of My Boyhood Days"	Howley, Haviland	Kittiebelle Stirling
	"He Brought Home Another"	Howley, Haviland	
	"He Fought for the Cause He Thought Was Right"	Howley, Haviland	
	"The Honest Little Dollar" (melody from "Just Tell Them That You Saw Me"; words by Monroe H. Rosenfeld for Republican national campaign)	Howley, Haviland	
	"I Wish That You Were Here Tonight"	Howley, Haviland	Georgia A. Stirling

Year	*Title*	*Publisher*	*Dedicated To*
	"I Wonder If She'll Ever Come Back to Me"	Howley, Haviland	Patsy Shepard
	"I'se Your Nigger If You Wants Me Liza Jane"	Howley, Haviland	
	"Say Yes, Love"	Howley, Haviland	
	"Show Me the Way"	Howley, Haviland	
	"Yes! I'll Wait Awhile"	Howley, Haviland	
1897	"Coontown Capers" (music by Theodore F. Morse)	Howley, Haviland	Homer Howard
	"If You See My Sweetheart"	Howley, Haviland	
	"In the Sweet Summer Time"	Howley, Haviland	Mary M. Howley
	"On the Banks of the Wabash, Far Away"	Howley, Haviland	Mary E. South
	"A Sailor's Grave by the Sea"	Howley, Haviland	My Sister, Mary
	"You're Going Far Away Lad; or, I'm Still Your Mother, Dear"	Howley, Haviland	
1898	"Come, Tell Me What's Your Answer, Yes or No"	Howley, Haviland	Theodore F. Morse
	"Every Night There's a Light"	Howley, Haviland	J. Duke Murray
	"The Old Flame Flickers, and I Wonder Why"	Howley, Haviland	
	"On the Shores of Havana, Far Away" (words by Andrew B. Sterling)	Howley, Haviland	
	"Our Country May She Always Be Right but Our Country, Right or Wrong"	Howley, Haviland	The Heroes Who Fought in the Name of Humanity
	"The Path That Leads the Other Way"	Howley, Haviland	
	"Perhaps You'll Regret Some Day" (music by Theodore F. Morse)	Howley, Haviland	Mai Monica Birs
	"Sweet Savannah"	Howley, Haviland	Joseph B. Maxwell
	"We Are Coming Cuba, Coming"	Howley, Haviland	

Year	Title	Publisher	Dedicated To
	"We Fight Tomorrow Mother"	Howley, Haviland	H. L. Kramer
	"Your God Comes First, Your Country Next, Then Mother Dear"	Howley, Haviland	Bertha M. Eppinghausen
	"You'se Just a Little Nigger, Still You'se Mine, All Mine"	Howley, Haviland	Benjamin A. Jefferson
1899	"Ave Maria"	Howley, Haviland	The Knights of Columbus of America
	"Come Home, Dewey, We Won't Do a Thing to You"	Howley, Haviland	
	"The Curse of the Dreamer"	Howley, Haviland	
	"Darktown after Dark" ("A Bunch of Niggerism" for piano solo)	Howley, Haviland	
	"Gath'ring Roses for Her Hair"	Howley, Haviland	Katherine P. Christopher
	"Good Bye for All Eternity"	Howley, Haviland	
	"I Wonder Where She Is Tonight"	Howley, Haviland	Anna B. MacDonald
	"In Good Old New York Town"	Howley, Haviland	
	"There's Where My Heart Is Tonight"	Howley, Haviland	Judge and Mrs. Rabb
	"We Came from the Same Old State"	Howley, Haviland	Judge and Mrs. McCabe
1900	"The Blue and the Gray; or, A Mother's Gift to Her Country"	Howley, Haviland	Gen. and Mrs. Oliver Roberts
	"Calling to Her Boy Just Once Again"	Howley, Haviland	Al Smith
	"Give Us Just Another Lincoln"	Howley, Haviland	Arthur Brisbane
	"The Green above the Red"	Howley, Haviland	
	"I'd Still Believe You True"	Howley, Haviland	Kate Waters
	"When de Moon Comes Up behind de Hill"	Howley, Haviland	

Year	*Title*	*Publisher*	*Dedicated To*
	"When Mammy's by Yo' Side"	Howley, Haviland	
	"Wrap Me in the Stars and Stripes"	Howley, Haviland & Dresser	
1901	"I Just Want to Go Back and Start the Whole Thing Over"	Howley, Haviland & Dresser	
	"In the Great Somewhere"	Howley, Haviland & Dresser	
	"Mr. Volunteer; or, You Don't Belong to the Regulars, You're Just a Volunteer"	Howley, Haviland & Dresser	Will D. Cobb
	"My Heart Still Clings to the Old First Love"	Howley, Haviland & Dresser	C. S. Crane
	"There's No North or South To-Day"	Howley, Haviland & Dresser	Mr. and Mrs. R. J. Jose
	"Way Down in Old Indiana"	Howley, Haviland & Dresser	
	"When the Birds Have Sung Themselves to Sleep"	Howley, Haviland & Dresser	Little Isabelle O'Keefe
1902	"The Army of Half-Starved Men"	Howley, Haviland & Dresser	Arthur Lynch of the Boer Army
	"Glory to God"	Howley, Haviland & Dresser	
	"In Dear Old Illinois"	Howley, Haviland & Dresser	The People of Illinois
	"When You Come Back They'll Wonder Who the ——— You Are"	Howley, Haviland & Dresser	
1903	"The Boys Are Coming Home Today"	Howley, Haviland & Dresser	Eva Mudge
	"Lincoln, Grant and Lee; or, The War Is Over Many Years"	Howley, Haviland & Dresser	
	"Paul Dresser's Battle Hymn"	Howley, Haviland & Dresser	
	"The Voice of the Hudson"	Howley, Haviland & Dresser	

Year	Title	Publisher	Dedicated To
	"Where Are the Friends of Other Days?"	Howley, Haviland & Dresser	
1904	"Mary Mine"	James H. Curtin	James H. Curtin
	"She Fought On by His Side"	James H. Curtin	
	"She Went to the City"	James H. Curtin	
	"When I'm Away from You, Dear"	Howley-Dresser	
	"Your Mother Wants You Home, Boy (And She Wants You Mighty Bad)"	Howley-Dresser	
1905	"After the Battle"	Paul Dresser	
	"The Day That You Grew Colder"	Paul Dresser	
	"Jim Judson"	Paul Dresser	My Friend "Judson"
	"My Gal Sal; or, They Called Her Frivolous Sal"	Paul Dresser	Nan Baker
	"Niggah Loves His Possum; or, Deed He Do, Do, Do"	Jerome H. Remick	
	"Sousa's Band Is on Parade Today"	Paul Dresser	
	"The Town Where I Was Born"	Paul Dresser	
	"When Zaza Sits on the Piazza"	Paul Dresser	
1906	"The Judgment Is at Hand"	Paul Dresser	Frank A. Mullane

APPENDIX 3

Undated Songs

The Theodore Dreiser Collection at the Van Pelt–Dietrich Library Center, University of Pennsylvania, Philadelphia, includes a list of undated Paul Dresser songs that someone—perhaps Dreiser himself—compiled. For most titles, the list provides a publisher and a range of possible publication dates. The author was able to find missing information for some of these songs and has included them in appendixes one and two. Others eluded his searches and are presented below.

Title	*Publisher*	*Dates*
"Always Show Respect, Joe"	Willis Woodward	1888–93
"Bethlehem"	Howley, Haviland & Dresser	1901–3
"Come Back to the Land of Cotton"	Paul Dresser	1904–6
"Come Home with Me, Dear Brother"	Willis Woodward	1888–93
"Evelyne"	Paul Dresser	1904–6
"The Glad Hand"	None given	None given
"I Hate to Leave You Behind"	Paul Dresser	1904–6
"Would I Were a Child Again" (but see appendix four)	Paul Dresser	1904–6

APPENDIX 4

Unpublished Compositions

Several Paul Dresser song sketches are held in the Theodore Dreiser Collection at the Van Pelt–Dietrich Library Center, University of Pennsylvania, Philadelphia. Some of these sketches contain both melody and words, while others include only words. It appears that none of these ever reached finished form for publication.

"At Rest": words handwritten in highly decorative form; no music found; two verses; "By Paul Dresser—1901" at bottom of page.

"Baby Mine": words and music in manuscript form; two verses and chorus; undated.

Untitled, but beginning with "Boys, don't you know that without her this life would be nothing at all": handwritten words only; no music found; undetermined number of verses; undated.

"Drink to Your Sweethearts Dear": handwritten words only; no music found; one verse and chorus; undated.

Untitled, but beginning with "Father again I come to thee": handwritten words only; no music found; undetermined number of verses; undated.

"Good Night Little Girl Good Night": typewritten words only; no music found; two verses; undated.

"The Great Old Organ": words and music in manuscript form; Paul Dresser listed as composer, but "Paola Rossi" written over Dresser's name with "Dresserissimo" written under names; two verses and chorus; undated.

"I Hate to Leave You Behind": typewritten words only; no music found; two verses and chorus; undated.

"Marching through Georgia; or, To the Tune(s) of Dixieland": words and music in manuscript form; two verses and chorus; undated.

"Mother's Picture": no words found; music in manuscript form; undated.

"The People Are Marching By": words and music in manuscript form; two verses and chorus; undated, but probably ca. 1904.

"See Them on the Avenue": typewritten words only; no music found; two verses; undated, but probably ca. 1904.

"Would I Were a Child Again": words and music in manuscript form; two verses and chorus; copyrighted 1905 by the Paul Dresser Publishing Company, but probably never engraved.

"Ye Wolves of Finance": typewritten words only; no music found; four verses; undated, but probably ca. 1904.

"You Are My Sunshine Sue": words and music in manuscript form; two verses and chorus; undated.

Notes

Preface

1. Clayton W. Henderson, "The Slippery Slopes of Fame: Paul Dresser and the Centennial of 'On the Banks of the Wabash, Far Away,' " *Traces of Indiana and Midwestern History* 9 (fall 1997): 4–13.

Introduction

1. For more details, see especially Charles Hamm, *Yesterdays: Popular Song in America* (New York and London: W. W. Norton and Co., 1979), and Lawrence W. Levine, *Highbrow/Lowbrow: The Emergence of Cultural Hierarchy in America* (Cambridge: Harvard University Press, 1988).

2. For another look at "Dixie," see Howard L. Sacks and Judith Rose Sacks, *Way Up North in Dixie: A Black Family's Claim to the Confederate Anthem* (Washington, D.C.: Smithsonian Institution Press, 1993).

3. "Gone to the Heavenly Garden" (New York: J. L. Peters, 1872), words by S. N. Mitchell, music by J. C. Chamberlain.

4. Two major studies of this material include Hamm, *Yesterdays,* and Jon W. Finson, *The Voices That Are Gone: Themes in Nineteenth-Century American Popular Song* (New York: Oxford University Press, 1994).

5. Letters and newspaper clippings are located primarily in the Theodore Dreiser Collection in the Van Pelt–Dietrich Library Center, University of Pennsylvania, Philadelphia (hereafter cited as Dreiser Collection); in the Emma Rector Flanagan Manuscripts in the Lilly Library, Indiana University, Bloomington; in the Vigo County Public Library, Terre Haute, Ind.; and in the Vigo County Historical Society, Terre Haute.

6. Paul Dresser was not the only victim of Theodore Dreiser's notorious inaccuracies. Writing in *A Hoosier Holiday* (1916; reprint, with an introduction by Douglas Brinkley, Bloomington and Indianapolis: Indiana University Press, 1997), 393, Dreiser recalls that "the fourth eldest [child], and one of the most interesting of all, as it seemed to me, a railroad man by profession, finally died of drunkenness (alcoholism is a nicer word) in a South Clark Street dive in Chicago, about 1905." Later, in *Dawn: A History of Myself* (New York: Horace Liveright, 1931), 11, Dreiser has the same brother drinking "himself into failure if not death." In both instances he is referring to his brother Rome, the second oldest child, who, in fact, lived until 1940 and to whom Theodore gave considerable financial support.

7. Theodore Dreiser, "My Brother Paul," in *Twelve Men* (New York: Boni and Liveright, 1919), 108, 105.

8. Theodore Dreiser, *Newspaper Days,* ed. T. D. Nostwich (Philadelphia: University of Pennsylvania Press, 1991), 424–25.

9. Theodore Dreiser, "Concerning the Author of These Songs," in *The Songs of Paul Dresser* (New York: Boni and Liveright, 1927).

10. Theodore Dreiser, "Whence the Song," in *The Color of a Great City* (New York: Boni and Liveright, 1923); Dreiser, *A Hoosier Holiday*; [Pencil Sketch Biography of Paul Dresser], Dreiser Collection. By late 1905 Dresser was living with his sister Emma Dreiser Nelson at 203 West 106th Street in New York City. During the last couple of months of his life he shared some of his memories with his brother Theodore. Those memories constitute a five-page untitled document that Theodore made in pencil.

11. H. L. Mencken to Theodore Dreiser, 1 Oct. 1923, quoted in Val Holley, "H. L. Mencken and the Indiana Genii," *Traces of Indiana and Midwestern History* 3 (winter 1991): 10.

12. Dreiser, *Dawn,* 154.

Prelude

1. Unidentified newspaper clipping, Theodore Dreiser Collection, Van Pelt–Dietrich Library Center, University of Pennsylvania, Philadelphia (hereafter cited as Dreiser Collection); Theodore Dreiser, "Concerning the Author of These Songs," in *The Songs of Paul Dresser* (New York: Boni and Liveright, 1927), vii; H. L. Mencken, quoted in Val Holley, "H. L. Mencken and the Indiana Genii," *Traces of Indiana and Midwestern History* 3 (winter 1991): 10; unidentified newspaper clipping, Dreiser Collection; *Indianapolis News,* 31 Jan. 1906; unidentified newspaper clipping, Dreiser Collection.

2. *New York Telegram,* 31 Jan. 1906.

3. *New York Clipper,* 10 Feb. 1906.

4. All information from Patricia O'Neill, *The Church of St. Francis Xavier, 1882–1982* (New York: Park Publishing Co., [1985]).

5. *New York Daily News,* 2 Feb. 1906. Another obituary, in an unidentified newspaper in the Dreiser Collection, indicates the song was sung before the funeral procession "by the many friends of the dead song writer present." This is unlikely because the song was not yet in circulation, and the "many friends" would not have known it.

6. "The Judgment Is at Hand" (New York: Paul Dresser Publishing Co., 1906), words and music by Paul Dresser. Joseph W. Stern and Company, 34 East Twenty-first Street, New York, is given as the "Exclusive Selling Agents."

7. Theodore Dreiser, "My Brother Paul," in *Twelve Men* (New York: Boni and Liveright, 1919), 108.

Chapter 1

1. Edwin G. Burrows and Mike Wallace, *Gotham: A History of New York City to 1898* (New York: Oxford University Press, 1999), 456, 738. Much of the Dreiser family history can be found in Richard Lingeman, *Theodore Dreiser: At the Gates of the City, 1871–1907* (New York: G. P. Putnam's Sons, 1986).

2. H. C. Bradsby, *History of Vigo County, Indiana, with Biographical Selections* (Chicago: S. B. Nelson and Co., 1891), 746.

3. Theodore Dreiser, *Dawn: A History of Myself* (New York: Horace Liveright, 1931), 4.

4. Ibid., 7.

5. "Appendix of Baptisms Omitted," in Record Book of Baptisms, St. Joseph Catholic Church, Terre Haute, Ind., 197. The entry was signed by J. A. Koenig.

6. Charles Blanchard, ed., *History of the Catholic Church in Indiana,* 2 vols. (Logansport, Ind.: A. W. Bowen and Co., 1898), 1:441, 442.

Chapter 2

1. *Sullivan Democrat,* 12 May 1864.

2. Thomas J. Wolfe, ed., *A History of Sullivan County, Indiana: Closing of the First Century's History of the County, and Showing the Growth of Its People, Institutions, Industries, and Wealth,* 2 vols. (New York: Lewis Publishing Co., 1909), 1:167.

3. Ibid.

4. *Sullivan Democrat,* 3 Nov. 1864.

5. Wolfe, *A History of Sullivan County,* 1:169–70.

6. Ibid., 1:167–68.

7. *Sullivan Democrat,* 24 Nov. 1864.

8. Wolfe, *A History of Sullivan County,* 1:169.

9. [Pencil Sketch Biography of Paul Dresser], 1, Theodore Dreiser Collection, Van Pelt–Dietrich Library Center, University of Pennsylvania, Philadelphia.

10. Paul Dresser to Mamie Coffman, 10 Nov. 1903, ibid.

11. Unidentified newspaper clipping, James Brian Maple Scrapbook, Sullivan County Public Library, Sullivan, Ind. (hereafter cited as Maple Scrapbook).

12. Unidentified newspaper clipping, ibid.

13. *Sullivan Democrat,* 3 May 1866.

14. Theodore Dreiser, *Dawn: A History of Myself* (New York: Horace Liveright, 1931), 5.

15. Ibid., 5–6.

16. Unidentified newspaper clipping, Maple Scrapbook.

17. "This indenture, witnesseth, that we Hardy Hill and Ally Hill of Sullivan County, in the State of Indiana, convey and warrant to Paul Dreiser of Sullivan County, in the State of Indiana, for the sum of One hundred and forty dollars the receipt of whereof is hereby acknowledged . . . Lots Number three and four . . . in Snows and Cochrans addition to the Town of Sullivan." Deed to Property, 20 July 1867, Sullivan County Public Library.

18. Richard Lingeman, *Theodore Dreiser: At the Gates of the City, 1871–1907* (New York: G. P. Putnam's Sons, 1986), 23.

19. *Sullivan Daily Times,* 14 June 1937.

20. Alerding was consecrated bishop of Fort Wayne on 30 Nov. 1900.

21. Wolfe, *A History of Sullivan County,* 1:169.

22. *Sullivan Democrat,* 14 Feb. 1867.

23. Written comment by an unidentified Sullivan schoolmate, Clyde S. Crawford File, Indiana State Library, Indianapolis (hereafter cited as Crawford File). Crawford's mother had been a Sullivan neighbor of the Dreisers and had worked with Dresser in the Sullivan Woolen Mills.

24. *Sullivan Daily Times,* 14 June 1937.

25. Unidentified newspaper clipping, Maple Scrapbook.

26. Dreiser, *Dawn,* 41.

27. Ibid.

28. Elizabeth Akers Allen, "Rock Me to Sleep," in *Yale Book of American Verse*, ed. Thomas R. Lounsbury (New Haven, Conn.: Yale University Press, 1912), 395. Numerous composers, including George F. Root, John H. Hewitt, Ernest Leslie, Isaiah Ickes, Daniel K. O'Donnell, George R. Poulton, and A. Von Smit, set these popular words to music in the early 1860s.

29. "Twenty Years Ago" (Cleveland: S. Brainard, 1856), words and music by William Willig.

30. "Oh! Susanna" (New York: C. Holt, Jr., 1848), words and music by Stephen C. Foster.

31. Unidentified newspaper clipping, Maple Scrapbook.

32. Ibid.

33. "Ralph Thompson and wife Mary J. to Paul Dreiser: Lot No. 2 in Snow and Co's. addition to the town of Sullivan. Recorded Jan. 14th, 1869." Warranty Deed Record, Sullivan County Public Library.

34. Mary Frances Brennan to A. R. Markle, 13 Jan. 1946, A. R. Markle File, Vigo County Public Library, Terre Haute, Ind. (hereafter cited as Markle File).

35. Lingeman, *Theodore Dreiser*, 25; other information in unidentified *Sullivan Democrat* clipping, Maple Scrapbook.

36. *Sullivan Democrat*, 10 May 1871.

37. Unidentified newspaper clipping, Crawford File. The article may have been written by Maude McConnell, whose name appears handwritten in a margin.

38. *Sullivan Daily Times*, 14 June 1937.

39. Mary Frances [Mame] Dreiser Brennan, "The Home of My Early Childhood," in letter to Gertrude Nelson, copy in Markle File.

Chapter 3

1. Albert Kleber, *History of St. Meinrad Archabbey, 1854–1954* (St. Meinrad, Ind.: A Grail Publication, 1954), 180.

2. Peter Behrman, "St. Meinrad Abbey: An Historical Sketch of Its Foundation and Development, 1853–1928" (master's thesis, University of Notre Dame, 1928), 16.

3. Kleber, *History of St. Meinrad Archabbey*, 218.

4. Mary Dreiser Brennan, "A Memory of Paul Dresser," unpublished typescript, n.d., Theodore Dreiser Collection, Van Pelt–Dietrich Library Center, University of Pennsylvania, Philadelphia (hereafter cited as Dreiser Collection).

5. Gertrude Cronin, "Have You Heard about This?," unidentified newspaper clipping, ca. 1941, James Brian Maple Scrapbook, Sullivan County Public Library, Sullivan, Ind.

6. *Terre Haute Tribune*, 25 Apr. 1909. The Lyceum, also referred to in newspaper articles as St. Bonaventure's College and St. Bonaventure's Asylum, was founded in 1872 at the northwest corner of Fifth and Walnut Streets. Operated by the fathers of the Franciscan order, it had a brief life, probably closing after the 1875–76 academic year. I wish to thank B. Michael McCormick, Vigo County historian, for sharing this information with me. Surprisingly, neither Paul Dresser nor Theodore Dreiser ever mentioned St. Bonaventure in their letters, interviews, or written reminiscences. Perhaps Paul's stay at the Lyceum was so brief that neither thought it worth commenting on in later years.

7. Indiana Census for 1860 and Terre Haute city directories for 1868, 1871–77.

8. "Making Songs for the Million: An Unconventional Chapter in the Biography of the Man Whose Songs Have Sold to the Extent of Five Million Copies," *Metropolitan Magazine*, ca. 1900, Dreiser Collection.

9. [Pencil Sketch Biography of Paul Dresser], 1, ibid.

10. Ibid.

11. "The Path That Leads the Other Way" (New York: Howley, Haviland and Co., 1898), words and music by Paul Dresser.

12. [Pencil Sketch Biography of Paul Dresser], Dreiser Collection.

13. Ibid., 2.

14. Ibid.

15. Ibid.

16. Ibid.

17. Ibid.

18. Ibid.

19. Ibid., 4. Unless Paul walked quite slowly or took a slow train, it is likely that he would have reached Indianapolis more quickly than Theodore Dreiser indicates. Perhaps in telling this story to Theodore, Paul misremembered, or exaggerated, the amount of time it really took.

20. Ibid.

21. Ibid., 5.

22. *Terre Haute Express*, 22 Feb. 1876.

23. Ibid.

Chapter 4

1. Unidentified Terre Haute newspaper clipping, 5 Mar. 1911, Community Affairs File, Vigo County Public Library, Terre Haute, Ind. (hereafter cited as Community Affairs File). The author has the Lemon brothers forming their troupe in the early 1880s, but because Dresser was already an experienced entertainer by that time, that date must have been earlier, perhaps as early as 1875.

2. [Pencil Sketch Biography of Paul Dresser], 5, Theodore Dreiser Collection, Van Pelt–Dietrich Library Center, University of Pennsylvania, Philadelphia (hereafter cited as Dreiser Collection).

3. Unidentified Terre Haute newspaper clipping, 5 Mar. 1911, Community Affairs File.

4. Brooks McNamara, *Step Right Up*, rev. ed. (Jackson: University Press of Mississippi, 1995), 64.

5. Hamlin Wizard Oil pamphlets, Warshaw Collection of Business Americana, Archives Center, National Museum of American History, Smithsonian Institution, Washington, D.C.

6. George D. Bushnell, "Chicago's Miraculous Patent Medicines," *Chicago History* 3 (fall 1974): 79.

7. Ibid., 82.

8. "Humorous and Sentimental Songs As Sung throughout the United States by Hamlin's Wizard Oil Concert Troupes in Their Open Air Advertising Concerts" (undated pamphlet), Chicago Historical Society.

9. McNamara, *Step Right Up*, 47.

10. [Pencil Sketch Biography of Paul Dresser], 5, Dreiser Collection.

11. Ibid. The author has been unable to locate any copies of the songbook.

12. Ibid.
13. McNamara, *Step Right Up,* 71.
14. *Terre Haute Saturday Evening Mail,* 31 Aug. 1878.
15. Unidentified Terre Haute newspaper clipping, 5 Mar. 1911, Community Affairs File.
16. Ibid.
17. Ibid.
18. *Terre Haute Saturday Evening Mail,* 28 Sept. 1878.
19. Unidentified *Terre Haute Mail* clipping, Community Affairs File.
20. *Evansville Daily Journal,* 14 Dec. 1879. While it is entirely possible and even likely that Dresser went with Barlow, Wilson, Primrose, and West, the author has not been able to confirm it, for his name appears neither on playbills nor in reviews. In itself, that would not have been unusual since Dresser would have been one of the troupe's lowest-ranking members.
21. Unidentified *Terre Haute Daily Tribune* clipping, [before 28 Apr. 1898], Paul Dresser Manuscripts, Lilly Library, Indiana University, Bloomington.
22. "Life on Broadway," reprinted in *Gaslight New York Revisited,* ed. Frank Oppel (Secaucus, N.J.: Castle, 1989), 35, 41.
23. Theodore Dreiser, "Concerning the Author of These Songs," in *The Songs of Paul Dresser* (New York: Boni and Liveright, 1927), v.
24. Theodore Dreiser, *Newspaper Days,* ed. T. D. Nostwich (Philadelphia: University of Pennsylvania Press, 1991), 582.
25. *Evansville Daily Journal,* 8 Dec. 1880.

Chapter 5

1. *Evansville Daily Journal,* 27 May 1879.
2. Ibid., 28 Sept. 1879.
3. Ibid., 14 July 1883.
4. *Evansville Courier,* 1 Feb. 1906.
5. *Evansville Sunday Journal,* 15 Oct. 1922.
6. Unidentified newspaper clipping (written in connection with Paul Dresser Day, April 1940), Paul Dresser File, Evansville Public Library, Evansville, Ind.; *Evansville Sunday Courier and Press,* 1 June 1952. If Dresser, in fact, worked for the Lightning Linament Company, it might account for a strange listing for him in the Terre Haute city directory for 1882. There his occupation is given as "lightning rod agent," and he resides at 205 North Thirteenth Street. Perhaps the directory compiler misunderstood Dresser's work as an agent for the Lightning Linament Company and recorded it as "lightning rod agent," or perhaps someone was pulling his leg. Dresser appears in the Evansville city directory for the first time in 1883, where his name is misspelled Paul P. Drieser and where he is listed as residing at 1413 East Franklin Street and working as a songster. At best, however, these city directories are somewhat misleading. In the same year that Dresser is listed for Evansville, the directory lists father Paul Dreiser, weaver, as living at the 1413 East Franklin Street address, even though he still resided in Terre Haute. In the Terre Haute directory he is listed as Paul Dreiser, laborer for G. F. Ellis, boarding at 118 South First Street. The Evansville directory for 1883 does not mention Sarah, even though it is clear that she resided at the 1413 East Franklin Street address.

7. Various authors have associated Dresser with different minstrel troupes before his days in Evansville, but none has documented any of these activities. Vera Dreiser claims her uncle was "both end and middle man with as many as three different minstrel companies of repute." (Vera Dreiser and Brett Howard, *My Uncle Theodore* [New York: Nash Publishing, 1976], 72.) At some time Vera Dreiser began researching her musical uncle and made some abbreviated notes about him and minstrelsy. She suggests a connection, beginning in March 1876, between Dresser and a troupe she identifies as "BWP & W." Although she later identifies the "B" variously as Benbo or Benbow, she probably means Barlow. She also writes: "Joined Billy Rice Minstrels" in 1885. From time to time she gives dates for various *New York Clipper* articles, but a search for Dresser's name in these articles was fruitless. Additionally, the dates of some of the articles coincide with dates when the author has documented that Dresser was elsewhere, usually performing as a solo act. (Vera Dreiser Notebooks, Theodore Dreiser Collection, Van Pelt–Dietrich Library Center, University of Pennsylvania, Philadelphia [hereafter cited as Dreiser Collection].) W. A. Swanberg has Dresser with "a Cincinnati minstrel show, . . . [and later as] end man for Thatcher, Primrose and West's famous minstrel show, drawing a handsome salary." (W. A. Swanberg, *Dreiser* [New York: Charles Scribner's Sons, 1965], 12.) Richard Lingeman also asserts that Dresser "put in a stint with the Thatcher, Primrose and West Minstrel Show." (Richard Lingeman, *Theodore Dreiser: At the Gates of the City, 1871–1907* [New York: G. P. Putnam's Sons, 1986], 48.) Theodore Dreiser claims only that his brother had been "both end- and middle-man with one, two or three different minstrel companies of repute." (Theodore Dreiser, "My Brother Paul," in *Twelve Men* [New York: Boni and Liveright, 1919], 76.) That Dresser did work in minstrelsy is certain, but the author has found no documentation for it.

8. *Evansville Daily Journal,* 26 Sept. 1880.

9. Ibid., 16 Nov. 1880.

10. Ibid., 23, 28 Oct. 1880.

11. Ibid., 8, 12 Dec. 1880.

12. During the years the Dreisers lived in Terre Haute, city directories displayed an inconsistency in the spelling of their last name. The name appeared as Dresser (1858, 1863, 1864, 1874, 1877); Dreiser (1872, 1878–84); Dreser (1874), and Drieser (1874); and Dusser (1873).

13. *Evansville Daily Journal,* 13 Dec. 1880.

14. John Mackey to Theodore Dreiser, 1 Dec. 1926, Dreiser Collection.

15. Phil Hacker to John H. Mackey, 28 Mar. 1921, ibid.

16. John W. Grant to Theodore Dreiser, 6 Sept. 1931, ibid.

17. Mackey to Dreiser, 1 Dec. 1926, ibid.

18. Ibid. Mackey is recounting to Dreiser what Kane had written to Paul Dresser.

19. Dreiser, "My Brother Paul," 79.

20. Theodore Dreiser remembered it as being before the end of Paul's first winter in Evansville (i.e., the winter of 1880–81). Theodore Dreiser, *Dawn: A History of Myself* (New York: Horace Liveright, 1931), 146.

21. *Evansville Daily Journal,* 9 Apr. 1882.

Chapter 6

1. *Evansville Daily Journal,* 6 Mar. 1881.

2. *Chicago Tribune,* 13 Mar. 1881.

3. Ibid., 12 Mar. 1881.
4. *Indianapolis Sentinel,* 24 June 1881.
5. Ibid., 22 June 1881.
6. Ibid., 23 June 1881.
7. Program for H. C. Miner's New Theatre, 5 Sept. 1881, Harvard Theatre Collection, Nathan Marsh Pusey Library, Harvard University, Cambridge, Mass. (hereafter cited as Harvard Theatre Collection).
8. B. F. Keith, "The Vogue of the Vaudeville," in *American Vaudeville as Seen by Its Contemporaries,* ed. Charles W. Stein (New York: Da Capo Press, 1985), 18.
9. Edwin Milton Royle, "The Vaudeville Theatre," *Scribner's Magazine,* Oct. 1899, p. 489.
10. Program for H. C. Miner's New Theatre, Harvard Theatre Collection.
11. W. A. Swanberg, *Dreiser* (New York: Charles Scribner's Sons, 1965), 70.
12. Program for H. C. Miner's New Theatre, Harvard Theatre Collection.
13. Royle, "The Vaudeville Theatre," 495.
14. *New York Clipper,* 22 Oct. 1881.
15. Program for New National Theatre, 18 Oct. 1881, Harvard Theatre Collection.
16. *New York Clipper,* 22 Oct. 1881.
17. Program for New National Theatre, Harvard Theatre Collection.
18. *New York Clipper,* 4 Nov. 1881.

Chapter 7

1. Theodore Dreiser, *Dawn: A History of Myself* (New York: Horace Liveright, 1931), 109.
2. Ibid., 113.
3. Ibid., 114.
4. Ibid., 114–15.
5. Ibid., 153–54.

Chapter 8

1. Theodore Dreiser, *Dawn: A History of Myself* (New York: Horace Liveright, 1931), 114.
2. "My Gal Sal; or, They Called Her Frivolous Sal" (New York: Paul Dresser Publishing Co., 1905), words and music by Paul Dresser.
3. *Evansville Journal,* 7 Sept. 1882. Evansville city directories include the names of the following known prostitutes: Fine: 1876–78, 1880–81, 1883; Holland: 1879–81, 1883; Griffith: 1880–81, 1885–86; Caldwell: 1876, 1880, 1884; Lockwood: 1879, 1883.
4. Dreiser, *Dawn,* 114.
5. *Evansville Journal,* 2 Sept. 1883.
6. Dreiser, *Dawn,* 142.
7. Ibid.
8. Ibid.
9. Ibid., 154.
10. Richard Lingeman, *Theodore Dreiser: At the Gates of the City, 1871–1907* (New York: G. P. Putnam's Sons, 1986), 54.

Chapter 9

1. *Chicago Tribune,* 2 Oct. 1882.
2. *New York Clipper,* 29 Sept. 1883.
3. *Chicago Tribune,* 8 Oct. 1882.
4. Ibid., 16 Oct. 1882.
5. Ibid., 6 Oct. 1882.
6. Ibid.
7. Ibid.
8. *New York Clipper,* 25 Nov. 1882.
9. Ibid., 12 Jan. 1884.
10. Ibid., 5 June 1883.
11. Armond Fields and L. Marc Fields, *From the Bowery to Broadway: Lew Fields and the Roots of American Popular Theater* (New York: Oxford University Press, 1993), 61.
12. Otis Skinner, *Footlights and Spotlights: Recollections of My Life on the Stage* (Indianapolis: Bobbs-Merrill Co., 1924), 139.
13. *Chicago Tribune,* 3 June 1883.
14. Ibid., 5 June 1883.
15. Ibid., 3, 10 June 1883.
16. *Evansville Daily Journal,* 18 Aug. 1883.
17. Theodore Dreiser, "Concerning the Author of These Songs," in *The Songs of Paul Dresser* (New York: Boni and Liveright, 1927), vii.
18. *Chicago Tribune,* 9 Sept. 1883.
19. Ibid., 6, 9 Sept. 1883.
20. *Evansville Daily Journal,* 21, 22 Sept. 1883.
21. *Terre Haute Evening Gazette,* 27 Nov. 1889.

Chapter 10

1. Theodore Dreiser, *Dawn: A History of Myself* (New York: Horace Liveright, 1931), 154.
2. Ibid., 171.
3. Unidentified *Terre Haute Gazette* clipping, Dresser File, Vigo County Public Library, Terre Haute, Ind.
4. Edward Bennet Marks and Abbott J. Liebling, *They All Sang: From Tony Pastor to Rudy Vallee* (New York: Viking Press, 1934), 126.
5. Unidentified newspaper clipping, 11 Oct. 1951, James Brian Maple Scrapbook, Sullivan County Public Library, Sullivan, Ind. Actress Ingrid Bergman had recently left her physician husband for the Italian movie director Roberto Rossellini.
6. Ronald L. Davis, *A History of Music in American Life,* 2 vols. (Huntington, N.Y.: R. E. Krieger, 1980–82), 2:182.
7. *New York Clipper,* 5 Jan. 1889.
8. Ibid., 25 Jan. 1890.
9. Ibid., 20 July 1889.
10. "The Curse" (New York: Willis Woodward and Co., 1887), words and music by Paul Dresser.
11. Ibid.
12. *New York Clipper,* 17 Aug. 1889.

13. "I Can't Believe Her Faithless; or, Since Nellie Went Away" (New York: Willis Woodward and Co., 1889), words and music by Paul Dresser. The second song was "The Blind Mother" (New York: Willis Woodward and Co., 1889), words and music by Paul Dresser.

14. Theodore S. Charrney to Frank D. Chandler, 14 Dec. 1988, Willard Library, Evansville, Ind.

Chapter 11

1. *New York Clipper,* 9 Feb. 1884.
2. Ibid., 5 Mar. 1887.
3. Ibid., 19 Dec. 1885.
4. Ibid., 24 Nov. 1888.
5. Theodore Dreiser, *Dawn: A History of Myself* (New York: Horace Liveright, 1931), 154.
6. *New York Clipper,* 28 Aug. 1886.
7. Ibid.
8. Dreiser, *Dawn,* 360–62.
9. Ibid., 360, 361.
10. *New York Clipper,* 8 Mar. 1884.
11. Dreiser, *Dawn,* 361–62.
12. *New York Clipper,* 1 Mar. 1884.
13. Program for Lyceum Theatre, 11 Dec. 1882, Chicago Historical Society.
14. *New York Clipper,* 3 Apr. 1886.
15. Ibid., 6 Mar. 1886.
16. Ibid., 23 Oct. 1886.
17. Ibid., 27 Nov. 1886.
18. Ibid., 11 Dec. 1886.
19. Ibid., 30 Oct. 1886.
20. *Terre Haute Evening Gazette,* 27 Nov. 1889.
21. "The Letter That Never Came" (New York: T. B. Harms Co., 1886), words by Paul Dresser, music by Max Sturm. While this Harms edition gives Dresser as the author and Sturm as the composer, Theodore Dreiser's reprint of the song for his edition of *The Songs of Paul Dresser* (New York: Boni and Liveright, 1927) credits Dresser with both words and music.
22. *New York Clipper,* 27 Nov. 1886.
23. Ibid., 4 Dec. 1886.
24. *The Songs of Paul Dresser,* 1.
25. "Making Songs for the Million: An Unconventional Chapter from the Biography of the Man Whose Songs Have Sold to the Extent of Five Million Copies," *Metropolitan Magazine,* ca. 1900, Theodore Dreiser Collection, Van Pelt–Dietrich Library Center, University of Pennsylvania, Philadelphia.
26. *Terre Haute Express,* 10 Jan. 1902.
27. *New York Clipper,* 25 Aug. 1883.
28. Ibid., 20 Oct. 1888.
29. Ibid., 6 Oct. 1888.
30. George C. D. Odell, *Annals of the New York Stage,* 15 vols. (New York: Columbia University Press, 1927–49), 14:163.
31. *New York Clipper,* 15 Dec. 1888.

32. Ibid., 22 Sept. 1888.
33. Ibid., 29 Sept. 1888.
34. Ibid., 17 Nov. 1888.
35. *New York Dramatic Mirror,* 22 Dec. 1888.
36. *New York Clipper,* 5 Jan. 1889.
37. Ibid., 26 Jan. 1889.
38. Ibid., 23 Feb. 1889.
39. Ibid., 13 Apr. 1889.
40. Ibid., 29 Dec. 1889.
41. Ibid., 9 Feb. 1889.
42. Ibid.
43. Ibid., 13 Apr. 1889.
44. Ibid.
45. Ibid., 22 June 1889.
46. Ibid., 15 June 1889.
47. *New York Dramatic Mirror,* 15 June 1889.
48. *New York Clipper,* 20 July 1889.

Chapter 12

1. *Terre Haute Evening Gazette,* 27 Nov. 1889.
2. Gerald Martin Bordman, *American Musical Theatre: A Chronicle,* 2d ed. (New York: Oxford University Press, 1992), 96; *New York Dramatic Mirror,* 1 Dec. 1900.
3. Bordman, *American Musical Theatre,* 87.
4. *Indianapolis News,* 5 Dec. 1956.
5. *New York Dramatic Mirror,* 7 Sept. 1889.
6. *New York Clipper,* 30 Nov. 1889.
7. Ibid., 21 Dec. 1889.
8. Ibid.
9. Ibid., 31 Aug. 1889.
10. Ibid., 14 Sept. 1889.
11. Louis Wesley played the part of Rats. *New York Dramatic Mirror,* 28 Sept. 1889.
12. Ibid., 12 Oct. 1889.
13. Ibid., 2 Nov. 1889.
14. Ibid., 16 Nov. 1889.
15. *New York Clipper,* 16 Nov. 1889.
16. Ibid., 30 Nov. 1889.
17. Ibid., 16, 23, 30 Nov. 1889.
18. Ibid., 25 Oct. 1890.
19. *New York Dramatic Mirror,* 8 Dec. 1900.
20. *New York Clipper,* 1 June 1889.
21. Ibid., 23 Nov. 1889.
22. Ibid., 9 Nov. 1895.
23. *Terre Haute Evening Mail,* 23 Nov. 1889.
24. *Terre Haute Evening Gazette,* 27 Nov. 1889.
25. Ibid.
26. *New York Clipper,* 7 Dec. 1889.

27. Ibid., 14 Dec. 1889.
28. Ibid., 21 Dec. 1889.
29. Ibid., 4 Jan. 1890.
30. Ibid., 11 Jan. 1890.
31. Ibid., 25 Jan. 1890.
32. Ibid.
33. Ibid., 3 May 1890.
34. Ibid., 1 Feb. 1890.
35. Ibid., 8 Feb. 1890.
36. Quoted in John Burke, *The Legend of Baby Doe: The Life and Times of the Silver Queen of the West* (New York: Putnam Press, 1974), 63.
37. Ibid., 63–64.
38. *New York Clipper,* 6 Apr. 1889.
39. Ibid., 17 Apr. 1890.
40. Ibid., 5 July 1890.
41. Ibid., 13 Sept. 1890.
42. *New York Dramatic Mirror,* 13 Sept. 1890.
43. *New York Clipper,* 27 Sept. 1890.
44. Ibid., 11 Oct. 1890.
45. Ibid.
46. Ibid., 25 Oct., 1 Nov. 1890.
47. Theodore Dreiser, *Dawn: A History of Myself* (New York: Horace Liveright, 1931), 511.
48. Ibid., 514.
49. Paul Dresser to Jesse and Julia Rector, 19 Nov. 1890, Emma Rector Flanagan Manuscripts, Lilly Library, Indiana University, Bloomington.
50. Dreiser, *Dawn*, 516.
51. Ibid., 519.
52. Ibid., 520, 521.
53. George C. D. Odell, *Annals of the New York Stage,* 15 vols. (New York: Columbia University Press, 1927–49), 14:582.
54. *New York Clipper,* 10 Jan. 1891.
55. *New York Dramatic Mirror,* 10 Jan. 1891.
56. Program for Windsor Theatre, 5–10 Jan. 1891, Harvard Theatre Collection, Nathan Marsh Pusey Library, Harvard University, Cambridge, Mass.
57. *New York Clipper*, 24 Jan. 1891.
58. *New York Dramatic Mirror,* 11 Apr. 1891.

Chapter 13

1. *New York Clipper,* 30 May 1891.
2. Ibid., 12 Sept. 1891.
3. George C. D. Odell, *Annals of the New York Stage,* 15 vols. (New York: Columbia University Press, 1927–49), 15:70.
4. *South Bend Daily Tribune,* 18 Apr. 1893.
5. Ibid., 9 Apr. 1894.
6. "Music and Drama: The Danger Signal," unidentified newspaper clipping, Theodore Dreiser Collection, Van Pelt–Dietrich Library Center, University of Pennsylvania, Philadelphia (hereafter cited as Dreiser Collection).

7. "'Danger Signal' at the New Theatre," unidentified newspaper clipping, ibid.
8. *New York Clipper,* 28 Dec. 1895.
9. All information from the Harvard Theatre Collection, Nathan Marsh Pusey Library, Harvard University, Cambridge, Mass.
10. "Music and Drama."
11. "'Danger Signal' at the New Theatre."
12. *New York Clipper,* 12 Sept. 1891.
13. *New York Dramatic Mirror,* 12 Sept. 1891.
14. "I Told Her the Same Old Story" (New York: Willis Woodward and Co., 1893), words and music by Paul Dresser.
15. Theodore Dreiser, *Newspaper Days,* ed. T. D. Nostwich (Philadelphia: University of Pennsylvania Press, 1991), 432.
16. *New York Clipper,* 10 Oct. 1891.
17. *New York Dramatic Mirror,* 24 Oct. 1891.
18. *New York Clipper,* 14 Nov. 1891.
19. Ibid.
20. *New York Dramatic Mirror,* 12 Dec. 1891.
21. *New York Clipper,* 12 Dec. 1891.
22. *New York Dramatic Mirror,* 19 Dec. 1891.
23. Odell, *Annals of the New York Stage,* 15:77, 244.
24. *New York Dramatic Mirror,* 5 Mar. 1892.
25. *New York Clipper,* 5 Mar. 1892.
26. Unidentified newspaper clipping, Dreiser Collection.
27. *New York Clipper,* 21 May 1892.
28. Ibid.
29. Ibid., 6 Aug. 1892.
30. Ibid., 16 July 1892.
31. Ibid., 29 Oct. 1892.
32. Ibid., 21 Jan. 1893.
33. Ibid., 15 Apr. 1893, 17 Dec. 1892.
34. Ibid., 10 Feb. 1894.
35. Ibid., 26 Aug. 1893. The other songs: "Strangers," "Sitting by the Kitchen Door," "Fallen by the Wayside," "Only a Tangle of Golden Curls," "Can Hearts So Soon Forget," "You'll Never Know," "School Bells," and "Sleep, My Baby Boy."
36. Ibid., 19 Aug. 1893.
37. Ibid., 18 Mar. 1893.
38. Ibid., 26 Aug. 1893.
39. Frederick Jackson Turner, *The Significance of the Frontier in American History* (Madison: State Historical Society of Wisconsin, 1894).
40. *New York Clipper,* 5 Jan. 1884.

Chapter 14

1. *New York Clipper,* 8 Apr. 1893.
2. Ibid., 16 Sept. 1893.
3. Ibid., 17, 24 Feb., 3 Mar. 1894.
4. Theodore Dreiser, *Newspaper Days,* ed. T. D. Nostwich (Philadelphia: University of Pennsylvania Press, 1991), 431, 432.
5. Ibid., 433, 435.

6. Ibid., 431.
7. Ibid., 439–40.
8. Ibid., 434.
9. Ibid., 436.
10. Ibid., 439.
11. Ibid., 440.
12. Ibid., 440–41.
13. Nick Salvatore, *Eugene V. Debs: Citizen and Socialist* (Urbana, Chicago, and London: University of Illinois Press, 1982), 127.

Chapter 15

1. Theodore Dreiser, *Newspaper Days,* ed. T. D. Nostwich (Philadelphia: University of Pennsylvania Press, 1991), 562.
2. Ibid., 563.
3. Ibid., 565.
4. Theodore Dreiser, *Sister Carrie: An Authoritative Text, Backgrounds, and Sources Criticism,* ed. Donald Pizer (New York: Norton, 1970), 17.
5. Theodore Dreiser, "My Brother Paul," in *Twelve Men* (New York: Boni and Liveright, 1919), 90.
6. Ibid., 91.
7. Theodore Dreiser, "Concerning the Author of These Songs," in *The Songs of Paul Dresser* (New York: Boni and Liveright, 1927), vi.
8. Dreiser, "My Brother Paul," 82.
9. Dreiser, *Newspaper Days,* 589.
10. Ibid., 590.
11. Ibid., 592–94.
12. Edwin G. Burrows and Mike Wallace, *Gotham: A History of New York City to 1898* (New York: Oxford University Press, 1999), 1169.
13. Dreiser, *Newspaper Days,* 572.
14. Ibid., 574.
15. Ibid., 602.
16. Ibid., 603.
17. Patricia O'Neill, *The Church of St. Francis Xavier, 1882–1982* (New York: Park Publishing Co., [1985]), [8].
18. Dreiser, *Newspaper Days,* 572.
19. Dreiser, "My Brother Paul," 97.

Chapter 16

1. Theodore Dreiser, *Newspaper Days,* ed. T. D. Nostwich (Philadelphia: University of Pennsylvania Press, 1991), 609.
2. Phil Hacker to John H. Mackey, 28 Mar. 1921, Theodore Dreiser Collection, Van Pelt–Dietrich Library Center, University of Pennsylvania, Philadelphia.
3. *New York Clipper,* 29 Dec. 1894.
4. Paul Dresser, *A Green Goods Man,* Act III (n.p., 1894), manuscript in Rare Book and Special Collections Division, Library of Congress, Washington, D.C. A search for any published versions of Dresser's plays proved fruitless.
5. Ibid.

6. Ibid.
7. *New York Clipper*, 12 Jan. 1895.
8. Ibid., 19 Jan. 1895.
9. Ibid., 16 Feb. 1895.
10. Ibid., 16 Mar. 1895.
11. Ibid., 13 Apr. 1895.
12. Ibid., 27 Apr. 1895.
13. Ibid., 25 May 1895.
14. Edwin G. Burrows and Mike Wallace, *Gotham: A History of New York City to 1898* (New York: Oxford University Press, 1999), 585.
15. Quoted in Gerald Martin Bordman, *American Musical Theatre: A Chronicle,* 2d ed. (New York: Oxford University Press, 1992), 19–20.
16. *New York Clipper,* 1 June 1895.
17. Ibid., 27 July 1895.
18. Ibid., 3 Aug. 1895.
19. Theodore Dreiser, "My Brother Paul," in *Twelve Men* (New York: Boni and Liveright, 1919), 99.

Chapter 17

1. *New York Clipper,* 31 Aug. 1895.
2. Ibid., 21 Sept. 1895.
3. Ibid., 26 Oct. 1895.
4. Ibid., 10 Aug. 1895.
5. Ibid.
6. Theodore Dreiser, *Newspaper Days,* ed. T. D. Nostwich (Philadelphia: University of Pennsylvania Press, 1991), 609.
7. *Ev'ry Month,* Oct. 1895, p. 26.
8. Paul Dresser to Emma Rector Flanagan, 10 Nov. 1895, Emma Rector Flanagan Manuscripts, Lilly Library, Indiana University, Bloomington (hereafter cited as Flanagan Manuscripts).
9. Because of his schedule with *The Danger Signal,* the only Sundays in November that Dresser could have been in New York would have been the eleventh or the eighteenth. Theodore Dreiser recounts the story twice (with slightly different words) of his brother trying out "Just Tell Them That You Saw Me." Theodore Dreiser, "My Brother Paul," in *Twelve Men* (New York: Boni and Liveright, 1919), 98, and "Concerning the Author of These Songs," in *The Songs of Paul Dresser* (New York: Boni and Liveright, 1927), viii.
10. "Just Tell Them That You Saw Me" (New York: Howley, Haviland and Co., 1895), words and music by Paul Dresser.
11. Dreiser, "My Brother Paul" and "Concerning the Author of These Songs."
12. All in Theodore Dreiser Collection, Van Pelt–Dietrich Library Center, University of Pennsylvania, Philadelphia (hereafter cited as Dreiser Collection).
13. *Ev'ry Month,* Feb. 1897, p. 35.
14. Ibid., 38.
15. Dresser to Flanagan, 26 Apr. 1896, Flanagan Manuscripts.
16. "The Honest Little Dollar" (New York: Howley, Haviland and Co., 1896), words by Monroe H. Rosenfeld, music by Paul Dresser.
17. Ibid.

18. Dreiser, "My Brother Paul," 98–99.

19. *Terre Haute Express,* 10 Jan. 1902.

20. Carroll Fleming, "Popular Songs and Their Writers," *Junior Munsey,* no date, Dreiser Collection.

21. Paul Dresser to Jeannette Rector, 1 Mar. 1896, Flanagan Manuscripts.

22. Theodore Dreiser, "Whence the Song," in *The Color of a Great City* (New York: Boni and Liveright, 1923), 244–45.

23. Ibid., 249.

24. Ibid., 242.

25. Theodore Dreiser to Sara Osborne White, 18 May, 21 Sept. 1896, Dreiser Collection.

26. I thank Thomas Riis, director of the American Music Resource Center at the University of Colorado, Boulder, for bringing these pieces to my attention.

27. "Sweet Rosie O'Grady" (New York: Joseph W. Stern and Co., 1896), words and music by Maude Nugent.

28. "Writes Home and Mother Songs but He Is No Sentimentalist, Paul Dresser Says—Facts That Contradict Him," unidentified newspaper clipping, 29 May 1904, Dreiser Collection.

29. Dresser to Flanagan, 26 Apr. 1896, Flanagan Manuscripts.

Chapter 18

1. Paul Dresser to Mary South, 2 Aug. 1897, Paul Dresser Manuscripts, Lilly Library, Indiana University, Bloomington (hereafter cited as Dresser Manuscripts).

2. Theodore Dreiser, "My Brother Paul," in *Twelve Men* (New York: Boni and Liveright, 1919), 78.

3. *Ev'ry Month,* Apr. 1897, p. 154.

4. In October 1902 *Ev'ry Month* was absorbed by the J. W. Pepper piano music magazine and then merged into the *Household Ledger* in June 1903.

5. Dreiser, "My Brother Paul," 100.

6. Ibid.

7. Ibid., 100–101.

8. Donald Pizer, "'Along the Wabash': A 'Comedy Drama' by Theodore Dreiser," *Dreiser Newsletter* 5 (fall 1974): 2. The letter, dated 31 May 1895, is typed on Howley, Haviland and Company stationery. Dreiser's name (misspelled Dreisser) is handwritten by someone other than Dreiser or Dresser.

9. Ibid., 4.

10. Theodore Dreiser to Sara Osborne White, 23 Jan. 1898, Theodore Dreiser Collection, Van Pelt–Dietrich Library Center, University of Pennsylvania, Philadelphia (hereafter cited as Dreiser Collection).

11. Dreiser, "My Brother Paul," 101.

12. Ibid., 102.

13. Ibid.

14. Richard W. Dowell, "'On the Banks of the Wabash': A Musical Whodunit," *Indiana Magazine of History* 66 (June 1970): 109.

15. Unidentified newspaper clipping, Dreiser Collection.

16. Isidore Witmark and Isaac Goldberg, *Story of the House of Witmark: From Ragtime to Swingtime* (New York: L. Furman, 1939), 170–71.

17. Ibid.
18. Ibid.
19. Charles K. Harris, *After the Ball: Forty Years of Melody* (New York: Frank-Maurice, 1926), 135.
20. Ibid., 135–36.
21. *Terre Haute Daily Tribune,* 19 Apr. 1898.
22. Dresser to South, 24 July 1897, Dresser Manuscripts.
23. Dresser to South, 2 Aug. 1897, ibid.
24. Dresser to South, 6 Sept. 1897, ibid.
25. Dresser to South, 12 Mar. 1898, ibid.
26. Dreiser Collection.
27. *Chicago Tribune,* 23 Oct. 1897.
28. Sylvia Dreiser to Theodore Dreiser, 1 Nov. 1897, Dreiser Collection.
29. Dresser to South, 5 Nov. 1897, ibid.
30. Ibid.
31. Unidentified Attica, Indiana, newspaper clipping, 15 Apr. [1898?], ibid.
32. Unidentified *Chicago Record* clipping, ibid.
33. *LaGrange Standard,* 5 Aug. 1897.
34. Unidentified Bloomfield, Indiana, newspaper clipping, 31 July 1897, Dreiser Collection.
35. Unidentified *Terre Haute Daily Tribune* clipping, [before 28 Apr. 1898], Dresser Manuscripts.
36. "On the Banks of the Wabash, Far Away" (New York: Howley, Haviland and Co., 1897), words and music by Paul Dresser. For further discussion, see Clayton W. Henderson, "The Slippery Slopes of Fame: Paul Dresser and the Centennial of 'On the Banks of the Wabash, Far Away,'" *Traces of Indiana and Midwestern History* 9 (fall 1997): 4–13.
37. Dreiser, "My Brother Paul," 96–97, and "Concerning the Author of These Songs," in *The Songs of Paul Dresser* (New York: Boni and Liveright, 1927), vii.
38. *Chicago Record,* 15 Apr. 1898.
39. Unidentified newspaper clipping, [ca. 1897], Dreiser Collection.
40. Ibid.
41. *New York World,* 18 June 1900.
42. Unidentified newspaper clipping, Dreiser Collection.
43. *New York Sun,* 29 June 1898.
44. *New York Dramatic Mirror,* 8 Mar. 1902.
45. Daniel Gilbert to Louise Dresser, 16 Feb. 1906, Dreiser Collection.
46. Unidentified newspaper clipping, Special Collections, Vigo County Public Library, Terre Haute, Ind. The clipping is undated, but the article appeared sometime after the summer of 1924.
47. *Indianapolis Star,* 31 Jan. 1923.
48. *Terre Haute Tribune,* 9 July 1923.
49. Ibid., 13 June 1923.
50. Parody of "On the Banks of the Wabash, Far Away," words by E. P. Moran, Sam DeVincent Collection of Illustrated American Sheet Music, National Museum of American History, Smithsonian Institution, Washington, D.C.
51. Parody of "On the Banks of the Wabash, Far Away," words by John W. Bratton, ibid.

Chapter 19

1. "May Irwin's 'Bully' Song" (Boston: White-Smith Music Publishing Co., 1896), words and music by Charles E. Trevathan.

2. John Jakes, *Homeland: The Crown Family Saga, 1890–1900* (New York: Bantam Books, 1994), 673.

3. "Darktown after Dark: A Bunch of Niggerism" (New York: Howley, Haviland and Co., 1899), words and music by Paul Dresser. A copy of the song is in the Sam DeVincent Collection of Illustrated American Sheet Music, National Museum of American History, Smithsonian Institution, Washington, D.C.

4. Jacob A. Riis, *How the Other Half Lives: Studies among the Tenements of New York* (New York: Charles Scribner's Sons, 1890). See also *Humanities* 19 (May/June 1998): 16–21.

5. Theodore Dreiser, "My Brother Paul," in *Twelve Men* (New York: Boni and Liveright, 1919), 84.

6. Ibid., 85.

7. Paul Dresser to Mary South, 17 Mar. 1898, Paul Dresser Manuscripts, Lilly Library, Indiana University, Bloomington (hereafter cited as Dresser Manuscripts).

8. This quotation appeared on a souvenir tin distributed at Mudlavia. An illustration of the tin appears in Jane Nolan and Linda Weintraut, "The Right Water, the Right Mud, and the Right Place," *Traces of Indiana and Midwestern History* 4 (winter 1992): 23.

9. Nolan and Weintraut, "The Right Water, the Right Mud, and the Right Place," 23.

10. Ibid.

11. Ibid., 27.

12. Dresser to South, 1 Apr. 1898, Dresser Manuscripts.

13. Nolan and Weintraut, "The Right Water, the Right Mud, and the Right Place," 27.

14. Dresser to South, 1 Apr. 1898, Dresser Manuscripts.

15. Advertisement for Mudlavia, Theodore Dreiser Collection, Van Pelt–Dietrich Library Center, University of Pennsylvania, Philadelphia (hereafter cited as Dreiser Collection).

16. *Terre Haute Evening Gazette,* 18 Apr. 1898.

17. *Chicago Record,* 28 Apr. 1898.

18. *Terre Haute Evening Gazette,* 19 Apr. 1898.

19. *Terre Haute Express,* 19 Apr. 1898.

20. Ibid.

21. *Terre Haute Evening Gazette,* 19 Apr. 1898.

22. Ibid., 20 Apr. 1898.

23. Dresser to South, 11 Aug. 1898, Dresser Manuscripts.

24. David A. Jasen, *Tin Pan Alley: The Composers, the Songs, the Performers, and Their Times: The Golden Age of Popular American Music from 1886 to 1956* (New York: D. I. Fine, 1988), xxii.

25. Theodore Dreiser, *Newspaper Days,* ed. T. D. Nostwich (Philadelphia: University of Pennsylvania Press, 1991), 439.

26. Paul Dresser to Tillie Dreiser Gormley, 31 Jan. 1899, Dreiser Collection.

Chapter 20

1. Louise Dresser, [Reminiscences of Paul Dresser], 1, Paul Dresser Manuscripts, Lilly Library, Indiana University, Bloomington.
2. Ibid., 2.
3. Ibid., 3.
4. Ibid.
5. Ibid.
6. Ibid.
7. Ibid.
8. Ibid., 4.
9. *Evansville Courier,* 4 Sept. 1899.
10. Ibid.
11. Ibid.
12. Ibid.
13. "Hello! Ma Baby" (New York: T. B. Harms and Co., 1899), words by Ida Emerson, music by Joseph E. Howard.
14. Armond Fields and L. Marc Fields, *From the Bowery to Broadway: Lew Fields and the Roots of American Popular Theater* (New York: Oxford University Press, 1993), 167.
15. *New York Dramatic Mirror,* 26 Mar. 1900.
16. Ibid., 30 June 1900.

Chapter 21

1. *Hits and Hitters: Secrets of the Music Publishing Business* (New York: Herbert H. Taylor, [1900?]), reviewed in *New York Dramatic Mirror,* 17 Oct. 1900.
2. *Dwight's Journal of Music, a Paper of Art and Literature,* 19 June 1869, p. 55.
3. W. J. Henderson, "Music," *New York Times Illustrated Magazine,* 25 Oct. 1898, p. 4, quoted in Lawrence W. Levine, *Highbrow/Lowbrow: The Emergence of Cultural Hierarchy in America* (Cambridge: Harvard University Press, 1988), 216–17.
4. "Making Songs for the Million: An Unconventional Chapter in the Biography of the Man Whose Songs Have Sold to the Extent of Five Million Copies," *Metropolitan Magazine,* ca. 1900, Theodore Dreiser Collection, Van Pelt–Dietrich Library Center, University of Pennsylvania, Philadelphia (hereafter cited as Dreiser Collection).
5. Unidentified newspaper/magazine clipping, ibid.
6. Paul Dresser to editor of the *Syracuse (N.Y.) Post Standard,* Oct. 1900, ibid.
7. Ibid.
8. *Richmond Palladium,* 15 May 1899, quoted in Elizabeth J. Van Allen, *James Whitcomb Riley: A Life* (Bloomington and Indianapolis: Indiana University Press, 1999), 269.
9. Theodore Dreiser, *Sister Carrie: An Authoritative Text, Backgrounds, and Sources Criticism,* ed. Donald Pizer (New York: Norton, 1970), 434.
10. Ibid., 448.
11. *New York Dramatic Mirror,* 1 Dec. 1900.
12. Gerald Martin Bordman, *American Musical Theatre: A Chronicle,* 2d ed. (New York: Oxford University Press, 1992), 733.
13. *New York Dramatic Mirror,* 1 Dec. 1900.

14. Theodore Dreiser, *Newspaper Days,* ed. T. D. Nostwich (Philadelphia: University of Pennsylvania Press, 1991), 306.

15. Paul Dresser to Jesse Rector, 26 Dec. 1900, Emma Rector Flanagan Manuscripts, Lilly Library, Indiana University, Bloomington (hereafter cited as Flanagan Manuscripts).

16. Unpublished Paul Dresser poem, Dreiser Collection.

17. *New York Dramatic Mirror,* 2 Mar. 1901.

18. Ibid.

19. Armond Fields and L. Marc Fields, *From the Bowery to Broadway: Lew Fields and the Roots of American Popular Theater* (New York: Oxford University Press, 1993), 169.

20. *New York Dramatic Mirror,* 2 Mar. 1901.

21. *New York Sun,* 23 Feb. 1901.

22. *New York Dramatic Mirror,* 16 Mar. 1901.

23. Fields and Fields, *From the Bowery to Broadway,* 170.

24. Paul Dresser to Julia and Jesse Rector, 2 Apr. 1901, Flanagan Manuscripts.

Chapter 22

1. "The Path That Leads the Other Way" (New York: Howley, Haviland and Co., 1898), words and music by Paul Dresser.

2. *Terre Haute Express,* 10 Jan. 1902.

3. Ibid., 11 Jan. 1902.

4. "Way Down in Old Indiana" (New York: Howley, Haviland and Dresser, 1901), words and music by Paul Dresser.

5. "Mr. Volunteer; or, You Don't Belong to the Regulars, You're Just a Volunteer" (New York: Howley, Haviland and Dresser, 1901), words and music by Paul Dresser.

6. "I Just Want to Go Back and Start the Whole Thing Over" (New York: Howley, Haviland and Dresser, 1901), words and music by Paul Dresser.

7. *Terre Haute Evening Gazette,* 26 Feb. 1902.

8. Unidentified newspaper clipping, Theodore Dreiser Collection, Van Pelt–Dietrich Library Center, University of Pennsylvania, Philadelphia (hereafter cited as Dreiser Collection).

9. Music Publishers Association of the United States to Paul Dresser, 16 June 1902, ibid.

10. Charles Bayly to Paul Dresser, 16 June 1902, ibid.

11. *New York Dramatic Mirror,* 9 Aug. 1902.

12. Tim Gracyk and Frank Hoffmann, *Popular American Recording Pioneers, 1895–1925* (New York: Haworth Press, 2000), 203.

13. Paul Dresser to Albert Beveridge, 2 Feb. 1903, Dreiser Collection.

14. Ibid.

15. Theodore Dreiser, *Dawn: A History of Myself* (New York: Horace Liveright, 1931), 41.

16. Albert Beveridge to Paul Dresser, 6 Feb. 1903, Dreiser Collection.

17. *New York Times,* 25 Feb. 1903.

18. Ibid., 10 Mar. 1903.

19. Ibid., 25 Mar. 1903; in the chapter "My Brother Paul" in *Twelve* Men (New York: Boni and Liveright, 1919), 83, Theodore Dreiser writes that Bulger's death

sentence was commuted to life imprisonment, and in *Dawn,* 41, he writes that Bulger was electrocuted at Sing Sing, both examples of his misremembering or playing loose with the facts.

Chapter 23

1. *New York Dramatic Mirror,* 28 Mar. 1903.
2. Ibid., 25 Apr. 1903; *New York Record* advertisement, 5 Apr. 1903.
3. *New York Dramatic Mirror,* 6 June 1903.
4. Ibid., 17 Jan. 1903.
5. Ibid., 13 June 1903.
6. One of many instances appears in ibid., 23 May 1903.
7. Ibid., 30 May 1903.
8. Ibid., 14 Mar. 1903.
9. Ibid., 25 Aug. 1900.
10. Ibid., 28 Feb. 1903.
11. Theodore Dreiser, *Sister Carrie: An Authoritative Text, Backgrounds, and Sources Criticism,* ed. Donald Pizer (New York: Norton, 1970), 367.
12. Theodore Dreiser, *An Amateur Laborer,* ed. Richard W. Dowell, James L. W. West III, and Neda M. Westlake (Philadelphia: University of Pennsylvania Press, 1983), 53.
13. Theodore Dreiser, "My Brother Paul," in *Twelve Men* (New York: Boni and Liveright, 1919), 103.
14. Dreiser, *An Amateur Laborer,* 53.
15. Ibid., 54.
16. Ibid.
17. Ibid., 61.
18. *New York Clipper,* 4 May 1889.
19. Theodore Dreiser, "Culhane, the Solid Man," in *Twelve Men,* 134.
20. *New York Clipper,* 25 Oct. 1890.
21. Austin Brennan to Paul Dresser, 25 Apr. 1903, Theodore Dreiser Collection, Van Pelt–Dietrich Library Center, University of Pennsylvania, Philadelphia.
22. Dreiser, "Culhane, the Solid Man," 137–38.

Chapter 24

1. Theodore Dreiser, "My Brother Paul," in *Twelve Men* (New York: Boni and Liveright, 1919), 85.
2. Theodore Dreiser, *Dawn: A History of Myself* (New York: Horace Liveright, 1931), 117.
3. Vera Dreiser and Brett Howard, *My Uncle Theodore* (New York: Nash Publishing, 1976), 74.
4. Paul Dresser to Tillie Dreiser Gormley, 14 June 1903, Theodore Dreiser Collection, Van Pelt–Dietrich Library Center, University of Pennsylvania, Philadelphia (hereafter cited as Dreiser Collection).
5. Paul Dresser to Theodore Dreiser, 22 June 1903, ibid.
6. Dresser to Dreiser, 26 June 1903, ibid.
7. Dresser to Dreiser, 31 July 1903, ibid.
8. Dresser to Dreiser, 11 Aug. 1903, ibid.
9. Dresser to Dreiser, 2 Sept. 1903, ibid.
10. Dresser to Dreiser, Oct. 1903, ibid.

11. Dresser to Dreiser, 18 Oct. 1903, ibid.
12. *Indianapolis News,* 20 May 1898.
13. Dresser to Dreiser, 18 Oct. 1903, Dreiser Collection.
14. Dresser to Dreiser, Oct. 1903, ibid.
15. Unidentified *New York Telegraph* clipping, ibid.
16. Ibid.
17. Unidentified newspaper clipping, ibid.
18. Dresser to Dreiser, 18 Oct. 1903, ibid.
19. Ibid.
20. Paul Dresser and Robert H. Davis, *After Many Years: A Melodrama in Four Acts,* Act II (n.p., 1903), ibid.
21. Ibid.
22. Dresser to Dreiser, late Nov. or early Dec. 1903, ibid.
23. Quoted in unidentified newspaper clipping, 7 Nov. 1946, James Brian Maple Scrapbook, Sullivan County Public Library, Sullivan, Ind.

Chapter 25

1. Paul Dresser to Theodore Dreiser, 12 Dec. 1903, Theodore Dreiser Collection, Van Pelt–Dietrich Library Center, University of Pennsylvania, Philadelphia (hereafter cited as Dreiser Collection).
2. *"Lest We Forget": Chicago's Awful Theater Horror, by the Survivors and Rescuers . . .* ([Chicago?]: Memorial Publishing Co., 1904), 84.
3. Ibid.
4. Paul Dresser to Bob [Davis?], 18 Jan. 1904, Dreiser Collection.
5. *New York Dramatic Mirror,* 9 Jan. 1904.
6. Ibid., 16 Apr. 1904.
7. Ibid., 30 Apr. 1904.
8. Ibid., 26 Mar. 1904.
9. Ibid., 2 Apr. 1904.

Chapter 26

1. Paul Dresser to Austin Brennan, 19 May 1904, Theodore Dreiser Collection, Van Pelt–Dietrich Library Center, University of Pennsylvania, Philadelphia.
2. "Writes Home and Mother Songs but He Is No Sentimentalist, Paul Dresser Says—Facts That Contradict Him," unidentified newspaper clipping, 29 May 1904, ibid.
3. Ibid.
4. Ibid.
5. Ibid.
6. Unpublished manuscript, ibid.
7. Unidentified newspaper clipping, ibid.
8. Ibid.
9. "Writes Home and Mother Songs but He Is No Sentimentalist, Paul Dresser Says—Facts That Contradict Him."

Chapter 27

1. *New York Dramatic Mirror,* 11 June 1904.
2. Charles Ives, *Memos,* ed. John Kirkpatrick (New York: W. W. Norton, 1972), 105.

3. Paul Dresser to Tillie Dreiser Gormley, no date, Theodore Dreiser Collection, Van Pelt–Dietrich Library Center, University of Pennsylvania, Philadelphia (hereafter cited as Dreiser Collection).
4. Paul Dresser to Mame Dreiser Brennan, 4 Dec. 1904, ibid.
5. Paul Dresser to Austin and Mame Brennan, 10 Jan. 1905, ibid.
6. *New York Dramatic Mirror,* 14 Jan. 1905. The James Curtin Company is given as the publisher for some of Dresser's songs around this time; the name may have been a pseudonym, designed to protect Dresser.
7. Ibid., 25 Mar. 1905.
8. Mai Dreiser to Helen Dreiser, 11 Jan. 1947, Dreiser Collection.
9. *New York Dramatic Mirror,* 7 Jan. 1905.
10. Ibid., 11 Feb. 1905.
11. Ibid.
12. Ibid., 18 Feb. 1905.
13. Ed Dreiser to Theodore Dreiser, Oct. 1906, Dreiser Collection.
14. Dresser to Austin and Mame Brennan, 11 Mar. 1905, ibid.
15. Paul Dresser to Theodore Dreiser, 12 May 1905, ibid.
16. Ibid.
17. *New York Dramatic Mirror,* 10 June 1905.
18. Dresser to Theodore Dreiser, [June?] 1905, Dreiser Collection.
19. Paul Dresser to Austin Brennan, 11 Aug. 1905, ibid.
20. *New York Dramatic Mirror,* 26 Aug. 1905.
21. Dresser to Mame Dreiser Brennan, 10 Dec. 1905, Dreiser Collection.
22. Charles K. Harris, *After the Ball: Forty Years of Melody* (New York: Frank-Maurice, 1926), 139.
23. Louise Dresser, [Reminiscences of Paul Dresser], 7–9, Paul Dresser Manuscripts, Lilly Library, Indiana University, Bloomington.

Chapter 28

1. Paul Dresser to Mame Dreiser Brennan, 10 Dec. 1905, Theodore Dreiser Collection, Van Pelt–Dietrich Library Center, University of Pennsylvania, Philadelphia (hereafter cited as Dreiser Collection).
2. Paul Dresser to Theodore Dreiser, Dec. 1905, ibid.
3. Theodore Dreiser, "My Brother Paul," in *Twelve Men* (New York: Boni and Liveright, 1919), 105.
4. Ibid, 105–6.
5. Ibid., 106.
6. Ibid.
7. "Where Are the Friends of Other Days?" (New York: Howley, Haviland and Dresser, 1903), words and music by Paul Dresser.
8. Mai Dreiser to Helen Dreiser, 11 Jan. 1947, Dreiser Collection.
9. Dreiser, "My Brother Paul," 107.
10. Ibid., 106–7.
11. Ibid., 107.
12. Theodore Dreiser, "Whence the Song," in *The Color of a Great City* (New York: Boni and Liveright, 1923), 255–56.
13. From time to time, Dreiser thought he would write a book about Dresser, but all that came from those thoughts were a few sketches.

14. State of New York: Certificate and Record of Death, Certificate no. 3493, New York Department of Health, Municipal Archives, New York City.

15. Dreiser, "My Brother Paul," 91.

16. Ibid., 108. Dreiser made a number of errors in his recollection: he wrote that Dresser died in "late November" (he died on 30 January) and that he "died at five in the afternoon" (he died at 6:23 P.M.). In "Concerning the Author of These Songs," published as a preface to *The Songs of Paul Dresser* (New York: Boni and Liveright, 1927), Dreiser wrote that Dresser was "not quite fifty-five when he died" (he was just shy of forty-eight).

17. Theodore Dreiser, *Newspaper Days*, ed. T. D. Nostwich (Philadelphia: University of Pennsylvania Press, 1991), 427.

18. *The Music Trades*, 3 Feb. 1906.

19. Unidentified newspaper clipping, Dreiser Collection.

20. Unidentified newspaper clipping, ibid.

21. *New York Dramatic Mirror*, 10 Feb. 1906.

22. Ibid., 24 Feb. 1906.

Chapter 29

1. *New York Dramatic Mirror*, 12 May, 9, 23 June 1906.

2. Vera Dreiser and Brett Howard, *My Uncle Theodore* (New York: Nash Publishing, 1976), 127.

3. Ibid.

4. Mame Brennan to Theodore Dreiser, [2?] Mar. 1906, Theodore Dreiser Collection, Van Pelt–Dietrich Library Center, University of Pennsylvania, Philadelphia (hereafter cited as Dreiser Collection).

5. Inscribed on the gravestone for Johann Paul and Sarah Dreiser in St. Boniface Cemetery, Chicago.

6. Carl Dreiser Kishima to Theodore Dreiser, 16 Oct. 1908, Dreiser Collection.

7. Austin Brennan to Theodore Dreiser, 27 June 1906, ibid.

8. Theodore Dreiser to Dreiser family members, 29 June 1906, ibid.

9. Mame Brennan to Theodore Dreiser, 5 July 1906, ibid.; as late as 1922, no one had yet paid Huhna for his work.

10. Ibid.

11. Ed Dreiser to Theodore Dreiser, 8 Oct. 1906, ibid.

12. Theodore Dreiser to Mame Brennan, 16 Oct. 1906, ibid.

13. Al Dreiser to Theodore Dreiser, 20 Nov. 1906, ibid.

14. Theodore Dreiser to Al Dreiser, 29 Nov. 1906, ibid.

15. Thomas McKee to Theodore Dreiser, Sept. 1907, ibid.

16. Much of this correspondence is in the Dreiser Collection.

17. Mai Dreiser to Helen Dreiser, 11 Jan. 1947, ibid.

18. *Terre Haute Tribune*, 1 Dec. 1928.

19. Unidentified Terre Haute newspaper clipping, ca. 1922, Special Collections, Vigo County Public Library, Terre Haute, Ind.

20. The film was *Remember the Night*, released in 1940.

21. "Indiana" (New York: Shapiro, Bernstein and Co., 1917), words by Ballard MacDonald, music by James F. Hanley; "On the Banks of the Wabash, Far Away" (New York: Howley, Haviland and Co., 1897), words and music by Paul Dresser.

22. Letters dating from 29 Apr. 1940 to 7 Nov. 1940 to and from Max Mayer, Theodore Dreiser, Helen Dreiser, and Stanley Moffat, Dreiser Collection.

23. *Terre Haute Tribune,* 9 July 1923.

24. Dreiser Collection.

25. Theodore Dreiser to H. L. Mencken, 1 Nov. 1920, in Thomas P. Riggio, ed., *Dreiser-Mencken Letters: The Correspondence of Theodore Dreiser and H. L. Mencken, 1907–1945,* 2 vols. (Philadelphia: University of Pennsylvania Press, 1986), 2:405.

Chapter 30

1. *Terre Haute Express,* 10 Jan. 1902.

2. Unidentified *Metropolitan Magazine* clipping, Theodore Dreiser Collection, Van Pelt–Dietrich Library Center, University of Pennsylvania, Philadelphia (hereafter cited as Dreiser Collection).

3. Unidentified *Junior Munsey* clipping, ibid.

4. *Terre Haute Express,* 19 Apr. 1898.

5. Unidentified *Metropolitan Magazine* clipping, Dreiser Collection.

6. "Writes Home and Mother Songs but He Is No Sentimentalist, Paul Dresser Says—Facts That Contradict Him," unidentified newspaper clipping, 29 May 1904, ibid.

7. Unidentified *Junior Munsey* clipping, ibid.

8. Theodore Dreiser, "My Brother Paul," in *Twelve Men* (New York: Boni and Liveright, 1919), 96.

9. Ibid., 97.

10. Ibid., 98.

11. Ibid.

12. Theodore Dreiser, "Birth and Growth of a Popular Song," *Metropolitan Magazine* 8 (Nov. 1898): 497–502, reprinted in *Selected Magazine Articles of Theodore Dreiser: Life and Art in the American 1890s,* ed. Yoshinobu Hakutani, 2 vols. (Rutherford, Madison, and Teaneck, N.J.: Fairleigh Dickinson University Press; London and Toronto: Associated University Presses, 1985–87), 2:21–22.

13. Theodore Dreiser, "Whence the Song," in *The Color of a Great City* (New York: Boni and Liveright, 1923), 244–45.

14. Ibid., 254.

15. "Writes Home and Mother Songs but He Is No Sentimentalist, Paul Dresser Says—Facts That Contradict Him."

Chapter 31

1. "Never Speak Again" (New York: Willis Woodward and Co., 1887), words and music by Paul Dresser.

2. "I Long to Hear from Home" (New York: Willis Woodward and Co., 1888), words and music by Paul Dresser.

3. "I Wonder Where She Is Tonight" (New York: Howley, Haviland and Co., 1899), words and music by Paul Dresser.

4. "The Curse of the Dreamer" (New York: Howley, Haviland and Co., 1899), words and music by Paul Dresser.

5. James Whitcomb Riley, "How It Happened," in *The Complete Poetical Works of James Whitcomb Riley* (Bloomington and Indianapolis: Indiana University Press, 1993), 416.

6. "Old Folks at Home: Ethiopian Melody as Sung by Christy's Minstrels, Written and Composed by E. P. Christy" (New York: Firth, Pond and Co., 1851), words and music by Stephen C. Foster. Foster allowed E. P. Christy to claim authorship and the music for this song at its first publication in 1851.

7. James Whitcomb Riley, "When My Dreams Come True," in *The Complete Poetical Works of James Whitcomb Riley*, 394.

8. "On the Banks of the Wabash, Far Away" (New York: Howley, Haviland and Co., 1897), words and music by Paul Dresser.

9. "I Believe It for My Mother Told Me So" (Chicago: Lyon and Healy, 1887), words and music by Paul Dresser.

10. "I Long to Hear from Home" (New York: Willis Woodward and Co., 1888), words and music by Paul Dresser.

11. "My Gal Sal; or, They Called Her Frivolous Sal" (New York: Paul Dresser Publishing Co., 1905), words and music by Paul Dresser.

12. "On the Banks of the Wabash, Far Away."

13. "Tramp! Tramp! Tramp! The Prisoner's Hope" (Chicago: Root and Cady, 1864), words and music by George F. Root.

14. "The Battle-Cry of Freedom" (Chicago: Root and Cady, 1862), words and music by George F. Root.

15. "Old Folks at Home."

16. "Massa's in de Cold Ground" (New York: Firth, Pond and Co., 1852), words and music by Stephen C. Foster.

17. "Show Me the Way" (New York: Howley, Haviland and Co., 1896), words and music by Paul Dresser.

18. "Kathleen Mavourneen" (Richmond, Va.: George Dunn and Co.; Columbia, S.C.: Julian A. Selby, 1840), music by F. N. Crouch.

19. "The Letter That Never Came" (New York: T. B. Harms and Co., 1886), words by Paul Dresser, music by Max Sturm. In *The Songs of Paul Dresser* (New York: Boni and Liveright, 1927), Theodore Dreiser credits Dresser as the author of both the words and music.

20. "The Day That You Grew Colder" (New York: Paul Dresser Publishing Co., 1905), words and music by Paul Dresser.

21. "Love's Promise" (St. Louis: Balmer and Weber, 1887), words and music by Paul Dresser.

22. "I Wonder If There's Someone Who Loves Me" (New York: Willis Woodward and Co., 1890), words and music by Paul Dresser.

23. "My Gal Sal."

24. Ibid.

25. "The Curse of the Dreamer."

26. Ibid.

Chapter 32

1. "He Loves Me, He Loves Me Not" (New York: George T. Worth Co., 1893), words and music by Paul Dresser. George T. Worth was a pseudonym for the company that became Howley, Haviland and Company by the end of 1893. Later printings of the song bore the Howley, Haviland designation.

2. "He Brought Home Another" (New York: Howley, Haviland and Co., 1896), words and music by Paul Dresser.

3. "If You See My Sweetheart" (New York: Howley, Haviland and Co., 1897), words and music by Paul Dresser.

4. "I Wonder If She'll Ever Come Back to Me" (New York: Howley, Haviland and Co., 1896), words and music by Paul Dresser.

5. " 'Tis All That I Have to Remember Her By" (New York: Howley, Haviland and Co., 1895), words and music by Paul Dresser.

6. "My Heart Still Clings to the Old First Love" (New York: Howley, Haviland and Dresser, 1901), words and music by Paul Dresser.

7. "Gath'ring Roses for Her Hair" (New York: Howley, Haviland and Co., 1899), words and music by Paul Dresser.

8. "When I'm Away from You, Dear" (New York: Howley-Dresser Co., 1904), words and music by Paul Dresser.

9. "Rosie, Sweet Rosabel" (New York: George T. Worth Co., 1893), words and music by Paul Dresser.

10. "Jean" (New York: Howley, Haviland and Co., 1895), words and music by Paul Dresser.

11. "Little Fannie McIntyre" (New York: Willis Woodward and Co., 1890), words and music by Paul Dresser.

12. "When Mother First Taught Me to Pray" (New York: Willis Woodward and Co., 1892), words and music by Paul Dresser.

13. "Show Me the Way" (New York: Howley, Haviland and Co., 1896), words and music by Paul Dresser.

14. "Ave Maria" (New York: Howley, Haviland and Co., 1899), words and music by Paul Dresser.

15. "In the Great Somewhere" (New York: Howley, Haviland and Dresser, 1901), words and music by Paul Dresser.

16. "Bethlehem" (New York: Howley, Haviland and Dresser, n.d.), words and music by Paul Dresser.

17. "The Judgment Is at Hand" (New York: Paul Dresser Publishing Co., 1906), words and music by Paul Dresser.

18. "What a Wonderful World It Would Be!" (New York: Willis Woodward and Co., 1889), words by J. S. G. [John Stewart Crossy?], music by Paul Dresser.

19. "The Band Played Annie Laurie; or, To Hear Them Tell It" (New York: Willis Woodward and Co., 1890), words and music by Paul Dresser.

20. Ibid.

21. "The Limit Was Fifty Cents" (New York: Willis Woodward and Co., 1890), words and music by Paul Dresser.

22. "Three Old Sports from Oklahoma" (New York: Howley, Haviland and Co., 1894), words and music by Paul Dresser.

23. "The Battery" (New York: Howley, Haviland and Co., 1895), words and music by Paul Dresser.

24. *New York Dramatic Mirror,* 12, 26 Nov. 1898.

25. "Jim Judson" (New York: Paul Dresser Publishing Co., 1905), words and music by Paul Dresser.

26. *New York Clipper,* 29 Oct. 1892.

Chapter 33

1. "The Lone Grave" (New York: Willis Woodward and Co., 1890), words and music by Paul Dresser.

2. "I Was Looking for My Boy, She Said; or, Decoration Day" (New York: Howley, Haviland and Co., 1895), words and music by Paul Dresser.

3. "We Are Coming Cuba, Coming" (New York: Howley, Haviland and Co., 1898), words and music by Paul Dresser.

4. "Your God Comes First, Your Country Next, Then Mother Dear" (New York: Howley, Haviland and Co., 1898), words and music by Paul Dresser.

5. "We Fight Tomorrow Mother" (New York: Howley, Haviland and Co., 1898), words and music by Paul Dresser.

6. Ibid.

7. "On the Shores of Havana, Far Away" (New York: Howley, Haviland and Co., 1898), words by Andrew B. Sterling, music by Paul Dresser.

8. "In Good Old New York Town" (New York: Howley, Haviland and Co., 1899), words and music by Paul Dresser.

9. "Come Home, Dewey, We Won't Do a Thing to You" (New York: Howley, Haviland and Co., 1899), words and music by Paul Dresser.

10. H. W. Brands, *The Reckless Decade: America in the 1890s* (New York: St. Martin's Press, 1995), 326.

11. "Our Country May She Always Be Right but Our Country, Right or Wrong" (New York: Howley, Haviland and Co., 1898), words and music by Paul Dresser.

12. "Mr. Volunteer; or, You Don't Belong to the Regulars, You're Just a Volunteer" (New York: Howley, Haviland and Dresser, 1901), words and music by Paul Dresser.

13. "There's No North or South To-Day" (New York: Howley, Haviland and Dresser, 1901), words and music by Paul Dresser.

14. "She Fought On by His Side" (New York: James H. Curtin, 1904), words and music by Paul Dresser.

15. "The Green above the Red" (New York: Howley, Haviland and Co., 1900), words and music by Paul Dresser.

16. "The Army of Half-Starved Men" (New York: Howley, Haviland and Dresser, 1902), words and music by Paul Dresser.

17. "When You Come Back They'll Wonder Who the —— You Are" (New York: Howley, Haviland and Dresser, 1902), words and music by Paul Dresser.

18. "Where Are the Friends of Other Days?" (New York: Howley, Haviland and Dresser, 1903), words and music by Paul Dresser.

Chapter 34

1. "What Is Home without a Mother" (Philadelphia: Lee and Walker, 1854), words and music by Alice Hawthorne [Septimus Winner].

2. "There Is No One Like a Mother" (Philadelphia: J. E. Gould, 1862), words and music by Septimus Winner.

3. "Mother on the Brain" (New York: H. De Marsan, n.d.), words and music by John C. Cross.

4. "Rock Me to Sleep Mother" (Cincinnati: J. Church, Jr., [ca. 1860]), words by Florence Percy [Elizabeth Akers Allen], music by George R. Poulton. Several composers set Allen's poem to music, and the verses vary slightly from source to source. The lyrics presented here match those of the sheet music cited.

5. Shari L. Thurer, *The Myths of Motherhood: How Culture Reinvents the Good Mother* (New York: Houghton Mifflin, 1994), 217.

6. "As Some Fond Mother" (New York: Dubois and Stodart, 1828), words and music by C. E. Horn.

7. "Long Years Have Passed My Willie" (Boston: George P. Reed, 1845), words and music by Theodore T. Baker.

8. Ibid.

9. "Who Will Care for Mother Now" (Richmond, Va.: George Dunn and Co.; Columbia, S.C.: Julian A. Selby, 1863), words by C. C. Sawyer, music by C. F. Thompson.

10. "The Soldier to His Mother" (Philadelphia: Lee and Walker, 1862), words by Thomas Mackellar, music by William U. Butcher.

11. "My Mother's Memory" (New York: William A. Pond and Co., 1855), words and music by John S. Cox.

12. "The Day Our Mother Died" (Philadelphia: William H. Shuster, 1856), words and music by William R. Hart.

13. "Mother Would Comfort Me" (Brooklyn, N.Y.: Sawyer and Thompson, 1863), words and music by Charles Carroll Sawyer.

14. "A Boy's Best Friend Is His Mother; or, You'll Find Your Best Friend Is Your Mother" (Cleveland and Chicago: S. Brainard's Sons, 1884), words and music by Ben Williams.

15. "I'll Weep No More for Mother Dear" (Philadelphia: Charles W. A. Trumpler, 1865), words and music by C. Everest.

16. "Days Gone By" (New York: Willis Woodward and Co., 1890), words and music by Paul Dresser.

17. Joy S. Kasson, *Marble Queens and Captives: Women in Nineteenth-Century American Sculpture* (New Haven, Conn.: Yale University Press, 1990).

18. "A Dream of My Boyhood Days" (New York: Howley, Haviland and Co., 1896), words and music by Paul Dresser.

19. "I Believe It for My Mother Told Me So" (Chicago: Lyon and Healy, 1887), words and music by Paul Dresser.

20. "Don't Tell Her That You Love Her; or, Mankind Is Seldom True" (New York: Howley, Haviland and Co., 1896), words and music by Paul Dresser.

21. Ibid.

22. "When Mammy's by Yo' Side" (New York: Howley, Haviland and Co., 1900), words and music by Paul Dresser.

23. "I Believe It for My Mother Told Me So."

24. Theodore Dreiser, *Dawn: A History of Myself* (New York: Horace Liveright, 1931), 467.

25. Unidentified newspaper clipping, Theodore Dreiser Collection, Van Pelt–Dietrich Library Center, University of Pennsylvania, Philadelphia.

26. *New York Dramatic Mirror,* 10 Feb. 1906.

27. Dreiser, *Dawn,* 150–51.

28. Ibid., 7.

29. Theodore Dreiser, "My Brother Paul," in *Twelve Men* (New York: Boni and Liveright, 1919), 93, 95.

30. "The Path That Leads the Other Way" (New York: Howley, Haviland and Co., 1898), words and music by Paul Dresser.

31. "The Convict and the Bird" (New York: Willis Woodward and Co., 1888), words and music by Paul Dresser.

32. "She Went to the City" (New York: James H. Curtin, 1904), words and music by Paul Dresser.

33. "I Just Want to Go Back and Start the Whole Thing Over" (New York: Howley, Haviland and Dresser, 1901), words and music by Paul Dresser.

34. "I Send to Them My Love" (New York: Willis Woodward and Co., 1888), words and music by Paul Dresser.

35. *Indianapolis News*, 20 May 1898.

36. "Just Tell Them That You Saw Me" (New York: Howley, Haviland and Co., 1895), words and music by Paul Dresser.

37. "You're Breaking Mother's Heart" (New York: Willis Woodward and Co., 1890), words and music by Paul Dresser.

38. "I Wonder If There's Someone Who Loves Me" (New York: Willis Woodward and Co., 1890), words and music by Paul Dresser.

39. "The Blind Mother" (New York: Willis Woodward and Co., 1889), words and music by Paul Dresser.

40. "The Outcast Unknown" (New York: Willis Woodward and Co., 1887), words and music by Paul Dresser.

41. "I Just Want to Go Back and Start the Whole Thing Over."

42. "Way Down in Old Indiana" (New York: Howley, Haviland and Dresser, 1901), words and music by Paul Dresser.

43. "In Dear Old Illinois" (New York: Howley, Haviland and Dresser, 1902), words and music by Paul Dresser.

44. "Sweet Savannah" (New York: Howley, Haviland and Co., 1898), words and music by Paul Dresser.

45. "The Town Where I Was Born" (New York: Paul Dresser Publishing Co., 1905), words and music by Paul Dresser.

46. Elizabeth J. Van Allen, *James Whitcomb Riley: A Life* (Bloomington and Indianapolis: Indiana University Press, 1999), 13.

47. Alan Trachtenberg, *The Incorporation of America: Culture and Society in the Gilded Age* (New York: Hill and Wang, 1982).

48. "On the Banks of the Wabash, Far Away" (New York: Howley, Haviland and Co., 1897), words and music by Paul Dresser.

Chapter 35

1. "In the Good Old Summer Time" (New York: Howley, Haviland and Dresser, 1902), words by Ren Shields, music by George Evans.

2. "Meet Me in St. Louis, Louis" (New York: F. A. Mills, 1904), words by Andrew B. Sterling, music by Kerry Mills.

3. "In My Merry Oldsmobile" (New York: M. Witmark and Sons, 1905), words by Vincent Bryan, music by Gus Edwards.

4. "Hello! Ma Baby" (New York: T. B. Harms and Co., 1899), words by Ida Emerson, music by Joseph E. Howard.

5. "Under the Bamboo Tree" (New York: Joseph A. Stern and Co., 1902), words and music by Bob Cole and John Rosamond Johnson.

6. "Old Folks at Home: Ethiopian Melody as Sung by Christy's Minstrels, Written and Composed by E. P. Christy" (New York: Firth, Pond and Co., 1851), words and music by Stephen C. Foster.

7. "On the Banks of the Wabash, Far Away" (New York: Howley, Haviland and Co., 1897), words and music by Paul Dresser.

8. Charles Hamm, *Yesterdays: Popular Song in America* (New York and London: W. W. Norton and Co., 1979), 302.

9. Val Holley, "H. L. Mencken and the Indiana Genii," *Traces of Indiana and Midwestern History* 3 (winter 1991): 9–10.

10. Joel Whitburn, *Joel Whitburn's Pop Memories, 1890–1954: The History of American Popular Music: Compiled from America's Popular Music Charts, 1890–1954* (Menomonee Falls, Wis.: Record Research, 1986). Myers's version of "Just Tell Them That You Saw Me" was number one for six weeks, beginning 1 August 1895 (p. 333); Gaskin's version of the same song enjoyed a peak position of number two for three weeks, beginning 15 August 1896, and his "On the Banks of the Wabash, Far Away" was in first position for ten weeks, beginning 6 November 1897 (p. 171). Porter's recording of "Wabash" was in first place for four weeks, beginning 8 January 1898 (p. 355); Myers's "Way Down in Old Indiana" was number one for five weeks, beginning 15 May 1902 (p. 333); and Jose's interpretation of "The Day That You Grew Colder" peaked at number three on 15 April 1905 (p. 243).

Bibliography

Appelbaum, Stanley. *The Chicago World's Fair of 1893: A Photographic Record, Photos from the Collections of the Avery Library of Columbia University and the Chicago Historical Society*. New York: Dover Publications, 1980.

Atherton, Lewis. *Main Street on the Middle Border*. Chicago: Quadrangle Books, 1966.

Badger, Reid. *The Great American Fair: The World's Columbian Exposition and American Culture*. Chicago: N. Hall, 1979.

Bancroft, Hubert Howe. *The Book of the Fair: An Historical and Descriptive Presentation of the World's Science, Art, and Industry, as Viewed through the Columbian Exposition at Chicago in 1893*. New York: Bounty Books, 1894.

Bode, Carl. *The Anatomy of American Popular Culture, 1840–1861*. Berkeley and Los Angeles: University of California Press, 1959.

Bordman, Gerald Martin. *American Musical Theatre: A Chronicle*. 2d ed. New York: Oxford University Press, 1992.

Brands, H. W. *The Reckless Decade: America in the 1890s*. New York: St. Martin's Press, 1995.

Burrows, Edwin G., and Mike Wallace. *Gotham: A History of New York City to 1898*. New York: Oxford University Press, 1999.

Csida, Joseph, and June Bundy Csida. *American Entertainment: A Unique History of Popular Show Business*. New York: Watson-Guptill Publications, 1978.

Dowell, Richard W. "Ask Mr. Markle?" *Dreiser Newsletter* 8 (spring 1997): 9–14.

———. "Dreiser vs. Terre Haute, or Paul Dresser's Body Lies A-Molderin' in the Grave." *Dreiser Studies* 20 (fall 1989): 9–20.

———. "'On the Banks of the Wabash': A Musical Whodunit." *Indiana Magazine of History* 66 (June 1970): 95–109.

Dreiser, Theodore. *An Amateur Laborer*. Edited by Richard W. Dowell, James L. W. West III, and Neda M. Westlake. Philadelphia: University of Pennsylvania Press, 1983.

———. *American Diaries, 1902–1926*. Edited by Thomas P. Riggio. Philadelphia: University of Pennsylvania Press, 1982.

———. *The Color of a Great City*. New York: Boni and Liveright, 1923.

———. *Dawn: A History of Myself*. New York: Horace Liveright, 1931.

———. *A Hoosier Holiday*. 1916. Reprint, with an introduction by Douglas Brinkley, Bloomington and Indianapolis: Indiana University Press, 1997.

———. *Newspaper Days*. Edited by T. D. Nostwich. Philadelphia: University of Pennsylvania Press, 1991.

———. *Selected Magazine Articles of Theodore Dreiser: Life and Art in the American 1890s*. Edited by Yoshinobu Hakutani. 2 vols. Rutherford, Madison, and Teaneck, N.J.: Fairleigh Dickinson University Press; London and Toronto: Associated University Presses, 1985–87.

———. *Sister Carrie: An Authoritative Text, Backgrounds, and Sources Criticism*. Edited by Donald Pizer. New York: Norton, 1970.

———. *Twelve Men*. New York: Boni and Liveright, 1919.

Dreiser, Vera, and Brett Howard. *My Uncle Theodore*. New York: Nash Publishing, 1976.

Dresser, Paul. *The Songs of Paul Dresser: With an Introduction by His Brother, Theodore Dreiser*. New York: Boni and Liveright, 1927.

Elias, Robert H. *Theodore Dreiser: Apostle of Nature*. Ithaca, N.Y.: Cornell University Press, 1970.

Fields, Armond, and L. Marc Fields. *From the Bowery to Broadway: Lew Fields and the Roots of American Popular Theater*. New York: Oxford University Press, 1993.

Finson, Jon W. *The Voices That Are Gone: Themes in Nineteenth-Century American Popular Song*. New York: Oxford University Press, 1994.

Freemont, Robert A., ed. *Favorite Songs of the Nineties: Complete Original Sheet Music for Eighty-Nine Songs*. New York: Dover Publications, 1973.

Gerber, Philip L. *Theodore Dreiser*. New York: Twayne Publishers, 1964.

Goldberg, Isaac. *Tin Pan Alley: A Chronicle of American Popular Music*. New York: F. Ungar Publishing Co., 1961.

Haley, Carmel O'Neill. "The Dreisers." *Commonweal*, 7 July 1933, pp. 265–67.

Hamm, Charles. *Yesterdays: Popular Song in America*. New York and London: W. W. Norton and Co., 1979.

Harris, Charles K. *After the Ball: Forty Years of Melody*. New York: Frank-Maurice, 1926.

Henderson, Clayton W. "The Slippery Slopes of Fame: Paul Dresser and the Centennial of 'On the Banks of the Wabash, Far Away.'" *Traces of Indiana and Midwestern History* 9 (fall 1997): 4–13.

Holley, Val. "H. L. Mencken and the Indiana Genii." *Traces of Indiana and Midwestern History* 3 (winter 1991): 4–15.

Homberger, Eric. *Scenes from the Life of a City: Corruption and Conscience in Old New York*. New Haven and London: Yale University Press, 1994.

Jasen, David A. *Tin Pan Alley: The Composers, the Songs, the Performers, and Their Times: The Golden Age of Popular American Music from 1886 to 1956*. New York: D. I. Fine, 1988.

Key, Susan. "Sound and Sentimentality: Nostalgia in the Songs of Stephen Foster." *American Music* 13 (summer 1995): 145–66.

Kleber, Albert. *History of St. Meinrad Archabbey, 1854–1954*. St. Meinrad, Ind.: A Grail Publication, 1954.

Lingeman, Richard. *Small Town America: A Narrative History, 1620–the Present*. Boston: Houghton Mifflin, 1981.

———. *Theodore Dreiser: At the Gates of the City, 1871–1907*. New York: G. P. Putnam's Sons, 1986.

McConachie, Bruce A. *Melodramatic Formulations: American Theatre and Society, 1820–1870*. Iowa City: University of Iowa Press, 1992.

McNamara, Brooks. *Step Right Up*. Rev. ed. Jackson: University Press of Mississippi, 1995.

Marks, Edward B. *They All Had Glamour: From the Swedish Nightingale to the Naked Lady*. New York: J. Messner, 1944.

Martin, John Bartlow. *Indiana: An Interpretation*. 1947. Reprint, with an introduction by James H. Madison, Bloomington and Indianapolis: Indiana University Press, 1992.

Matlaw, Myron, ed. *American Popular Entertainment: Papers and Proceedings of the Conference on the History of American Popular Entertainment*. Westport, Conn., and London: Greenwood Press, 1979.

Moers, Ellen. *Two Dreisers*. New York: Viking Press, 1969.

Morris, Lloyd R. *Incredible New York: High Life and Low Life of the Last Hundred Years*. New York: Random House, 1951.

Nasaw, David. *Going Out: The Rise and Fall of Public Amusements*. New York: BasicBooks, 1993.

Nolan, Jane, and Linda Weintraut. "The Right Water, the Right Mud, and the Right Place." *Traces of Indiana and Midwestern History* 4 (winter 1992): 20–26.

Odell, George C. D. *Annals of the New York Stage*. 15 vols. New York: Columbia University Press, 1927–49.

O'Neill, John P. " 'My Brother Paul' and *Sister Carrie*." *Canadian Review of American Studies* 16 (winter 1985): 411–24.

Oppel, Frank, ed. *Gaslight New York Revisited*. Secaucus, N.J.: Castle, 1989.

Pizer, Donald, " 'Along the Wabash': A 'Comedy Drama' by Theodore Dreiser," *Dreiser Newsletter* 5 (fall 1974): 1–4

Riggio, Thomas. "The Dreisers in Sullivan: A Biographical Revision." *Dreiser Newsletter* 10 (fall 1979): 1–12.

———, ed. *Dreiser-Mencken Letters: The Correspondence of Theodore Dreiser and H. L. Mencken, 1907–1945*. 2 vols. Philadelphia: University of Pennsylvania Press, 1986.

Root, Deane L. *American Popular Stage Music, 1860–1880*. Ann Arbor, Mich.: UMI Research Press, 1981.

Rubin, Joan Shelley. *The Making of Middlebrow Culture*. Chapel Hill and London: University of North Carolina Press, 1992.

Ryan, Mary P. *The Empire of the Mother: American Writing about Domesticity, 1830 to 1860*. New York: Institute for Research in History and Haworth Press, 1982.

Salvatore, Nick. *Eugene V. Debs: Citizen and Socialist*. Urbana, Chicago, and London: University of Illinois Press, 1982.

Schmidt–Von Bardelben, Renate. "Dreiser on the European Continent." *Dreiser Newsletter* 2 (fall 1971): 4–10.

Scott, Derek B. *The Singing Bourgeois: Songs of the Victorian Drawing Room and Parlour*. Milton Keynes, England, and Philadelphia: Open University Press, 1989.

Stein, Charles W., ed. *American Vaudeville as Seen by Its Contemporaries*. New York: Da Capo Press, 1985.

Swanberg, W. A. *Dreiser*. New York: Charles Scribner's Sons, 1965.

Tawa, Nicholas E. "Serious Songs of the Early Nineteenth Century: Part 2, The Meaning of the Early Song Melodies." *American Music* 13 (fall 1995): 263–94.

———. "Songs of the Early Nineteenth Century: Part 1, Early Song Lyrics and Coping with Life." *American Music* 13 (spring 1995): 1–26.

Taylor, Robert M., Jr. "Soaking, Sluicing, and Stewing in Hoosier Mineral Waters." *Traces of Indiana and Midwestern History* 4 (winter 1992): 4–9.

Thurer, Shari L. *The Myths of Motherhood: How Culture Reinvents the Good Mother*. Boston: Houghton Mifflin, 1994.

Toll, Robert C. *On With the Show! The First Century of Show Business in America*. New York: Oxford University Press, 1976.

Trachtenberg, Alan. *The Incorporation of America: Culture and Society in the Gilded Age*. New York: Hill and Wang, 1982.

Van Allen, Elizabeth J. *James Whitcomb Riley: A Life*. Bloomington and Indianapolis: Indiana University Press, 1999.

Vanausdall, Jeanette. "'A Miracle of Rare Device': Images of the West Baden Springs Hotel." *Traces of Indiana and Midwestern History* 4 (winter 1992): 10–18.

Whitburn, Joel. *Joel Whitburn's Pop Memories, 1890–1954: The History of American Popular Music: Compiled from America's Popular Music Charts, 1890–1954*. Menomonee Falls, Wis.: Record Research, 1986.

White, Avron Levine, ed. *Lost in Music: Culture, Style, and the Musical Event*. London and New York: Routledge and K. Paul, 1987.

Wilmeth, Don B. *The Language of American Popular Entertainment: A Glossary of Argot, Slang, and Terminology*. Westport, Conn., and London: Greenwood Press, 1981.

———. *Variety Entertainment and Outdoor Amusements: A Reference Guide*. Westport, Conn., and London: Greenwood Press, 1982.

Wolfe, Thomas J., ed. *A History of Sullivan County, Indiana: Closing of the First Century's History of the County, and Showing the Growth of Its People, Institutions, Industries and Wealth*. 2 vols. New York and Chicago: Lewis Publishing Co., 1909.

Index